Praise for *BEYOND PROFIT*

"A foundational book for tomorrow's leaders. Reinventing the master discipline of capitalism is the most profound challenge facing 'Homo economicus'. *Beyond Profit* maps the profound global shift underway - how to be part of leading for it."

John Elkington, Founder and recaller of the Triple Bottom Line

"For too long we have been playing at the edges - getting lost in the noise, all the while watching what we love be destroyed. *Beyond Profit* helps us see the common ground and lead for radical change – an imperative that has never been so urgent."

Hunter Lovins, President and Founder of Natural Capitalism Solutions, Co-founder of Rocky Mountain Institute, and Founding Professor of Sustainable Management at Bard MBA

"Holistic and practical, *Beyond Profit* reminds us that compassion, responsibility and ethics must power the engine of our economy, not stand on the sidelines. Because far from idealism, this is the only pragmatic path that makes economic, social and planetary sense. *Beyond Profit* guides us to action – for the benefit of all."

Paul Polman, Author, Philanthropist and Activist. Former CEO, Unilever

"We must move beyond profit as the purpose of business, or any organization. Marketing, when used wisely, can be a powerful force for shaping a better world – one that prioritizes the common good over short-term gain. This book sets the frame for that role."

Philip Kotler, Professor Emeritus of Marketing at the Kellogg School of Management, Northwestern University. The founding father of modern marketing

"What makes *Beyond Profit* especially powerful is that it's not just theoretical, it's deeply human. It speaks to the part of us that knows we were meant to lead differently. It helps us remember that long-term wellbeing for all is not just a lofty ideal, it's our shared purpose. It doesn't offer easy answers, but it offers the right questions, sharp insights, and a profoundly hopeful vision. If you're serious about contributing to a world that thrives beyond profit, start here."

Wakan Wahohipi Win, Co-organizer of World Peace and Prayer Day

"*Beyond Profit* helps us see a way out of the dominant global financially oriented economy that is driving us in ecologically and societally unsustainable directions. Market creativity and employee motivation is stimulated by active governance of our common purpose and a focus on meaningful results, not shareholder profitability or growth. The book does not demonise profit, acknowledging that all organisations, whether "for profit" or "not for profit" need sustainable financial surpluses for investment in change. *Beyond Profit* shows us that movement to this new paradigm is already underway and how we might make it the new norm."

Mark Moody Stuart, KCMG Former Chairman of Royal Dutch Shell and Former Chairman of the UN Global Compact Foundation

"To have a chance at a thriving future, it's essential to create organizations, economies and approaches to leadership that are regenerative and distributive in their very design. And as Victoria Hurth and her colleagues powerfully point out, these will not be based on extraction and profit maximisation. New designs are fast emerging and this book masterfully helps to unpack their key traits and the opportunities for transformation that they bring."

Kate Raworth, creator of the Doughnut of social and planetary boundaries, and co-founder of Doughnut Economics Action Lab

"*Beyond Profit* is a timely and inspiring contribution to the global leadership conversation. It places governance and purpose where they belong - at the heart of operationalizing our transition to a sustainable, inclusive, and hence wellbeing-focused future. By highlighting the pivotal role of international standards, this book demonstrates how global consensus can be translated into practical action. I recommend *Beyond Profit* to all who believe that purpose-driven leadership and strong governance are essential foundations for better world."

Sergio Mujica, Secretary-General, International Organization for Standardization (ISO)

"The major barrier preventing progress toward a better world today is the lack of a truly shared vision of a sustainable wellbeing world well beyond unsustainable GDP growth. This book will help everyone to see the choices more clearly and make the right ones."

Robert Costanza, University College London, Winner of the Blue Planet Prize 2024

"*Beyond Profit* shines a light on governance – the unsexy yet unquestionably greatest leverage point we can use to align our systems with our values. If we want an economic system built on a foundation of care, then we must be clear about ends and means and we must redesign governance to evolve our fiduciary duty of care to put the wellbeing of people, and life on earth, above profit."

Jay Coen Gilbert, Co-Founder, the B Corporation movement

"As the world moves beyond Western domination and unipolarity toward a more multipolar global order, the urgency for an alternative to the prevailing profit-driven growth model has never been greater. *Beyond Profit* offers a compelling vision and clear direction for a more balanced path of development – one that prioritizes environmental sustainability and human well-being over short-term profits for a privileged few."

Asoka Bandarage, Ph.D. Author of *Sustainability and Well-Being: The Middle Path to Environment, Society and the Economy*

"Profit is not an end in itself - it's the lifeblood of companies and markets but the rules by which profit is defined shape what those companies and markets deliver to society as a whole. The lazy assumption that profit maximisation will be good for society regardless of those rules has led to social and environmental outcomes that no 'hand of god' would have chosen. The authors use the 3-Horizons framework to lay out the flaws in current systems of governance, illustrate a plethora of examples of new approaches and sketch a future where reformed governance leads to prosperity for all. A timely and practical guide."

Nigel Topping, Former UN Climate Change High-Level Champion COP26, Member UK Climate Change Committee, Founder Ambition Loop

"*Beyond Profit* is book of wisdom and common sense. Victoria, Lorenzo and Ben are practical visionaries. They make a compelling case that economy needs to have a greater purpose than making money. If by the endless and meaningless economic growth planet Earth is put in peril and if humanity suffers from the lack of fulfilment, then what is the point of such economic growth? Every economist, every politician and every business leader should read this book. It will help them to transform their economic outlook and make them act with greater responsibility."

Satish Kumar, Editor Emeritus, Resurgence & Ecologist and Founder of Schumacher College

"Thinking about purpose driven leadership is the business idea of the century."

R Edward Freeman, Professor at University of Virginia. Founding father of 'Stakeholder Value'

Beyond Profit offers a practical blueprint for redefining success around long-term wellbeing for all. From my experience as Federal Chief Sustainability Officer in the Obama White House to advancing infrastructure delivery in the Biden administration, I've seen how urgently we need purpose-driven leadership. The book moves beyond critique, to offer a powerful vision and actionable frameworks for creating systems that are governed for the well-being of all. It is both a call to action and a practical guide – one that could not be more timely, or more necessary."

Christine Harada, Former Federal Chief Sustainability Officer, Obama White House; Executive Director, Federal Permitting Improvement Steering Council, Biden Administration

"For anyone interested in understanding and driving wellbeing economies, *Beyond Profit* is essential reading written by leading experts in the field."

Colin Mayer, Professor of Management Studies, University of Oxford and Academic Lead for the British Academy Future of the Corporation Programme

"We're trapped by an economic logic of short-term profit that is failing us all. *Beyond Profit* argues that incremental changes are insufficient. The book presents a powerful alternative: a 'purpose-driven' model that realigns our entire system, from global economies to individual businesses, around the long-term well-being of people and the planet as the core objective. It's a necessary shift from a flawed past to a thriving future."

Joram Mwinamo, Chief Executive Officer - SNDBX International, Global Advisory Board Member and East Africa Chair - Aspen Network of Development Entrepreneurs (ANDE)

"In the ever-tightening grip of the Nature and climate crisis, a liveable and thriving future is still within our grasp, if we act now. But what to do, and where to begin? *Beyond Profit* presents answers and maps a practical route forward. This is a must read for leaders who wish to secure a legacy that will count."

Tony Juniper CBE, Chair Natural England, UK. Author of *Just Earth*, Ex CEO Friends of the Earth UK

"Vnokeckvn etemocet fulletvt owēs pumvhatokhoyvnts (They instructed us to go about having love for all)... *Beyond Profit* ushers back in this sacred ancestral memory of prioritizing the livelihoods of all living beings. Whether you are a descendant of an Indigenous culture of the distant-past somewhere in the world that no longer exists, or you are a leader of an extant Indigenous community with contemporarily adopted economic and governance models that contribute to ecological degradation, reading this book will undoubtedly set you on a healing path toward living in right relationship with all life!"

Marcus Briggs-Cloud, Ph.D., Co-director, Ekvn-Yefolecv Maskoke Ecovillage

"This is a superb primer for the Next Generation of Directors. It rises high above the old concept of corporate governance being bounded by finance, 'bottom lines', stultifying Codes, and risk aversion. It focuses on an organisation's primary Purpose, to rise above current uncertainties and align with a future where we all thrive. This is a future that seems increasingly out of reach – but which *Beyond Profit* makes practically achievable."

Bob Garratt, Author of *The Fish Rots from the Head*, Director of Good Governance Development. A founding father of Corporate Governance

"The economy requires massive change: in its purpose, composition, and impact. Achieving that change is the goal of the Wellbeing Economy movement, a diverse suite of actors working in different ways and in different spheres to realign economic activity with what people and planet need. The book *Beyond Profit* shows how these various parts can come together to deliver the transformation the economy so urgently required. Crisply written and peppered with case studies which prove the possible, this is critical reading for change agents, wherever in the system they may be."

Katherine Trebeck, University of Edinburgh. Co-founder of the Wellbeing Economy Alliance and Wellbeing Economy Governments

"*Beyond Profit* brilliantly articulates how leaders can create cultures that drive sustainable success and foster long-term wellbeing for all."

Paul J. Zak, PhD, Author of *Immersion: The Science of the Extraordinary and the Source of Happiness*

"I am now convinced that in order to stabilize health and health systems in the face of ecological and social crisis, we need to make long-term wellbeing for all our explicit goal. This calls to the best in humanity, uniting us in our joint project. *Beyond Profit* fills a critical gap - it shows how guided by skilful governance, we can turn destruction into an abundance of wellbeing for all, now and into the future."

Courtney Howard MD, MPP, Emergency Physician, Chair, Global Climate and Health Alliance, Founder of POWER--PlanetaryHealth Organizations for Wellbeing, Equity, and Regeneration

"The wilful blindness around the failure of our economic and business leadership to produce lasting benefits for the world as a whole has gone on long enough. The change required is daunting, but this book lays out in clear and pragmatic terms the resources and choices we have."

Margaret Heffernan, Author of *Wilful Blindness: Why We Ignore the Obvious at our Peril*

"*Beyond Profit* is a timely and necessary contribution to the discourse on ethical governance, purpose-driven leadership, and collective wellbeing. It thoughtfully interrogates the underlying assumptions that have shaped our economic and organizational systems and provides a comprehensive roadmap for transitioning from extractive to regenerative practice. As a leader committed to social inclusion, equity, and the democratization of opportunity, I see this work as a foundational resource for practitioners, policymakers, and changemakers looking to embed justice, access, inclusion, diversity, decolonization, and equity into the core of institutions. It is not only a powerful call to action – it is a practical guide for systemic transformation."

Victor Beausoleil, Board President of The Canadian Community Economic Development Network and Executive Director of Social Economy Through Social Inclusion (SETSI)

"Leadership is what we focus on and pursue in the new era, and *Beyond Profit* offers a fresh perspective on what leadership can be. 领导力是新时代我们所关注与追求的,《超越利润》给我们展现了一种新型领导力。"

Mingzheng Xiao, Professor of Leadership and Human Resource Development at the School of Government Management, Peking University

"As someone privileged to work with governance leaders across continents and sectors, I know that governance is a foundational function and skill, essential to building the nuts and bolts of a sustainable future. Yet, it too often remains out of view. *Beyond Profit* brings governance to the forefront, powerfully demonstrating that without mastering governance (of the self, our organisations, and our economies), the future we aspire to cannot be achieved or sustained. This book is a timely and necessary contribution to the global governance dialogue, offering clarity, relevance, and practical insight for leaders at every level."

Carolynn Chalmers, CEO, The Good Governance Academy founded by Professor Mervyn King

"*Beyond Profit* is a timely guide for leaders who want to embed purpose at the heart of complex organisations and deliver lasting value for communities and the planet. A thought-provoking and practical read."

John Holland-Kaye, Chair, Sizewell C

"The #climatemajority is emerging into self-consciousness. This book holds a mirror up to the world to accelerate into consciousness how governance for profit is driving us into an abyss - and what good governance looks like. The laws/regulations that we actually need - if our civilisation is not to collapse beyond recall - will only become law if and when norms and practices of a desired future become clear enough. For that reason, we need foundational literacy in purpose and governance. So this is a book to help set the stage for better, faster laws of the kind that the silent majority is already latently aware are required. *Beyond Profit* is not a book for the faint-hearted!"

Rupert Read, Emeritus Prof. Co-Director of the Climate Majority Project, and Author of *Why Climate Breakdown Matters*

"This is the practical and integrative thinking that we need - and we do not have time to waste."

David Orr, Paul Sears Distinguished Professor of Environmental Studies and Politics Emeritus at Oberlin College, and Professor of Practice at Arizona State University

"Literally everything we know and love is at stake. If we can't shake our suicidal profiteering, we will simply not have a civilization in a few decades. Which of us could possibly want that? *Beyond Profit* shows us why we are stuck and more importantly how to break free. Read it - then let's act to make 'Logic 3' our new reality as soon as possible."

Phoebe Barnard, Former lead scientist at the South African National Biodiversity Institute and past CEO of the Pacific Biodiversity Institute

"*Beyond Profit* is not just a book, it is an essential tool for all our existence, it is transcendental universal Indigenous knowledge in contemporary practical and academic language. Environmental and social, purpose based, rationalization in a state of wellbeing...in Tupi this is Marangatú."

Lic. Pedro Mojica, Embassador Emeritus Ngäbe-Buglé Nation, ABLA-YALA. UNHC- Indigenous Issues Special Rapporteur & Independent Expert. UCLA-NAID Centre Contributing Researcher

"*Beyond Profit* is the question of our time. Critically, it leads us to the task of breaking the dominance of finance over business, so as to make purpose-driven leadership possible. In this book, Victoria, enriched by her colleague's insights, masterfully draws from her decades of insights to guide businesses and society on this urgent journey."

Erinch Sahan, Associate Director for Investment, Joseph Rowntree Foundation and former Business & Enterprise Lead at Doughnut Economics Action Lab

"An inspiring and practical path to update our economic system so it represents what we all really care about.

Mark Gough, CEO and Founder, Capitals Coalition

"Clear, practical, and quietly radical – *Beyond Profit* belongs on the bedside table of every leader. In an age of ecological collapse and political fragmentation, the book calls us to the one identity we all share – as humans on planet Earth – and offers a clear and grounded framework to govern for our collective future. With humility and precision, the book doesn't tinker at the edges – it redraws the map. The authors weave micro, meso and macro insights into a practical agenda for reorienting leadership, power, and purpose. More than a book, this is an operational tool for those bold enough to lead towards long-term well-being and intergenerational responsibility."

Otti Vogt, former COO and Chief Transformation Officer in ING, Co-Founder of Global Society for Good Leadership

"Wellbeing has long been recognised as the essential goal, yet it continues to be overshadowed by a narrow focus on profit and growth, especially in how economics is taught. *Beyond Profit* equips students with the tools to understand and question this imbalance and shows how education itself can become part of the solution. It challenges universities to reflect on the values they promote – and offers a framework to help them centre long-term wellbeing for people and planet – in other words a sustainable future."

Shloka Murarka, Economics student. Student Advisor at Association for Quality Economics

"Sadly, the sustainable business movement has failed to address the terrible challenges faced by our planet. *Beyond Profit* articulates the path forward for a much-needed new vision and course correction."

Jeffrey Hollander, Co-Founder and Former CEO of Seventh Generation, Adjunct Professor, NYU Stern

"If governance is 'how we do things round here', then our current systems, which reward financial self-interest, have spectacularly failed to deliver for the majority of humanity. *Beyond Profit* is a breath of fresh air - a manual for change showcasing inspirational leadership shifting us to a fairer future. Read and be inspired. Then act."

Jane Davidson, Author of *#futuregen: Lessons from a Small Country*, Chair Wales Net Zero 2035. Ex Welsh Government Minister.

"*Beyond Profit* represents a gathering together of thinking that takes us outside of our comfort zone. To quote Albert Einstein "we cannot solve our problems with the same thinking we used when we created them." Well-being for all is surely the key indicator of success in a world that needs to wake up. As the World Benchmarking Alliance states: "we do not need to take a linear approach, nor can we afford one stakeholder group or region waiting for another to act first. Instead, we need everyone, everywhere to act all at once."

Paul Druckman, Chairman of the World Benchmarking Alliance, Honorary Professor at Durham Business School, and Former CEO of the International Integrated Reporting Council (IIRC)

"I stumbled into the deep problems of profit-first economy as an entrepreneur in Kenya. I managed to navigate a purpose-driven route beyond, unlocking the innovation needed - but many just get stuck. This is what makes *Beyond Profit* so important. It delivers the clarity, courage, and coherence needed to show, practically, how to shift from these profit-first models to purpose-driven systems; an urgent transformation our world can no longer afford to delay."

Tayba Hatimy, Co-Founder Baus Taka Enterprise, Kenya

"*Beyond Profit* is a book that combines truly systemic, holistic thinking with practical, focused advice. This is quite a feat! A must read for anyone seeking hope for the future."

Alison Taylor, Clinical Professor at NYU stern and Author of *Higher Ground*

"Humanity has been stuck on the fast track to disaster because we have been stuck in the narrow logic of profit, and the even narrower story of ourselves as consumers. This book plays a vital part in opening the way, equipping anyone willing to engage with the tools and frameworks to do better. It's no longer possible to claim that there is no alternative - there manifestly is."

Jon Alexander, Author *Citizens: Why the Key to Fixing Everything is All of Us.*
Co-founder New Citizen Project

"The wellbeing of all life on earth can never be achieved unless we align our worldview and decision making with the process that describes how it works – the regenerative process. If we want to enable the regenerative mindsets and practices that honor the entanglement of life then we cannot just wish this into being – we need to govern for it. *Beyond Profit* helps us take shared steps to governance literacy for a regenerative future where we all thrive."

John Fullerton, Founder & President Capital Institute

"In a time when cascading crises on planet Earth demand bold systemic change, *Beyond Profit* delivers a thoughtful and inspiring framework for anyone ready to help shape a better future. It reconnects purpose, governance, and wellbeing in a way that is both visionary and deeply grounded in practical action."

William J. Ripple. Distinguished Professor of Ecology, Oregon State University, USA;
Director of the Alliance of World Scientists and lead Author of 'World Scientists'
Warning to Humanity: A Second Notice'

"Moral leadership is nothing more than the love child of bravery and doing the right thing-intelligently and with drive. It is not about hair shirted sanctimony because that has never been a successful leadership model. However, pragmatism with a heart of gold-has! Read this book and don't treat it like a New Age Bible. Read it as the serious person you are looking for guidance to build on the strengths you already have. Treat it as a thought-provoking friend and mentor reminding you always that the Future Remains ours to Make."

Tim Smit, KBE. Co-founder of the Eden Project. Environmental Entrepreneur

"*Beyond Profit* is not just a book – it's a systemic intervention. It names the invisible structures that have quietly governed our decisions and reorients leadership toward a radically necessary horizon: long-term wellbeing for all. With clarity and courage, it challenges the myth that financial self-interest will lead us to collective flourishing and provides the theoretical and practical scaffolding to lead differently. In a world that's tipping between breakdown and breakthrough, this is the roadmap we need, not to reform what's broken, but to govern for what truly matters."

Hans Stegeman, Chief Economist Triodos Bank

"*Beyond Profit* focuses on core issues, provides powerful insights and gives clear messaging that can really help sustainability professionals, and all leaders, see a positive way forward. The book helps us to collectively see and name the systemic changes needed and how they can be adopted, now, to meet the existential challenges of our time. No quick fixes – but long-term actions and outcomes designed to result in a good life for everyone forever."

Gwyn Jones, Founder, Association for Sustainability Professionals (ASP)

"At a time when 'purpose' and 'sustainability' is being diluted, *Beyond Profit* cuts through. It is not yet another book, it should be placed squarely at the centre of strategy meetings, cabinet discussions, board agendas and leadership retreats. A manual not only for reforming capitalism, but to redefine what it means to lead responsibly in the 21st century."

John O'Brien MBE, Founder of Anthropy, the UK's largest cross-sector national
leadership gathering

"This book is brutally honest and asks some tough questions that will inspire leaders to reflect on how their organisations, and themselves as leaders and citizens, can better position their role in improving the wellbeing of people and the planet. After all, all organizations, including business, are about people coming together to create something of value. Purpose-driven models frame value creation and its governance in the broadest of ways. In a world where many are searching for meaning, this book can act as a map towards the hidden treasure."

Michael Ristaniemi, EU official, Professor of Practice, University of Eastern Finland,
former Vice President, Sustainability, Metsä Group

"As greenhouse gas emissions continue to rise and we cross six out of nine of our planetary boundaries, it's clear the system we have is no longer the system we need. We urgently need to embed new approaches to governance and find new ways to lead. *Beyond Profit* offers an alternative way forward to support leaders to create value that matters now, for the long-term and for wellbeing for all."

Matt Scott, Executive Director of UK Centre for Greening Finance & Investment,
Senior Advisor at Chapter Zero and former Head of Climate, Bank of England

"*Beyond Profit* is not only a compelling call to shift our economy to one that drives long-term well-being for all but also offers a blueprint to drive the necessary transformations at the personal and organizational levels, as well as in how we govern and structure our economies. It's essential reading for any executive serious about shaping a purpose-first system that genuinely serves people and planet."

Catherine Wood, Chief Product, Marketing and Wealth Officer, Coast Capital
Savings, Canada

"*Beyond Profit* goes right to the heart of the challenge facing the humanity and every living creature on Earth: we have prioritized profits over everything else, and this short-termism has driven us to the edge of planetary "boundaries. *Beyond Profit* calls out the flaws of our unsustainable economy and provides an inspired solution of purposeful leadership as the way forward."

Chris Coulter, CEO, GlobeScan

"*Beyond Profit* dares to name the elephant in the boardroom: that financial self-interest has been mistaken for collective wisdom for far too long. This is the handbook we need for rewiring leadership logic from profit to purpose, from red tape to right action, from paralysis to progress."

Solitaire Townsend, Chief Solutionist, Futerra

"This is a book that seeks to bridge many divides – a hard but necessary task. It may not, therefore, be the most accessible read for some and may in parts feel quite technical. Though without doubt Victoria is a visionary thinker and powerful actor who has created a guide for leaders across all sectors that, if consciously applied, offers a path away from the current domination of fear, hate and division, to love, respect and wellbeing uniting us as a global family."

Cindy Forde, Author, Founder of Planetari

Beyond Profit captures both the urgency of our moment and the profound opportunity before us, giving us a practical blueprint for building the Wellbeing Economy our world desperately needs. At its heart, this is about purpose-driven leadership – the kind that transforms – and governance that helps Purpose-Driven Organizations perform as we would want to perform on a best day, every day, for all."

Shari Slate, Former Chief Inclusion and Collaboration Officer and Senior Vice President of Inclusive Future and Strategy, Cisco

"*Beyond Profit* is a transformative guide for leaders seeking to inspire meaningful change.

Richard E. Boyatzis, PhD. Author of *The Science of Change*

"*Beyond Profit* provides a thoughtful and thought-provoking book by three leading voices in the field of transformational system change. The suggestions for governance that structures our simultaneous transition at the macro (country), meso (business) and micro (personal) level resonated very deeply for me."

Rutger Hoekstra, Author of *Replacing GDP by 2030*

"Leadership for purposeful and meaningful change requires: 'Critique' of current practice - which must be convincing; 'Vision' of necessary alternatives - which must be inspiring; and 'Design' - which must be practicable. *Beyond Profit* clearly illuminates each of these keys, providing a carefully argued analysis and an action guide to help make its wisdom manifest - in pursuit of systemic breakthrough to a wellbeing economy and a safe future. At this 'eleventh hour' our priority must be to unlearn unexamined deep-grained toxic assumptions and habits and learn governance for human and planetary wellbeing. This very timely book elaborates the meaning and implications of Donella Meadow's plea to work 'for the good of the whole'. It makes personal sense, it makes economic sense, and crucially, it makes planetary sense. There is no time to lose!"

Stephen Sterling, Emeritus Professor, Sustainable Earth Institute, University of Plymouth. Author of *Learning and Sustainability in Dangerous Times*

"This book is desperately needed by leaders at all levels of society – in business as well as government. When we first realize that the world is crashing against environmental and social limits, many of us tend to hope that governments will come to the rescue. By themselves, they can't and won't. As the authors of this timely book argue, what's required is a whole-system reset, and that requires identifying the bug in our current operating program. Profit is the system's measure of success, and it sets us on a path for more climate change, economic inequality, toxic pollution, resource depletion, and disappearance of wild nature. Getting beyond profit is humanity's only hope of shifting the incentives and disincentives that lock us on a course of mutual assured destruction. The alternative to our current death march is to flourish together in a world that's recovering its innate beauty and abundance."

Richard Heinberg, Senior Fellow, Post Carbon Institute. Author of *Power: Limits and Prospects for Human Survival*

"We live in a complex, turbulent and fast changing world, full of challenges, risks and opportunities. A proper multidimensional view is needed in order to nurture well-being across people, organizations and societies. Defining and implementing proper purpose-driven approaches is core to inspiring and delivering the solutions we must build together. This wonderful book is a must-read compass to inspire and guide all of us, at many different levels, in the identification and creation of this future!"

Pedro Saraiva, Director of PLANAPP – Centre for Planning and Evaluation of Public Policies for Portugal

"As a Chief Sustainability Officer in a company which has changed its Articles of Association to put environmental and social prosperity at its heart, I have been working hard over the last five years to operationalise our approach to the wellbeing economy and demonstrate true value generation. Wow, how I wish I had been able to read this book at the start of that journey. Luckily, I have worked closely with some of the authors over that time and I can tell you; their thinking has been instrumental in making the shift to a purpose driven organisation a success. This is a must-read book for all CSOs and CEOs/CFOs for that matter."

Andy Brown, Group Chief Sustainability Officer - Anglian Water Group Chair of the British Standards Institute Mirror Committee on Purpose-Driven Organisations

"Over the past decade, I've had the privilege of working alongside Victoria and witnessing the evolution of the ideas that *Beyond Profit* now brings to life. This book is the product of years of rigorous thought, practical application, and principled leadership. The authors' clarity in redefining how purpose, governance, and leadership intersect with long-term wellbeing makes this essential reading for any leader seeking to navigate today's complex sustainability landscape with integrity and foresight."

Beth Knight, Board advisor and sustainability director. Great British Businesswoman of the Year, 2022

"'Beyond' is the key word, as it embodies evolution. Profit has driven human progress for centuries, but the time has come to redefine it in alignment with today's societal and environmental priorities. We are grateful to Victoria, Ben, and Lorenzo for leading the way in accelerating this essential transformation."

Eric Ezechieli and Paolo Di Cesare, NATIVA

"What will be the epitaph for my generation of business leaders? That we were wilfully blind to the unfolding polycrisis? Or that we were well-intentioned but too wedded to Business as Usual? These are the questions that came to mind as I studied this comprehensive, practical and readable roadmap of the business journey ahead. The authors formidably and irresistibly marshal the overall agenda – and by questioning the assumptions and details of our current system and exposing their own, enable the reader to do the same."

Mark Goyder, Founder, Tomorrow's Company

"*Beyond Profit* is a clarion call and practical guide for Purpose-driven Leaders to embrace a governance model focused on serving others, and to achieve a long-term collective wellbeing. It is both a diagnostic and a roadmap for the new leaders, as it outlines a vastly superior model for individuals and society to the current narrow-minded self-interest and zero-sum game economics."

Luca Zerbini, CEO Una Terra Early Growth Fund, and Sustainability Operating Advisor at Advent International

"We are living at a time of profound change across multiple dimensions – decisions made today are likely to have significant consequences for generations to come. Those with the responsibility of holding decision-making roles during this time will find in this book the thought-provoking questions, stimulus and practical guidance to navigate towards a better future for us all."

Sarah Gillard, CEO Blueprint for Better Business, Former Director of Purpose and Special Projects, John Lewis Partnership

"*Beyond Profit* is a transformative guide for leaders seeking to move beyond profit-first thinking and toward purpose-driven governance that prioritizes long-term wellbeing for all. The book details the broader global context for how creative, resource-efficient solutions can drive sustainable impact when aligned with a clear sense of purpose. It offers practical frameworks and real-world examples to empower leaders at every level – economy, organization, and individual – to make this future a reality, unlocking creativity, resilience, and collaboration for a thriving future."

Jaideep Prabhu, Professor of Marketing, University of Cambridge. Co-author of *Frugal Innovation: How to Do More with Less*

"*Beyond Profit* reminded me of Keynes who said the difficulty lies not so much in developing new ideas, as it is in escaping from old ones. It is a poignant & practical reminder that the economy, and marketing as part of it, needs to work for people and the planet, never the other way around. *Beyond Profit* gives us the practical tools to urgently unite for action to the benefit of long-term well-being for all."

Rupen Desai, CMO Una Terra and Co-founder The Shed 28. World Federation of Advertisers, VP Asia-Pacific.

"Here's a book that takes a leap forward towards an exciting phase in the human story, from an ever-rising material progress for some towards a more widely distributed well-being for many. We have become an insatiable society, racing against each other to earn more and more to buy stuff we don't need, whilst neglecting our shared, common, wealth. *Beyond Profit* to me opens up opportunities for growth in knowledge, life chances, healthy lifestyles, a revitalisation of our common goods: nature, liveable communities, beauty, the arts and culture. Profit is good and necessary if it is produced by worthy activities, reinvested in socially useful purposes, not earned at the expense of the planet or people and more fairly distributed. *Beyond Profit* does not deny this reality, but it deepens the meaning of profit and offers reflections, models and inspirations to leaders who grasp the civilsational tipping point we face."

Marcello Palazzi, MSc MBA, Co-Founder, B Corps in Europe, For Good Leaders Cooperative, NOW Partners, Progression Foundation

"For too long our global economic system has been driving profits for some rather than wellbeing for all. *Beyond Profit* is a guide for leaders who want to reverse this."

Jeremy Nicholls, Social Value International Co-Founder. Former UNDP Impact Standards assurance framework lead

"*Beyond Profit* brilliantly articulates the imperative shift from profit maximization to wellbeing maximization, guiding leaders with compelling clarity toward a thriving future. It serves as a compelling catalyst for systemic change, empowering leaders to shift entrenched economic paradigms and build resilient governance structures aligned with long-term wellbeing for all."

Kirsten Wright, Managing Director of the Waterloo Institute for Complexity and Innovation (WICI) at the University of Waterloo

"*Beyond Profit* is more than just essential reading for today's business leaders; it lays out the fundamental change in economic thinking needed for almost all environmental of societal transitions we could hope to achieve. By dissecting strategies narrowly pursuing profit, it reveals how they ultimately lead to systemic unravelling. And as a guide to a positive future, it shows how a new economic logic - centred in long-term wellbeing for all - leads to a credible, resilient and desirable economy that can work better for everyone."

James Vacarro, CEO Re:Pattern. Former Strategy Director, Triodos Bank

"*Beyond Profit* is a bold and thoughtful piece of work. It tackles the big questions, reframes the role of leadership, and lays out a path many instinctively know is necessary – but few are equipped to articulate. Importantly, it also brings to life the critical role that co-created global standards – especially ISO 37011 – can play in turning that vision into a shared and actionable future."

Neil Gaught, FRSA, Author of *CORE: How a Single Organizing Idea Can Change Business For Good*

"*Beyond Profit* is a timely and visionary tour de force which reorientates purpose and leadership away from profit to wellbeing for all. We should all use it to guide our work and our lives."

Jules Peck. ex-Chair of the first UK Quality of Life Commission, ex board member at the New Economics Foundation and the Center for Thriving Places.

"*Beyond Profit* is a highly pragmatic book, proclaiming a vitally needed refreshed purpose. Governments the world over are desperately staking their credibility on more growth of their financial income - at whatever cost. So long as GDP rises, wages increase, jobs are created, investments flow, and wealth spreads, they blindly assume that global wellbeing will magically result. This is a chimera. Growth as it is currently pursued is systematically destroying universal wellbeing. Victoria Hurth and her colleagues are reaching out to the crest of a truly transformational wave to address this. They have articulated an ongoing global movement for enabling wellbeing to become the purpose of all organisations through enlightened governance in all sectors. There is a restless but hopeful recognition of this transformation, expressed particularly by the young. If we are to survive as a moral and decent species on a unique planet, the message of this important book needs to get under our skin."

Tim O'Riordan, OBE DL FBA, PhD. Emeritus Professor of Environmental Sciences, University of East Anglia

"*Beyond Profit* not only provides a practical guide to leaders willing to drive the world to the future we need, but also provides a profound challenge to our deep beliefs in recent past (current?) leadership attributes: it clearly stimulates the sense of need for a shift from a 'master of the universe' and 'success self-identification only type of leadership, towards new leaders with self-awareness in relation with the whole world."

Michele De Capitani, Former CFO and CSO Italian Export Credit Agency - SACE

"*Beyond Profit* is a call to reimagine the purpose of enterprise and governance – where the measure of success is not how much we take, but how well we care. It's about shifting from a logic of extraction to one of regeneration – for the wellbeing of all. The Common Good calls."

Christian Sarkar, co-author of *Brand Activism: From Purpose to Action*

"A boardroom literate bridge between high intention and the grit of corporate reality. This is a book for people ready to remake business."

Chris Nichols, Visiting Professor, and Co-Founder of GameShift

"In the spirit of the best horror movies, the sustainability community prophesied an end-of-the world monster so terrifying that we all hid behind the sofa and hoped it would go away if we ignored it. *Beyond Profit* charts a genuine and pragmatic path out of the horror we all know we are in yet feel powerless to act on. Quite simply the right book at the right time!"

Paul Randle, Co-author of *Sustainable Marketing: The Industry's Role in a Sustainable Future* (Leonard Berry Book Award Winner). Co-founder of the Sustainable Marketing Compass

"The authors have done a remarkable thing: they have forced us to think harder about governance and how it could make a tangible difference to the impact business has on the world. This book contains lessons which business leaders cannot duck."

Stefan Stern, former *Financial Times* columnist and Visiting Professor at Bayes Business School, City St. George's, University of London

Beyond Profit

Purpose-Driven Leadership for a
Wellbeing Economy

Victoria Hurth
Ben Renshaw
Lorenzo Fioramonti

First published in Great Britain by John Murray Business in 2025
An imprint of John Murray Press

2

A CIP catalogue record for this title is available from the British Library

Hardback ISBN 978 1 399 82248 0
ebook ISBN 978 1 399 82249 7

Typeset by KnowledgeWorks Global Ltd.

Printed and bound in India by Manipal Technologies Limited

John Murray Press
Carmelite House
50 Victoria Embankment
London EC4Y 0DZ

www.johnmurraybusiness.com

John Murray Press, part of Hodder & Stoughton Limited
An Hachette UK company

The authorised representative in the EEA is Hachette Ireland, 8 Castlecourt Centre,
Dublin 15, D15 XTP3, Ireland (email: info@hbgi.ie)

To the many, many people out there dedicating their energy to leading for a future of collective wellbeing for all life on Earth. This book is for you.

Disclaimer

Throughout this book, we reference real-world examples and share testimonials to illuminate the diverse global efforts being made towards developing Purpose-Driven Organisations and long-term wellbeing for all. These examples are intended purely to illustrate the range of ideas, experiments and practices at play across industries and geographies. We remain neutral to any individual organisation's work and recognise that there is no single example of definitive best practice. Our purpose is to inspire thoughtful reflection and collective progress beyond profit.

Contributors

The following people gave their insight and time with incredible generosity, providing in-depth interviews or insightful quotes. They will be referenced by name and title in the book:

Amy C. Edmondson, Novartis Professor of Leadership and Management, Harvard Business School

Andy Brown, Group Chief Sustainability Officer, Anglian Water Group

Andy Cosslett CBE, Chair, ITV plc

Angela Monaghan, Founder a m impact

Brandon Peele, Author of *Purpose Work Nation*

Brian Woodhead, Former Director, Terminal 2 Programme and Operations, Heathrow

Carlota de Paula Coelho, Senior Policy Manager, B Lab

Catherine Wood, Chief Product, Marketing and Wealth Officer, Coast Capital Savings

Coro Strandberg, Board Director and Governance Committee Chair, BC Lottery Corporation

Dora Gudrun Gudmundsdottir, Director of Public Health, Directorate of Health in Iceland, Founder and Chair of Wellbeing Economy Forum

Emily Chang, Chief Executive Officer, VML West

Enrico Giovannini, Professor, University of Rome Tor Vergata and LUISS Guido Carli University

Geoff McDonald, Former Global VP HR, Unilever

Jamie Bunce, Entrepreneur in Later Living

Jane Davidson, Chair, Wales Net Zero 2035 and Pro Vice-Chancellor Emeritus, University of Wales Trinity Saint David

Jeffrey Hollander, Adjunct Professor, NYU Stern and Founder and Former CEO, Seventh Generation

Jeremy Nicholls, Founder of SVI and Independent Advisor

Jin Montesano, Director, Representative Executive Officer, Chief People Officer, LIXIL Corporation

Joachim Froment, Co-founder and Creative Director, Futurewave

Jon Alexander, Co-Founder, New Citizen Project

Joel Burrows, Chief Executive Officer, Lindt UK and Ireland

Juan Diego Mujica Filippi, Impact Law lead, NATIVA

Justin Banini, Chief Executive Officer and Co-Founder, ClearScore

Justin Reese, Chief Executive Officer, Ghirardelli

Katherine Trebeck, Advisor and Champion for a Wellbeing Economy

Laura Miller, Former Executive Vice President, Chief Information Officer, Macy's

Luca Zerbini, CEO and Managing Director, Una Terra Venture Capital Fund

Matt Palmer, Executive Director, Lower Thames Crossing

Nick Dent, Director of Customer Operations, London Underground at Transport for London

Paolo Di Cesare and Eric Ezechieli, Co-Founders, NATIVA

Paul Snyder, Executive Vice President Stewardship, Tillamook County Creamery Association

Paul J. Zak, Author of *Immersion: The Science of the Extraordinary and the Source of Happiness*

Pedro Saraiva, Director, PLANAPP (Centre for Planning and Evaluation of Public Policies), Portuguese Centre of Government

Richard E. Boyatzis, Professor, Departments of Organisational Behavior, Psychology and Cognitive Science, H. Clark Ford Professorship, Case Western Reserve University

Richard Solomons, Chairman, Rentokil Initial plc

Roland Fasel, Chief Operations Officer, Maybourne Hotel Group

Rupen Desai and Ranjit Jathanna, Co-founders, The Shed 28

Ryan Turnbull, Member of Parliament for Whitby, Parliamentary Secretary to the Minister of Finance, and Parliamentary Secretary to the Minister of Innovation, Science and Industry

Sandrine Dixson-Declève, Honorary President, The Club of Rome and Executive Chair, Earth4All

Tayba Hatimy, Founder, Baus Taka Enterprise

Tony Juniper CBE, Chair, Natural England UK and Former CEO, Friends of the Earth UK

Wakan Wahohipi Win, Co-organiser, World Peace and Prayer Day

Zoë Arden, Leadership Communications Expert

Contents

Foreword

Coming out of college, I had the great joy of working as an engineer for Buckminster Fuller, the remarkable 20th-century inventor, designer, systems thinker and educator. My job included geodesic dome calculations, engineering drawings, and building scale models for new geodesic dome designs. It was a memorable experience; I loved the work and believed it mattered. I was moved by Fuller's larger vision of making the world a better place, but slowly concluded that I would never be a good enough engineer or architect to make a contribution to the world in the way he had. At the time, it was not at all clear to me what my future work would be, nor how I would figure it out.

This started a journey of self-reflection on what I was able to do and what I was drawn to that might make a tangible difference in the world. The next step seemed to be one of giving back, in a small way, to try to repay the debt I felt I owed for the good fortune of working with Fuller. I decided to write a book to clarify Buckminster Fuller's intricate geometric work, making it accessible to a wider audience, because his own books on the subject (*Synergetics* and *Synergetics 2*) were extraordinarily dense. This experience taught me that I enjoyed the process of writing and teaching. But I still had to figure out the academic field where I could make a contribution.

At this time, I was fortunate to meet Larry Wilson, a thinker and successful serial entrepreneur, who had recently started a new business in organisational development. I went to work for Larry, doing research and consulting, and loved the work. The job thus opened a new door – giving me an opportunity to study organisations, and to help people and teams make the work better while trying to do the right thing for customers and communities. After almost four years, I went on to pursue a PhD in Organisational Behavior. When I graduated, I was offered a faculty job at Harvard Business School where I have been for over 28 years.

As a second-year graduate student in the early 1990s, I joined an interdisciplinary team of researchers undertaking a groundbreaking study of medication errors in hospitals. As part of the study, trained nurse investigators painstakingly gathered data about these potentially devastating human errors over a six-month period, hoping to shed light on their actual incidence in hospitals. Meanwhile, I observed how care-givers in hospital units worked as teams. My research question was simple: did better teams have lower error rates? It was easy to under-stand how errors might happen in these busy, life-or-death, highly var-iable and customised operations, where transfer of tasks to others was frequent and important.

Through this work, I accidentally stumbled into the importance of psychological safety, broadly defined as a context in which people are comfortable speaking up – for instance about mistakes – despite the interpersonal risk of doing so. When people work in psychologically safe environments, they feel able to ask for help, express concerns and admit mistakes without fear of embarrassment or retribution. They are confident that speaking up won't lead to humiliation or rejection. They believe they can ask questions when they are unsure about something. They trust and respect their colleagues. When a work environment has reasonably high psychological safety, good things happen: mistakes are reported quickly so that prompt corrective action can be taken; coordination across groups or departments is enabled, and potentially game-changing ideas for innovation are shared.

My accidental discovery of this interpersonal context factor occurred when survey data I collected suggested that better teamwork (itself enabled by more coaching-oriented team leaders) was associated with higher, not lower, error rates. This surprising result started me think-ing. It simply didn't make sense that better teams make more mistakes; I realised better teams may simply be more willing and able to speak up about mistakes. Of course, this meant that the error data for the larger study might be biased and incomplete. More research was needed to establish support for this new interpretation of the results, which I have described in detail in prior writings.[1] For the purposes of this foreword,

1 Edmondson, A. (2023) *Right Kind of Wrong: Why Learning to Fail Can Teach Us to Thrive*. London: Penguin; Edmondson, A. (1996) Learning from mistakes is easier said than done: Group and organisational influences on the detection and correction of human error. *Journal of Applied Behavioral Science*, 32 (1): 5–28.

I note simply that psychological safety, which facilitates openly sharing failures, is crucial for individuals, teams and organisations to learn and work effectively together to serve clients and customers.

This formative research informed my 2023 book, *Right Kind of Wrong – Why Learning to Fail Can Teach Us to Thrive*. I dub "intelligent failure" the "right kind of wrong". To be intelligent, a failure must take place in new territory, in pursuit of a goal, with adequate preparation and tolerable risk. Intelligent failures are essentially the experiments that don't pan out: new ideas and solutions that fail to work as hoped. Intelligent failures are essential for developing new knowledge.

Failures are an unavoidable part of progress. This is true for science, for technology, for the vital institutions that shape society, as well as in our personal lives. This is why it's so important – and ultimately so rewarding – to learn about the science of failure. Psychological safety is an antidote to the interpersonal fear that prevents us from failing well. My research has shown that psychologically safe environments help teams avoid preventable failures. They also help them pursue intelligent ones. Psychological safety helps people do and say the things that allow learning and progress. This interpersonal climate factor turns out to be crucial in predicting team performance in challenging environments, ranging from those in leading academic medical centres to Fortune 500 companies to your family. It is leadership responsibility to build fearless organisations – but everyone in an organisation can contribute to doing so, when they show up with curiosity and respect, interested in what others have to say and willing to listen.[2] Organisations with low interpersonal fear are those where people are willing to speak up with ideas, concerns, questions, and to experiment and team up with one another for the greater good. It's where the focus is on accomplishing something that matters; where it is not about *me* but about *us*.

As we consider the severe challenges and problems humanity must now solve under considerable time pressure, questions about how we can fail fast so as to arrive at the very best solutions seem more pertinent than ever. *Beyond Profit* helps us recognise this challenge and highlights the requirement for leaders to minimise fear and unleash

2 Edmondson, A.C. and M.J. Kerrissey (2025) What people get wrong about psychological safety: Six misconceptions that have led organisations astray. *Harvard Business Review*, May–June, pp. 52–59.

love – from within themselves all the way to how our economies are structured. The authors set out what we know to be the case – that as humans we are disposed to work harder when, and we get more joy from, pursuing meaningful goals that serve the good of others – in other words, love. As the book sets out, seeking to be in service of the good of others, which is anchored to our long-term collective wellbeing, is the essence of what it means to be purpose-driven. The authors take us on a global and system-wide journey that starts with the premise that the economy, and by extension the organisations that enable it, exists to transform shared resources for collective long-term wellbeing. There is nothing new in this. However, we often ignore that the system of governance we have created to achieve this outcome relies on economies, organisations and leadership that are self-interested and prone to focusing on short-term financial gain. We have been led to believe that this is the best way to serve our wellbeing, but it is increasingly clear to many observers that this has created, in aggregate, the opposite effect.

Beyond Profit challenges us to confront a technical reality: if we are to survive and move beyond this phase of dangerous unsustainability, we need leadership that creates efficient and effective economies, organisations, and teams that are governed to serve others. This requires building Wellbeing Economies anchored on achieving long-term wellbeing for all, Purpose-Driven Organisations that contribute to this shared goal, and Purpose-Driven Leadership that unlocks meaningful work and lives, igniting the energy to drive these outcomes.

To unleash a purpose-driven market economy, it is vital to work to reduce fear at all levels. Psychological safety is a part of the conditions that allow purpose-driven work to flourish and, as the book will outline, a key tool of Purpose-Driven Leaders. The authors offer a powerful roadmap for navigating today's profound leadership challenges. They offer steps to develop your leadership potential to support our collective wellbeing.

In today's complex and ambiguous world, continuous learning and agility are vital to our collective success. The best leaders are those who are truly aware of the interconnected systems in which they operate, understand their own limitations, and have the humility to admit their mistakes, accept when they are wrong, and desire more to understand reality than to be right. *Beyond Profit* outlines the decision-making frame our organisations rely on and how it's brought us to this point.

Leading others out of the decision-making box we have created for ourselves, at all levels of the system, will require new degrees of bravery and vulnerability and it will require courage and curiosity to create meaningful connections with others.

This book was written to help you take that first step.

Amy C. Edmondson
Novartis Professor of Leadership and Management
Harvard Business School
November 2024

About the Authors

Every book has a story, and *Beyond Profit* is no exception. This book is born from the collaboration of three distinct voices, each with primary experiences that span the interconnected levels of leadership required to drive meaningful change. Between us, we bring decades of lived, global expertise across the three system levels essential for purpose-driven leadership: Lorenzo at the Macro economy level, Victoria at the Meso organisational level, and Ben at the Micro leadership and team level. What unites us is a shared commitment to assuring long-term wellbeing for all by working for Wellbeing Economies, Purpose-Driven Organisations and Purposeful Work and Lives. Below, we share brief glimpses into our personal journeys and expertise, setting the stage for the different perspectives and styles you'll notice throughout the chapters on the Macro (Chapter 2), Meso (Chapter 3) and Micro (Chapter 4) levels.

Victoria Hurth

I began life as a curious and persistent child, puzzled by the way adults, outside the family, made decisions at odds with their wellbeing. Advice from them revolved around acquiring big houses, cars and expensive holidays – but even then, I knew that a good life did not rely on these status symbols. That set me on a lifelong journey to find out what was wrong, what could change and what I could do to bring it about. I never realised what this 35-year "action learning" journey would reveal to me and I had no idea until 2002 just how much current and future wellbeing was being destroyed by our collective decisions.

I started investigating business and company decision-making via a degree in Management Sciences and jobs at 3M and Accenture as a management consultant in retail strategy. In a bid for greater impact I volunteered in South Africa and Ghana. A chance brush with the World Summit on Sustainable Development in 2002 in Johannesburg opened up the world of sustainability science and philosophy. From there, I spent 20 years spanning academia and practice following all the "but why?" "but how?" questions I could. My continued parallel work as an independent management consultant allowed me to learn from, and test, conclusions with global executives – and 12 years leading the development of national and international standards in sustainability and governance have given me the chance to listen to and synthesise the global views of experts from the pool of 174 national members of ISO. My five years of co-convening the International Standard in Governance of Organizations (ISO 37000) and my current role leading the development of the most critical standard: ISO 37011 in Purpose-Driven Organisations have been particularly insightful.

About six years ago my research, interactions and relentless questioning kept leading back to the same fundamental insights that I was hearing across sectors, nations and leaders. While I will never stop questioning, I realised that decades as a pracademic had led me to deeply transformative and stable conclusions that could unite the energy of people working hard to make the world better. I recognised that these insights were hard-won and probably just out of reach of leaders caught in the demands of the day to day. Even the simplest – like how the goal of the economy and the goal of sustainability are in essence the same – took years to crystallise. How could busy leaders be expected to arrive at the same place in time to address the ultra urgency of our unsustainability? I had to be bolder in helping leapfrog leaders of all kinds. And if I was wrong, then it would be a way to learn and refine my conclusions. This book is a core part of my journey and that mission: to make visible what remains just beyond sight and to accelerate the shift towards Purpose-Driven Leadership that serves long-term wellbeing for all of us.

I now have a broad portfolio as an Independent Pracademic. I spend most of my time presenting key notes and supporting the world to crystallise and live out the consensus that is often just beyond sight. This includes working hands on with leaders and organisations – such as educating global senior executives as a Fellow at the University of Cambridge Institute for Sustainability Leadership (CISL), being an impact advisor for Una Terra, a non-executive director of the UK's major organic standards company (Soil Association Certification Ltd), an academic lead for Common Ground Research Networks and the Head Tutor for CISL's online Sustainable Marketing course – amongst other things.

Ben Renshaw

My journey began at the world-renowned Yehudi Menuhin School, a prestigious institution nestled in the picturesque Surrey countryside outside London, where I trained as a classical violinist. It was here that I first witnessed the profound connection between craft and wellbeing. One vivid memory stands out: observing the school's founder, the visionary Lord Menuhin, in the later stages of his life. Despite struggling with his health, Lord Menuhin would place a violin under his chin and be transported into a state of flow. The transformation was remarkable – his energy would return, and his playing would radiate magic, touching everyone in the room. However, the passion to dedicate my life to mastering the next concerto was missing.

After leaving the school, I embarked on a gap year to travel and reflect. In Israel, arriving from cold and rainy London with only my violin and a backpack, I found myself overlooking the Mediterranean Sea. In that moment of stillness, I felt a profound sense of peace and realised there was more to life than playing the violin. A few months later, I began a performance degree at The Guildhall School of Music but soon left to pursue a new path. My curiosity about what drives human behaviour and my desire to solve meaningful problems led me into the world of personal development. It was here that I found my calling. Stumbling into the field of executive coaching, I was fortunate to be mentored by Graham Alexander, the pioneer of business coaching in Europe.

In 2005, Graham introduced me to Andy Cosslett, then CEO of InterContinental Hotels Group (IHG). Cosslett, together with Tracy Robbins, IHG's Executive Vice President of Human Resources, crafted the company's core purpose: *Great Hotels Guests Love*, and committed to developing Purpose-Driven Leaders. I vividly recall sitting in Tracy's office to discuss creating what would become the *Leading with Purpose* programme. Though I was new to the concept of purpose at the time, the idea captivated me. Over the following years, I worked with IHG to develop more than 1,000 leaders globally, helping them discover and lead with purpose – a transformative experience that deeply influenced my own sense of purpose.

Since then, I have partnered with organisations such as A&O Shearman, BT, Diageo, Ghirardelli, Heathrow, Hermes, HSBC, Lindt Canada, Lower Thames Crossing, Maybourne Group, M&S, National Highways, Sainsbury's, Sky, Transport for London, Unilever, Virgin Media, and Whole Foods Market to develop Purpose-Driven Leaders. My work has become a core expression of my own purpose, inspiring leaders to connect what matters most to meaningful outcomes. Alongside my coaching work, I have authored 11 books, including *How to Be a CEO*, *LoveWork*, *Purpose*, and *LEAD*, which have shaped my thinking and methodology. These efforts have culminated in *Beyond Profit*, a testament to my lifelong dedication to unlocking the potential of purpose-driven leadership.

Lorenzo Fioramonti

I landed on the term "Wellbeing Economy" after reaching the summit of Tiger's Nest, the famous Buddhist temple in Bhutan. For years, I had been focusing on the flaws of the current economic system and had been chipping away at developing a feasible and implementable alternative to the status quo. It was only when I reached the top of the mountain, roughly 5,000 metres above sea level, that I realised how powerful the concept of wellbeing could be in triggering change at the political level. An historian and political scientist by education, I had already written several books on national statistics and economic policy. Now I needed a narrative that could help motivate leaders at all levels to change: the Wellbeing Economy was it.

Since that pivotal moment, I have developed a number of internationally renowned research centres in both the Global North and the Global South. I was appointed policy advisor by presidents and prime ministers the world over. Due to my commitment to wellbeing in national politics, I was then elected Member of Parliament and national Minister in my home country, Italy, which – along with the work of my colleagues – has pioneered the adoption of Wellbeing Economy frameworks and policies. My work has been published in over 80 scientific articles (with thousands of citations) and several books (which have been reviewed, by, among others, *Financial Times*, *Harvard Business Review, Bloomberg* and the World Economic Forum) and has inspired three film documentaries, the latest of which is titled *Purpose* (https:// purpose.film/).

The Overview

Beyond Profit offers both a vision and practical guide for building better governance in a world where narrow and unhelpful assumptions have made sustainability feel out of reach. Around the globe, leaders are working to shift systems towards collective long-term wellbeing, yet the movement remains fragmented and difficult to join. Despite widespread efforts, progress is slow.

Unless we clearly define the core change we seek across economies, organisations, and daily life, the status quo will prevail. Leaders we meet from all walks of life seem to intuitively agree on what is wrong, recognise the deeper problems and understand the necessary solutions, yet they speak about this in different ways and focus on different parts of the puzzle. What's missing is a shared picture: a map we can all navigate by which can achieve effective and sustained change. Others we meet are convinced humanity is on a cliff edge but even the most powerful of them can't see a way forward. Without shared clarity, we remain in a vacuum where harmful or misleading alternatives can flourish.

Beyond Profit offers clear language and practical steps to help leaders, and others, to bring clarity and move in the same direction. Ushering in the deliberate governance of Wellbeing Economies through Purpose-Driven Organisations (including governments) – and via a critical mass of Purpose-Driven Leaders is not an easy or partial solution. It calls on the best of the human spirit – something we have systematically forgotten how to nurture. Yet, we believe it is the only effective route forward because it tackles the root cause, unleashing the level of energy and creativity required, and enables parts of the global system to work for the good of the whole in a virtuous cycle.

If what we present here as our collective, unspoken, direction isn't valid – we invite you to ask, "If not this, then what?" If there is no better proposal then using this as our guide is a logical next step. We recognise that putting the good of others at the heart of decisions may not seem practical to everyone straight away – and that's okay. What we need first is a critical mass of leaders working together to change governance at all levels so that new norms, laws, routines, institutions can be built – where acting for the good of all becomes simply "how it is" – even on a bad day.

The first collective step is to acknowledge that we have reached a turning point where we must confront the issue systematically making our world unsustainable: the profit-maximisation motive. We have deliberately built governance systems to maximise financial self-gain, based on the shared assumption that this would optimise our collective wellbeing. Instead, making money the core measure has delivered the opposite outcome: it locks in harm and blocks real solutions. A world driven by profit-first thinking doesn't just stall progress – it accelerates the decline of wellbeing for all life on earth. It breeds unhelpful bureaucracy that constrains innovation and props up a failing system.

In short, our economy, systems and lives rest on faulty assumptions – that profit is a proxy for the wellbeing we seek. These and related beliefs are now so deeply embedded in governance that most leaders don't even notice how they shape decisions and our world. The "logic" of these assumptions makes unsustainable investments seem rational, while sustainable investments appear irrational.

If profit is the problem, the solution lies in changing the logic behind it – and governing for the future we want. That means naming and addressing the flawed decision systems we call Logic 1 (short-term financial self-interest), recognising that Logic 2 (long-term financial self-interest) is an unhelpful distraction, and deliberately shifting governance into a new frame: Logic 3 – Purpose-Driven – where we directly deliver the end goal of the economy. This shift takes us from the primacy of profit and self-interest to prioritising the good of others, recognising that our wellbeing is intertwined with the long-term wellbeing of everything else. Humanity is now in the driving seat for the planet's future – it is vital we know where we are going and how to get there.

We live in a tightly connected world. To shift the system, change must happen on three levels at once: the economy, organisations, and individuals. Since each level is locked into unsustainable decision-making, Purpose-Driven Leadership is the only way to bring about governance change across all three:

MACRO: shifting from a GDP-based model to a Wellbeing Economy.

MESO: moving from Profit-Driven to Purpose-Driven Organisations – including Purpose-Driven governments designing and operating Wellbeing Economies.

MICRO: redefining work and life from financially driven – to purposeful and meaningful and underpinned by our capacity to be Purpose-Driven Leaders.

Unless we address the governance of all three levels together, we face bleak outcomes: red-tape overload; a drift from market freedom to central control; and runaway risks of "intelligent tech", amplified by financial self-interest and governance misaligned with our collective good. We are entering a world where hard choices must be faced head on. Logic 3 governments, economies, organisations and individuals are equipped to make those choices peacefully, with a real chance of increasing our wellbeing over time.

The alternative – continuing to act in financial self-interest in a time of great challenge – can only ever lead to far worse outcomes. Remaining where we are is also not an option – a system that is destroying us cannot endure. The question is whether we can create the alternative in time.

Hence, we face a stark choice: follow those offering comforting illusions that prop up a harmful system and in fact move us assuredly towards centrally controlled systems – or step up together to make lasting governance change where we all win by serving each other.

We believe that we agree on far more than we think – but we need to embed that agreement in a shared governance frame for it to bear fruit. Differences are usually about approach or strategy, not foundations. We do not need to agree on every step; diversity of approach is the heartbeat within the shared frame. Purpose-Driven governance provides that frame – orientating our deliberations so they drive, rather than undermine, long-term wellbeing for all. With it, we can vigorously debate laws to pass or repeal, weigh stakeholder claims, decide which organisations can be temporarily allowed to cause harm, and determine which products and services are worth their true cost. A shared governance frame channels and amplifies collective energy towards a positive future.

It starts with seeing that our current BAU approach is destroying the very goal it is supposed to achieve. The science of social and

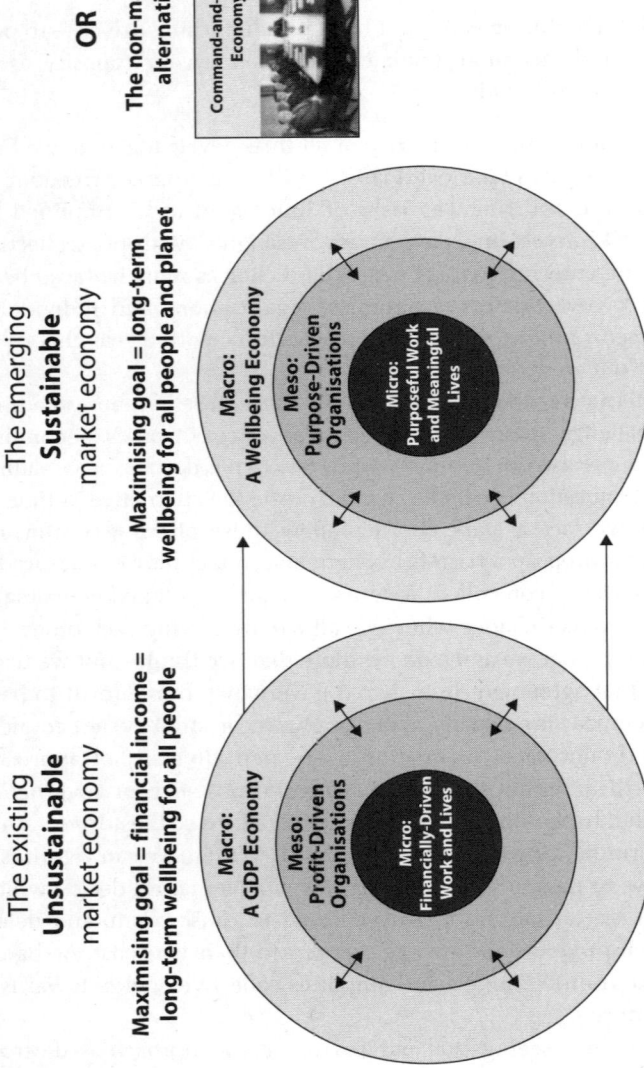

Figure 0.1 The new market economy and the unwanted alternative

environmental system breakdown offers a clear performance indicator: as GDP, profits, and wages rise, so does damage to our shared future – pulling us further away from our real goal: long-term wellbeing for all.

We have worked with leaders at all levels – and we see just how many are ready to act. Whether named explicitly or felt as growing discomfort, they recognise the problem: the focus on finance as if it were the end goal, and a reliance on self-interest incentives and survival-focused measures that reinforce it. They are also clear that change will require bold and brave leadership – beyond what has been considered normal.

As you are already reading this book, the above may resonate with you. You may find it harder than ever to ignore the science behind humanity's crises, and be increasingly uneasy with our slow and complacent responses. You may know we are only around 17 per cent[1] of the way to achieving the 2030 Sustainable Development Goals; that inequality is rampant; that keeping planetary warming below a life-sustaining 1.5 degrees is becoming almost impossible and that we are heading fast to an uninsurance world – or that we are in the midst of the sixth mass extinction, the last fifth one being when the dinosaurs met their fate.

Perhaps you've tried for years to make the case for doing good, only to meet resistance. Perhaps you believed in hopeful ideas like "long-term thinking" or "balancing profit with purpose" only to watch them stall. You may have pinned hopes on ESG, only to see it reduced to a tick-box "audit game" that distracted people from real innovation. You may have seen Corporate Social Responsibility, the Triple Bottom Line, or the Strategic Development Goals – adopted with good intentions – only to see them co-opted as tools for short-term profit. Maybe you are ready to give up on the spirit of humanity you know is everywhere – concluding that we are simply too selfish.

If all that feels familiar, this book will help you make sense of what's gone wrong and will equip you to lead towards something better.

The practical power of seeing the landscape properly can't be underestimated. As Angela Monaghan, former Head of Purpose and Impact, and reviewer of this book said: *"I've spent my life solving problems for positive change – yet everywhere, from academia to government, good ideas hit walls of apathy and siloed thinking. Even my PhD solution went unfunded because it didn't 'fit' a department. The problem wasn't the ideas – it was the system. I almost quit, until I realised I was missing a map: a way to see the hidden rules that put profit before sustainability. Understanding governance and the flawed economic ideas driving destructive patterns finally gave me the power to challenge the toxic frame holding us back."*

Before mapping the problem and the solution, we will explore two key ideas: the value of *Purpose-Driven Leadership*, and what we mean by *profit*.

INTRODUCING PURPOSE-DRIVEN LEADERSHIP

We have long been told that the most powerful way to improve our own wellbeing is to help others. Serving others gives us a deep sense of meaning and worth – the essence of a good life. Yet today's systems often tell us that self-interest matters more, that it's naïve to put values, ethics and the services of others at the heart of decision-making.

Purpose-Driven Leadership flips that logic. It draws on our innate drive to serve the good of others, knowing that this is the surest way to true wellbeing. It is about governing ourselves to become the person we want to be – and inspiring others to do the same. Further, it is about using that energy to embed the purpose-driven governance in ourselves, organisations and economies so that serving others is normal – even for those who might be disinclined.

A great leader helps people believe in a future that doesn't yet exist and motivates them to help build it – and bring others along the journey. It starts with a clear direction: What do we want to achieve with our economy, our organisations, our lives? A great leader explains why the challenges along the way matter – and why the journey is worth the effort. It's not about micromanaging the path, but about illuminating the destination, clarifying the boundaries we need to respect in the process – and setting the human spirit free.

Purpose-Driven Leaders are also students of human nature. This is not an easy task: we can be easily distracted, short-termist, biased, contradictory and excitable. Our hunger for certainty and hope makes us vulnerable to simple promises. In a world of risk and instability, many turn to leaders who offer short-term comfort that ignores root problems – mirages that provide only surface stability. Deep down we sense these are false answers, but without clear alternatives we can feel stuck.

To lead towards long-term wellbeing, leaders need to feel ownership of a shared vision that's clear, compelling and sensitively adaptive – and it must have a real chance of working. Financial self-interest driven by fear may seem the pragmatic, or only, way to continue – but it is an empty idol. It is based on the false belief that there is no other way. We create the future. What we believe about the past and future shapes what we see as possible now – and becomes a self-fulfilling prophecy. That's why good theory matters. As pioneering psychologist Kurt Lewin put it: "There is nothing as practical as a good theory." This book offers a theory of the future that is profound, but can work – a clear, practical narrative about why we are stuck, where we can go, and how to get there, so that our laws, systems, and strategies align in service of future we want. A frame that we hope helps bring together leaders doing inspiring work on inclusive learning, regenerative futures, sustainable finance, circular economy (to name a tiny fraction).

British futurist Bill Sharpe described three "horizons" leaders should hold in mind:

- Horizon One – today's path
- Horizon Two – near-term adjustments
- Horizon Three – the emerging, transformative future.

Beyond Profit orientates leaders in all three – and outlines in rich detail what 'Horizon Three' could look like – so that we might, together, bring it about as quickly as possible.

INTRODUCING WHAT WE MEAN BY PROFIT

There are many forms of profit, but in this book, we're talking about financial profit (the money left over after costs). We can define "financial profit" as "monetary gain, especially the difference between the amount earned and the amount spent in buying, operating, or producing something"[2] – noting that true financial profit should, of course, include costs incurred that are not paid for, e.g. pollution.

Sometimes income and profit are used interchangeably as core motivational goals of our current system – though technically they differ. Our underlying aim is to challenge entrenched assumptions about financial capital and clarify the alternative: money is not a reliable indicator for human wellbeing. We need to focus directly on wellbeing.

To be clear from the start: this isn't about demonising profit. Quite the opposite. We want to set profit free, to play its proper role as a vital tool that is a means to a meaningful end.

Any organisation (business, charity, government, household) needs enough money, at the right time, to function. This is "healthy" profit – a necessary enabler to run any form of organisation. It has not been helpful that our current system pits "for-profit" against "not-for-profit" – somehow implying that profit is unimportant in some contexts. Even charities and NGOs need surplus funds to survive. "Not-for-profit" just means they don't distribute profits to outsiders – not that they don't need them.

The idea that profit is "bad" arises only because its role has become distorted. We made profit the main goal, treating it as if it were a proxy for wellbeing – this has caused great harm and labelled profits the enemy.

We have collectively come to believe that if we focus on money, wellbeing will follow – without questioning whether this is true. We are all complicit in our lack of governance – as individuals, citizens, companies, or governments. We all tend to treat money as the primary measure of success: whether for a country (GDP), a business (share price, margins), or ourselves (salary). Governments do it. Organisations do it. Many of us do it.

But focusing on money as the goal points decisions in the wrong direction – and undermines the collective long-term wellbeing we seek. As the costs become clear, organisations, including governments, often dig their heels in – as if more financial growth will resolve things. Yet that road leads nowhere.

So, when we say "beyond profit", we do not mean that financial capital is unimportant, or that money doesn't matter. We are saying: stop treating it as the reason any organisation exists.

Profit is a tool. What matters is how we put it to use. Since money is a human invention, we can – and must – decide how best to use it. The ultimate purpose of any organisation should be to build long-term wellbeing; profit, when managed well, is one of the means to achieve that.

MOVING THE MOVEMENT FORWARD

Once we remember that money is symbolic of what we truly value we can limit it to being a powerful social tool – never the ultimate end. If we ask, "What is the end goal?", the answer is hiding in plain sight. It is the underlying aim of economies, sustainability, and governance. It is the closest we have to a meta-purpose for humanity It is long-term wellbeing for all:

- **Wellbeing** (not just any outcome);
- **For everyone** (not just a few, and including non-human life, with which our collective wellbeing is intertwined);
- **Over the long term** (not just for the present moment, but for the long term and including current and future generations).

Today's economic logic has left what we value most to the whims of financial self-interest and questionable ideas about how markets and humans work. Instead, we must bring the true point of an economy back to the centre of all our decisions – and govern this with skill.

Leaders across the world have long sensed both the problem of profit and the need for sustainability, where long-term wellbeing is created for everyone. Yet real progress remains elusive. Why? Because we have lacked a shared language to name the problem and the way forward.

Our destination can never be fixed on specific products or services. These are merely strategies that must constantly evolve and adapt – to be the subject of vigorous debate, free from ideological angst. Instead. The destination can only be a system of governance that:

- Clarifies our shared goal
- Enables open, ongoing debate about how to achieve it
- Ensures decisions serve it rather than undermine it

Once we master the fundamentals of this kind of governance, we can align existing global movements and build the momentum and system change we urgently need.

GOVERNANCE – THE LOCK AND KEY

Governance creates the structure for routine decision-making. All systems are governed, even the most distributed. A governance system establishes what an economy, organisation, team or individual exists to achieve, and the important lines that shouldn't be crossed when achieving that goal. It checks that the system is on course, and that the course is correct, continually adjusts behaviour if not and is accountable for the governance system. It is therefore governance that most powerfully structures our relationships with ourselves and others. Hence governance is also the most influential shaper of "how things are done around here". In other words governance shapes culture. This culture is made up of both the cultural hardware including structures, processes and artefacts as well as the cultural software, such as ways of thinking, feeling and acting.

Governance creates the internal logic of an organisation, defining what a "rational" decision is and what isn't. It sets the frame for all strategic decisions that are made. At its best, governance helps us to perform as we would want to perform on our best days – every day. It is our greatest tool to develop creative and wise systems that can adaptively align with collective long-term wellbeing. But if based on bad goals, misguided assumptions or a lack of sensitivity to context, it locks in toxic decisions and puts alternatives out of sight. Therefore, if we want to understand how we are locked into unsustainable decisions that prioritise profit and undermine our collective long-term wellbeing and understand how to overcome this in practical and effective terms, then we need to be governance-literate. If we want to repair our relationships with ourselves, others and living systems, then we need to direct, oversee and account for our routine decisions so that this moves from hope or desire to reality.

Logic 1 governance and why it is undermining us

Our current decision-making, as described above, is bounded by a governance box which we call Logic 1. Based on a series of interdependent and deeply held assumptions, Logic 1 functions as a coherent "business-as-usual" (BAU) decision-making paradigm, a comfortable, invisible box that abstracts the world and orientates and constrains our decisions.

This is the "Horizon 1" system. This BAU Logic 1 box places financial income as the core maximising goal of economies, organisations and individuals – long-term wellbeing for all is left outside of this governance frame.

As well as money being the goal, the Logic 1 box designates the stocks and flows of financial capital as the key resource – the key means – to achieve the goal of profit maximisation. It is not by accident but design that financial capital is the resource that we oblige organisations of all kinds to measure, report and create decision-making parameters around, in order to ensure healthy stocks and flows of it. In contrast, other critical forms of capital – such as human, social and natural as well as the health of stakeholders and foundational social and environmental systems – are outside this box. Mandatory multi-capital accounting, such as Integrated Reporting on the Johannesburg Stock Exchange in South Africa, remains the exception to aspects of this. As a result, organisations are encouraged, or even feel obliged, to maximise profits by treating these systems as infinite resources or limitless sinks.

The basis of our wellbeing is therefore systematically liquidated and turned into financial capital which we then celebrate as success. Those that do this best are those that we feel encouraged to invest in, work for and buy from. This comfortable but deeply flawed Logic 1 decision-making box has dictated the rules of how to be a successful leader, country or person.

As the economy has rocketed in size, the issues have therefore also exploded. In effect, we created the most inefficient and ineffective economy, where the goal we all assume the economy creates (our collective wellbeing) isn't being optimised but is in fact being systematically destroyed.

Logic 1 governance systems constrain decisions to goals and parameters based on financial income. The actual goal of the economy isn't then what drives the innovative strategy of government, organisations or individuals. Decisions therefore aren't designed to ensure that what underpins our wellbeing is in a good state of health. We just hope this is the end result. The problems created by this Logic 1 decision-making box compound when the resulting unsustainability problems hit this decision-making box. When faced with such critical problems, we are stuck trying to solve them within the same decision-making box that created them. If there isn't a short-term financial self-interest business case for it, it is not rational to act. Placating powerful stakeholders makes sense with this investment case frame. Dealing with or even reporting on the issues faced or created just doesn't make sense.

There is a palpable tension building as Logic 1 firms are unable to act on unsustainability – because it is irrational to do so. We are therefore stuck creating the problems with no means to address them. Lacking the confidence to visualise an alternative to work towards, leaders, understandably, retract to Logic 1 comfort where they are rewarded and loved.

Throughout history, we have repeatedly made and remade the economy. Yet, faced with the highest stakes imaginable, and overwhelming evidence of its harm, why have we failed to change this current form of market economy? First, the Logic 1 decision-making box is a comfortable place that keeps the fog of complexity outside. It is going to take a lot of courage, or palpable threat, to let the chaos in. Second, the simple and potent "super-assumption" of BAU Logic 1 is that it equates our least favourable short-term selfish urges with a moral sense that we are doing good. This assumption creates a rationale that the more financial capital we can accumulate (profits), the more wellbeing we create for everyone. We have made greed good. In other words, we have come to unquestioningly believe that financial income = success = development = flourishing = the good life = wellbeing.

Supporting this is a further assumption that we are rational, self-interested driven beings who know what wellbeing is and act to maximise it, and that the best place for this is the formal market: we therefore need more money so we can buy more wellbeing on the market. The key to this assumption consists in self-interested organisations that, by seeking to outwit competition and capture financial income from buyers, do their very best job to meet our wellbeing demands. A profitable organisation, a high-GDP country and a person with a high wage must be doing a lot of "good" by others, by enabling us to buy more wellbeing.

Because we moralise financial income, we squeeze a couple more per cent out of manufacturers in the supply chain, attracting positive performance reviews and bonuses, with little or no question as to the effect this could have on livelihoods. We attract more research sponsorship and consider this an indicator of success even if from highly polluting industries. We celebrate the bonus a friend was given by driving down costs in their department without reflecting on the collateral damage of longer hours. We celebrate an inward investment deal secured through subsidies, without considering the impact on smaller companies. This is not just true for businesses. All organisations have, to varying degrees, bought into this logic. Governments focus on GDP and its drivers. Individuals focus on increasing their financial income so that they can buy their wellbeing on the market, and we are all incentivised to accumulate enough stock of money as the basis to drive more income.

The incentives to keep inside the Logic 1 box, combined with the difficulty to even perceive that the box exists, help explain why we have had to wait until the chaos comes through the doors, the windows and the floorboards before starting to act *en masse*. Now is the time for leaders to see this dangerous false simplicity for what it is – to recognise that this governance box is no longer safe or useful and so start the urgent work to actively dismantle it.

Logic 2 and its limits

As the science of system breakdown has become starker, combined with a number of unforeseen global financial crashes, we have witnessed global efforts to make changes to Logic 1.

However, rather than address the root assumptions about how a market economy is designed, we have told ourselves that if we take a longer-term approach, we can keep the assumptions. We can stem the harm by focusing on the long-term rather than short-term issues. This is a long-term self-interest 'enlightened' approach that ushers in concepts like "Stakeholder Capitalism", "ESG" and "Creating Shared Value" – because by thinking long-term we start to understand that we need to protect and regenerate the health of the resources and systems that enable our financial self-interest. Logic 2 is the "Horizon 2" system.

An organisation moving from BAU Logic 1 to BAU Logic 2 will start experimenting with multi-capital/full-cost accounting and will seek to understand and improve the health of stakeholders. Additionally, it will start implementing transition plans to move parameters for decision-making to a place where system health thresholds are respected – for example, to net or absolute zero carbon emissions over a defined period of time. For truly enlightened self-interested organisations, hard parameters to protect the health of non-financial capitals (human, social and natural), the health of stakeholders and the health of social and environmental systems are regarded as just as critical as the health of financial capital.

Whereas the Logic 1 investment case revolves around protecting short-term financial self-interest, e.g., placating powerful stakeholders, Logic 2 governance systems make it logical to pass investment cases that divert financial capital and innovation efforts in order to restore and protect the underpinning resources, stakeholders and system health.

The mantra we have coined that underpins this Logic 2 long-term financial self-interest is "doing good is good for business". But by doing good, what we nearly always mean is in fact doing "less harm" – in other words "don't kill the golden goose".

That is not to diminish the importance of this shift to long-term thinking and protecting what sustains us. The shift from short-term to long-term thinking is a vital component of making wise and sustainability-aligned decisions. There are, however, challenges that make Logic 2 a very hard place for leaders to try to create a sustainable world from, including because:

1. Science tells us some hard truths and more information throws up more challenges. Therefore, most organisations are only motivated to be somewhat enlightened, some of the time – for instance, having science-aligned net zero or absolute zero targets or committing to paying a living wage. However, we urgently need full enlightenment.

2. Most operating models are heavily incentivised to asset-strip fundamental environmental and social systems for profit. Complying with parameters that stop this harm is not minor or easy. Ensuring operations are within thresholds of health for important resources and systems, including human diversity, equality and inclusion, fresh water supply and ecosystem functioning, is not just a tick-box compliance activity but a whole business model transformation agenda. This scale of change requires very creative ways of thinking and acting, and the BAU assumptions that still underpin Logic 2 prevent this.

3. Logic 1 organisations, and politicians, see efforts to change the parameters away from short-term financial self-interest as an illogical burden on making as much money as quickly as possible.

Because Logic 2 organisations share the same BAU assumptions as Logic 2 organisations, it takes an extremely enlightened organisation to sustain the journey.

Very strong, informed, collaborative and persistent leadership will be required to speed up the legal, governance and management changes needed. It is hard to see how we will achieve this level of leadership within Logic 2. What is required is to tap into a new source of energy and innovation other than that of self-interest.

The invitation to the power of Logic 3

A fundamental shift has been underway over the past few decades to envision and design a new market economy. This goes beyond establishing strong values or projects as a means to do some good, while maximising profits. It goes beyond putting profit and doing good on an equal footing. These are stepping stones on the journey to Logic 3 – where we govern our economies, organisations and ourselves for the end goal of the economy: long-term wellbeing for all (sustainability). Here serving the good of the whole is deliberately put at the heart of our practice, norms, laws and institutions. Here we enable and structure our decisions to be literally *driven* by purpose – by design. Financial capital will continue to be very important but as a means to a meaningful end: governed and managed to invest in this goal, pay the bills and to meet the expectations that have been created with stakeholders (including shareholders).

This is the Horizon 3 system striving to be born or, more accurately, reborn in a conscious way. It is the Logic 3 system: a Wellbeing Economy, made real by Purpose-Driven Organisations and powered by Purposeful Work and Lives. This is the destination we have been intuiting action on, at all three levels, for many decades:

Macro: At the Macro economy level, 35 years ago the UN created its Human Development Index, and 17 years ago Bhutan decided to measure its progress using its Gross National Happiness Index. In 2009 the EU published the report 'GDP and beyond: Measuring progress in a changing world'.[3] Now over 70 per cent of all OECD countries have frameworks that at least measure wellbeing in one form or another, even though the metrics are fragmented and the connection with the governance system needs leadership. The Wellbeing Economy Governments (WEGo) group was formed in 2018 to bring leading countries in this agenda together and create the conditions for accelerated global change.

Meso: At the Meso organisational level, while change has been happening in governments, universities, charities and a range of other organisations, the corporate realm has been demonstrating that even in extreme Logic 1 conditions, change towards Logic 3 is possible. Decades ago leaders of companies like The Body Shop, Interface Flor, Wholefoods, Ben & Jerry's, Seventh Generation, Green & Blacks, Whole Foods Market, Natura, Patagonia and huge numbers like them went on a journey to cut loose from Logic 1. CEOs of large corporations began making statements like: "The business of business is to improve the world" (Anita Roddick, The Body Shop); "To be truly successful, companies need to have a corporate mission that is bigger than making a profit" (Marc Benioff, Salesforce); "Just as people cannot live without eating, so a business cannot live without profits. But most people don't live to eat, and neither must businesses live just to make profits" (John Mackey, Whole Foods Market). Purpose was further propelled from 2018 by Larry Fink, the CEO of the world's largest asset manager BlackRock and his letters to CEOs about the need for them to serve a social purpose. Then in 2018, the US Business Roundtable stated that the role of US business was to serve all Americans and not profit maximisation for shareholders. The focus on purpose has continued apace over the decades through a wide range of mechanisms, including legal innovations which straddle Logic 1 and Logic 2, and inch towards Logic 3. For instance, Public Benefit Corporations (California, 2010), Società Benefit (Italy, 2016), Loi Pacte (France, 2019), Ley de Economía Social (Spain, 2011) and similar laws in Colombia, Ecuador, Panama, Peru and Uruguay. Similarly, Community Interest Companies were first enacted in the UK in 2005. These legal options, plus increasing pressure for mainstream law to change, start to open the door to fully Purpose-Driven Organisations. Here, financial capital for any stakeholder or the company itself is firmly placed as serving the shared purpose – not equal partners. As we will outline in the book in detail, we are moving swiftly to a place where we can clarify and argue for Logic 3 organisations because of a globally co-created ISO standard in Purpose-Driven Organisations (ISO 37011) that the world can co-own globally and refine as we learn.

Micro: At the Micro level, push-back against Logic 1 has been happening in the academic and practice sphere for decades. Whole movements have been created by leadership experts and coaches to counter the overuse of financial incentives, the treatment of humans like machines, fear-based environments, and values being left at the office door. The organisational and leadership literature is littered with all the reasons why it makes no real-world sense to treat people this way – they become unproductive, stressed and unable to make wise decisions. The movement to counter these common workplace realities for many continues to grow in networks of coaches like Global Purpose Leaders and the Forward Institute.

On the one hand these efforts are growing, and on the other they are hardly discernible within the mainstream. The idea that we can move, collectively and at speed, to Logic 3 could therefore be dismissed as not "pragmatic" or "feasible". However, this idea of feasibility has been created from within the Logic 1 box. The real "pragmatic" and "feasible" approach lies outside of Logic 1. It is getting difficult to ignore this "real reality" and the current solutions are starting to show themselves to be well short of the mark. The more we ignore what is truly pragmatic, the more the pressure to do so will build. The chance this results in losing the freedom, democracy and efficiency aspects of the market economy is real if we consider the response to the pandemic. When the realities of crises hit, we are all too quick to hold up our hands and give over the market to central decision-makers. One of the authors of this book, Lorenzo, was sitting as a Minister of the Italian Government when the pandemic unfolded and experienced the instant pivot from Logic 1 individuals: "Let's keep the market economy unregulated" to "Let's close down the free market". This act shows how, in a crisis, losing the market economy and moving to a centrally planned system is only a few decisions away.

To those who say that this three-level system of a Wellbeing Economy, made real by Purpose-Driven Organisations and powered by Purposeful Work and Lives, is wishful thinking, our response is that we either come together to make this happen or lose the market economy and our ability to organise ourselves in a potentially adaptive way, when we need it most. Either way, a BAU market economy which is causing an existential threat to our collective long-term wellbeing cannot persist. To those who say we need laws we say, yes we do. But these laws are less likely to happen, and may do far more harm than good, if we don't build solid norms about the Logic 3 governance we actually need. Laws to stop harm, imposed on a majority that cannot fathom their point, will never work. Furthermore, whatever levels of challenge are coming our way, understanding and governing for Logic 3 economies, organisations and individuals will be needed, so that long-term wellbeing for all is deliberately generated – and the systems underpinning it and brought back to a state of natural regeneration and protected. We cannot envisage any scenario where we will not need to be skilled at purpose-driven governance – of ourselves and of the collectives we create. The future trying to be born is now discernible; we need to work together, at speed, to make it real.

How this book will help you

Leadership has always been challenging, but today, it is even more so as leaders strive to make decisions for the world we need while navigating governance systems that are anchored in profit-driven priorities. This book will help you recognise the invisible barriers holding us all back, understand why progress has been slow, distinguish signals from noise and learn how to dismantle these obstacles to build a governance framework that truly works.

Without recognising these decision-making structures, meaningful change remains out of reach and we continue to bang into the walls of the Logic 1 box. Just as important, it is hard to see each other in the fog. We miss the great efforts others are making around the world who are awake to the urgency of needing a different way of leading and who are doing their best to respond. We can feel more isolated than ever and less connected to what it means to be human in our work. The ability to define a new sense of clarity and certainty to create a better future can appear beyond reach. At best this can cause immense frustration, at worst, burnout, and other personal challenges. This is true for leaders from Directors, CEOs and community activists to government staff, university leaders or entry-level executives. Chief Sustainability Officers are at the forefront of these frustrations, and we are starting to hear them say "enough is enough". If this connects with some aspects of how you feel, or if in reading this you recognise how the Logic 1 box has constrained your leadership, then this book is for you.

Understanding the problem is, however, step one. We also need to be able to describe, in precise terms, the unifying governance frame that can create the outcomes and impact we want. We then need to realise this ambition. The work to drive new governance at all three levels is the work we all need to do as leaders, regardless of where we primarily lead from. Amongst other things, this book sets out the basics of governance and gives you key tools to start working actively through your personal governance, the governance of your organisations and of the economy you are a part of. Good governance is not easy – and governance that does not shy away from the real reality, especially so. But with the right problem at the centre of the room, we can create positive flywheels of progress.

One of the primary reasons for writing *Beyond Profit* is to help shine a light on the movement for positive change and address the fragmentation within it. This fragmentation is affected by different languages and by geographic distances but most of all by the silos and relational walls created by the all-encompassing power of Logic 1. Across the world we see weak connections within the Macro, Meso and Micro levels, and between them the links are almost non-existent. What is exciting is that, with a clear lens, it becomes possible to see not three or 5000 separate movements – but to begin to see one. This book is therefore not about introducing something new, but rather holding up a mirror to what we see is already unfolding, uniting the energy and solutions that are already in motion.

While the Wellbeing Economy, a network of Purpose-Driven Organisations and a global talent pool of Purpose-Driven Leaders, is underway, fully realising these is not possible while Logic 1 dominates. Hence, while we will share inspiring stories from the Macro, Meso and Micro levels of leadership in action, there are no perfect cases that fully exemplify what it looks like to govern under Logic 3.

Whether you are just beginning your purpose-driven sustainability leadership journey or have been on this path for a very long time, *Beyond Profit* is your handbook and roadmap for the shared journey. It is written to help navigate the choices we have at this incredible moment in human history.

Structure of the book

The book is organised as follows.

CHAPTER 1

This chapter provides the foundational ideas that the other chapters rest on. It invites readers to consider how governance systems at all levels is THE task at hand for Purpose-Driven Leaders. Specifically, to consciously design governance at the levels of the self (MICRO), the organisations we lead (MESO) and the economies we operate within (MACRO) to move beyond profit and instead to anchor to long-term wellbeing for all. We start with a precise description of the Logic 1 box of decision-making, the role of "profit", and how governance systems of the economy, organisations and the self hamstring our efforts to stem the harm and often increase our problems. The chapter goes on to explain how the governance system, at all three levels, changes when moving from Logic 1 to Logic 2. Finally, it lays out the starting point for understanding Logic 3 governance as the only logical approach to routine decision-making that is aligned with a sustainable future. To be successful this needs Purpose-Driven Leaders to help implement change at three levels, simultaneously at the:

- **MACRO level** – to create a Wellbeing Economy through Purpose-Driven Governments that move deliberately away from GDP economies
- **MESO level** – to move from profit-maximising organisations to Purpose-Driven Organisations – organisations that can realise the Wellbeing Economy at the MACRO level and unleash and enable the MICRO level
- **MICRO level** – to build our capacities as Purpose-Driven Leaders and enable Purposeful Work and Lives

CHAPTERS 2–4

These chapters dive into what is required to RETHINK and RETOOL as a Purpose-Driven Leader for the Macro, Meso and Micro levels as well as the benefits that will be REALISED if you do. It describes what

Logic 3 practice at each level looks like and how this contrasts with the dominant Logic 1 reality around us.

These chapters draw on real-world experiences of the authors and via direct accounts of leaders who have been at the forefront of change in different parts of the system. The Macro, Meso and Micro levels are intricately interconnected and therefore so are the chapters. For example, if you work in government then you may have a role to directly create and implement economy-wide governance for a Wellbeing Economy. Chapter 2 (MACRO) outlines what this looks like. At the same time, government is an organisation, and everything in Chapter 3 (MESO) is equally relevant to governments – it could be argued that governments should be the archetypal Purpose-Driven Organisation. Everyone who works in government or any other organisation has the opportunity to develop their Purpose-Driven Leadership and influence their teams, organisations and the economy as outlined in Chapter 4 (MICRO). No matter where you lead, each chapter is for you.

As authors we have collectively spent over 90 years working to identify the root issues, clarify the solutions and unlock the human potential and organisational systems needed to build a better future – at all three levels. We have brought our different theory building and hard-won practical insights to this book. Hence, you may notice a difference in tone, style and context in parts of the text.

Chapter 2: MACRO – a Wellbeing Economy

This chapter describes the features of a Logic 3 Wellbeing Economy. It starts by challenging us to rethink some core features of Logic 1: firstly, to resituate GDP from the GOAL to a PARAMETER and second, to bring WELLBEING from a side topic to THE POINT and for us to all see the economy as not just for POLITICIANS BUT FOR ALL LEADERS. Three tools essential for a Wellbeing Economy are then introduced: GOVERNANCE for a Wellbeing Economy, National WELLBEING ACCOUNTABILITY and FISCAL POLICY for wellbeing. While there are many benefits that will be realised from moving to a Wellbeing Economy, we highlight three: CITIZENSHIP, WELLBEING and PURPOSE-DRIVEN ORGANISATIONS. This final result of a Wellbeing Economy provides a bridge to the next chapter.

Chapter 3: MESO – Purpose-Driven Organisations

This chapter explores what it means to make decisions as a Logic 3 Purpose-Driven Organisation. It explains that to become Purpose-Driven Leaders shaping Purpose-Driven Organisations, we must RETHINK three key areas. First, we must redefine the organisation's point of being, shifting from financial CAPTURE to wellbeing CREATION. Second, we need to move beyond a focus on STRATEGY and recognise quality GOVERNANCE as the overarching decision frame that ensures strategy can help the organisation adapt choices to the dynamic context. Third, we must transition from market RESPONSE to actively MAKING markets. To RETOOL, the chapter introduces three essential frameworks. First, there is the watershed International ISO standard in Governance of Organizations (ISO 37000), which provides a universal foundation for understanding governance. Second, there are the national (PAS 808) and forthcoming international (ISO 37011) standards in Purpose-Driven Organizations, outlining how such organisations should be governed. Third, there is the Evolved Value Framework (EVF), which defines six marketing principles that align value generation efforts with governance goals in a Purpose-Driven Organisation. When implemented effectively, the benefits of Purpose-Driven Organisations are numerous, but this chapter highlights three key outcomes – COHERENCE, CREATIVITY and COMMITMENT.

Chapter 4: MICRO – Purposeful Work and Lives

The transition from an unsustainable to a sustainable market economy via Purpose-Driven Organisations will only be possible through Purpose-Driven Leadership. A focus on this vital change is woven throughout our book but is brought to life very specifically at the MICRO level chapter.

This chapter shows how to develop as a Logic 3 Purpose-Driven Leader who works actively at all three levels by tapping into our purpose-driven energy as humans. Rethinking leadership enables us to be more conscious of the beliefs we hold about what is valuable. The chapter starts by challenging us to RETHINK three of the most fundamental shifts required to be a Purpose-Driven Leader, moving from MONEY to MEANING, DOING to BEING and ME to WE. This gives us the opportunity to question the paradigms we use to make leadership decisions and to create a future-aligned coherent mental map to move forwards with. The RETOOL section focuses on ways for making the transition to enable us to LEAD with LOVE, LEAD with VISION, and LEAD with PERSPECTIVE. It is vital to have these skills to unlock our potential to progress the fundamental objective that unites us all – our long-term wellbeing for all. Realising our leadership brings to life three of the greatest benefits of being a Purpose-Driven Leader: ENERGY, FLOW and IMPACT, enabling us to govern ourselves to create purposeful work and a meaningful life and support others to do the same.

CHAPTER 1

Beyond the Box

Why Leading Beyond Profit is The Leadership Agenda of the 21st Century

● ● ●

What unites us?

We start this book with a focus on purpose – a profound concept that lies deep at the heart of humanity, philosophy and the logic underpinning a Wellbeing Economy, Purpose-Driven Organisations and Purposeful Work and Lives.

The history and thought surrounding the concept of purpose in an organisational sense are long and winding, and there are many references in our bibliography that help reveal this background. In summary, purpose has two key features that are consistent in theory and practice. Firstly, it is a reason to exist – the fundamental point of action – for a nation, an economy, an organisation, brand, project, team or individual. Secondly, the reason to exist is anchored in serving the good of others and, by extension, ultimately our collective long-term wellbeing.

To understand what it means to be purpose-driven we must define what it means to do "good". You might wonder why we are starting our book with such a philosophical and difficult task. The reality is that it is necessary and we cannot move forwards as leaders without this foundation.

The global breakdown of the basis of wellbeing requires us to work collectively in communities, nations and as a planetary community. We cannot collectively endeavour towards anything if we don't have a shared sense of direction. As humans with the ability and obligation to make conscious choices, it is not a question of if we direct ourselves, but how. While focusing on money is easier than defining what collectively matters, the evidence tells us that we have reached the edge of this experiment.

The facts show that we can't continue on the basis that what we value is too highly fragmented to unite around and is something that just emerges from our choices. Nor can we continue trying to unite our efforts around terms like "sustainability", "values", "prosperity" or "regenerative" without being really clear what value we are seeking to generate and protect through them. Devising yet another new term and pinning our hopes on this moving us beyond the status quo won't work. If we don't define and govern for what matters most we will lose it – perhaps forever. Fortunately, when we look, it seems that humanity *already seems to know* its foundational value, its "meta-purpose" – it has been articulated time again across cultures, philosophies, and traditions.

Long-term wellbeing for all – our shared goal?

The "meta-purpose" that is revealed all around us has three key aspects:

1. Wellbeing (not just any goal)
2. For all (not just for some)
3. Over the long term (not just for now)

We can consider "long-term wellbeing for all" as a powerful working definition of a "meta-purpose" when we review the answers to these core questions:

What is the point of an economy?	Economic textbooks tend to say the same thing in varying lengths and language; however, Goodland and Ledec in 1987 boiled this down to: "allocating the resources available to society in a way that maximises social wellbeing".[1] After all, economics, as a discipline, was summarised in 1980 by Alfred Marshall as: "a study of mankind in the ordinary business of life; it examines that part of individual and social action which is most closely connected with the attainment and with the use of material requisites of wellbeing".[2]
What is the goal of "sustainability"?	The definition of sustainability, achieved through sustainable development, established via international consensus, is: "meet(ing) the needs of the present without compromising the ability of future generations to meet their own needs" (WCED 1987).[3] Long-term wellbeing, for all, is therefore the overarching frame for the UN Sustainable Development Goals, as also remarked on by Robert Costanza, Jacqueline McGlade, Hunter Lovins and Ida Kubiszewski in 2014.[4]
What is the most basic question that philosophers and religions seek to answer for us?	Foundational to philosophy and spirituality is the enduring question of how to attain wellbeing (eudaimonida/human flourishing/a good life) as an individual in respect to the collective.
What is the core delegated role of governments by citizens, which every other function in their remit, like the economy, is a tool to achieve?	As stated by the International Public Sector Accounting Standards Board: "The primary function of governments and other public sector entities is to provide services that enhance or maintain the wellbeing of citizens and other eligible residents."[5]

What are the shared aspects of written international norms or international and national constitutions of what "good" looks like?	These tend to prioritise equal rights of everyone to a good life as outlined in the international human rights law and the UN Guiding Principles.

Another way to explore our "meta-purpose" is to repeatedly ask: "Why does this matter?" We find this invariably leads to the conclusion of long-term wellbeing for all. If we are wrong, and a different shared destination consistently emerges, then that should be the anchor we collectively align to. In the distant past we may have had the luxury to live in flow with the world around us, not requiring such deliberate consciousness. However, in an increasingly interconnected world facing existential challenges, we must urgently decide what matters most, to the majority of us, before we lose the opportunity to achieve it.

The three elements of our apparent meta-purpose: 1) wellbeing; 2) for all; 3) long-term, are the most foundational subjects for us to debate. They will always remain subjective to the consensus of the current generation – including how we might perceive and represent non-human wellbeing. If we want long-term wellbeing for all then we can't leave these topics on the sidelines; they must be brought to the centre of our debates and collective problem-solving. While these three core elements are subjective, we also have strong starting points, developed and refined over millennia.

Wellbeing.[6] An umbrella term for the meeting of universal human needs that allow us to live a "good life". Understanding what wellbeing is and how to attain it is perhaps the most important and never-ending philosophical and spiritual question of humanity and vast amounts have been published on it over the centuries. As Katherine Trebeck, instigator of Wellbeing Economy Governments (WEGo), notes: "The conceptualization of wellbeing aligns closely with indigenous wisdom, such as the Indigenous Australians' long-term thinking and prioritisation of connection with each other and country. *Buen vivir* (living well), from Indigenous Andean cultures that emphasises collective wellbeing and harmony with nature and with the African principles of *ubuntu*, which highlights that humans cannot thrive in isolation." Indigenous conceptualisation of wellbeing includes "all parts of the self" – the spiritual, physical, emotional and mental aspects of being as outlined by Jacquelyn Cardinal Naheyawin in her paper "A Guide to Indigenous Concepts of Wellness & Wellbeing".[7]

While the term happiness is often used as a similar concept, it is well established that living well is not the same as "being happy". We may experience moments of unhappiness when all our needs are met or, by contrast, feel happy in conditions of deprivation. Happiness is a personal journey, whereas wellbeing is a collective one. Although we all aspire to be personally happy, living well is a collective objective and the goal of development policy. Wellbeing is a concept that is intricately connected to meaningfulness and purpose – serving the wellbeing of others through purpose drives our own wellbeing, through making our lives meaningful. Wellbeing has been measured subjectively regarding how we feel at any particular time, but we also know there are objective determinants of wellbeing, which are common to all human beings and universal needs such as good food, enough time to spend with friends and in the community, and proximity to well-preserved natural ecosystems. We also know that as social animals, relationships are core to our wellbeing – positive and mutually supportive relationships with each other, with nature and with ourselves. While the foundations of wellbeing may be shared, the ways to achieve it are shaped by infinite possibilities of context-specific strategies that develop in place and in relationship. The rituals, norms, artefacts and products and services found over the millennia and across cultural groups reflect this diversity. As we will reveal, a huge amount of work has been, and is being, done to decide how to evaluate and account for wellbeing at the Macro economy, Meso organisational and Micro personal levels. At the same time, our understanding of wellbeing is constantly evolving with scientific progress, societal explorations and remembering past forgotten wisdom – which means that we can continuously improve our development process and the best ways to attain a good life.

For all. Any shared ethic will logically include all involved. While some may try to support long-term wellbeing for themselves and those they identify with, this narrowed conceptual vision doesn't lead to a shared ethic or a shared ethic that recognises that our fates are intricately intertwined. As we will expand on throughout this book, to serve others is the basis of being purpose-driven and what makes us human. As Adam Smith concluded in *The Theory of Moral Sentiments*:[8] "it is the great precept of nature to love ourselves only as we love our neighbour, or what comes to the same thing, as our neighbour is capable of loving us" – our ability to have wellbeing is fundamentally entwined with the wellbeing of others. But we now know this interdependency transcends those we see and touch. While our decision-making box may have allowed us to ignore the interdependency between life on Earth, we are now in a period where this interrelatedness is starkly apparent: either we take care of the wellbeing of all of us or we all have none. As people begin to move beyond the artificial separation of humans and nature, the idea that the wellbeing of non-human life is an end in its own right is gaining ground. Hence, when we say long-term wellbeing for all, by "all" we mean people and planet, with the planet representing non-human species and ecosystems. This places people and nature as both a means to the end of long-term wellbeing for all, as well as being equal beneficiaries of this goal.

Over the long term. Wellbeing is not just important for today or next week. There are no shared global norms that state or imply that progress is only for those that happen to be around now, or just for them at the moment. We generally recognise the fact that as life forms, we are just passing beneficiaries and stewards. How "long-term" we mean also needs careful consideration and inclusive debate. Some of the most powerful decision-makers on our planet are openly, but without global consensus, pursuing strategies based on a philosophy called "longtermism" championed by thinkers including Scottish academic William McAskill. An effect of this is to relegate planet Earth to a stepping stone to be used up in pursuit of fulfilling our "destiny" in the wider universe. Resources, including people, therefore become expendable in pursuit of the distant future. Accelerating resource use is sign of success. If the majority of citizens of planet Earth do not buy into this view then we need to be very clear about this – and what view of long-term we instead support.

Long-term wellbeing for all, then, is a three-pronged unifying goal. It is the goal of the economy, the goal of sustainability and (therefore unsurprisingly) the shared goal of humanity.

Therefore, if the economy had achieved its objective, we would not need a word called "sustainability". If you delve into the Brundtland Report that was published in 1987 by the United Nations, and we highly recommend you do, it is clear that the movement for

Sustainable Development is about how we create long-term wellbeing for all through a change in how we enact the economy.[9] Hence, while it is vital to start with a clear shared view of the goal, to lead, we also need a shared robust understanding of how the current design of the economy has resulted in rampant unsustainability. Without both we believe it is not possible to change course. Much has been expressed, of varying angles and quality, about the issues and potential ways out. This book aims to cut through what can feel like a fog of discussion to provide a roadmap that focuses on what matters and shine a light on shared wisdom that is often lurking in these conversations.

The need for change hinges on the threats to our collective long-term wellbeing that our economic development approach has driven, which is why denying these threats is the easiest way to stop change. Let's reflect on how far away from ensuring long-term wellbeing we are.

A world of withering wellbeing and woeful responses

At this point of a book or presentation, people usually find it necessary to caveat how many great things we have achieved through our economy and the positive trends that seem underway. If we don't do this it is easy to be accused of being pessimistic "doom and gloomers" who are in denial of the great things humans and our economy have achieved. Aligned with this, we would not deny that there are pockets or trends of "good news", or that for some people, things are going well at the moment. We recognise that aspects of our wellbeing have got significantly better on some critical fronts. Leaders like Bill Gates and the late Hans Rosling have done a very good job pointing out these positive trends, e.g. huge reductions in child mortality rates, many more children accessing education, especially girls, and a step change in mechanisms for global cooperation.

While these aspects of progress are positive and give us some hope that change in the right direction is possible, they distract us from the central governance issue. We can only assess how well we have transformed resources into useful outcomes and impacts by analysing the changes against the actual goal: long-term wellbeing for all. Hence the key questions we should ask ourselves before we celebrate are:

Wellbeing. What level of long-term wellbeing for all might we have achieved with the resources used if we had done a better job to govern and manage for this outcome? How much wellbeing have we destroyed through this process of "development"?

For all. How far has wellbeing been achieved for everyone? Who has primarily benefited? Have we all had access to wellbeing, or have some had a lot of access, some a bit, some not so much and some not at all? How many experience their wellbeing as net negative?

Over the long term. How resilient is the wellbeing we have created? Are these trends in "good news" durable, or are they a "flash in a pan" – here today and gone tomorrow?

Of course, no one is in a position to definitively know how much wellbeing could have been created – and the fact that no one knows the answer is revealing in and of itself. While we can't answer the question, as we move through this book it will become easier to see what might have been possible, and what is still within our reach once we put the right problem at the centre of our decision-making.

However, the science is clear: whatever wellbeing has been created has primarily benefitted a few, with others gaining only marginally – and some not at all, or gaining on one hand and losing on another. Even when these margins improve individual wellbeing, the overall trajectory remains unsustainable. Any progress made will not endure unless we shift to a fundamentally different path.

An unsustainable world was surely inevitable: we have not directed, overseen or held to account whether or not our decisions optimise for long-term wellbeing for all and used this as our Key Performance Indicator (KPI). Instead, we directed our decisions to maximising profits – and we never took the care to oversee or account for whether these financial metrics actually achieved the goals they were meant to – we just blindly assumed they would. As a result, although we haven't asked for the data, the answers are banging down our door. Scientists have had to resort to, in effect, screaming at society to wake up – up to 15,364 scientists across 184 countries when they issued their three "Warning to Humanity" open publications in 1992, 2017 and 2019. UN Chief António Guterres regularly highlights the critical emergency we face. He has warned, for example, that: "With our bottomless appetite for unchecked and unequal economic growth, humanity has become a weapon of mass extinction" and that "Multinational corporations are fill-ing their bank accounts while emptying our world of its natural gifts".

A SYSTEMIC PROBLEM

It is easy to jump to the problem of climate change, and stay there. There are a number of ways to avoid this "climate myopia". The Planetary Boundaries work by Johan Rockström at the Stockholm Resilience Centre alerts us to nine key environmental system thresholds, of which six, and potentially seven, have been breached. The food–energy–water nexus is also a popular way to broaden the analysis as well as integrating the social crises. Another way is to start from what is harming these systems. It is useful to consider that ultimately, everything we do requires energy and how we source energy, i.e. fossil fuels, and how we use energy, i.e. natural habitat change, drive the unsustainability of the systems above.

The energy sources we rely on and how we use that energy both create distinct yet interconnected consequences. It is important to consider them separately because addressing one without the other still leaves us facing an existential threat. Even if we achieved zero carbon tomorrow, many critical issues would remain unresolved because of how we use the energy at our disposal. Hence how much energy we use, and how we use it, is just as important as where we get it from. As Dr Nate Hagen highlights, financial income growth (GDP) is approximately 98 per cent correlated with energy use.[10] If global financial income grows by 3 per cent per year, world energy consumption will double roughly every 23 years.

Amongst a raft of negative consequences from what energy source we depend on, and how we use that energy, there are a number of "super-issues". These issues on their own have been identified by scientists to derail, possibly permanently, our chance of long-term collective well-being and are in "red alert" states. Below, we outline these super-issues – and others that could emerge as super-issues – within the categories of where we, as humans, source energy and how we use it.

Issue 1 – where we get our energy from

Greenhouse gas emissions (super-issue). As outlined in a joint 2024 paper by leading climate scientists authored by William Ripple and colleagues – for 50 years, global warming has been accurately forecasted prior to its observation, and this has been recognised not just by independent academic researchers but also by fossil fuel companies.[11] Nonetheless, we have failed to do what is needed to save ourselves from the consequences. As a result, the paper outlines that: "Fossil fuel emissions have increased to an all-time high, the three hottest days ever occurred in July of 2024, and current policies have us on track for approximately 2.7 degrees Celsius (°C) peak warming by 2100. We are at a tipping point with the impact on our climate". As reported in the Financial Times Special Report on Renewable energy in 2024: "Clean tech investment set to hit \$2tn in 2024 – but spending is still at less than half of estimated level needed by the early 2030s to achieve net zero targets."[12]

Air pollution. Outdoor air pollution is a major problem affecting the wellbeing of people and non-human life across the world. According to the World Health Organization (WHO) outdoor air pollution is "estimated to have caused 4.2 million premature deaths worldwide in 2019; [a death rate] due to exposure to fine particulate matter, which causes cardiovascular and respiratory disease, and cancers".[13] While everyone is affected to varying degrees, people in lower-income countries disproportionately suffer. The WHO assesses that 89 per cent (of the 4.2 million premature deaths) occurred in these areas, particularly in Southeast Asia and the Western Pacific Regions. There is worrying new research linking different types of air pollution with the brain and mental health issues. This includes dementia. A 2019 meta-analysis of research by Ruth Peters and colleagues concludes that: "Evidence is emerging that greater exposure to airborne pollutants is associated with increased risk of dementia."[14] Additionally, the huge problem of micro plastic pollution is now shown to also be an airborne one. Tiny toxic plastic fibres from, for example, our polyester clothes can be inhaled and have effects on our respiratory system but emerging research also shows they have a route directly to our brain via our noses to the olfactory bulb with effects as yet unknown.

Carbon dioxide absorption by our oceans (super-issue). Ocean acidification is known as "the other carbon problem". Ocean acidification refers to a reduction in the pH of the ocean over an extended period of time. This is caused primarily by uptake of carbon dioxide (CO_2) from the atmosphere – an effect that helps shield us from the effects of our emissions but with a devastating knock-on effect. As reported by the National Ocean Service in an article entitled "What is ocean acidification", 16 June 2024: "Ocean acidification is affecting the entire world's oceans, including coastal estuaries and waterways. Many economies are dependent on fish and shellfish and people worldwide rely on food from the ocean as their primary source of protein."[15] Through a combination of acidification and ocean warming, it is estimated that coral reefs could decline by up to 70–90 per cent if current trends continue.

Geopolitical instability. It has long been known that the uneven geographical spread of fossil fuel reserves is a key driver of global conflict and instability. This is exacerbated by the fact that most fossil fuels are located in politically unstable countries.

Deaths from hazardous working in fossil fuels. As summarised in a 2008 paper by Burgherr and Hirschberg, deaths related to the energy sector, of which the vast majority are fossil fuel related, are reported to form the second biggest direct man-made cause of deaths after transport-related deaths.[16] While the transition to renewable energy has many hazards related to raw material extraction, the majority of fossil fuel-related risks comes from issues specific to the source, such as gas explosions and the fact that these energy sources need ongoing extraction and transportation.

Nitrogen disruption (super-issue). Our food and ecosystems rely on just the right type of nitrogen being available at the right time in the right place. The academic paper "Global nitrogen: Cycling out of control" by Scott Fields in 2004 summarises the magnitude of the issue, even more than 20 years ago – when it was not as extreme.[17] Our economic system has resulted in more disruption to nitrogen than any other basic element, mainly by using fossil fuels to create huge quantities of artificial fertilizers and as a by-product of burning fossil fuels. The 2011 European Nitrogen Assessment noted that this has acted to "convert atmospheric di-nitrogen (N_2) into many reactive nitrogen (Nr) forms, doubling the total fixation of Nr globally in our natural systems and more than tripling it in Europe".[18] This, they say, threatens water quality, air quality, greenhouse balance, ecosystems and biodiversity, and soil quality. At an estimated cost of €70–320 billion per year in Europe this outweighs the direct economic benefits of the use of Nr in agriculture.

Issue 2 – how we use the energy

We currently use 75 per cent more biocapacity than can be sustained on an ongoing regenerative basis. The Ecological Footprint overshoot varies greatly amongst different peoples and countries with the US using over five Earths' worth of resources if everyone did the same, India operating within one planet and many other countries using far less. However, we need to go beneath these headline figures to see what damage is caused by how we decide to use the energy we create – something we can enable AI to help or harm further.

Destruction of biological diversity (super-issue). Biodiversity loss means the loss of genetic diversity on the planet. Drivers include habitat fragmentation and change, direct species consumption, climate change and pollution and disruption of habitats, for example from plastics and invasive species. Loss rates are now so high that the emerging consensus is that we are in the sixth mass extinction phase, the last being when the dinosaurs left Earth. Given its rapid decline and foundation of life, biodiversity loss is largely assessed by scientists to be the most urgent and problematic for life on Earth. The WWF Living Planet report concludes that: "Between 1970 and 2020, the size of wildlife populations plummeted by 73% on average."[19] Biodiversity loss is a consequence of how we use energy as individuals, organisations and governments. As the WWF report outlines, "Global public explicit subsidies to sectors driving nature's decline ranged from $1.4 trillion to $3.3 trillion per year in 2022 and total public funding for environmentally harmful subsidies has increased by 55% since 2021." It is important to note that the IPBES in 2019 assessed that "35% of the areas formally protected and 35% of all remaining terrestrial areas with very low human intervention are traditionally owned, managed, used, or occupied by Indigenous peoples".[20]

Undermining ecosystems (super-issue). Ecosystems are coherent clusters of living organisms combining with non-living elements of the natural world including atmosphere, geology and water. They can adapt to change to a point but if their integrity goes beyond a certain point they collapse. As Tony Juniper, Chair at Natural England, UK and former CEO, Friends of the Earth UK, described to us, the role the Amazon plays in global weather we depend on examples how its perpetual piecemeal loss could lead to its collapse with grave consequences: "Forests are one of the major ecosystem types that we depend on. Rainforests like the Amazon are core to the Earth's hydrological system – recycling water drawn off the ocean in what are termed by some to be 'Sky Rivers'. You can trace a chain of events of rainfall and evaporation, which begin to unravel once the forest is fragmented, and so there is a danger that the entire system collapses beyond a certain threshold. Scientists estimate that the Amazon system could collapse if only one quarter of it is cleared, making its biological and cultural diversity non-viable. Judging by the scale and intensity of the fires and droughts, which are becoming more frequent and more intense across the Amazon, that point may be approaching, which is terrifying."

Misuse of soil (super-issue). We directly depend on the top 30 centimetres of soil on our planet for 95 per cent of our food. It takes around 1,000 years to produce 2–3 cm of soil. Every five seconds, the equivalent of one football pitch of soil is lost. The rate is 100–1,000 times higher on intensively grazed or arable land. Where soil is eroded the loss in crop yields can be up to 50 per cent, leading to billions of dollars in losses. The UN Food and Agriculture Organization (FAO) estimates that by 2050 around 90 per cent of top soil could be eroded. Soil erosion is just one of ten key issues threatening soil health.[21]

Misuse of water (super-issue). In its 2021 report titled "Water in circular economy and resilience" (WICER), the World Bank Group stated: "The ongoing water crisis represents one of the most significant challenges of our time."[22] As WWF summarises, while water makes up 70 per cent of our planet, only 3 per cent of it is freshwater, and two-thirds is frozen or inaccessible. They also outline how agriculture accounts for 70 per cent of the world's freshwater usage, however, current demand is outstripping supply, the Rio Grande is overutilised by 50 per cent.[23] The World Bank highlights the dependency of GDP on water: "some regions could see their (GDP) growth rates decline by as much as 6 percent of GDP by 2050 as a result of water-related losses."[24] They also note water as a critical equity issue, with around 2 billion people lacking access to safely managed drinking water services, 3.6 billion without safely managed sanitation services, and 2.3 billion who do not have basic hand-washing facilities.

Misuse of antibiotics (super-issue). The World Health Organization, and other experts, see antimicrobial resistance (AMR) as one of the most urgent and threatening issues to humanity.[25] They estimate that "bacterial AMR was directly responsible for 1.27 million global deaths in 2019 and contributed to 4.95 million deaths". New vaccines are being searched for all the time but are not able to keep up with the rate of resistance. This means that some believe that it could be only a couple of decades before we could die of minor scratches. The number one cause of AMR is overuse, teaching bacteria how to respond. While overuse in humans is a major issue, the biggest use and misuse of antibiotics is in the food sector. In its 2017 report "Drug resistant infections: A threat to our economic future", the World Bank Group stated that in 2010 the animal production sector consumed "63,200 tons of antibiotics and probably far more, exceeding total human consumption".[26] They also noted the intersection between GDP and antibiotics, estimating that AMR could result in US$ 1 trillion additional healthcare costs by 2050, and US$ 1 trillion to US$ 3.4 trillion GDP losses per year by 2030 – as large as in the 2008 financial crisis.

Misuse of chemicals (super-issue). The number of persistent toxic chemicals in our environment and their interaction poses one of the greatest threats to human wellbeing. Carcinogens and toxic residues from industrial processes have been found in the blood and tissues of all populations. An NYU study, published in *Lancet Planetary Health*, analysed a group of over 5,000 mothers in the US, finding that chemicals found in plastic food packaging were associated with 10 per cent of pre-term births in 2018.[27] The societal costs stemming from this issue alone could reach up to $8 billion – let alone the huge direct wellbeing impacts. We depend heavily on flying insects for our food and for our food industries to function. In another of many examples, research published in *Science* by Mitchell and colleagues in 2017 found that chemicals that are toxic to bees have been found in 75 per cent of honey globally, providing one clue as to why 48 per cent of US colonies prematurely died off in 2023.[28] In financial terms alone, this is irrational, as Dennis and Kemp published in *PLOS One* in 2016: "In current financial terms, and in the U.S. alone, the estimated wholesale value of honey, more than $320 million dollars in 2014, pales in comparison to aggregate estimated annual value of pollination services, variously valued at $11–15 billion."[29] One of the biggest harms from plastics is the chemicals used in their production including many PFAS (per- and polyfluoroalkyl substances) known as "forever chemicals". There are more than 4,700 types that are produced. They take more than 1,000 years to break down and during that time concentrate up the food chain, meaning that higher concentrations are found in predators including humans via, for example, food, dust and water. One academic study, by Guomao Zheng and colleagues published in 2021, reported levels 2,000 times higher than considered safe in drinking water were found in all 50 women they sampled.[30] They can be actively destroyed but the cost of doing so is estimated in a 2024 academic paper by Alison Ling to be more than one year of GDP (106 trillion USD).[31] We produce more than 100,000 tons of PFASs per year and despite it only being less than 120 years since the first plastic product hit the shelves, production of plastics has rapidly increased from 50 million metric tons a year in 1976 to over 400 million in 2023. Roland Geyer and colleagues have estimated that only 9 per cent of plastic actually gets recycled – which does not actually mean turned back into itself but normally into a lesser quality material.[32] The UN has forecast that there will be more plastic than fish in the ocean unless we stop using single-use plastic.

Stresses on mental health (super-issue). The United Nations put mental health as a global priority. The World Health Organization estimates that a staggering one out of the 8 billion people on planet Earth, including one out of every seven teenagers, have a mental health disorder.[33] The OECD states that half of all people will have an adverse mental health condition at some point in their life.[34] However, few people have access to quality mental health services. The repercussions of mental ill-health on individuals, families, communities and workplaces are severe, contributing to financial costs that reach above 5 per cent of GDP in some countries.

Isolation. The OECD, in its 2021 paper "All the lonely people", defined loneliness as "a subjective emotional state, characterised by a longing for human contact.[35] It is the discrepancy between a desired and actual level of social contact". Loneliness has always been a human issue, but in recent decades, due to the way humans interact in the modern economy, and despite there being more humans on Earth to interact with than ever before, it has reached chronic levels, for example, increasing 8–15 per cent between 2003 and 2018 across the 38 countries in the OECD. Mareike Ernst and colleagues conclude that "social isolation and loneliness were becoming major public health and policy concerns, largely due to their serious impact on longevity, mental and physical health".[36] The 2023 US Surgeon General's Advisory report entitled "Our epidemic of loneliness and isolation" concluded that "a significant portion of Americans lack adequate social connection", a trend that continues to grow, increasing by a massive 24 hours in an average month between 2003 and 2020.[37] For people aged between 15 and 24 the shift has been dramatic, with in-person time with friends reducing by nearly 70 per cent in only two decades. The US is not alone in such shocking trends: Gallup's inaugural 2024 survey on global loneliness found that "the share of adults who felt lonely exceeded 30% in 22 countries, over half of which are located in Africa".[38] The WHO assesses that rates and prevalence mean that loneliness should be considered an issue of grave global concern and has set up a commission on social connection to prioritise resolving it.[39]

Social exclusion and fragmentation. A related but different issue is social exclusion which refers to the process by which individuals or groups are systematically blocked from various rights, opportunities, and resources that are normally available. This has implications for citizenship, democracy and social cohesion as well as mental health. A 2024 paper by Cuesta and colleagues in *PLOS One* estimates that around 2.33 to 2.43 billion people across the globe (approximately 32 per cent of the total population) are at risk of being socially excluded.[40] The South Asia and East Asia and Pacific regions together account for 1.3 billion of these individuals, with India and China alone hosting 840 million. Sub-Saharan Africa has the highest proportion, with 52 per cent of its population at risk of exclusion.

Financial debt levels. The IMF reports that private debt as a percentage of GDP tripled between 1960 and 2022.[41] The UN 2024 report "A world of debt" outlines that global financial debt (private and public) rose almost every year from 2010 to 2023 – nearly doubling in that time.[42] This helps create the financial vicious cycle which propels the need to chase further GDP growth and higher wages in order to service this debt and reduce interest payments. Financial debt underpins social inequity. According to the World Bank's 2024 International Debt Report, developing nations diverted money from public spending to allocate a record $1.4 trillion managing their foreign debt, with interest costs alone now at a 20-year peak totalling $406 billion.[43]

Rampant inequality. We live in a time of shocking inequality of opportunity, income and access to clean and green environments to name a few. Given our current economic system (as we will outline in detail), financial income has systematically become the main way people can access wellbeing, hence it tells us more about access to wellbeing than it should. Jason Hickel points out the fact that the wage gap between the Global North and Global South is increasing, not decreasing, across all sectors, even as the share of highly skilled labour and manufacturing has increased dramatically over the same time frame.[44] Tony Juniper, famous for his advocacy and political work on environmental issues, has published the book *Just Earth* detailing the intricate connection between social and environmental crises. In this 2025 book he summarises that "Currently [...] ten per cent take 52 per cent of global income, whereas the poorest half of the population has 8.5 percent of it. On average, an individual from the top ten per cent of the global income distribution earns US$122,100 per year, whereas an individual from the poorest half makes US$3,920 per year."[45] He goes on to draw from the World Bank's World Inequality Report of 2022, which revealed how "between 1995 and 2021 the top one percent captured 38 per cent of the global increment in wealth, while the bottom 50 percent captured just two per cent between them".

Unplanned levels of population. The level of human population is known to be a direct result of our use of cheap fossil fuels to turn non-arable land into food-growing areas via what is known as the Green Revolution. While it is easily calculated that if there were fewer people consuming in different ways it would almost certainly be easier to achieve long-term wellbeing for all, the impact of human population is intricately connected with patterns of consumption – many, including the World Resources Institute, estimate we could all have durable high levels of wellbeing even at the UN-projected peak of 9.7 billion, if we consumed in a different way.[46]

FACING FACTS

Together these major issues paint a severe picture of a world where our wellbeing is on the brink – driven there by our decisions about how we organise and enact our economy. These statistics also clearly reveal the fallacy at the heart of the system: the costs of the issues created by this economy are set to wipe out any financial benefits we are counting.

This is our operating context and it is the role of leaders today to understand the severity of these issues which shape the stakeholder, legislative, regulatory, cost base and most other leadership pressures faced. The tension and pressure to change will only get stronger (and be amplified by AI) until we understand and use this knowledge to act. If the state of these base systems as described above is not front of mind when decisions are made, then how can the result be anything other than dangerously wrong strategy?

In summary, we have designed an economy that is perhaps the most inefficient and ineffective possible – because it has created the very opposite outcome to its intended result. We wouldn't need a word called "sustainability" if the economy had been working. Instead, we are in a state of urgent and "end game time unsustainability" – an existential crisis of our collective long-term wellbeing. Reflecting soberly on the facts, and not just pockets of short-term good news, must be the basis of a wake-up call. If the economy's goal is right but it has just been governed and enacted badly, then this is where we need to focus.

'IT'S THE ECONOMY (AND GOVERNANCE), STUPID'

The economy is one of the most powerful human-created organising systems that exists. As outlined previously, it shapes how we allocate our precious shared resources to optimise wellbeing for the collective over the longer term. In this way the goals of the economy are aligned with the goals of sustainability and sustainable development. It also means the economy is purpose-driven. In other words, it is aligned with serving the good of others – it exists and is driven by maximising goal that is other-serving. If the economy was doing its job well, how is it that we as humanity have ended up with our toes hanging over the cliff edge and with any chance of long-term wellbeing for all slipping over into the abyss? If it isn't the idea of the economy that is the problem, which is ostensibly about achieving society's best interest, then the issue must lie with how we have organised the economy and the collective worldviews we hold about it.

LOGIC 1: THE ECONOMY WE HAVE DESIGNED

While many forms of economy exist, our current globally dominant economy is a particular form of capitalism. There are different definitions of capitalism which can get unnecessarily nuanced. We feel that the most practical way to think about capitalism is in contrast to centrally controlled economies.

Whether an economy relies on governed markets for allocation and transformation of resources, or direct allocations made by a central group of people, is the core economic design choice. All economies are recognised to be a mix of these. However, an economy dominated by carefully governed markets is a very different choice to an economy dominated by central control regarding who gets access to which resources – with an almost absence of market allocation. A definition of capitalism we find useful from the Merriam-Webster dictionary is: "An economic system characterised by private or corporate ownership of capital goods, by investments that are determined by private decision, and by prices, production, and the distribution of goods that are determined mainly by competition in a free market."

The definition does not mention profit maximisation, or determination of the level or type of governance frame that shapes those markets. This helps reveal that short-term financial self-interest is just one *form* of market capitalism that has come to dominate. When the Berlin

Wall fell, the idea of serious alternatives for organising the economy fell with it. This was not just a story about capitalism winning over communism, it was also about a particular form of market capitalism winning over any other alternative that might have existed. Even before the Iron Curtain fell, and particularly in the post-war period, a specific form of profit-maximising capitalism was being written into rules of international governance and capital allocation like the WTO, the IMF and other such bodies.

The use of "free" in the definition is a relative term, because all markets are in some way regulated by governments that dictate aspects of what can and cannot happen. A central premise of our book is the recognition that markets are vital and need to work well. The ability to "freely" move capitals of all kinds, whether they are natural, human, financial or social, within specific governance frames is deeply human, as McMillan summarises in his book on the history of markets: "Markets have been around as long as history and have been incessantly reinvented."[47] He goes on to state that the antithesis of a market economy is central planning. While many protest and call for the end of capitalism, in our observation they are generally not calling for the end of a market economy and the ability to exchange resources liberally within a well-governed frame. What they are calling for really seems to be the end of the short-term financial self-interest form of capitalism which is harming our collective long-term wellbeing. In our view, the core choice is a new form of capitalism based on a market economy deliberately governed for long-term wellbeing for all, or a command-and-control economy that centrally allocates resources. The latter is not an outside possibility – industry leaders are already beginning to warn that climate change alone could undermine the entire market economy.[48]

It is lamentable that a lack of clarity about these choices often leads to an unhelpful divide between those on both sides who want to see deep change, but use different language to argue for an economy that serves our collective long-term good. We hope to shine a light on the already existing frame that transcends this polarity in a way that takes us beyond "left" and "right" politics and reminds us that this is about something deep and unifying. As unsustainability moves us into dangerous territory, the lure of handing over allocation decisions to a central body rapidly increases. The risk is that by rejecting our unworkable form of capitalism because it doesn't align with long-term wellbeing for all, we reject a market economy entirely and hence lose the freedom, democracy and efficiency effects just when we need them most.

THE FORM OF CAPITALISM WE LIVE WITH

We will refer to the current, globally dominant form of economy, as the "business-as-usual" (BAU) Logic 1 economy. This is often referred to as a "neo-liberal" version of market capitalism, mainly designed by American and UK political actors (notably US President Ronald Reagan and UK Prime Minister Margaret Thatcher) in the 1980s. It was built on the foundation of unifying the world post-war through trade as the harmoniser with the Bretton Woods system of global financial governance a core part of this. The BAU Logic 1 approach rests heavily on neo-classical economic thinking and the thought leadership of Milton Friedman and the Chicago School of Economics. Its early adoption by countries such as General Pinochet's regime in Chile via what is known as the "Chicago Boy" regime underpinned the Washington Consensus in 1989, formalising its global influence.

We are keenly aware of the complexities and contested history of the economy we live with. We are not in a position to cover the detailed, nuanced history of the evolution of the economy. Lorenzo and Victoria have written at length about the history of economics as well as the role of marketing in extending its reach into society. You can find some of these references in the chapter bibliography. We don't seek to deny important nuances, or any other debate, but rather to draw attention to the core unified aspects that materially affect all of us and all types of organisations, on a daily basis.

It is easy to spend time pointing out exceptions but we ask you to deliberately look beyond these when they distract from the "rule". Whilst sophisticated thinking is vital, a focus on the exceptions, at the expense of first principles, has not served us well. A focus on exceptions to the rule has led to more and more silos being created to the "extent that we forget what unites across these divides". Universities are society's "thought leaders" and the divisions and disciplines that are created reflect this focus on sub-divisional thinking. Yet complex adaptive system theory, as summarised by John Holland who coined the term, tells us living systems (like global or national economies) despite their incredible complexity "have enough significant characteristics in common to make it possible, even probable, that common general principles explain their dynamics".[49] It is time to focus on the rule and not just the exceptions.

With this in mind we will simply set out the well-documented generalised core assumptions of this BAU Logic 1 economy. They represent "generalised truths" which are deeply held, and which affect all economies, organisations and individuals in the world in one way or another. These assumptions have gradually formed the silent structure of the world around us. They create "hidden in plain sight" barriers for leaders. Therefore, naming these assumptions, the role they play in our current crises, and how they are locked in through governance systems is the foundation for understanding why leading beyond profit at the levels of the economy, organisation, team and self is THE task of today's leaders.

Below is an adapted table from the first paper in the University of Cambridge Institute for Sustainable Leadership Unleashing the Sustainable Business series that Victoria wrote with Aris Vrettos. The table summarises some of the most important and flawed assumptions that underpin the BAU economy (both Logic 1 – short-term self-interest, and Logic 2 – long-term self-interest, as we will cover later). These have come to powerfully shape our actions at the economic, organisational and individual levels. The evidence for the assumption in the table can be found in the book's Chapter 1 bibliography which can be found at https://nblibrary.papertrell.com/id008068019/Beyond-Profit-Bibliography

TABLE 1.1 KEY FLAWED ASSUMPTIONS OF THE BAU LOGIC 1 "PROFIT-FIRST" ECONOMY

ASSUMPTION	WHAT THIS MEANS
Self-interest	Humans are primarily motivated by egoistic self-interest and are endowed with fear-based instincts to protect this. The self-interest that humans are seeking is what economists term "utility". This is something "useful", because it (what is sought) will ultimately support their wellbeing. Hence, in this view, the best place to increase wellbeing is through buying products and services on the formal market, and citizens are more usefully understood as consumers.

(Continued)

ASSUMPTION	WHAT THIS MEANS
	Therefore, financial income is what allows us to achieve higher levels of wellbeing and the main constraint to this is income. This self-interest and focus on financial income as the means to achieve it is mirrored at the organisational level where financial self-interest, in other words profit maximisation, is the main motivation.
Theory of rational behaviour (or bounded-rationality)	Individuals are rational or rational to a point known as "bounded-rationality", where they are driven to maximise wellbeing and know how to achieve it in the optimal way. They are generally able to see through marketing messages and understand what will really make their lives better.
Financial investors own the company and invest for financial gain (shareholder primacy)	Shareholders are the owners of a company and are the "principals". Governing bodies and management are the "agents" acting on their behalf to maximise shareholder interests. However, as self-interested human beings, management will naturally act to maximise their own interests and therefore must be closely monitored by the governing body. What investors care about – and what agents are expected to maximise – is by default assumed to be financial profit. Hence, only by aligning the financial self-interest of both parties can financial performance be effectively pursued.
Competition helps well-being	Competition is the core mechanism that keeps self-interest in check through external threats that force companies to pass enough value onto customers and not retain it all as financial capital. This also minimises government regulation. Therefore, executives should be resolutely focused on out-competing others in the market.

ASSUMPTION	WHAT THIS MEANS
Government intervention and spending would, ideally, be zero to optimise wellbeing	A perfectly running free market that optimises wellbeing for everyone would not need any government intervention. Government intervention is the result of a failure of the market economy. Where market failures happen, laws are the way that society makes its discontent known through the democratic process. This then changes the laws and so also the rules of the game (hard decision parameters) for organisations. Voluntarily changing behaviours in a way that reduces profit maximisation, e.g. choosing to apply a law from one country on worker protection in a country that doesn't require it, or transitioning to "Net Zero" emissions where no law requires it, would be bypassing the democratic system and be against the perceived fiduciary duty to maximise owners' financial returns.
Perfect information is the goal	If everyone in a market has complete information then the market will run properly and wellbeing for everyone will be optimised. Consumers will then know all choices open to them and be able to action their rational choice. Well-run companies will know what their competitors are doing and what consumers want. Trying to create perfect information is therefore a core policy goal and removing imbalances in what is known (asymmetry) is vital. Providing more information is the obvious government market correction where people are making choices that harm their wellbeing, e.g. people are obese because they don't have enough information about the food choices available.

(Continued)

ASSUMPTION	WHAT THIS MEANS
Wellbeing is subjective to the individual. The customer is king (consumer sovereignty)	The best way for an individual to maximise their wellbeing is entirely subjective but stable and knowable through market demand. People will spend more money on something that gives them more wellbeing benefit. Hence, if profit-maximising companies try to supply what individuals demand in the market (consumer sovereignty) and shape their decisions around these customer demands then wellbeing is optimised. This has been the essence of the "marketing concept" of business since the 1950s (aligned with neoclassical economics). Those companies that meet customer demands the best will be rewarded with superior profits. Therefore, how much profit and growth a company achieves is a proxy for how effectively they are supplying wellbeing. Whilst the customer may be king, this is in fact only a means to the end of profit maximisation.
Wellbeing is not the rightful remit of a company	It is not necessary to understand what underpins people's preferences in order to deliver them. Preferences are revealed through consumer choice in the market combined with consumer insight research. As consumers are rational, self-interested utility maximisers, they are best placed to know how to improve their lives – hence a company should concentrate on its self-interest and let consumers focus on theirs. Any attempt to "educate" or alter preferences is a distortion of the market and will result in sub-optimal wellbeing outcomes. Those companies that do best at meeting the wellbeing of society will be rewarded by increased demand and profit. Another way companies contribute to wellbeing is through the direct and indirect jobs they create which allow people to buy more wellbeing on the market.

ASSUMPTION	WHAT THIS MEANS
Values and responsibilities neutral	A business cannot have values and responsibilities, only a person can, and the proper way for these to be expressed is through democratic government processes. If an individual expresses these through their decision-making at work (as employees) then they are abusing the resources given to them in trust by owners to maximise profits and instead using them for something they personally decide is 'valuable'. For this reason, values and business should be kept entirely separate.
Maximum levels and freedom of choice	The wider the choice of products and services available to consumers, the more likely they are to be able to meet their preferences and optimise their wellbeing. Choice editing therefore limits companies' ability to freely meet consumer demand and consumers' autonomy to decide how to optimise their wellbeing. Anything that limits the range of choice or people's ability to freely choose from them will reduce wellbeing optimisation – other than financial capital which is a justifiable limitation.
Trickle down	Wealth created at the top income levels is one of the best ways to ensure wealth is created at the bottom income levels because those with money create jobs and increase GDP and contribute to the country's balance of payments.
Globalisation (economic)	The concept of a free market is a global one and not confined to national borders to trade. Protectionism or other regulations that create barriers to trade, enforced by governments, reduce the freedom of the market to optimise for wellbeing and therefore reduce global wellbeing outcomes.

(Continued)

ASSUMPTION	WHAT THIS MEANS
Increasing prices as a way to decide who gets what	When demand rises and supply can't keep up, prices should rise to decide who gets access. This means that those who have money are able to access scarce resources more easily than those that don't. This aligns with the view that pricing should be focused on maximising profit based on what people are willing to pay alone. Inequality of wellbeing is a necessary means to achieving optimal wellbeing for everyone.
Short-termism (not an assumption)	Short-termism isn't a condition of an effective market but it is a natural consequence of financial self-interest aided by trading rules and technology. As trading has sped up, helped by new technology, money and "ownership" changes in nano seconds to try to find the best and least risky financial returns. This means that companies, especially those with a large number of non-institutional investors, experience high pressure for shorter and shorter returns, although institutional investors have themselves been cited as part of the short-term problem.

Source: Adapted from Hurth, V. & Vrettos A. (2021) "Unleashing the sustainable business: how purposeful organisations can break free of business-as-usual". Cambridge, UK: University of Cambridge Institute for Sustainability Leadership.

PROFIT AS THE GOAL

Together, these assumptions represent our collective deep beliefs about how to best achieve collective long-term wellbeing through the economy, organisational and individual decisions. Over time we have forgotten the point of these assumptions, or some of us didn't know they existed. Hence, we don't question them. Either way, they create the walls of the decision-making box that we are bound by. They sit deep within us and structure the world around us, shaping the decisions we make – or even just what actions feel comfortable or not.

The BAU assumptions that guide behaviour are often only revealed when Logic 1 behaviour is challenged, with responses that imply that "it is just the way it is": "Unfortunately humans are just selfish"; "We are at our best when we compete and so it is the best way to get results"; "We are a useful company and deserve tax breaks because we are making massive profits and creating jobs." The conversation rarely goes deeper: we tend not to explain to ourselves or others why actually making as much money as possible and creating jobs (regardless of the type) is actually a good thing and what the downsides might be or what science tells us are other ways to think about human behaviour. Terms like "value", "economy", "growth" and "performance" are steeped in BAU assumptions. Even in universities – the places where we should question everything – they are rarely exposed and challenged but just taken for granted from the start and end point of the majority of all mainstream academic research and teaching – especially in business schools where we train some of our most powerful leaders. Questioning Logic 1 has become out of reach, but we cannot create a sustainable world if we don't.

The super-assumption

At the heart of these BAU assumptions is one super-assumption that emerges as the most powerful driver of unsustainability:

FINANCIAL CAPITAL ACCUMULATION (PROFIT) = WELLBEING IMPACT

Adam Smith coined the term "invisible hand" to describe how markets work their magic to produce collective wellbeing from individualised self-interest. We can think of the collection of BAU assumptions as the conditions for enabling the market to act as a "wellbeing machine" – if everyone plays their role in making the assumptions true, then the wellbeing of everyone is automatically optimised. As long as we all play our role and the market is acting as close to the idea as possible, the only factor that really affects the level of wellbeing a citizen can attain is how much financial income they can capture from the market, which is mainly a function of their capacity and hard work (merit). Hence how much money we as individuals earn is key to buying more wellbeing in the market. This is the basis of the financially-driven work and lives that pervade global societies. This makes profit, or markers of it, appear as though it is an end in and of itself – and the best way in which we judge all types of organisations' contribution to society and judge our own, and others', self-worth.

Macro. At the economic level this, in turn, puts pressure on governments to maximise how much money is in the pockets of citizens, how much our money can buy (including vis a vis other countries) and how many jobs exist as their primary concern. Governments then play this narrative back to citizens via an almost singular focus on GDP and jobs as the two key markers of success and the lack of them a deep fear. Governments account to society by measuring and reporting production, consumption and financial income (this is what the gross domestic product, GDP, measures) as success, without questioning whether this reflects wellbeing and the best routes to it. A clear illustration of how the Logic 1 box leads to illogical conclusions for long-term wellbeing for all can be found in the Nobel prize winning economist William Nordhaus' conclusion that a global average temperature increase of 4°C is "optimal". This conclusion was drawn from his modelling which suggested that a 3°C rise would only reduce global economic output by 2 per cent, and even a significant increase to 6°C would result in just an 8 per cent decline. In contrast, many scientists view a world with a 4°C increase as fundamentally disastrous and insurers say that even 3 degrees would mean an uninsurable world.

Meso. At the Meso level we measure profits in organisations as the marker of success and the way of assessing the success of an organisation, without questioning or accounting for whether those profits reflect increases in collective wellbeing over time. While the BAU assumptions are intended to be geared primarily to business, all other kinds of organisations have moved into the orbit of serving this Logic 1 economy in the assumption that our lives will be improved by it. Just as governments gear their strategy and policy to short-term financial interest (GDP), many universities also prioritise actions based on maximising research income and student numbers, and charities chase donations at the expense of impact. All types of organisations display one or more Logic 1 assumptions and behaviours – even some organisations that are specifically established in law not to maximise financial self-interest but benefit a third party, such as charities or social enterprises. But don't take our word for it. As we outline the system in the rest of the book, consider for yourself the influence you notice regarding how we are all incentivised to fit these assumptions about how wellbeing is optimised.

Micro. At the Micro individual level, success for us and those of others is how much money we are paid and the goods and services we are therefore able to consume. As money equals wellbeing we also seek financial gains as quickly as possible. For this kind of "homo economicus", a bird in the hand is always better than two in the bush – and it makes perfectly rational sense to sacrifice future collective gains for immediate personal satisfaction.

GROWING THE WRONG THING

The assumption that financial income is a proxy for wellbeing outcomes and impact has become so deeply accepted and absorbed into our global cultures that we have collectively forgotten what the purpose of maximising financial income is. We are so certain about this working that we don't govern whether the goal is being achieved or not. Hence in a mental shortcut, growing the wellbeing machine is accepted as the route to higher wellbeing: the size of an economy or an organisation is equal to how valuable it is to society. Therefore, when we talk about "growth" what we nearly always mean is financial income growth – in the assumption this will grow wellbeing (i.e. prosperity, the good life, thriving, etc). And because it is wellbeing that we truly value, it becomes natural to equate financial growth with "performance", "development" and "success". Therefore, financial income in the pockets of citizens becomes the most important thing to grow; the financial income and profits of organisations become paramount; business (and finance) become the most important sectors that need to be free to make as much money as possible; and GDP growth becomes the pinnacle goal of the economy. It is clear how "growth" (of financial income) has become the ultimate "good".

Motivating unsustainable lives. As a result, we have become entrenched in high-consumption lifestyles in the search for increasingly elusive wellbeing – this could be small families sacrificing family time for work in order to live in large houses with massive mortgages, high school fees and annual long-haul holidays, or a rural villager in somewhere like Ladak now feeling they need to drink a particular fizzy drink to be respected. These effects are enhanced because we live in a postmodern world where our identities and our source of meaning have moved from communities and occupations – to what we consume.

As we strive to service lifestyles that, we are told, our wellbeing and very sense of self rely on, we become more and more isolated from each other, working longer and longer hours and feeling worse for it. The global effects of this on our mental and physical health are massive as we outlined in the World of Withering Wellbeing section in Chapter 1. Even Adam Smith, assumed architect of the Logic 1 economy, knew the fallacy of looking to material goods for wellbeing: "The pleasures from which we propose to derive our real happiness are almost always the same with those which, in our actual though humble station, we have at all times at hand and in our power."[50]

This creeping appropriation is evident in the expanding "marketisation" of life where the economy has created more and more markets for products and services that were once freely created outside of the formal market: Why cook when you can buy pre-made meals? Why care for parents when you can hire someone? Why drink freely available water when bottled water exists? As marketing departments come up with more and more ways to grow their company income, a price is now attached to many things we used to give and receive informally. As the dependency on the market to access foundational goods and services has grown and replaced non-material routes, our wellbeing has become increasingly tied to earning money to meet our needs. The shadow of this is that if you create wellbeing in ways that don't have a price tag, e.g. home-based care, community support or informal charitable acts, then your efforts are not counted in the nation's success (GDP) with important effects on areas like social inclusion, self-esteem and the ability to access basic wellbeing services.

Some argue that our problem is that we are greedy and don't know when to say "enough". Having enough means for our needs to be satisfied. However, we haven't even begun to understand what it is to really satisfy our needs and create true wellbeing. At every turn are dead ends and distractions as organisations are incentivised to shape and tempt us into consuming what makes them the most money.

Locked into destruction. We have locked this BAU Logic 1 way of making decisions into layers of governance systems. As Jeffrey Hollander, a pioneering Purpose-Driven Leader and founder of the early Purpose-Driven Organisation, Seventh Generation, summarised in our conversation: "We've designed a system that generates a host of unintended negative consequences – and embedded it deeply into the fabric of society, whether it's through laws, norms or accounting practices or through legislation and regulations. Our culture is saturated with this way of thinking and acting. We've built an incredibly elaborate architecture that keeps us locked on the path that we're on, where maximising profit is the point."

A BAU Logic 1 economy is shown to concentrate wealth and power in a small group of society. These, in turn, benefit from it and are motivated, able, and morally sanctioned to hold it in place. This reinforces our lack of capability to address the Logic 1 lock-in.

There are further ways that BAU assumptions reduce our ability to deal with the issues it creates: Logic 1 is an individualistic economy where BAU assumptions tell us that our wellbeing depends on beating the global competition, running faster and working harder to earn more money. This creates a fear-based system that pits us against each other in zero-sum competitive games.

As humans we are all capable of greed, individualism and self-promotion – traits that, as we will detail later, are enhanced when we are fearful. However, we have formally created an economy that relies upon and amplifies these negative traits – to enhance our wellbeing. The rationale for this was a genuine assessment that this would optimise collective wellbeing. As Friedman expressed in an interview with Phil Donahue in 1979: "The world runs on individuals pursuing their separate interests ... The record of history is absolutely crystal clear that there is no alternative way, so far discovered, of improving the lot of the ordinary people that can hold a candle to the productive activities that are unleashed by a free enterprise system."[51] By free enterprise system, Friedman of course meant the sort that runs on individual pursuit of financial self-interest.

The paradox at the heart of this form of capitalism was apparently summarised by Keynes when he said it was based on "the astounding belief that the most wickedest of men will do the most wickedest of things for the greatest good of everyone". Friedman himself was not unaware of this problem: "The great virtue of capitalism is that it encourages people to be self-interested. The great vice of capitalism is that it encourages people to be self-interested." It is perhaps not surprising that the Lakota indigenous people describe "Westerners" as *Wasichu* relatives, which is not translated as "white" as many believe, but in fact, "the ones who steal the fat".

Compounding this problem, BAU assumptions make it hard for society to question and arrive at new ways forward. This is because BAU Logic 1 in effect relegates deeper questions about what is valuable and unnecessary to the market. If all consumers (citizens) make consumption decisions that maximise their own wellbeing, then as long as the market is working well what is valuable will be revealed and society as a whole can avoid such contentious and philosophical arguments. We can leave the puzzle of wellbeing for the "Wellbeing Machine" to solve. As Milton Friedman argued in 1993 about this version of a market economy: "The great virtue of a free-market system is that it does not care what color people are; it does not care what their religion is; it only cares whether they can produce something you want to buy. It is the most effective system we have discovered to enable people who hate one another to deal with one another and help one another."[52] This approach may reduce friction but it also reduces the relevance and potency of philosophical and ethical debates in society. It also means that what unites us as a global community is relegated outside of decision-making. Being fractured, pitted against each other and lacking in important social conversations about what is really important is a toxic combination – one that has inevitably led to growing the destruction of what matters – and calls this growth "success".

PROFIT AS THE *MEANS* TO ACHIEVE THE GOAL

Due to BAU assumptions, financial capital hasn't just become the goal. It is also the most important means to achieve the goal of financial self-interest. Together, money as the goal and as the means to achieve the goal, is the reason why we live in a Logic 1 "hyperfinancialised" world where the relentless and myopic pursuit of short-term financial gains dominates decisions.

In today's world, making enough money to continue to run an organisation is vital – an organisation can't persist as a going concern without enough to pay the bills, meet the expectations of stakeholders and invest in its goal. To ensure that we make enough money, parameters[53] are put in place to our spending decisions that will maintain sufficient stores (stocks) at the right time (flows). Decision-making parameters include, for example: "don't spend more money than X or Y projects this year", or "ensure the financial margins are at least Z". If an action breaches these parameters and will use too much money, or too quickly then the answer to whether we can make the investment or not should be "no".

The importance of having sufficient profit to enable healthy stocks and flows of financial capital is vital whether you are a government, executive or household. Some different rules apply to governments as they are able to create money, but they are still bound by current "cash flows". The fact that experts in finance and accounting (and the Treasury) now tend to hold the most powerful positions in *strategic* decision-making in governments and other organisations is bound up in the problems of our fixation on profit.

The assumption that financial capital is the most important resource to protect is embedded in global legal requirements. For example, the balance sheet reporting that the law requires all organisations, including governments, to provide annual financial statements. These are important to help protect investors and other stakeholders who invest their financial, and other, resources. We have all witnessed the massive scandals in governments (e.g. Iceland), commercial companies (e.g. Enron in the US) and charities (e.g. The Kids Company in the UK) which wiped out savings, donations and other resources.

The problem is not the attention given to financial resources, but the fact that it is often the only resource that is properly valued – and so cared for, counted and accounted for by economies, organisations and citizens. This means that the health of everything that underpins financial capital is generally unnoticed, uncounted, unreported and therefore uncared for. This is a grave problem, because financial capital is only a symbolic good. Money *represents* value – it does not *embody* it. What is actually valuable is what money depends on:

- **Resources:** The healthy stocks and flows of human, natural[54] and social non-financial capitals including human capital (e.g. personnel), natural capital (e.g. raw materials) and social capital (e.g. loyalty to the organisation).

- **Systems:** The healthy, regenerative functioning of the social and environmental systems that support these foundational and financial capitals (e.g. a healthy climate, ecosystems, water systems, social trust and community inclusion).

- **Stakeholders:** The healthy, regenerative, functioning of stakeholders that gatekeep, embody and enable these systems and capitals to function.

SEEING THE WHOLE: THE ADAPTED DALY TRIANGLE

We have created a hyperfinancialised system where both the goal and parameters of our decisions are about financial capital: profits and profitability. We tell ourselves that the reason an organisation exists is primarily for maximising short-term financial self-interest, and the main parameter for this is the health of financial capital.

It is important to remember that these two core aspects of decision-making – the maximising goal of making as much money as possible and the parameter of carefully managing how much money is coming in and out in order to achieve the goal – are not the same thing. It is the difference between the skills of strategic marketing which pursues a value generation goal through developing products and services at a certain price, place and promotional activity, and the skills of accounting and finance (or the Government Treasury) which determine how much money is needed to pay for these market activities. They are of course intricately connected, but they are different functions.

This is a key point that needs to be understood by leaders if we are to recognise what is wrong with our current unsustainable system and how to fix it through new ways of making decisions. We routinely state "profits are vital", but we are rarely clear if we mean profit as a maximising goal or profitability as a resource. This obscures the difference between the way that profit is a problem (profits as a maximising goal that innovation is pointed at) and instead, how profit remains critical, as a means to an end – and therefore protecting stocks and flows of money will be vital for all organisations.

In the model below we see what we have outlined in this section, including the two aspects of goal and parameters. This figure has been adapted from the seminal work of Herman Daly[55] and subsequently Donella Meadows when her, and her colleagues, concluded that it was the best way of representing what a sustainable economy looks like, and what is wrong with the current one: we are stuck in BAU Logic 1, as shown in the middle of this triangle (Figure 1.1).

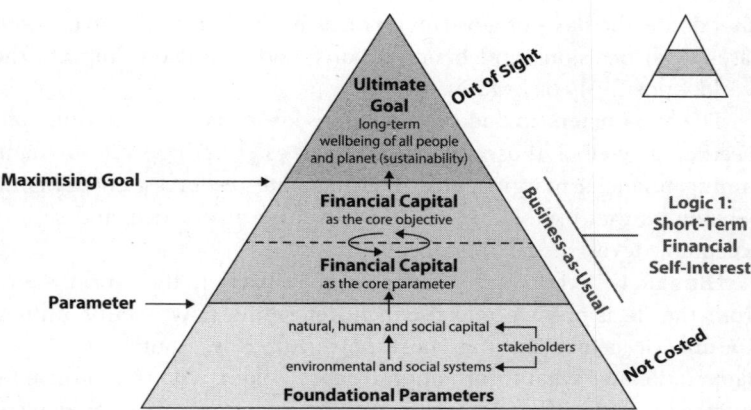

Figure 1.1 An adapted Daly Triangle depicting Logic 1 – short-term financial self-interest as our dominant economic logic which constrains governance direction to optimising for financial ends and protecting financial means

In summary, BAU assumptions, which underpin our dominant Logic 1 economy, form the invisible, silent boundaries of our thinking and action. If we are going to be able to empathetically and effectively lead for a sustainable future, then we need to soberly recognise the silent power that these assumptions have over the decisions we and others make, or don't make, and on the unsustainability crises we now face. We need to understand the mechanics of how these assumptions structure our routine decisions through being embedded in governance, and then very deliberately, through the leadership of each one of us, mount a united global effort to implement a system of governance that is aligned with long-term wellbeing for all.

Governance – the key to good (or bad) decisions

To become leaders in building a sustainable future, we must prioritise developing "governance literacy" – and quickly. The optimisation goal we choose to pursue and the parameters that constrain how this is done are fundamental; together they form the direction that we make decisions to achieve. They form governance direction. Governance

35

direction is the basis of governing policy, business models, investment cases – all decisions and hence actions, and ultimately impacts the world – positively or negatively.

The parameters include those imposed on us, such as time and weather, as well as those we choose, such as adhering to laws, maintaining financial margins, ensuring adequate resources, encouraging behaviours that uphold organisational values in practice, and setting acceptable levels of risk tolerance.

Ultimately, every human-influenced impact in the world stems from the decisions we make, which determine how actions unfold. Routine decisions are the most powerful. How routine decisions happen dictates what information reaches whom, who is authorised – overtly or implicitly – to access specific resources, and under what cultural conditions decisions are made. Governance structures and shapes these routine decisions.

The economy, organisations and ourselves are all governed to ensure the common goal is reached and common boundaries are not breached. These systems of governance at all levels, globally, are interconnected in various ways. The key formalised thread is this:

- Citizens of nations (nations being the current way we organise our world, though many critique[56] this) delegate and govern governments.
- Governments govern organisations as a whole.
- Governing bodies govern specific organisations through a nested thread of governance spanning the organisation.
- Individuals within organisations govern themselves in and outside of an organisational context.
- These individuals are also citizens, who together make up the ultimate governing body that governs governments.
- At the broadest level (and considering we are in the "Anthropocene"), we as humans – along with, and often on behalf of, other living systems – constitute the ultimate governing body of planet Earth.

The effect of the power of governance is compounded when we, as individual single entity organisms, come together to create larger organisations or organising systems. All things being equal, human beings operating in living systems will tend to self-organise and adapt to external feedback. Organisations, like a government, a company or a community group, are ways of *deliberately* bringing the energy of sometimes a few and sometimes hundreds of thousands of people together to make decisions as if they are of one mind and one body (encoded in law if you are "incorporated") for a deliberate goal and within agreed boundaries as well as emergent ones. This is true of ancient and more traditional first-nation cultures to more recent "Westernised" cultures. Indeed, McGee and Edson outline that all complex adaptive living systems are formed of agents that are "goal driven and their adaptation to changing conditions is often guided by their desire for goal attainment". Human societies of all kinds across nations have developed formalised organisations, including councils of elders, incorporated businesses but also governments, NGOs, partnerships and community groups, as the key tool to enact the economy and its goals of transforming shared resources for collective wellbeing, over time.

According to ISO 37000, the international multi-stakeholder consensus view on Organisational Governance is a "human-based system by which an organisation is directed, overseen and held accountable for achieving its defined purpose" (see Section Retool 1 in Chapter 3 for details of ISO 37000). If we want different outcomes, but they aren't reflected in the governance system, then we will either just be lucky to make them happen or we have to accept that they will remain just a nice idea. Governance has three core functions that, as leaders, we need to become very familiar with:

Direction: Define the organisational goal: the fundamental value you intend to generate through your reason to exist and clarify the value that will be protected in the process – via decision-making parameters that must be respected when making decisions.

Oversight: Monitor and adjust in an ongoing way so that the goal is optimally achieved within the parameters – and hence the value intended is generated and protected.

Accountability: Those given the obligation and authority to make decisions are answerable for how well they achieve the direction.

A quality governance system enables a group of complex, interacting humans to make decisions "as one entity" by structuring the basis of routine decisions and enabling corrective action and adaptation to external systems. Decisions are nearly always made under conditions of high variability and complexity, with partial information, so this will only ever be about maximising the probability that the purpose is optimised – achieved as fast and as much as is appropriate – depending on the nature of the purpose, and while protecting the intended value. This optimisation naturally includes building in necessary failure and redundancy because it is about continually doing the best job at the moment of decision-making.

Direction is the foundation of a governance system and determines what oversight and accountability are anchored to. Governance direction, in essence, translates worldviews (assumptions about what is valuable and how the world works) into a frame that determines how it is rational or irrational to act. For example, if purpose-driven worldviews need to be aligned with a regenerative approach – where we recognise that our wellbeing is positively enmeshed with the wellbeing of all living systems – then governance becomes the critical enabler of routine regenerative decisions, or the obstacle to them. By shaping what actions are validated as good, or seen as unwanted, governance profoundly shapes "the way things are done around here". Governance is therefore the basis of culture, which in turn continually influences worldviews in an ongoing feedback loop. This is true for an economy, an organisation (including government as an organisation), or an individual. In a well-governed system, the governing body establishes this organisational direction (goal and parameters) – with as much input from stakeholders, meaning those who affect and are affected by this system, as possible. This direction (goal and parameters) are then the basis of strategy, dynamically made in ever-changing contexts. See Figure 1.2.

Figure 1.2 Goal, parameters and strategy

Governance direction therefore serves as the foundation of governance and holds the greatest power to shape the operating (business) model, the investment cases, and the actions undertaken throughout the organisation, which determines the impacts an organisation has on the world. The larger and more influential the organisation the more power the governance system has on the world.

The goal and core parameters form the basis for deciding strategy. We tend to overcomplicate the concept of strategy, but at its core it can be summarised as: "How we can optimally maximise the goal while respecting the parameters, considering the dynamic context we face." For those that don't like the overly military or business implication of the term strategy – it can be simply replaced with "approach". Every strategic context is unique and that strategy needs to be as free and adaptive as possible. There is no way to learn the best strategies but there is a way to be armed with information and ways of processing that to make the best strategic decision possible. Strong, useful parameters should provide a relevant, safe space for creativity.

Organisational strategic deliberation results in top level strategic sub-goals (or objectives and sub-parameters). This is then encoded as direction within policies which are passed down to more specific parts of the organisation and elaborated in greater levels of strategy and policy as appropriate. We can think of this nesting of governance direction through policy as the thread of governance that all organisational decision-makers will be involved in.

The layers of detail form the structure of the governance system – flat systems may only have one or two layers (or none if the governing body is the entire executive), as opposed to many, sometimes very complex, layers. The more layers that exist in a system, the more distant the policy in one part can be from the organisational-wide goal and parameters that it is ultimately serving. As we will discuss later, sometimes new layers or divisions can provide a richer and more context specific identity and decision-making context that is welcomed. This can enable strategy to be more adaptive – but done badly layers and divisions create unhelpful boundaries that subvert useful and agile decision making.

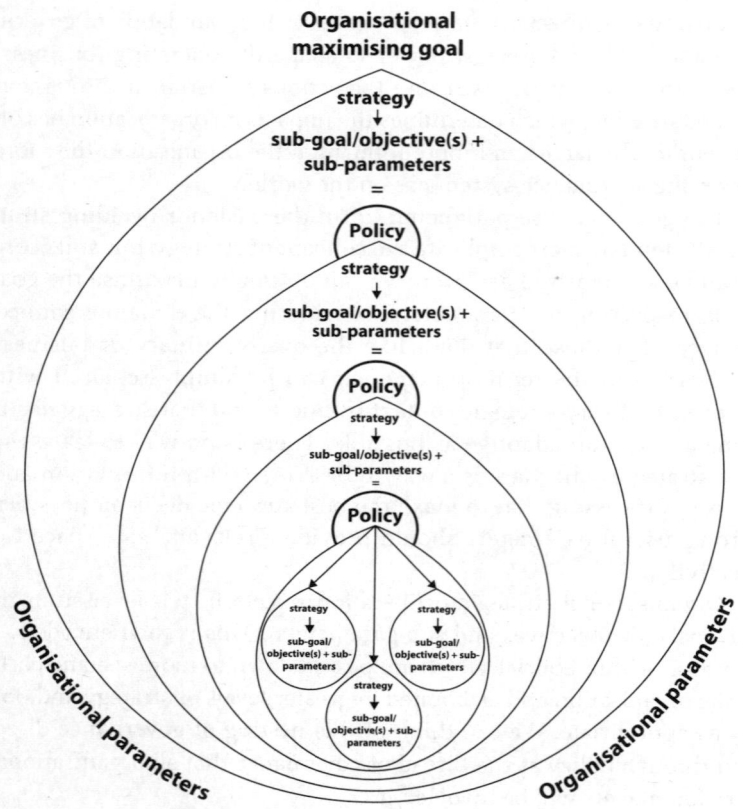

Figure 1.3 Governance, strategy, policy relationship

The governance direction is, therefore, logically cascaded throughout the organisation, through more specific translation of the organisational purpose and parameters.

Although governance is nested throughout an organisation (and beyond), and stakeholders should be central to setting the governance frame that they then make real and or experience the wellbeing consequences of, the ultimate accountability always lies with the most senior group of decision-makers – the governing body (see section Retool 1 in Chapter 3 for details). All organisations will have one governing body that is ultimately accountable for all actions. An individual or a sole trader will encompass the governing body as well as the CEO and other executives. Even where ultimate governance accountability appears to be shared across more than one system, ultimately it isn't.

For example, in a "two tier" of "dual board" governance system, for example in China, Germany and Indonesia, the supervisory board has ultimate accountability and other board types can be considered "governing groups" that have been delegated responsibilities for governing. The seven governing groups of the indigenous Oceti Sakowin peoples – the Seven Council Fires of Teton, Yankton, Yanktonai, Sisseton, Wahpeton, Mdewakanton, and Wahpekute – come together as a governing body to discuss and make collective decisions on matters affecting the whole nation. Decisions are made only when every group agrees. The existence of an ultimate accountable decision-making unit is true whether or not the governance is distributed (e.g. Distributed Autonomous Organisations or DAOs), collective, participatory, hierarchical or heavily rules-based.

GOVERNANCE AND MANAGEMENT

Organisations come in many forms, but a useful generalised perspective is to see the governing body as having the default accountability and responsibility for all organisational activities. It is not possible for the governing body to know everything and normally it cannot do everything. It therefore delegates responsibilities to an executive – within incorporated organisations, this is normally via a single CEO, but this delegation can be primarily to small "on the ground" decision units that then decide what coordinating support they need from senior executives (as is the case with Buurtzorg – the Dutch homecare organisation). Regardless of how delegation happens, the norm for the relationship between the governing body and the executive is that the governing body devises sub-goals or objectives and key performance indicators (KPIs)) which, if achieved, are believed to optimise the goal within the parameters. The executive, then, proposes a strategy that can best optimise the objectives within the parameters. The governing body approves, oversees and supports the achievement of this. Even where all goals and parameters may appear to happen at the "lowest" levels (like with Buurtzorg), ultimately the governing body is required to approve this set up (decide direction), and then oversee and account for all actions and inactions to external parties. Hence, governance design can come in an infinite number of forms. Additionally, a governance system spans and involves the whole organisation: in effect, everyone in an organisation (or indeed an individual as a single entity) is going to wear two hats:

1. doing (executing direction)
2. governing (directing, overseeing and being accountable) – even if they work on their own and are just governing their own behaviour.

It is worth reflecting for a moment on how these roles of "governing" and "doing" apply to every human system you can think of – from a government to yourself.

GOVERNANCE AS FREEDOM

Thomas Paine, was one of USA's Founding Fathers and in 1791 he wrote "Man is not the enemy of man but through the medium of a false system of government". Good governance on the other hand, far from holding us back, unleashes the best of our energy and enables unhelpful or even toxic rules to be removed.[57] A common mistake people make is to think the opposite – associating governance with rules, lack of freedom, top-down hierarchy, layers of unhelpful bureaucracy and rigidity. However, as we will explain further in Chapter 3, good governance is the key to enabling the very opposite – complex systems that achieve their goal through dynamic adaptation and balancing exploitation of the current versus exploration of the new. In other words, systems that can be held firmly by a frame that allows the strategy to dance as needed with its context. Elinor Ostrom, Nobel award-winning economist, evidenced that the "Tragedy of the Commons" was avoidable – whereby individuals, acting in their own self-interest, overuse and deplete a shared, finite resource that no one owns exclusively, meaning that everyone's best interest is undermined.[58] She showed that common resources can be collectively managed in adaptive self-organising ways for the long term, as long as certain governance "design principles" are met, including: clear boundaries; appropriate localised rules; adaptive monitoring for accountability; stakeholder influence mechanisms; sanctions for non-compliance; conflict resolution mechanisms and the need for nested governance in larger enterprises. Combined, this reinforces the importance of having a clear, broad governance frame within which nested, adaptive decision-making can be made. Hence good governance enables the freedom for groups of people to adapt appropriately. In other words, decisions by people in an organisation can be self-directed, rather than dictated by more specific behavioural rules, when a clear overall direction supports confident, coherent and healthy decision-making.

The clearer and broader the governance frame the less decision-making processes and specific goals or objectives need to be dictated. With a shared view of the goal and parameters, participants can collaborate and devise strategy in agile ways that can learn and adapt to surrounding system dynamics. With an appropriate outer governance frame we can create the conditions for regenerative wisdom to flourish and intuitive strategies to flow.

Governance, when done well, is merely the ultimate accountable and enabling function that keeps us on track to achieve what we collectively want, in the way we want. Motivational theory tells us that as humans we want to feel good about ourselves – it gives us meaning and self-esteem to feel the world is a better place because we are in it. We want to feel autonomy and mastery over the decisions we make and we do not want those decisions to be judged by others as bad. On a philosophical level, because governance direction is about goals and parameters, it combines both ends (which is akin to utilitarianism) and means (akin to deontology). Therefore, as we outline in more detail later, we could see governance direction as creating the conditions for virtuous decisions – a frame within which the appropriate resolutions for achieving ends and protecting means through purpose-aligned decision-making. Hence, we can, in reverse, judge the quality of the governance system by the virtue of the decisions which result – does the decision create overall harm or benefit? Please keep this in mind as we take you through the toxic governance systems we have created and the logical consequences of them.

Effective governance is by extension crucial for eliminating unnecessary red tape and unhelpful bureaucracy which have accumulated as attempts to patch a system producing toxic results. We currently try to plug the holes of a dysfunctional system with more and more rules. These misdirected rules just further hem in our ability to move the system to align with our best interest. Furthermore, governments lurch from subsidising and legislating one "solution" to another. Well-designed governance can therefore unlock human ingenuity and intrinsic motivation which enables the creation of optimal solutions and their rapid delivery and move beyond more or no structure.

As Indy Johar summed up regarding his 2025 "Dark Matter Labs" report: "The old paradigm forces us to choose between more governance to control markets or deregulation to free markets from governance altogether. But this binary is obsolete. What we actually need is a third pole – where governance itself is radically transformed to operate within a landscape of large-scale turbulence, rapid innovation, and fundamental uncertainty."[59] We believe that Logic 3 governance sets the conditions for this by creating a strong outer governance frame that keeps us on track to what matters, and by doing that frees up the strategy to achieve it – while keeping the governing body sensitive to what the system needs.

Once we are clear what the core governance direction is, then we can think about how we want that governance to operate so that the direction is achieved optimally. Governance can encompass a highly fluid, participatory system or a more rigid, defined structure. To be able to decide on the current most optimal design will rely on ongoing experimentation about how best to optimise for long-term wellbeing for all, in context. As David Graeber and David Wengrow masterfully outlined in their 2021 book *Dawn of Everything: A new history of humanity*, humans have experimented with a wide range of approaches to governance practice. This includes the "right to disobey" where citizens could ignore rules or relocate if they disagreed.[60] It is helpful to consider that the broadest possible purpose-driven governance frame is one that sets the value generation goal as long-term wellbeing for all while setting parameters that ensure the protection, regeneration and enhancement of the foundations that sustain it – and with governance aligned with the long-term collective good, of course even this outer frame should be open to continual multi-stakeholder debate. As we will delve into further in Chapter 3, the type of organisational structure, incentives, ownership rights, stakeholder influence, and other factors needed to achieve the governance direction are questions of governance strategy – in other words, context-dependent choices about how best to deliver on that direction.

The governance system is (or should be) the most powerful lever for organisational decision-making. Hence, if an organisation's governance system is misaligned with the goal of long-term wellbeing for all, then there is nothing to say that its routine decisions are not leading to consequences that undermine this goal. Unfortunately, and in fact, what we have designed for ourselves, at scale, is governance systems within organisations across the world that almost certainly assure these negative wellbeing consequences.

LOGIC 1: Governance – the driver of unsustainability

Governance systems, based on flawed assumptions, have embedded the business-as-usual (BAU) hyper-financialised objectives and parameters into the routine decisions of hundreds of millions of organisations and individuals globally.

The reason this has inevitably led to unsustainability is because Logic 1 governance in zeroing in on short-term financial self-interest, it excludes sustainability from decision-making – both the pursuit of long-term wellbeing for all and the protection of its foundations – as is illustrated if we overlay governance onto the adapted Daly Triangle.

At the "top of the triangle", the ultimate objective of the economy and society – long-term wellbeing for all – is out of the sight of governments, organisations and individuals alike. At the "bottom of the triangle", the health of the social and environmental systems that underpin everything is not accounted for or included in decision-making. The healthy stocks and flows of non-financial capitals – which are critical inputs for an organisation's ongoing viability, and in turn depend on the health of social and environmental systems – are not governed. The same neglect applies to the health of stakeholders whose ability to function is not overseen or accounted for properly. These systems, resources and stakeholders are effectively treated as inexhaustible free resources and limitless sinks.

The governance direction of the goal and parameters establish the box within which decisions are made. In Figure 1.4 we can see the governance box that structures decision-making within a Logic 1 organisation.

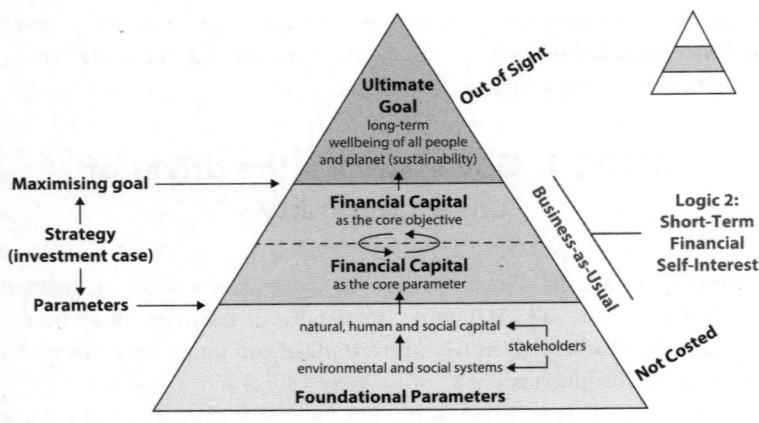

Figure 1.4 Logic 1 governance

Figure 1.4 not only illustrates the focus of decision-making but also highlights what lies outside the scope of strategic decision-making – the crucial elements that are routinely overlooked.

A GOVERNED CRISIS

By prioritising financial gain as the maximising goal and focusing on protecting financial capital as the only important parameter, the BAU Logic 1 governance system makes it normal and rational to make decisions that drive an unsustainable future – while making it irrational to address the root causes. Unsustainability, then, does not occur by chance; it is the result of deliberately governed systems designed to embed business-as-usual (BAU) assumptions into decisions made and opportunities forfeited.

Trillions of decisions across millions of organisations governed to varying degrees to this Logic 1 archetype, have collectively driven us to the brink of permanently losing the chance of wellbeing. Given that the Logic 1 economy has operated for decades excluding the advancement and protection of long-term wellbeing for all from its governance framework of decision-making, a state of extreme unsustainability was surely the only logical consequence. In other words, unsustainability should be understood as the inevitable result of the BAU economic assumptions we have embraced and embedded through Logic 1 governance systems.

Economies and organisations are society's innovation nerve centre. Yet, the innovation agenda they are made to work for drives destruction and forfeits the change we need – by design. The governance systems we have established not only suppress questions and solutions that can encompass the top and bottom of the triangle (see Figure 1.4) but actively disincentivise and penalise such "deviant" behaviour. This irony is stark: the very purpose of these Logic 1 assumptions – and the reason society has supported the Logic 1 market economy – was to produce collective long-term wellbeing. Instead, we have engineered perhaps the most ineffective and inefficient economy imaginable that drives the opposite.

Making mistakes is human, and we can all be forgiven for them. However, unsustainability stands out as the ultimate failure – the ultimate governance failure – because no one has thought to check whether the system was working and to course-correct when necessary. Properly governed economies would have had oversight – by governments as organisations and by citizens as the ultimate governing body – to evaluate whether the chosen goal was appropriate and the parameters sufficient. Instead, this critical responsibility has been neglected.

COMPOUNDING THE CRISES

It has been said that it is madness to try to solve a problem from within the same frame of thinking that created the problem. Yet this is exactly the trap we have fallen into with our Logic 1 governance box. Not only does a Logic 1 governance frame create unsustainability effects, but when the issues come back to hit the very same Logic 1 governance systems, they can only respond from within this logic. When collapsing systems hit us, Logic 1 governance responds from within its decision-making frame of short-term financial self-interest. This entrenched mindset renders innovative solutions to sustainability challenges irrational for most organisations. Decisions that align with long-term wellbeing for all don't just fail the rationality test in Logic 1; they also fail the morality test that many hold deep in their consciousness. After all, as Friedman argued, the best way to serve society is to pursue personal financial self-interest.

This helps explain why, despite how long we have known about dangerous climate change (or degraded soil quality, or inequality or any other major sustainability issue) and despite countless global meetings, agreements and plans, extending all the way to local and individual levels – we are still hurtling in the wrong direction on nearly all the indicators that matter, as outlined in this chapter.

Logic 1 is held in place at three nested levels of governance – Macro, Meso and Micro. These are the levels that we as leaders actively need to change simultaneously. We will now introduce how Logic 1 shows up at each level.

MACRO LEVEL LOGIC 1: GOVERNANCE OF THE ECONOMY

As the economy is central to our ability to progress wellbeing, the Logic of government and the Logic of the economy are intricately connected. Logic 1 economies, run by Logic 1 governments and based on BAU assumptions, are primarily focused on short-term financial self-interest. They have a maximising goal to grow financial income (i.e. GDP) and parameters based on keeping the stocks and flows of money healthy (national balance sheet). This results in policy that prioritises short-term financial gains over durable, equitable wellbeing impacts. While some policies may at first glance appear wellbeing-focused, they often tend to focus on GDP growth as the ultimate goal, neglecting the more efficient and effective routes to the ultimate goal of collective long-term wellbeing. Examples include:

Investing in GDP, not wellbeing. Tax breaks for landlords, reduced taxes for large companies regardless of what they are selling or their work environment, or relaxed rules e.g. in "enterprise zones" are all examples of common Logic 1 actions. These measures are based on the assumption that the resulting financial income will trickle down to benefit society, enabling citizens to purchase more wellbeing as a result. In reality, research, such as by Bouchard and Mézard, in 2000 has shown that a Logic 1 economy, shaped by such policies, will always result in the concentration of wealth – the only question is how quickly this happens, which is based on the number and speed of financial transactions.[61] This concentration of wealth accelerated following Jensen's 1986 paper which argued for better aligning executive pay with financial performance by increasing bonuses and reducing base salaries. In practice base pay remained – and bonuses soared.[62] Investing in GDP instead of wellbeing can result in altered citizen behaviour that reduces wellbeing, for example making fast food or fast fashion the only real choice. GDP may grow but much of this is through spending by society as a whole to clean up the mess or creating an unpaid ecological and societal "bill". Because Logic 1 provides the rationale for focusing on financial income to achieve wellbeing, governments, in turn, habituate citizens to prioritising their personal financial income over their wellbeing – and to judge the success of government in those terms. This combined with a goal of "small government" and low levels of trust in their competence and ethics, means that asking individuals to pay more taxes or accept lower salaries is unlikely to gain political support. Leaders are left with little option but to turn to the same GDP-focused approach, advocating for GDP growth as the only way to fund solutions for the problems created by the pursuit of GDP.

More rather than better jobs. A Logic 1 economy treats any job, operating within the law, as inherently beneficial, systematically overlooking the harms caused by low-quality or "bad" jobs. Toxic workplaces contribute to mental health issues and family breakdowns, yet the typical government response focuses on treating symptoms – such as funding mental health programmes – rather than addressing root causes like poor job quality. The result is a cycle of societal harm and organisational friction.

Self-regulation over better governance. When faced with "negative externalities" (unpaid for harms), an economy governed by Logic 1 will double-down on BAU assumptions to try to fix the market functioning as the go-to approach – and avoid imposing hard constraints/stronger decision-making parameters through changes in law or regulation. A classic example is trying to increase the quality and universal availability of information so that people can better rationalise and avoid harm – such as the range of anti-greenwashing laws that aim to correct information distortion. This is relatively comfortable ground for a Logic 1 government. While stopping misinformation is critically important for correcting wellbeing distortion, it is only really possible to legislate for factual inaccuracies rather than distortion of meaning – and focusing on greenwashing avoids the root cause of profit maximisation which underpins a cultural motivation to distort facts for profit.

Attracting investment at any cost. A Logic 1 government relies on attracting large amounts of financial inward investment as a way to bring financial income into the country. The economy is designed to seek out and incentivise inward investments regardless of their direct or indirect effect on wellbeing. The tax breaks and subsidies that often result can disadvantage smaller local businesses and can lead to other unaccounted for detrimental effects, such as housing stock being used as tax havens by overseas investors. This Logic 1 approach in government can also cause disproportionate harm in low-income countries – where governance of tax avoidance and corruption is typically less robust, but where the impact of that loss of revenue is significant.[63] In a Logic 1 economy, these knock-on effects won't be fully questioned or considered in decision-making.

Productivity above all. A Logic 1 governed economy will put a lot of emphasis on increasing "productivity" and this is normally reduced to mean financial output per capita. Therefore, economies that produce high margin goods and services will tend towards structurally higher levels of "productivity"; however, regardless of these dynamics the message from Logic 1 government leaders is usually that we all need to "work harder".

Short-term fixes for social investment. When an economy is governed by Logic 1, short-term policy solutions to maintain a functional workforce dominate. Investments in health for example, will therefore focus on treatments, like antibiotics or novel drugs (and often from Logic 1 companies that can profit heavily from them), rather than focusing on resolving underlying wellbeing issues often created by Logic 1. This includes stressful fear-based work environments driven by short-term financial motives or the loneliness that results from Logic 1 fuelled issues such as lack of time and social fragmentation.

Neglecting meaningful metrics. Underlying these challenges is a lack of a comprehensive purpose-aligned accounting system. While much work to evaluate wellbeing is happening in governments across the globe, as will be outlined in Chapter 2, most governments do not consistently and proactively evaluate or report publicly on critical factors like mental health, social cohesion, or ecological health. The focus on GDP as the primary measure of success prevents meaningful accountability. By design, this GDP hides and even motivates many harms (an oil spill drives GDP but avoiding one doesn't), and it obscures many of the routes to wellbeing (such as care for children, the elderly and community action). Focusing on these financial income metrics perpetuates decision-making blindness to the real drivers of wellbeing.

MESO LEVEL LOGIC 1: GOVERNANCE OF ORGANISATIONS

Organisations make the economy real and are therefore the ways collective, long-term wellbeing is created or destroyed. Organisations are granted access to resources by governments, on behalf of citizens in order to fulfil this purpose. However, in a Logic 1 governance model, mirroring the Macro level, we ask organisations to prioritise short-term financial gains, making sustainability action largely irrational. Below are some logical consequences of a Logic 1 governance system:

Ignoring non-financial costs. In Logic 1 governed organisations, decision-making focuses narrowly on financial capital, neglecting the health of non-financial capitals, stakeholders or underlying social and environmental systems. Questions like "How much does it cost?" or "Will it cover its costs?" typically pertain only to assuring financial health. Non-financial considerations – such as employee wellbeing, supply chain resilience, or environmental impact – are often neglected, even when they directly support financial health. This system encourages competition and self-interest to turn freely available resources into profit as quickly as possible. We are then collectively encouraged, and encourage each other, to hold up this "asset-stripping" behaviour as success. For example, as reported by Bloomberg, many data centres (which are celebrated as economic success stories) are established in regions already facing severe water shortages.[64] The rapid expansion of AI infrastructure has exacerbated this with nearly 70 per cent of data centres constructed or planned since 2022 situated in areas where water demand exceeds supply. This happens because access to affordable, renewable electricity is prioritised above all else, with water availability frequently overlooked. Since the sunniest locations with abundant renewable power tend to be the most arid, this creates a significant but often ignored environmental vulnerability driven by narrow financial priorities.

Financially focused investment. Logic 1 organisations apply rigid financial parameters to investment decisions, prioritising rapid returns. Expectations of high, quick financial returns are built into project decisions via the "discount rate" and "go / no go" parameters, such as a two-year return on investment. This means that important projects that could reduce harm to collective long-term wellbeing or drive it are commonly rejected, even if at year three they would become profit making. This shortsighted approach often prevents even simple sustainability initiatives, such as upgrading inefficient boilers – let alone more innovative solutions that are urgently required but which are built out of the system. Lower margin, longer returning sustainability-focused initiatives may gain internal support but this will nearly always be because of a tenacious employee going against the governance system – or because of weak governance systems. Furthermore, diverting or delaying dividend payments in order to safeguard an ecosystem affected by the organisation's raw material extraction – would be judged as an irresponsible use of resources based on a Logic 1 view of fiduciary duty. The world is full of examples of profit as the goal being a barrier to truly useful innovation as we will explore in Chapter 3.

Keeping wellbeing impacts out of sight. The myopic focus on maximising financial income of a Logic 1 governance system shuts out negative impacts on wellbeing. For example, in a Logic 1 governance system, prices should be set so that maximum financial return can be ensured. With this logic, it makes sense (and is a common practice) to sell bread for a higher price in a corner shop of a council housing estate where people have little access to private transport, compared to an outlet in the centre of an affluent town or a drive-through shopping centre. In another example, veterinary surgeries have been targeted by hedge funds in the UK, who now own more than 60 per cent of the market. Seeking quick profits, the prices customers pay have increased in some cases by over 300 per cent in eight years. In order to maximise profits, it is also common to lean on people's fears, hopes and dreams in order to sell more products at a higher price – with almost no consequences for the organisation. The BAU assumption of "consumer rationality" provides a useful cover to argue away these impacts as voluntary "customer choices". These practices perpetuate inequality and erode public understanding of wellbeing, undermining individuals' ability to act in their own best interests. The fact that Logic 1 companies seek profits and not wellbeing, also helps us answer these questions:

- How is it that bread, the most staple of food, in many of the most financially wealthy countries is considered ultra-processed and negative for health – containing up to 30 ingredients.
- What caused shortages of saline in US hospitals?

- How did the Post Office workers IT scandal in the UK happen – where many people running Post Offices were fired and treated like criminals due to an easily discoverable IT failure.

Constrained by short-term self-interest. A well governed Logic 1 company can only act on sustainability issues if there is a short-term financial investment case. For instance, from powerful stakeholder pressure that threatens profits or to guard against risks to reputations that enable the organisation to have a social licence to operate and continue making money. The result is an often eclectic range of Corporate Social Responsibility (CSR) initiatives, ESG-friendly financial products, or marginally "green" offerings. These alleviate pressures which threaten profits, as well as enabling a foot in the door of growing "green" markets where there are profits to be made. These are defence and opportunistic acts. As such, there is no logical sense in retaining them if stakeholder pressure diminishes or the green market starts to seem less profitable – or those profits come with more risk versus other staple, but far less sustainable options. A determined employee that might have been able to take advantage of a weak governance system and get away with bold sustainability acts, are likely to be reined in by the governance system once the limits of win–win-wins are reached and "low-hanging fruits" exhausted. This roll back in ambition is inevitable and is often combined with doubling down on unsustainable, but profitable, business models.

Investing in unsustainability. If a product or service, merger or acquisition or new procurement contract can happen in a way that will increase profits – and there are enough stocks and flows of money to make this happen – then there is no rational reason for a Logic 1 organisation not to invest. Investment questions that are rational and common include: "Could we remove the contract clause to require the contractor, rather than us, be responsible for any human rights issues?", "Could we push the supplier to increase how long they wait for us to pay a bit longer?", "Could we pay off that person complaining about bullying with a gagging clause like we did the others", "Could we close that subsidiary, wipe the debt with our debtors and start up again under a different name"?, "Could we add text that suggests the product needs to be used more frequently to work properly - and so promote higher levels of purchase?", "Could we design the product in a way that it is less easy to repair and so promote re-purchase (in other words "planned obsolescence)?" "Could we deface the product so it can't be used – and so avoid discounting it or reducing brand value by giving it to charity?" (as evidenced in the Netflix documentary *Buy It* with #retailmademe sourcing experiences of workers made to do this).

Pretending profit isn't the priority. It is not attractive to ask customers, colleagues, suppliers, the government or anyone else to support the primary goal of financial self-interest. People are more likely to support an organisation that is acting for the best interests of others. For organisations governed by Logic 1 and seeking short-term financial self-interest there will be a strong incentive to appear to be acting for others, even though this is not the case. This, along with a lack of motivation to really understand unsustainability issues, fuels purpose-washing, green-washing and all other kinds of disconnects between "what is said" and "what is done". Vision and mission statements are, quite logically, crafted in a way that attracts loyalty and trust, masking the underlying focus on financial self-interest. Marketing departments play a crucial role in maintaining this illusion, fiercely guarding a strong "social licence to operate" that reduces scrutiny. This is highly problematic as it distorts public understanding of organisational intentions and erodes trust over time.

KPIs that prioritise profit over wellbeing. In a well-governed Logic 1 organisation, KPIs will be there primarily to keep track of whether financial income is being optimised, within the parameters of healthy stocks and flows of financial capital. The sources of financial income that often have KPIs attached to them will be different for different types of organisations, for example customers (for brands), donors (for charities), students or research funding (for universities). In Logic 1 organisations, short-term pursuit of these financial KPIs often overrules long-term strategy – even financially-focused strategy that is designed to achieve income over marginally longer periods.

Limited reporting. Logic 1 organisations focus their reporting on financial information, as if this is the only thing that matters. This limited scope obscures the broader impacts of their activities, leaving stakeholders without the information needed to drive meaningful change. Because, for Logic 1, the objective is to protect against threats to short-term financial self-interest, there is no rationale to report more than the law requires. Therefore, sustainability reports have been recognised as a way for Logic 1 organisations to highlight small but unimportant acts of good while hiding big acts of harm that could and should have been addressed. There is no core rationale for a Logic 1 governed organisation to do more, so it is hard to see that sustainability reporting can ever go beyond minimum required for stakeholder management.

MICRO LEVEL LOGIC 1: GOVERNANCE OF THE SELF

As individuals, householders and leaders, we are not separate from, or merely subject to, the governance system of Logic 1. Instead, we are the ones that enable and power it through the continuous decisions we make. Our individual upholding of Logic 1 is routinised at a deep and normally imperceptible level of our personal governance systems: the goals we set ourselves to achieve (e.g. get a certain promotion), the parameters we define (e.g. only drive a certain brand of car) and the ways we hold ourselves accountable so we don't stray (e.g. tell ourselves we didn't work hard enough when the promotion doesn't happen). This gives Logic 1 power and momentum over our decisions, and we include ourselves as authors in this.

The human tendency towards personal material greed and many of the behaviours outlined below is nothing new. For centuries, philosophical and spiritual traditions have explored how this impulse undermines our wellbeing and how deeper, more fulfilling paths can be found. While resistance is a continual challenge, what makes our current Logic 1 era so problematic is that we have not just embedded and normalised but also moralised, short-term self-interest – equating financial success with making an important contribution to overall societal wellbeing. Setting aside any concerns about how wrong this feels, acting in our short-term self-interest has become not only socially acceptable, but has been framed, in effect, as purpose-driven. This propels the negative and reduces the positive aspects of the humans we are capable of being.

Furthermore, Logic 1 has made any attempts to resist financial self-interest technically hard. We live in a world which relentlessly promotes the BAU assumption that financial self-interest equals success. Tailored advertising, cultural norms and institutional structures reinforce this message daily, making even a "normal" life one that liquidates the social and environmental systems that underpin our collective wellbeing and an aspirational one the very pinnacle of unsustainability. Meanwhile, the routes to maximising our actual wellbeing are distorted and obscured from view.

This perpetual normalisation is understandable. All of today's organisational leaders worldwide grew up when Logic 1 thinking was dominant or being embedded into our global systems. It can now feel like "just the way things are". The truth – that this economic and organisational design is relatively new but has been redefined countless times throughout history – is not part of our daily consciousness. We are left with a sense of reality that perpetuates problems we are increasingly concerned about, but with the only obvious "manual for life" being the one that perpetuates harm.

Efforts to reduce the tension are rife: for example, putting high walls between our work and lives so that we can "leave our values at the office door" and take on the Logic 1 governance system in the office. However, the reality is that Logic 1, and the BAU assumption underpinning it, are reinforced at every turn. It will take clarity, unity and the confidence of a critical mass of leaders to move beyond. This starts with naming how Logic 1 shapes our self-governance, including:

Money equals success. Mirroring what happens at the organisational and economy levels, for individuals in Logic 1, the focus rests on having enough stocks and flows of money, and using that resource to maximise the acquisition of more money. Earning more money than others signals a better life, regardless of the impact on our health, relationships or wellbeing. Choosing a higher-paying job, even one that strains our personal life, seems logical and supported by messages around us that valorise owning a bigger car, sending children to expensive schools, or consuming more goods and services. Conversely, sacrificing income for non-material goals like time, family, or community is traditionally viewed as irrational or even irresponsible and lazy. Those earning less are often judged as less clever, useful, or successful. In a Logic 1 world, GDP counts the value of the financially productive people and so these, in turn, can be positioned as fully valuable members of society who contribute to our GDP growth. Working for a highly profitable company, while earning lots of money, is even better.

Marketisation of life. Logic 1 self-governance supports the idea that consumption brings wellbeing. More money means the chance to buy more things to improve our wellbeing. Goods and services of course can do a lot to solve problems and improve our lives, but the issues with this include:

- Focusing on shopping our way to wellbeing, we spend time, energy and debt chasing a very inefficient "wellbeing-return-on-financial-investment".

- Designed primarily for profit, these goods and services often solve the wrong problem and/or create other problems for us directly for and for the longer term – many of which are complex to pin down and therefore equally difficult to resolve and avoid;

- Logic 1 governance drives the marketisation of life, replacing meaningful activities with paid offerings and erasing reflections on what wellbeing truly means. Instead of learning to meet our needs deeply, we're left with distorted, reactive tools such as: if we're lonely, watch porn; if we're hungry, order takeaway; if we're stressed, gamble.

- Marketing messages that we cannot avoid, even when we aren't shopping, are now at epic proportions. These act as invisible "wellbeing distorters", steering us towards consumption as the answer to everything. We run faster to keep up with these expanding, costly, ineffective and inefficient ways of consuming that have become essential (or feel essential) – and we chase expanding incomes and more time at work to keep up.

Someone else's problem. A Logic 1 self-governance system also helps absolve us from the responsibility of addressing our role in the system, or of trying to influence the system. For BAU all aspects of unsustainability are market failures. Hence, there is a strong motive to reduce the problem to something that requires a market correction, and not something we are qualified to involve ourselves in. At the very same time, we are made to feel that individuals acting within the micro sphere alone, are able to effect the change required. It is well documented that Logic 1 organisations, in trying to protect their financial income, will push responsibility for change in demand onto individuals. For example, BP have been accused of using the concept of carbon footprints as a tool for this.

Underappreciating the power of marketing. Logic 1 insists we are rational decision-makers, clever enough to "see through" marketing tactics. Advertisements are dismissed as harmless entertainment or sources of information, and any suggestion that our choices should be edited – for our own wellbeing – is framed as an attack on personal freedom. Curated within Logic 1 motives, we have come to agree that choice itself is sacred. More options are seen as inherently better, even if the range of products is designed to maximise profit, not wellbeing. With Logic 1 self-governance in place, it is easy to ignore the scientific reality: that marketing deeply shapes our preferences, decisions and cultural norms.

Judging our governments on GDP. From a Logic 1 perspective, a successful government grows the financial income achieved through economy (measured by GDP) and as a result ensures we have money in our pockets. Therefore, if GDP and money in our pockets are increasing then we feel, and are told by government and the media, that things are going well. We can feel positive – the more money flows, the more jobs are created, the more purchases are possible. If GDP goes down then we internalise the fear expressed around us that this can only be a bad thing – companies will close, jobs will be lost, and purchases will slow. It makes sense, then, for governments to demand productivity, demand more output, harder work and hence more sales, more financial income and more to spend on wellbeing. We see policy that reduces our income or restricts what we can buy as irrational and harmful. For goods and services that we can't afford, it's our responsibility to work harder to earn more money.

Driven by fear and mistrust. At its core, Logic 1 is a fear-based zero-sum system. It assumes humans are self-interested and motivated by personal financial gain and results in feeling that our loss is someone else's gain. If we need something, it's our job to earn the money to buy it. If others need something, that's their problem, not ours. Helping others is seen as risky and unnecessary; their route to wellbeing, like that for all of us, is to work more and purchase their way out. Voluntarily paying more tax when there's little trust in how it will be spent is illogical. Jumping queues, avoiding taxes, or criticising colleagues to get ahead is normalised if it is within the law because "everyone would do the same." Logic 1 messages resonate most when they promise to protect our short-term gains: keeping more money, growing GDP and stopping others from taking what is "ours". Leaders and politicians reinforce these fears, feeding a win-lose mindset and distancing us from the "others" who want what we have – keeps us locked into the Logic 1 system.

Defining success through wealth, seeking wellbeing through consumption, resisting regulation that restricts what we can buy, judging governments by GDP, and operating from fear – are deeply ingrained in our self-governance systems. They feel normal, logical and even moral. But this self-governance systematically undermines our own and our collective wellbeing. It both distorts our understanding of what truly matters, resulting in self-harm as we fail to put parameters in place to protect our personal resilience, and fuels unsustainable lifestyles that harm us and the systems we rely on. Recognising these patterns is the first step. Addressing them comes next, particularly where we have the opportunity not just to lead ourselves, but also others.

MICRO LEVEL LOGIC 1: GOVERNANCE – LEADERSHIP IMPACTS

Most of you reading this book will be organisational leaders of some kind or another across the globe. We end this section on Logic 1 and its governance, by showing the influences that Logic 1 will have on leadership specifically – and the barriers to your leadership progress which this creates.

The education system cementing Logic 1. Historically, early management scholars, like Chester Barnard (1886–1961), emphasised that organisations should engage in meaningful pursuits that connect with human values and purpose. In his 1953 article "Social responsibilities of the businessman", Bowen stated: "Within the past few years large numbers of business leaders publicly acknowledged and actively preached the doctrine that they are servants of society [beyond] management merely in the interests (narrowly defined) of stockholders."[65] Yet Logic 1, particularly since Milton Friedman's influential 1970 essay, served to solidify the mainstream view that serving society directly was, in fact, an ironic drag on societal wellbeing, arguing that financial self-interest pursued by specifically designed BAU markets is the most efficient path to collective wellbeing.[66] We argue that it was the lack of good Logic 3 governance (and clarity about what this looked like) that fuelled these arguments and enabled Logic 1 to take hold. Friedman's argument provided an alternative to government and management "whims", subject to corruption and mis-direction. Through systematic international "export", Logic 1 assumptions shaped the very heart of leadership education and training, and we live with this today. Alternative ways of thinking have been sidelined. If you are a leader today, in whatever sector, the management education you received and continue to encounter will almost certainly subtly, or overtly, rest on a Logic 1 worldview and related assumptions.

Leaning on self-interest. As Logic 1 assumes humans are driven by financial self-interest. It follows, then, that leaders should harness this motivation to drive profit-maximising behaviour from those they influence. Herein lies a core, well-recognised, tension: the Logic 1 governance system is designed to optimise financial return for itself (including member stakeholders) but financially self-interested employees are expected to be working hard all day in order to increase the financial spoils of someone else (this is known as the "principal-agent" problem). Not just that, they have more insider information than investors and the governing body that represents them (the "information asymmetry" problem). Given half a chance they would be expected to "run off with the family silver" and put in minimum effort, so the only way around that is to align the financial self-interests of the organisation and employees. This, as well as the assumption of financial motivation, is the reason that financial incentives are the primary way that Logic 1 organisations motivate and compensate employees. For example, CEOs are rewarded through lucrative compensation packages tied to short-term financial goals; HR systems prioritise financial incentives in recruitment, performance reviews and motivation strategies; managers offer bonuses or pay raises to drive results in their teams. While financial rewards are a known "hygiene factor" and will always play a motivational role, but beyond a certain point lose their power – evidence for this was summarised in Daniel Pink's book *Drive*. Furthermore, this hyperfinancial approach reduces intrinsic motivation for the deeper drive to create something meaningful.

Treating work as an unwelcome drudgery. Because the Logic 1 system serves the short-term financial interests of investors, and financial rewards are seen as primary, work is not designed to be meaningful or fulfilling – beyond what a short-term financial investment case will support because of expected marginal productivity gains. Work is simply a means to an end for employees to get the money they need to purchase their wellbeing on the market. This creates the foundation for disengagement and negative pressures on wellbeing from work. As one author recalls from time as a management consultant, junior staff would jokingly respond to questions about their day with, "Well, I heated the partner's swimming pool." This disconnect is reflected in global workforce statistics. According to Gallup's "State of the Global Workplace" 2024 report:

- 77 per cent of workers are disengaged or actively disengaged.
- One in five workers experience daily loneliness.
- Stress, sadness, anxiety and anger have reached their highest record-ed levels.[67]

In general, data shows that workplace realities contribute to worsening mental wellbeing worldwide, and this trend shows no signs of slowing.

Leaning on fear. Fear is the opposite motivator to love. Fear sits at the heart of how Logic 1 organisations engage with employees, customers and suppliers. For instance: Leaders develop a team identity by framing other internal teams as "failing" or "less capable", encour-aging competitive, in-group / out-group dynamics that play on people's concerns of being excluded; suppliers are pressured into unfavourable terms, while customers are targeted with, often very subtle, fear-based messaging to drive purchases. While this can create short-term results, it often breeds toxic cultures that are low in psychological safety that undermine real progress.

Dismissing values as a distraction to good decisions. As the point of leaders in Logic 1 is to ensure all efforts lead to profit maximisation, any discussions of reducing that in order to meet something an employee cares about would be a misuse of the responsibilities of the leadership role – unless there was a short-term financial case for it.

Logic 1 leadership concerns include:

- What is to say that one person's values are more important than another's?
- Is it the right of a manager to spend investors' money on "pet pro-jects" they care about?
- If something were truly important, would it not already be reflected in the law or in the governing body's decision-making parameters.

This was at the very heart of the BAU Friedman doctrine. Therefore, personal values are not relevant to discussion and can be excluded and left for people's lives outside of work.

Assuming business exists to "make as much money as possible". "Obviously, the point of a company is to make as much money as possible," said the 13-year-old son of one of the authors. Guided by his business studies class, he was already reflecting Logic 1. It may start with children's formal and informal education but this idea is the foundation of education systems up to the highest level of leadership training.

ACCEPTING THE REALITY OF LOGIC 1 – AND AVOIDING BAD BUREAUCRACY

We have outlined the archetypal behaviours of a well-governed Logic 1 system, at different levels of the economy, organisation and self, including the self as a leader. We cannot lead towards a future we collectively desire without first seeing, naming and resolving to change this Logic 1 governance box that has become our decision-making prison.

This "box" also results in masses of unhelpful bureaucracy as we try to fix all the problems that result, akin to spending most of our time plugging holes in a sinking ship rather than building a new ship. As Nobel prize winner, Elinor Ostrom, and colleagues noted in 2013: "The very concept of individual self-interest leading to societal dysfunction occupied a marginal position in the thought of many economic theorists. When this possibility [for social dysfunction] was acknowledged, privatization (when possible) or top-down regulation were envisioned as the only solutions."[68] Supporting the idea that trying to address unsustainability within Logic 1 is creatively constrained to adding more bureaucracy, a recent study conducted by IBM, which surveyed 5,000 C-suite executives, revealed: "Spending on sustainability reporting exceeds spending on sustainability innovation by 43%."[69] The researchers at IBM indicated: "Many organisations are approaching sustainability as an accounting or reporting exercise rather than a transformation play." We argue there is no logical reason for them to do otherwise if they are an average Logic 1 organisation.

Faced with the growing realisation of this impasse, even the mainstream started questioning Logic 1. Yet rather than undertaking the hard but necessary work of dismantling business-as-usual assumptions, the thrust of the focus has been on changing one main thing: extending the time horizon over which financial self-interest is optimised. In other words, shifting from short-term to long-term financial self-interest. We call this tweaked BAU system Logic 2.

LOGIC 2: Governance for long-term financial self-interest

THE RISING CRITIQUE OF LOGIC 1: A CALL FOR CHANGE

Logic 1 BAU thinking is coming under increasing fire via the alarming cascade of scientific data highlighting the breakdown of social and environmental systems and the efforts of leading thinkers and politicians tuned in beyond their immediate interests. Given the dominance of Logic 1, it isn't a suprise that the most impactful wake-up calls seem to have followed the dramatic global financial crashes, notably those in 1997/98 and 2007/08. These crises shook the very foundations of the Logic 1 system, forcing even its staunchest adherents to question how we organise and regulate the economy and even asking the question: what purpose does it ultimately serve?

For those looking towards the horizon, the primary critique of Logic 1 becomes clear: short-term thinking is sabotaging our ability to make sustainable decisions. Conversely, long-term thinking is the solution to systemic dysfunction.

THE PROBLEM WITH SHORT-TERM THINKING

Short-term thinking is a big problem and an easy candidate to focus on. The assessment is that this mindset prevents us from adequately assessing risks to our deeper ambition, such as:

- Causing politicians to chase quick GDP gains instead of creating the structural conditions for long-term sustained financial success.

- Preventing a proper assessment of the risks to our financial self-interest from the degradation of the very social and environmental systems that underpin these gains.

- Overriding carefully planned three-year strategies for market development in order to push for the "numbers to look good" and appease stakeholders who themselves have no reason not pursue their self-interest as quickly as possible.

- Promoting a transactional approach where there is no need to worry about how we treat suppliers and customers based on a belief that there will always be others to fill their place.

- Persuading us to go into debt to service our wellbeing now rather than save for the future and to consume products and services, like ultra-processed foods, that harm us over time or to put massive pressure on our teams to deliver as quickly as possible.

This myopic approach indeed undermines the foundations of our collective long-term wellbeing, creating a vicious cycle of crises and reactive measures.

THE CASE FOR "ENLIGHTENED" SELF-INTEREST

The main antidote to short-termism is what some call "enlightened financial self-interest": a governance approach that prioritises long-term financial self-interest. The rationale is simple: organisations are dependent on others for what they do. If organisations could act in a way that reflected this, then we would protect the interests of others in order to protect our own self-interest. This would assure long-term profit maximisation and also correct the market so that externalities would be internalised by extension of this logic. With this perspective, enlightened self-interest provides a decision-making framework for safeguarding the resources and relationships essential for sustained success and dissolving the pressure from society.

This makes good BAU sense. For example, if you can't access the resources needed for your products and services, if banks aren't functioning, if society doesn't trust you, if stakeholders aren't around to work for and with you, and if the climate or society is unstable - then your ability to maximise profits will be hindered, if not entirely curtailed. This could be considered a relatively easy sell to Logic 1 proponents.

SHIFTING FROM LOGIC 1 TO LOGIC 2

Specifically, the shift from Logic 1 to Logic 2 is a move in the parameters of governance to encompass the "bottom of the triangle" – in other words Logic 2 firms will create parameters to ensure the health of the systems, stakeholders and resources that an organisation's long-term financial self-interest relies upon.

The transition from Logic 1 (short-term self-interest) to Logic 2 (long-term or "enlightened" self-interest), while seemingly small, in fact represents a profound shift in perspective. Logic 2 encourages decision-

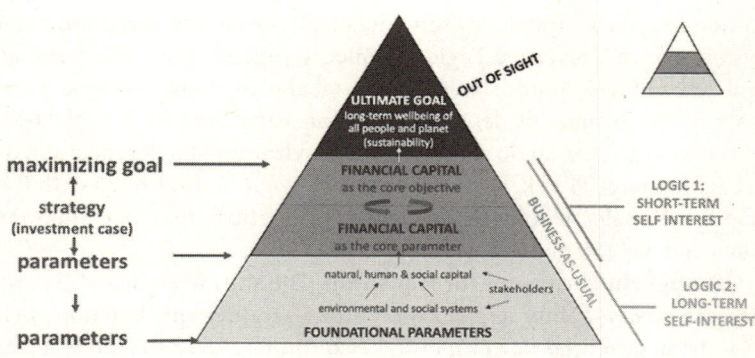

Figure 1.5 Logic 2 governance

makers to move beyond the immediate ("what is in front of my nose"), consider the foundational ("what lies beneath") and act to preserve it (Figure 1.5).

The shift in parameters: A fundamental change in decision-making

Moving from short-term to long-term self-interest creates some surprisingly large changes in decision-making including:

A rationale for protecting what society cares about. When governance systems embed the broader parameters of Logic 2 properly, they create a profound shift in decision-making and organisational culture. This long-term lens simultaneously widens the view, revealing the interconnected complexities that Logic 1 keeps out of view (and as a result compounds). The change in governance direction (via a shift in parameters) alters the strategic frame, changing what is considered logical and rational action. Strategy becomes bounded by governance parameters that are designed to ensure the health of everything that financial self-interest depends on: the health of non-financial capital inputs, the health of the stakeholders depended on and, most foundationally, the health of all social and environmental systems that underpin all else. Suddenly, there is a rationale, an "investment case", for understanding and protecting systems which we depend on. Instead of seeking to merely reduce the pressure created as a result of harm to non-financial capitals, stakeholders, and social and environmental systems, a well governed Logic 2 economy, organisation or individual, will actively seek to understand what stakeholders have to say and the state of the systems it depends on. Addressing the real complexities in the world, whether social inequality, environmental degradation, or systemic financial risk, becomes essential. Logic 2 also brings with it a strong rationale to lobby for changes to competitive market conditions that can level the playing field.

Thoughtful strategies for transition. The shift from harmful practices, to sustainability aligned ones, often requires quick action such as retiring coal-fired power plants, discontinuing harmful products, or switching to green energy suppliers. More frequently, it involves gradual, multi-year transitions because economies, organisations, and individuals are deeply embedded in systems that cause harm. Transitioning away from these entrenched practices requires long-term targets and plans, gradually aligning governance parameters with threshold conditions of health. For instance, at an organisational level, net-zero climate transition planning is designed to enforce decision-making that steadily moves towards a governance framework that has parameters aligned with a healthy climate system. These plans set incremental milestones to ensure progress, reflecting the complexity and scale of the challenge. Eventually organisational decisions, in aggregate, will need to respect this boundary.

Addressing systemic harm. As outlined in section x, the issues that need to be addressed go way beyond just climate change. Many pivotal systems, such as soil health, biodiversity loss and worker well-being are in critical condition. Nearly every decision we make today draws down from the health of these systems. We urgently need economies, organisations and individuals to implement governance systems that enforce decision-making parameters for all of these – and keep decisions within safe boundaries, as Doughnut Economics, for example, has convincingly argued. A fully enlightened Logic 2 governance system would require acknowledgement that sustaining every one of these systems is essential for long-term success.

For those starting out on their journey to Logic 2, this might seem like merely a reporting or compliance task. For certain, it is about compliance – but to comply in this case will require radical transformation. We need to start by acknowledging that most activities currently breach the thresholds of health that social and environmental systems require to function, let alone return to a natural state of regeneration.

EMERGING LOGIC 2 BEHAVIOURS

It is easy to look around and see many are taking steps to transition from Logic 1 to Logic 2 as the pressures from degraded systems compound. This will be made easier by those actors recognising that this is a shift in Logic and associated governance, as outlined in this book. To recognise when an organisation is in a movement from Logic 1 to Logic 2, we outline characteristic behaviours of this transition at the Macro, Meso and Micro levels. If you think when reading these that many are also behaviours of purpose-driven economies, organisations and individuals then you would be correct because preserving the health of underlying capitals, systems and stakeholders is also a core requirement of being purpose-driven, as we will come to in the following section.

MACRO LEVEL LOGIC 2: GOVERNANCE OF THE ECONOMY

How a shift from short- to long-term self-interest governance changes the economy

At a Macro economy level, the transition from Logic 1 to Logic 2 governance is centred around changes to governance requirements via legal systems. Starting with reporting harms (and benefits), these laws are designed to encourage embedding decision-making parameters in governance that results in decisions that do not harm the wellbeing of society and asset-strip the basis of this wellbeing. Below are key signals of governments becoming enlightened to the harms that undermine financial self-interest over the longer-term and hence seeking to address them through law:

Controlling brainprint harms. Recognising the cultural and societal harms caused by manipulative advertising and misinformation, many governments are cracking down on "brainprint" abuses. Across the world we see stricter regulations on greenwashing, bans on advertising harmful products like tobacco and fossil fuels, and restrictions on marketing to vulnerable groups, particularly children. Such measures aim to reduce the manipulation of consumer behaviour, promoting informed and rational choices that align with collective wellbeing.

Choice editing. Extremely difficult to justify in Logic 1, in Logic 2 a rationale exists for some level of government hand in shaping market choice, such as laws mandating the banning of inefficient cars, heating systems and appliances.

Giving stakeholders rights and voices. Ensuring the ongoing functioning of stakeholders, systems and capitals to support long-term financial self-interest requires understanding what is required for this healthy functioning – and in turn this requires bringing their voices into the governance decision-making system. In some nations, the most voiceless of stakeholders are now being recognised and given a voice, for example recognition of personhood rights for natural entities like rivers, e.g. the Whanganui River in New Zealand.

Changing corporate law and guidance. Logic 2 economies address how organisations are governed to make clear that the stakeholders and systems that the organisation depends on for its long-term interest can, and should, be protected, to at least a minimum level needed to regenerate. This is showing up in guidance and rules from stock exchanges and financial regulators. For example, in the UK, the Companies Act was amended (2006) to include at least the possiblity to consider other stakeholders, while pursuing benefits for the company and for members. Changes to corporate governance codes are progressing more quickly, such as Hong Kong's in 2012, Singapore's in 2018 and the Dutch Corporate Governance Code in 2016.

ESG reporting. One of the most prominent examples of Logic 2 governance in action has been the rise of the Environmental, Social and Governance (ESG) agenda. This was initially driven by investor demand to avoid harm while maximising financial returns. For these investors, it was no longer just profit maximisation within the parameters of the law. Instead, they sought profits within selected parameters that reflected concerns about their long-term returns – or, in a move towards purpose, acknowledged harms to wellbeing they were unwilling to accept creating. In doing so, investors were formally expressing that they valued something beyond profit. These investors required some assurance that the governance system was good enough to enact these wishes, which required proof in the form of information being systematically reported. As governments and society have increasingly understood the impact of organisational activity on collective long-term wellbeing, it has been recognised that this is the very same data that is required to make national, civic and individual decisions. Hence ESG reporting, starting mainly with reporting, has been progressing in guidelines, regulations and now hard law across the world. For mainstream Logic 1 leaders, Logic 2 efforts will naturally appear an irrational waste of time – hence the backlash from those trapped in Logic 1 that is now on full display is entirely normal. Having Logic 1 fully visible is useful, as it allows more honesty from those who were merely motivated or pressured into seeming to be enlightened. It also allows others to judge whether they find that acceptable and be frank about their own Logic. Recent evidence also shows that despite the opportunity and pressure to backtrack, voluntary ESG efforts seem to be quietly gaining pace across the world, suggesting Logic 2 may be gaining ground.[70]

While there are many variations of ESG, two approaches dominate, and reflect different logics:

1. **The International Financial Reporting Standards/ISSB global model:** Given this is an organisation with a traditional remit in financial reporting and hailing mainly from the US, it is perhaps not surprising that the ISSB approach is anchored in the Logic 1 governance system making the minimum requirements to placate broader stakeholder concerns. The standards focus on disclosure to financial investors regarding perceived risks to their financial returns in the short (Logic 1), medium and long term (Logic 2) – focusing mainly on climate change. The IFRS doesn't have a remit to embed its standards in law, but an increasing number of governments are taking this step.

2. **The European model:** This suite of laws and related standards make a break with Logic 1 – variously relying on a long-term self-interest (Logic 2), or an other-serving (Logic 3) rationale. While also addressing investors, they are designed to close information gaps for all stakeholders, including governments, citizens and companies. These focus on a range of unsustainability issues and include a requirement for assessment and reporting of significant harms by organisations on stakeholders and social and environmental systems. The disclosure standards and related law regarding any significant harms done to social and environmental systems are just some of a wide range of requirements for organisations under the EU's "Green New Deal".

Canada, China, Australia and a range of other countries are going beyond the IFRS approach and replicating many aspects of the EU approach.

The ESG end game. While the global ESG agenda is progressing at various speeds and trajectories, all are lacking the speed and systemic approach the science demands. It is important that Logic 2 organisations become fully enlightened as soon as possible and lobby hard to speed up the logical end point of ESG. This ESG end game is where society expresses, and enforces, the logical demand to organisations: "If you wish to exist as an organisation and access shared, fragile resources, you must prove you are, at least, not asset-stripping them and hence undermining collective long-term wellbeing." This logical trajectory is not progressing, and will not, without strong resistance from those in Logic 1 that see absolutely no rational reason for these laws other than annoying "do-gooders" undermining profit maximisation and hence social progress. In the US particularly, politicians and others have mounted significant backlash, including lawsuits against companies engaging in ESG reporting and actions. This is causing some to declare "ESG is dead". In reality, regardless of what we call it, there is in motion a logically unstoppable response to the unsustainability crisis being felt globally. ESG exists because we feel the harm to wellbeing from the collapsing systems. Only once we halt harm and regenerate these systems will there be a basis for the pressure for change to stop. Only then ESG will cease to be relevant. Neither politicians, nor anyone else, can wish the problems away.

MESO LEVEL LOGIC 2: GOVERNANCE OF ORGANISATIONS
A shift from short to long-term self-interest governance changes organisational behaviours in various ways:

Long-term governance redesign. Because the shift to Logic 2 necessitates a change to the core parameters that all decision-makers operate within – this has knock-on effects throughout the whole governance and management system. For example:

- **Risk governance and risk management.** These now need to include risks to all of the "bottom of the triangle" factors. As the underlying motivation is still financial self-interest, there is a keen focus on grasping the wide range of opportunities that will enhance profit maximisation. In other words, Logic 2 is where the language of financial risk and opportunity is prevalent.

- **Comprehensive oversight mechanisms.** These include internal and external due diligence and auditing able to accurately assess policy implementation in domains across the value network – from raw material production to customer use impacts and end of life – way beyond what is normal in Logic 1.

- **Aligned incentives.** Organisational goals, objectives and KPIs include "do no harm" intentions, with 100 per cent of bonuses tied to long-term financial returns *within* all parameters for long-term resource, stakeholder and system health.

Multi-capital accounting. Fully Logic 2 organisations logically treat human, environmental and social capitals with the same value and rigor as financial capital. Multi-capital accounting methods include tools like the MultiCapital Scorecard, Sustainability Balanced Scorecards and Triple Bottom Line Accounting along with a wide suite of support from organisations such as the Captials Coalition and the Future-Fit Foundation. These have varying levels of anchoring to the underlying system health. Multi-capital accounting should ideally ensure that investment cases evaluate the health of all capitals, not just financial, and that strategies meet "hygiene factors" for financial and non-financial capitals alike. For instance, an investment case must prove that water resources can be secured without depleting community reserves or goodwill, or that there are enough skilled staff for a project meaning that excessive overtime won't be necessary.

Stakeholderism. Logic 2 governance recognises that protecting stakeholders – suppliers, employees, communities and customers – is essential for profit maximisation. This is commonly known as stakeholder capitalism or at least the business-as usual interpretation of it. This was the core insight of Ed Freeman's stakeholder theory: you of course need to take care of your stakeholders and retain high quality relations with them if you want to secure your own best interest. In moving to being Logic 2, insights and questions that naturally result include:

- Usually if a supplier won't accept our terms, we cancel the contract and move to the next, but what if in a few years there are no viable suppliers to move to?

- What is the climate resilience of our raw material producers and how can we bolster that?
- Why are our staff stress levels so high?
- Are the communities we operate in happy that we are there?

Collaboration beyond the organisation. Logic 2 organisations understand they cannot regenerate shared systems alone. They collaborate with diverse entities to address systemic challenges, such as partnering with NGOs and governments to tackle issues like deforestation, water scarcity or community health in ways that wouldn't have happened in Logic 1.

Rethinking transactional arrangements with suppliers in favour of long-term collaborations that prioritise mutual sustainability. For instance, a company might fund solar cooking projects to simultaneously offset carbon emissions and improve community health in core supply chains.

The right kind of lobbying. Logic 2 organisations lobby not primarily to protect short-term financial gains but to drive systemic changes that secure long-term profit maximisation while also pursuing short-term gains where possible. This lobbying includes trying to "level the competitive playing field", ensuring that those who act to protect their long-term interests are not penalised by Logic 1 competitors who will fight for weaker regulations. Examples include:

- Advocating for stricter regulations on emissions or modern enslavement to prevent harm.
- Collaborating with groups like the UN Global Compact or The University of Cambridge Institute for Sustainability Leadership's Corporate Leaders Group to push for tighter governance that aligns with Logic 2 principles.

Working beyond "keep up compliance" towards "The ESG endgame". A well governed Logic 2 organisation will embrace the ESG agenda not just as a compliance tool but as a pathway to long-term financial maximisation. This means, for example: developing transition plans for every one of the breached thresholds. This would include a sense of adequate action which, given how other organisations are transitioning, would assure all stakeholders and systems can regenerate to an adequate level of health and continue to flourish independently into the future.

It would also include conducting "gap analyses". These would identify and close the gaps between current practices and a business model that is both financially viable now, as well as geared to maximising long-term financial returns.

Robust 360-degree information systems. Operating with a long-term financial self-interest perspective requires advanced data systems that provide comprehensive insights into stakeholder and system health. Logic 2 organisations therefore prioritise:

- *Stakeholder representation.* Boards and decision-making committees must genuinely reflect the views of diverse stakeholders, either through representation or robust reporting.

- *Collaborative data systems.* Organisations work together across sectors to share information, reducing data collection burdens on smaller entities in the value chain. For example, Italy's emerging collaboration between government, businesses and NGOs illustrates how unified data systems can enhance decision-making across entire economies.

MICRO LEVEL LOGIC 2: GOVERNANCE OF THE SELF

A shift to Logic 2, from short- to long-term self-interest governance changes individual behaviours. These include:

Investing in good. Actively seeking out products and services that minimise harm to environmental and social systems, recognising their reliance on these systems for their long-term self-interest. Logic 2 individuals are willing to pay more, if financially able, for alternatives that offer tangible benefits to protecting and restoring critical systems they know they depend on. Examples of Logic 2 choices include switching to organic food to support sustainable farming practices; choosing sustainable fashion brands over fast fashion; switching pension or saving accounts; switching to a renewable energy supplier or staying in hotels with credible green tourism certifications. For those unable to afford these alternatives, Logic 2 encourages people to seek ways to consume that align with healthy systems, often resulting in cost savings. Examples include taking local holidays instead of flying to reduce carbon emissions and reducing meat consumption to lessen environmental impact. As with the organisational and the economy level, the breadth and consistency of these decisions depend on an individual's understanding of the issues and the strength of their self-governance systems.

Citizenship. Logic 2 worldviews also spur greater political and social engagement. Individuals begin to see gaps between current government policies and the actions needed to protect and regenerate vital systems they depend on. This awareness prompts varying levels of political involvement, including:

Personal advocacy. Engaging friends and colleagues in conversations about necessary policy changes.

Digital campaigning. Supporting online political campaigns, signing petitions or amplifying causes through social media.

Community action. Participating in organised lobbying efforts, local protests or grassroots movements aimed at influencing government or corporate behaviour.

Driving accountability. Engagement extends to holding organisations accountable. Logic 2 individuals may boycott brands that fail to meet sustainability standards. They may also share critical information about harmful practices to raise awareness or support campaigns that pressure organisations to align with Logic 2 principles.

LOGIC 2: SELF-GOVERNANCE – WORKPLACE IMPACTS

Filtering employers. For individuals that recognise the risks posed by collapsing social and environmental systems and exploited stakeholders, working for organisations that contribute to these harms becomes very hard. This is especially true for young people entering the workforce, who are known to put greater effort into researching the impacts of potential employers. Many actively rule out certain sectors or companies known for their harmful practices even if it means sacrificing financial rewards. This trend is reported to be driving significant shifts in workforce decisions, particularly, but not only, among younger generations. Deloitte's "2024 Global Gen Z and Millennial survey" reported that "72% of Gen Zs and 71% of millennials say environmental credentials and policies are important when considering a potential employer".[71]

Distancing work from harm. For those already in the workforce, awareness of the long-term consequences of unsustainable practices often motivates career shifts. Deloitte's global survey found that "Two in 10 Gen Zs and millennials have already changed jobs or industries to better align their work with their environmental values, with another quarter of both cohorts planning to do so in the future". Logic 2 leaders and employees alike are increasingly leaving roles tied to system harm in favour of positions aligned with restoration and sustainability. The emotional burden of contributing to harm can be profound. Employees may feel disconnected from their values, particularly when facing questions from their children or peers, such as, "What are you doing about climate change?"

Leadership curiosity. Logic 2 leaders, informed by an understanding of the urgent need to restore shared systems, view traditional corporate social responsibility (CSR) efforts as inadequate. They will recognise CSR as reactive, addressing symptoms rather than the root causes of systemic harm. These leaders will ask deeper questions reflecting a shift from reacting to problems towards understanding and addressing their underlying drivers. For example:

- Why are regulators increasing pressure on businesses?
- What is driving increasing and wide-ranging protests?
- Why are net-zero commitments and nature-based solutions gaining momentum?
- Why are my children asking what I'm doing to help fix climate change?

Answering these questions is likely to fuel greater concern about the risks to long-term security and result in further momentum for leading change in their organisations and beyond.

Influencing governance parameters. Logic 2 leaders strive to instil a culture of long-term decision-making in themselves, their teams and their organisations. This will be grounded in a solid understanding of the risks posed by collapsing systems, fragile stakeholders and poor management of non-financial capital. Examples of their efforts may include sending staff to training programmes focused on the science behind a full suite of sustainability issues and encouraging them to propose innovative solutions to these problems; promoting awareness of the organisational risks associated with environmental and social harm; and developing a shared commitment to address them. Competent leaders will work to suggest, lobby for and enact changes to the governance systems they work within and can influence, either on their own or in collaboration with others so that they also move from Logic 1 to Logic 2, hence further reducing risks.

WHY LOGIC 2 ISN'T ENOUGH

Governing for the long-term rather than short-term self-interest is absolutely vital to create conditions for strategic decisions that do not harm long-term collective wellbeing, but it is not sufficient. Even in its best form, a Logic 2 governance system has inherent limitations that prevent it from fully achieving long-term sustainability. We outline the six key reasons why Logic 2 is not enough to align the economy, organisations or individuals with long-term wellbeing for all (sustainability).

Reason 1: It's the wrong problem. While short-term thinking is undeniably problematic and addressing it is critical, it is not the root cause of unsustainability, so it cannot be the solution. Tackling short-termism alone risks missing the deeper, structural issues driving harm to social, environmental and economic systems. When faced with clear evidence of climate breakdown, biodiversity collapse, extreme inequality and financial crises, the most pressing questions should include:

- Are our assumptions about how markets maximise wellbeing correct?

- Does treating people as primarily self-interested create a culture of fear and greed that limits human potential?

- Have we distorted our understanding of wellbeing and how best to achieve it?

- Has equating products and services with wellbeing distanced us from the consequences of our actions?

- How can the economy be redesigned to genuinely deliver long-term collective wellbeing?'

However, these are unlikely to be asked by those in Logic 2 – the assumptions that drive Logic 1 will remain relatively unchallenged. Only one of the assumptions is challenged – that of short-termism. However, this isn't really a challenge to Logic 1 as short-termism is not actually an expected requirement of Logic 1; rather, it is a natural consequence of a system where financial self-interest reigns supreme. Why wouldn't you want financial returns as quickly as possible, especially in a global system that enables "grab-and-run" investing, sometimes executed in nanoseconds? By focusing criticism on short-term thinking, Logic 2 avoids conflict and deflects attention from the more challenging questions about the fundamental flaws of BAU assumptions. Given the unquestioned power of BAU assumptions over our decisions, the shift to Logic 2 often feels intuitive, yet without real momentum that can sustain real change. This, along with the force and momentum of the status quo, makes it easy to see why the journey from Logic 1 to Logic 2 may be unlikely.

Reason 2: Creative myopia. Logic 2, driven by financial self-interest and shaped by BAU assumptions, inherently limits the potential for radical, integrated thinking. Addressing the systemic unsustainability crisis requires ultra-creative ideas that tackle all vital system issues simultaneously, often through persistent experimentation and risk-taking. While Logic 2 extends the timeline for financial self-interest, and shifts the resource-based parameters of decision-making, it leaves in place other unspoken parameters of what constitutes "acceptable strategy". This creates two significant boundaries to the creativity and systemic thinking needed to address existential threats to long-term wellbeing:

1. **Filtering ideas through financial self-interest.** Logic 2 governance still requires all decisions to pass through the lens of financial self-interest. Shifting the decision-making parameters for how resources are used can encourage a broader, longer-term perspective which sometimes align with stakeholder interests, for example through shared value initiatives or extended return-on-investment horizons. However, the vast majority of truly systemic and creative ideas needed to fix and advance long-term wellbeing for all will never be considered. For example, the Logic 2 investment case filtering process is likely to exclude ideas that involve unconventional or untested collaborations; require significant upfront investment with low or uncertain financial returns or challenge traditional competitive norms, such as pursuing innovations that competitors are not working on. The result is a cultural and cognitive lock-in. For example, while an organisation may adopt a construction project that includes affordable office space for future supply chain start-ups, it is unlikely to embrace riskier, more systemic ideas like redesigning entire business models to eliminate harm across all

systems. These paths are obscured by the Logic 2 governance system that prioritises financial returns, making leaders blind to what is truly possible.

2. **Partial and incremental enlightenment.** To transition towards Logic 2 requires being curious about all dependencies – but also actively engaged in learning about them. This often involves deep immersion in scientific data. Critically, it then requires channelling the resulting mental and emotional energy into transforming real-world governance systems. Without this, understanding the science of collapsing systems is of little use. In reality, leaders of organisations and economies driven by a vague sense that their organisations financial self-interest may be under threat, may only have the energy and desire to partially understand aspects of the systemic unsustainability crisis and potential systemic solutions. This is likely to be dominated by popularised topics. This limits the creative potential for change. Consider the World Economic Forum's "Global Risk Reports", which highlight the growing focus on environmental and social risks. While these reports reflect a shift from short-term economic or geopolitical concerns to broader systemic threats, they are a reflection of "perceptions" not actual scientific assessment of the risks and therefore remain filtered by mainstream norms, which in turn are held back by Logic 1 blinkers. As a result, unless a shift to "fully enlightened" Logic 2 has occurred, then strategies will be based on incomplete or biased data that limits the ability of strategy to address the full scope of systemic issues in a viable way for the organisation. Further consequences of this partial view include:

- *Tick-box compliance:* ESG metrics and laws are often treated as constraints on profit rather than opportunities for internal transformation, or an opportunity for engagement with economic decision-makers to help them go faster to bring on market adjustments that enable systemic transformation.

- *Missed thresholds:* Logic 2 organisations often fail to do their part to holistically address critical system thresholds – such as soil health, climate stability or worker wellbeing in supply chains – due to fragmented approaches that may well worsen these issues. Every harm that exceeds healthy threshold conditions matters, and therefore is material and needs to be dealt with. If we all do just a little bit of harm to a system it can still breach threshold conditions and collapse. Those partially enlightened confuse what matters with what to prioritise. They are not the same.

- *Celebrating second-rate action:* The pace of Logic 2 adoption becomes too slow to match the urgency of existential challenges, such as biodiversity collapse or climate breakdown. A sure sign of partial Logic 2 is when we celebrate action that is no-doubt incredibly hard and which can have important positive impacts on people's lives but in relation to the science, capacity and urgency, very small. Connected to this, partial enlightenment tethers decisions to underwhelming benchmarks of peer action, rather than the actual scientific requirements to achieve system functioning and flourishing. We then disproportionately praise ourselves, or others, for the benchmark beating actions. This then sets the evolved norm and "benchmark" for what "success" in sustainability looks like, when it is still so very far from what could and needs to be achieved. This misplaced peer satisfaction is one of the most potent risks to failure we face.

Reason 3: Semi-enlightenment creates harmful bureaucracy. As outlined previously, the risks of getting stuck in partial enlightenment on the journey to Logic 2 is high. This also creates a "worst of all worlds" piecemeal regulatory and operational context for organisations and leaders. Laws and regulation neither work comprehensively enough to motivate change against all system issues at once, nor deeply enough to establish the comprehensive, science-based governance necessary to ensure success in this journey. This results in a number of problems:

- **High bureaucratic costs.** Regulatory compliance under partial Logic 2 frameworks imposes significant administrative burdens without delivering the scale of change needed. Organisations are bogged down in processes that tick boxes but fail to drive genuine transformation.

- **Ambition gap.** The absence of a clear and comprehensive pathway to an "ESG end game" leaves systems stuck in semi-transformation, focused on insufficient and piecemeal ambition that fails to address systemic issues. Tackling thresholds one by one – first climate, then water, then biodiversity loss, then fair pay – is not only inefficient but also infeasible given the time pressures. Economies, organisations and individuals must undergo simultaneous, system-wide transformations, which are incompatible with fragmented approaches. Transforming to align with climate thresholds requires wholescale change. Sequential transformation creates a dangerous gap with science and a drag on time, resources and energy that we cannot afford.

- **Reduced strategic option:** The longer systemic issues remain unaddressed, the fewer viable solutions remain, increasing the complexity and cost of change.

Reason 4: It leaves too much to chance. Even the most progressive Logic 2 legal frameworks tend to focus on easily quantifiable and market-compatible system issues, such as climate change. Yes, climate change is beyond critical; however, equally critical challenges, like biodiversity loss or social inequity, are often placed in the 'too hard for now' category. The most likely reason that "climate tunnel vision" is a real issue is that emissions can be measured and traded, fitting neatly with Logic 1 and its BAU assumptions. This also limits the response – climate solutions are filtered through market-based mechanisms. Policies like cap-and-trade or Tradable Energy Quotas (TEQs), could enforce absolute emissions limits yet are bypassed in favour of trusting market mechanisms to find a "fair price for carbon". "Carbon myopia" (a blinkered singular focus on climate change) creates real inefficiencies. By delaying comprehensive action, semi-enlightened Logic 2 governance creates a cascade of inefficiencies:

Reason 5: Who will do the innovation? One of the most fundamental flaws of Logic 2 is its limited ambition; it is fundamentally a "do no harm" agenda. While this may seem like a step forward compared to Logic 1's unfettered pursuit of financial self-interest, it falls far short of what is required to address the pressing unsustainability challenges facing our collective wellbeing. In a Logic 2 economy, the message to organisations is simple: "Take these precious, limited and degraded resources and do what you like with them for your financial self-interest; as long as you can prove you are not harming them." For individuals, the message is equally restrictive: "Keep ideas that maximise for collective long-term wellbeing to yourself, unless they can also make your life financially better." This framework significantly limits the scope of innovation and creativity, particularly in the face of unprecedented global challenges. In reality, organisations are society's chosen innovation nerve centres. They are uniquely equipped for collective enterprise – to take resources and transform them into goods, services and solutions that drive economic activity and collective wellbeing. The "do no harm" agenda is inadequate at the best of times, but in the face of escalating existential crises, it borders on madness. At the moment when we face the most urgent and complex sustainability challenges to our collective wellbeing, what's needed is not innovation for self-interest while just not harming the systems we rely on. We require the full force of our enterprising spirit. If organisations aren't the ones to solve these problems using the efficiency, freedom and democratic effects of the market, who is? Where will we get the creativity, collaboration and persistence to transform the economy to address the harm?

Reason 6 Where will the persistence come from? When "do no harm" becomes the ceiling of ambition, we are discouraged from doing the hard work to tackle the root causes of harm – to take risks to develop solutions that go further than no additional harm and instead regenerate the systems we depend on. We exist within a deeply entrenched, inert Business-As-Usual (BAU) Logic 1 system, solidified through layers of governance built up over decades. Leaders at every level – individual, organisational and governmental – are surrounded by barriers that feel insurmountable. These systemic constraints create a sense of powerlessness, even among those who recognise the urgency of change. Furthermore, most leaders on the journey are likely to be only semi-enlightened. Hence, despite their intentions, the comfort and familiarity of BAU power dynamics and decision-making processes can easily overshadow the partial clarity they've achieved and makes them vulnerable to slipping back into Logic 1. We can all see the organisations either retreating (or never having moved from Logic 1). For example, ShareAction reports that those voting positively in response to shareholder resolutions to better steward resources through stronger governance for social and environmental systems hit a high in 2021 at 40 per cent By 2024, of 279 proposals, only 4 (under 2 per cent) had majority support.[72] Without strong systemic direction with clear milestones and rationales for long-term self-interest, leaders, then, remain trapped – observing the issues but lacking the systemic clarity or momentum to overcome them. As a result, Logic 2 leaders may continue to reinforce the very structures they seek to escape or not stretch their ambition to collaborate and involve themselves fully in the governance transformation required in organisation or at the macro economy level.

MOVING BEYOND FINANCIAL SELF-INTEREST

In summary, ensuring that economies operate within the healthy thresholds of social and environmental systems while maintaining adequate stocks and flows of financial capital is essential for long-term collective wellbeing. However, Logic 2, while theoretically aligned to this task, is insufficient to meet this challenge. Its focus on "do no harm" and its reliance on financial self-interest and other BAU assumptions falls far short of providing the transformational energy required to dismantle entrenched Logic 1 systems of governance that are driving humanity to the brink. The partial adoption of Logic 2 risks becoming a bureaucratic dead end, costing time, energy and resources we no longer have.

To overcome this inertia, we need a motivational agenda that fuels the courage and creativity needed to innovate solutions which not only function within today's constraints, but also are at least theoretically capable of realising the level of radical change needed.

Leaders, especially those at the vanguard, face immense resistance to necessary progress. This makes progress extraordinarily difficult if not enabled by a deep well of determination and persistence. Motivational research tells us time and again that the energy needed to sustain efforts of this level can only come from a place beyond financial self-interest. By continuing to rely on financial self-interest as its primary driver – as well as retaining other BAU assumptions as the rules of engagement – Logic 2 systematically limits this energy. It cannot possibly generate the persistent creativity, resilience and collaboration necessary to drive large-scale transformation.

A sustainable future hinges on routine decision-making at the Macro, Meso and Micro levels that creates, regenerates and protects long-term wellbeing for all. But this will remain a distant goal unless we focus our efforts on designing governance systems that objectively act to achieve, oversee and account for this.

Hence, the most critical question for leaders today to answer might be: What governance behaviours will enable organisations to routinely make decisions that maximise for long-term wellbeing for all while safeguarding the foundations of that wellbeing – and still generating sufficient financial and non-financial capitals to sustain the process? The answer to this question lies in Logic 3.

LOGIC 3: Governance beyond profit to purpose

A CALL TO ACTION: DELIBERATELY BUILDING GOVERNANCE SYSTEMS DESIGNED FOR LONG-TERM WELLBEING FOR ALL

This chapter has so far outlined in detail the nature of the governance that has created the problem and the inadequacy of the current ambition to change. At the heart of this book lies an urgent call to action: to do all we can to shift all governance systems so that they align routine decisions to drive and not harm, long-term wellbeing for all

Global efforts to make this happen have been underway for a very long time, at all levels of the system, and are gaining momentum. What has been missing within these humbling stories of action, is a clear framework to describe these efforts and define the problem being addressed – and the trajectory of change.

Hence, while the momentum is alive, it is in danger of failing and being overshadowed by Logic 1 fuelled narratives that provide a compelling, clear but utterly damaging, call to action. What can turn this tide, and where hope lies is not just in being able to name the problems of Logic 1 and 2 and the BAU assumptions that underpin them, but in being clear about what we are trying to achieve instead. Being able to name and visualise not just the rewards, but the system that will operationalise it, can propel a unifying agenda worthy of our efforts. When we, as individual leaders understand, can visualise and can share ownership of a future state, then we can shout loudly about the future we see and the path we want others to join us on to get there. Armed with this shared clarity and courage we can debate and create rapid change by moving from being 'annoying mosquitoes' to a "loud thunderclap" of Purpose-Driven Leaders that can break free of the status quo. As you read this book we invite you to consider what could be achieved if we collectively call out our ultimate (continually negotiated) destination as "the long-term wellbeing for all people and the planet", and shout loudly that to make this real requires Purpose-Driven Governance of all organisations.

The rest of this book is about drawing from the groundswell of work already being done, to clarify what this purpose-driven governance looks and feels like at the macro, meso and micro levels – and how it can be achieved.

LOGIC 3: THE ULTIMATE CORRECTION

Logic 3 provides the ultimate correction to the flaws of Logic 1 and Logic 2, that is, moving from serving the self to serving the good of others. Making this move aligns a reason to exist – for an economy, organisation or individual – with an optimal strategic contribution to long-term wellbeing for all. This goes beyond merely adding parameters that reflect values aligned with doing good in the process of maximising for self-interest. To fully align with a sustainable future requires rethinking both the point of our lives, an organisation or an economy, as well as how they are run. Hence, the key shift that comes with Logic 3 is the profound change in the maximising goal. At the same time, as with Logic 2, it results in the creation of clear parameters to ensure the health of stakeholders and resources (including enough financial resources). Logic 3 parameters ensure that the purpose can be achieved, but also ensure that the ultimate goal of collective long-term wellbeing is not inadvertently destroyed in the process.

LOGIC 3: WHOLE TRIANGLE GOVERNANCE

Returning to the triangle in Figure 1.6, Logic 3 is a whole-triangle approach that consciously aligns with a sustainable future. By shifting the goal and the parameters, Logic 3 overcomes not just the inadequacy of self-interest, but the hindrance of the other BAU assumptions because the current logic of how the market ought to work is leapfrogged. What needs to be firm is a purpose and parameters that direct our efforts in line with long-term wellbeing for all people and planet. Within this direction, we can then be freed to dynamically determine the best path – through continually adaptive strategy. This whole-triangle approach is not just an ideal. Rather, it is the practical foundation for navigating the

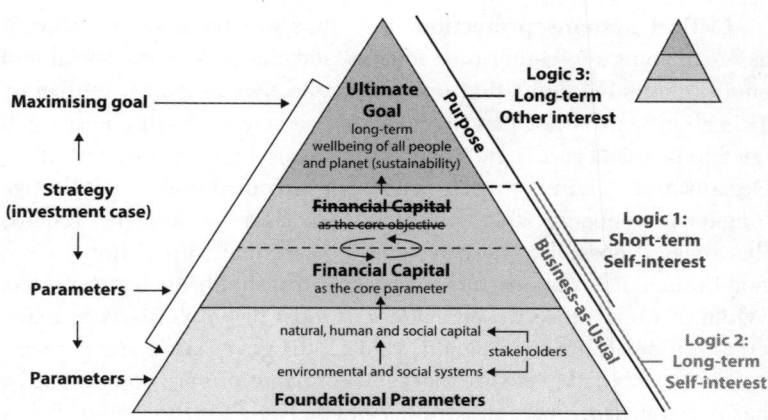

Figure 1.6 Logic 3 total sustainability governance

complexities of today's interconnected challenges. If not this, what? If and when fully implemented, it ensures that every effort has the maximum chance of contributing to building a resilient and flourishing global system, and that this can be overseen and accounted for.

Logic 3, therefore, establishes the foundation for a highly effective and efficient economy, one deliberately designed to align with its ultimate goal: long-term wellbeing for all. Governance systems, rooted in Logic 3, create:

Strong, safe frames. Carefully designed and accountable systems of decision-making that align us with a future we want – enabling us to tackle the hard choices with respect, transparency and justification. This includes enabling broad participation in deciding the right laws and rules and accepting the challenges in the short-term that these may bring.

Strategic agility. The flexibility to innovate and adapt creatively and boldly within strong and appropriate boundaries for decision-making and the ability to recognise and remove unhelpful bureaucracy – and increase rules or laws when needed.

Financial viability. Decisions are structured to maintain sufficient financial resources to pay bills, meet stakeholder expectations and reinvest in the organisation's purpose. Finance and financing as a whole is recognised to be directly in service of long-term wellbeing for all.

Critical systems protection. Decisions are bounded to prevent asset-stripping – whether of resources, stakeholders or the social and environmental systems that underpin collective long-term wellbeing. This alignment is not just practical, it is essential. Hard choices will need to be made and Logic 3 enables justice to be at the heart of them. Organisations cannot exist to maximise a contribution to collective long-term wellbeing while simultaneously undermining the systems that make it possible. These systems also are made up of human and non-human life that require wellbeing thresholds to be protected. While this may all seem self-evident, it must be emphasised, as many organisations claim to "do good" yet lack the governance and management rigor needed to ensure that their contributions are not undone by harm. In our conversation with Carlota de Paula Coelho, Senior Policy Manager, B Lab, she emphasised to us: "The shift to Logic 3 also holds true for organisations that have traditionally been mission-driven (e.g. charities, social enterprises and governments). To avoid unintended impacts which contribute to systemic risks, setting thresholds for healthy means is non-negotiable to ultimately contribute to long term wellbeing for all."

Beyond superficial "good". The Logic 3 approach explicitly addresses the gap between intent and action. While many economies, organisations and individuals aim to "do good", Logic 3 governance ensures that this intent is backed by structures, processes and accountability for this. This drastically reduces contradictions where good intentions are undone by practices that inadvertently, or deliberately, deplete resources, exploit stakeholders or destabilise systems.

Purpose-driven energy. The ability to untether and lean on the unlimited essential source of energy, the innate human desire to serve the greater good, which is known to be a far more powerful motivator than personal financial gain. The shift to Logic 3 governance is what will finally allow our values to enter our decision-making breaking us free from the limitations of self-interest.

A PHILOSOPHICAL NOTE

Purpose is centrally about serving the good of another, otherwise known as love. To live purposeful, meaningful lives requires knowing you are acting in ways that make others' lives better – that your decisions are "good" – or in other words "virtuous". What is a good versus bad action ultimately comes down to what we, as humans, judge. What appears to bind all views, though, is that "good" can be judged to achieve, or try to achieve, wellbeing benefits for others and "bad" is anchored to putting self-interest first. There are three mainstream schools of thought about how to make good decisions that can be assessed as "good"; 1) utilitarianism which prioritises good ends; 2) deontology, which prioritises good means and 3) virtue ethics prioritising the merits the person demonstrates when making the decision. If virtue ethics is about in-the-moment decision-making that optimises for the wellbeing of the collective, then Logic 3 is the governance system that works to optimise this possibility by creating a governance frame of virtuous ends and means.

A Logic 3 governance system aligns decisions within this frame, with the best interests of others, over the long-term. It does this by creating a governance direction that frames routine decisions so that they maximise ethical ends (utilitarianism) while at the same time ensuring ethical methods (deontology). This optimises the likelihood of virtuous decisions – where the decision-maker is both inspired, and able to, make decisions with the intent to do good. While a bad decision can happen in a virtuous governance frame and vice versa, Logic 3 governance maximises the chance of virtuous decisions happening. Even within this positive intent framework, once synergies ("win–wins") are exhausted, decisions made in dynamic real-world contexts will inevitably involve complex trade-offs and human deliberation at the moment they are taken. A Logic 3 purpose-driven governance system helps navigate this complexity by automatically excluding a range of options that lack virtue and creating a cultural norm aligned with virtue. It narrows the strategic discussion about what approach to take to a clear and communally-shared guiding question: "Which decision will best optimise long-term wellbeing for all?"

A THREE-LEVEL SHIFT

This is not a transformation where leaders can afford to contain their impact to the team, organisation or sector they work in. What is required is a critical mass of highly capable Purpose-Driven Leaders that work intentionally across scales, uniting energy around the shared ambition for Logic 3 governance. These leaders can perceive potential barriers and energy sources in detail – and at scale. They have informed views not just about what changes to the investment proforma may be needed in their organisations but what changes to government policies are required, what laws they need to lobby hard for and what changes to their mindset and skillset they need.

The levels – the Macro economy, Meso organisational and Micro individual levels – are not isolated; rather, they are deeply interdependent, and each demands a specific and deliberate redesign to enable the others to succeed. By addressing these three interconnected levels, leaders can drive systemic transformation, ensuring that economies, organisations, and individuals work in harmony to optimise long-term wellbeing for all.

Some believe that the choice we face is between staying where we are or taking on costly changes to BAU that may not work. We need to wake up to the reality that this is not the choice. Our real choice is, logically, between a rapid move to Logic 3 governance at the Macro, Meso and Micro levels or a loss of the market economy altogether when we need it most. As with the Covid 19 pandemic, when things get difficult central planning takes over, and things are going to get very, very difficult without change. This shift, and risk, is represented in Figure 1.7.

MACRO: A WELLBEING ECONOMY

At the Macro level the economy moves from being a GDP economy to a Wellbeing Economy. This is a global economy led by purpose-driven governments whose goal – and accountable measure of success – is to fulfil their mandate of enhancing wellbeing of its populations over the longer term. These are economies governed overtly with a maximising goal and parameters that are aligned with long-term wellbeing for all. GDP becomes one partial route and measure of success. Governments play a special role because, as well as being organisations and economic actors in their own right, they create the conditions for other organisations to be purpose-driven and to enable Purposeful Work and Lives. Governments also have the power to create nationwide parameters that ensure the health of the systems that underpin long-term wellbeing for all – hence levelling the competitive playing field and propelling change. This helpful purpose-designed bureaucracy can serve to clear out a raft of unhelpful red tape and organisational wasted effort.

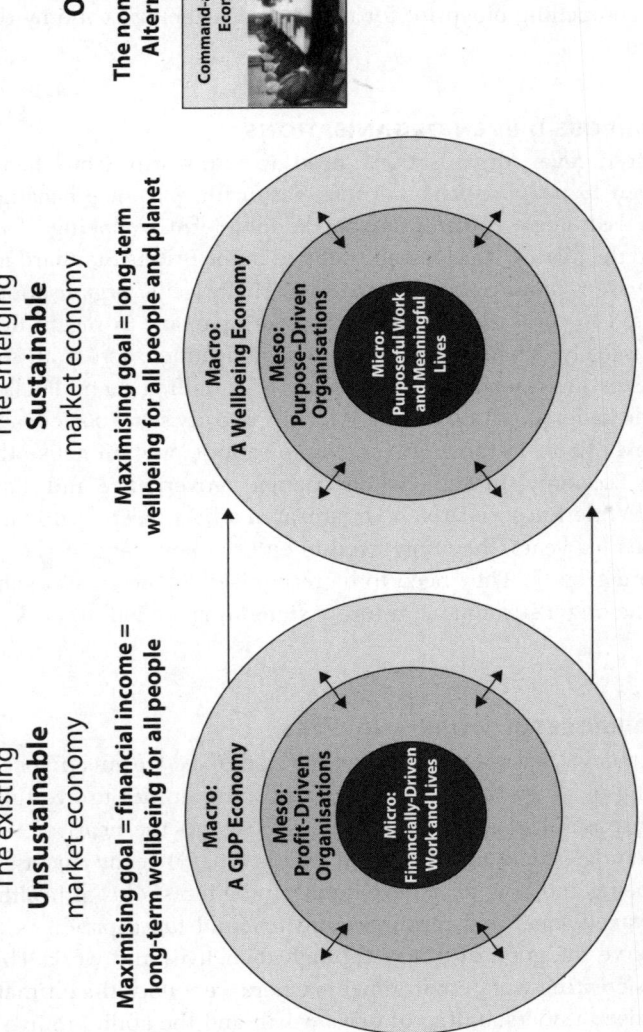

Figure 1.7 The move from an unsustainable to sustainable market economy and the unwanted but realistic alternative

As we will show in Chapter 2, the concept of a Wellbeing Economy is not theoretical; it is already taking shape, for example as the Wellbeing Economy Governments (WEGo) collaboration, which includes countries like New Zealand, Scotland and Iceland as well as aligned initiatives like Bhutan's Gross National Happiness framework. These efforts provide a compelling blueprint for making a Wellbeing Economy the global norm.

MESO: PURPOSE-DRIVEN ORGANISATIONS

At the Meso level, organisations need to transform from being profit-driven to purpose-driven. Their reason for existence becomes "an optimal strategic contribution to the long-term wellbeing of all people and the planet" – as formally defined in the British Standard for Purpose-Driven Organisations (PAS 808). Historically, organisations were created to serve the societies they were part of. In recent decades, a massively expanding number of organisations, across all sectors and sizes, are returning to these roots – or finding them. Fuelled by a deeper understanding of what it means to truly serve society and life on Earth, these Purpose-Driven Organisations operationalise the Wellbeing Economy through "whole triangle" governance and management. While Purpose-Driven Organisations have been a growing global focus for years, they now need to enter a new stage of clarity, support and growth. They need to be recognised as the critical vehicle for achieving a sustainable future – something we will unpack in Chapter 3.

MICRO: PURPOSEFUL WORK AND LIVES

At the Micro level, we require a shift in self and collective governance – empowering us as individuals, citizens and communities to live fully human, purposeful and hence meaningful lives. At the heart of this is emboldening people to debate and decide what it really means to have wellbeing and how to achieve it within the thresholds of healthy systems, stakeholders and resources and to build the capabilities to expertly serve the good of others through their lives and work. This also means creating work environments where we unlock the ultimate reward: a deep understanding of one's worth and the ability to live a life full of purpose that is able to drive system change at the Macro,

Meso and Micro levels. This requires a new type of leadership – Purpose-Driven Leadership – which is grounded in a genuine intent and capacity to serve the good of others. The virtuous cycle of rewards this generates, both personally and collectively, is the most important unlock of all – without it we cannot succeed. While this book provides tools and insights for leaders to act effectively at the Macro, Meso and Micro levels, it is the Micro level where the capacity for Purpose-Driven Leadership is built and Chapter 4 will focus on this as a core route to Purposeful Work and Lives.

The chapters ahead

The remaining three chapters of this book delve into practical insights on Logic 3 at the Macro, Meso and Micro levels. We organise these insights in each chapter using the following three sections:

RETHINK: What we as leaders need to deeply rethink.

RETOOL: The key tools we must acquire.

REALISE: The positive results we can expect will occur from making this change.

As authors, we draw on decades of experience in our respective domains, as well as much experience across them, to bring unique, grounded insights. Each chapter provides a deep and nuanced exploration of a focus area while reflecting the collective vision of this book. The overarching takeaway is that these levels are intricately connected and we authors represent this fully. We do not see three separate movements for change but one massive, coordinated movement from Logic 1 to Logic 3.

YOUR ROLE IN LEADING CHANGE

As you read, we invite you to reflect on the role you can play in driving change across all three levels based on where you sit right now and the capacities and influence you already have – or could have. Together, armed with this intention, we *can* tackle the hard work needed to create a future where long-term wellbeing for all is not just an aspiration but a reality.

CHAPTER 2

MACRO

Leading for a Wellbeing Economy

• • •

A Logic 3 economy is a Wellbeing Economy.[1] In other words, an economy designed by Purpose-Driven Governments to maximise (and protect) the long-term wellbeing for all those in its remit. This is rooted in the ultimate global purpose of long-term wellbeing for all people and planet. A move to a Wellbeing Economy requires a conscious pivot away from growth of Gross Domestic Product (GDP) as the economy's goal, parameter and marker of success. Instead, long-term wellbeing for all becomes the directly governed goal – a goal that is innovated for directly – not as an assumed result of innovating for GDP. This becomes the sign of success that we all focus on – and what government is held to account for.

A Wellbeing Economy can only become real when enacted by appropriate policy, strategy and action. This requires governments to govern the economy, and itself, as an organisation, through direction, oversight and accountability that ensures its decisions are aligned with long-term wellbeing for all – regardless of the current governmental cycle.

As part of this, governments themselves must be governed and held accountable by citizens and all stakeholders to be Purpose-Driven Organisations (see Chapter 3) – whose optimal strategic contribution to the long-term wellbeing of all, will be the long-term wellbeing of those in its remit. Governing the nation is the key task, with the economy as an appropriately designed tool for this mandate.[2] In addition, governments are at the very same time economic actors in their own right, operating within the economy they govern. Their role – whether as investors, service providers or employers, or stakeholder to other economic actors, must be shaped through deliberate strategy to achieve its purpose, within purpose-driven parameters (see Chapter 2 for detail about governing a Purpose-Driven Organisation).

As we will outline, the Wellbeing Economy movement is well underway. To support a swift move away from a BAU Logic 1 GDP model to a Wellbeing Economy, and resist the inenvitable backlash, we must recognise our role as leaders at all levels and actively engage in this transformation.

In this chapter, we will lay the foundations to RETHINK GDP, reframing it with wellbeing at the centre and seeing ourselves as catalysts for meaningful change. We will RETOOL by equipping ourselves with the knowledge and strategies needed to support new fiscal policies and national accounting systems that prioritise long-term wellbeing over short-term financial growth. Along the way, we will highlight pioneering initiatives already driving this shift worldwide. Finally, we will explore the key benefits we can REALISE when we accelerate the transition from GDP-centric decision-making to Wellbeing Economies at scale.

RETHINK

At the heart of a change from Logic 1 to Logic 3 is the ability to bring some assumptions we hold about the economy to the surface and actively realise that there is a different way to think about them. These shifts in beliefs are profoundly important to go on the journey of change needed for a world we want.

RETHINK 1: GDP – from goal to parameter

The first rethink underpinning the move to a Wellbeing Economy is to recognise that GDP should never have been an maximising goal and needs to, instead, be rethought as one, partial parameter. In other words, one *means* to achieve the goal of long-term wellbeing for all – which may, depending on the context, need to be increased, held constant or, as many argue, actively and systematically reduced. This shift from GDP as the goal to it being one potential means to achieve a purpose-driven goal, is essential to move beyond Logic 1 thinking, which mistakenly equates financial growth with growth in wellbeing.

WHY GDP IS JUST ONE IMPERFECT PARAMETER
OF PROGRESS – NOT THE GOAL

GDP is the standard indicator of national financial income and national success. GDP is a single indicator measured by the total monetary value of all goods and services produced within a country's borders, over a specific time period. Economies that move from Logic 1 to Logic 2, remain fixed on growing GDP as the maximising goal. While a Logic 2 economy that is focused on long-term financial self-interest, may, at best, be able to protect the foundations of long-term wellbeing from being harmed, it is not set up to enable decisions that proactively progress wellbeing.

As the foundation of governance direction, GDP influences nearly every policy and strategy decision. For example, governments allocate resources for essential services – schools, pensions, hospitals – based on GDP projections and estimates. However, when we examine what GDP measures and what it ignores, it becomes clear that this singular financial metric not only limits better policy decisions but actively drives unsustainable outcomes.

Pedro Saraiva, Director of PLANAPP, the Portuguese government's Centre for Planning and Evaluation of Public Policies, shared with us: *"To build a purpose-driven Portugal, we need to have very strong messages that citizens are able to understand, in line with themselves, about what we want to achieve as a society. GDP, is just one of the indicators out of 20 or 30 that we want to make sure we are developing in order to measure a balanced progress of our country."*

It is useful to realise that GDP was never supposed to be as powerful as it is today. It was always known to be a poor measure of the wellbeing which was always understood to be the real goal of the economy. As outlined in Lorenzo's 2013 book *Gross Domestic Problem*, GDP's dominance over global economic decision-making was more of an historical accident than a deliberate design.[3]

In 1934, economist Simon Kuznets was tasked by the US Congress to create national income accounts amidst the Great Depression and prospects of war where potential spending possibilities needed to be gauged. From there, GDP emerged as a single metric to measure economic recovery. The Second World War solidified GDP's political significance. The availability of a measure of potential spending helped the US government outpace its enemies in terms of munitions production, leading to unprecedented industrial growth. Post-war, GDP became a governance tool at the Bretton Woods Conference, influencing global economic systems and serving as a pivotal measure during the Cold War, where it was compared to the Soviet Union's 'material product'.

It is not widely known that Kuznets himself criticised the political use of GDP, arguing in front of Congress that it should not dictate peacetime policies. In 1934 he stated clearly: "The welfare of a nation can scarcely be inferred from a measurement of national income." He did not consider military expenses part of national income. For him, military spending was an absolute evil, perhaps necessary at times, but undeniably an evil. Yet, GDP depicted military growth as an indicator of economic strength and encouraged governments to increase rather than decrease the size of the military industrial complex.

Kuznets was attuned to the huge risks of growing something that could make wellbeing worse, not better. He pleaded with policy makers to distinguish between the gross quantity of growth and its actual quality, so they might clarify what type of growth they wanted, and for what reasons. As part of this, Kuznets was also worried about the way in which GDP growth affected the distribution of income. His famous "curve" showed how rapid growth is usually associated with rising inequality. Policies aimed at supporting GDP tend to destroy informal economic structures and replace them with formal systems of production. In the process, many people – especially those that are already marginalised – lose out. Thomas Piketty's bestselling book *Capital in the 21st Century* expands on Kuznets' analysis of growth and inequality by showing how, left unchecked, GDP growth widens inequality and concentrates wealth in a few hands.[4] Kuznets also raised doubts about the reliability of GDP accounting. Data was often missing, and he took great pains to point out the many different errors in international comparisons.

We can summarise the very problematic issues with GDP as five key factors:

1. **Environmental degradation ignored.** GDP treats all production as positive, even when it depletes natural material inputs to GDP, or harms the environmental systems that support it. For example, industries that generate significant pollution or social injustices, such as coal mining or oil extraction, contribute positively to GDP growth

while simultaneously degrading ecosystems and public health. The rapid industrialisation of countries like China and India has led to soaring GDP growth, but it has also caused severe environmental damage. More damagingly, this has the effect of promoting behaviour that harms the basis of our long-term wellbeing. Hunting rare species or causing an oil spill will raise GDP whereas protecting a forest, or stopping a spill, won't.

2. **Social costs neglected.** GDP growth can mask deep social inequalities and motivate them to be exacerbated. While some may feel their life is somewhat improved, others amass fortunes that increasingly can be used to subvert the very national governance that is supposed to benefit from this wealth. A 2024 Bloomberg article reveals an example of how big this accumulation is, even in "hard times": "Cargill Inc. is America's largest privately held company. After hitting all-time highs of $4.9 billion in 2020/2021 and then $6.7 billion in 2021/2022, the company's net profit for the fiscal year that ended in May was the lowest since 2015/2016. It still amounted to $2.5 billion, a number that Javier Blas got from an insiders-only report ... for the members of the Cargill-MacMillan family who own its shares, the company's profit decline means a sharp drop in dividend payouts that averaged about $1 billion a year over the past three years."[5] GDP also does not account for the quality of employment, working conditions or whether income growth is equitably distributed. Hence, a country's economy may grow rapidly and this is celebrated, while income disparities widen leaving many citizens behind. In the US, for example, there has been substantial GDP growth over the last few decades, but this has coincided with a widening wealth gap. This is unlikely to be a coincidence because, without corrective action, the dynamics of the economy are known to concentrate wealth, with more activity and speed increasing this effect. Wealth is increasingly concentrated in the hands of the top 1 per cent, while middle-class incomes have stagnated in many cases and lower incomes have fallen. This creates significant social tension, and these challenges remain hidden within GDP measurements. Additionally, as with the environment, there is a built-in incentive to harm. For example, more people, at a lower wage, working longer hours, is positive for GDP, just as would be the case for an organisation seeking to grow its financial income. Furthermore, GDP does

not reflect more effective and direct measures of economic success, such as mental health, work–life balance, community engagement and life satisfaction. This therefore helps illustrate why countries with high GDP often experience widespread issues like loneliness, stress and declining mental health.

3. **Financial costs of fixing harms can outweigh any financial gains.** We spend GDP gains in order to improve our wellbeing but the cost of fixing the resulting issues from this consumption often cost way more than the income gained even in GDP terms. For example, the Food System Economics Commission estimated that "The economic value of (the) human suffering and planetary harm" from food systems "is well above 10 trillion USD a year, more than food systems contribute to global GDP. In short, our food systems are destroying more value than they create".[6] Furthermore, a 2023 article by Newman and Noy in *Nature Communications* estimates the damage from extreme weather as a result of climate change to now be at least $16m an hour.[7] Yet, the WWF show there is also money left "on the table" from failing to act – if households in the UK utilised all available low-carbon technologies, they could have saved approximately £1,850 on energy bills in 2022 and nearly £1,900 in 2023, resulting in a total savings of £3,750 over two years.[8] A study also estimated that just the cost of decommissioning the UK's onshore oil and gas issues is triple the projected profits they are set to make, a burden that will be borne by taxpayers.[9]

4. **Non-market contributions overlooked.** GDP overlooks unpaid labour, such as caregiving, volunteer work and household activities, which are crucial to social cohesion and individual wellbeing. Because this does not generate a financial income, it literally isn't counted as part of economic activity. In other words, a crucial bedrock of our collective long-term wellbeing does not show up as part of national success. This also serves to embed and extend social exclusion. For example, women still perform most of the unpaid work, contributing to the economy in ways that are not recognised by GDP. International studies in more and less indus-trialised nations have estimated that unpaid labour, if monetised, would contribute billions of dollars to the economy, with benefits that naturally go well beyond a price tag. There are other aspects of social value as a means to our wellbeing that go beyond labour,

such as trust and security. Yet all this value that underpins the ultimate purpose of the economy is completely absent from the GDP measurements.

5. **Failure to reflect life satisfaction.** Studies have shown that GDP growth does not translate into proportionally higher levels of wellbeing, or even happiness. For example, research on the so-called "Easterlin Paradox" shows that after a certain point, higher income levels do not result in increased happiness. Recent studies suggesting that while GDP and subjective wellbeing are connected up to $20,000 USD, from then the link is much more uncertain. A recent paper by Kallis and colleagues reinforced that there are massive disparities between national GDP and wellbeing, and any wellbeing gains are resting on huge overshoot of what the planet can provide. In other words, GDP growth only provides direct wellbeing for a few and undermines the long-term wellbeing of all of us in the process. The disconnect between GDP growth and subjective wellbeing beyond a certain point is particularly evident in many wealthy nations where issues like mental health, loneliness, and work-related stress continue to worsen despite (or rather because of) economic expansion.[10]

CONCERNS WITH GDP ARE PERSISTENT AND WIDESPREAD

Kuznets was not alone in raising concerns about measuring economic success through financial income. In *The Wealth of Nations*, Adam Smith argued for a more nuanced understanding of success.[11] John F Kennedy, the 35th US president, understood the need for a Logic 3 world. In his inaugural speech in 1961 he famously expressed the need for a purpose-driven society: "Ask not what your country can do for you – ask what you can do for your country." In 1968, his brother Robert gave a famous speech that went into detail on the problems of the decision-making box of Logic 1 and the role of GDP (or Gross National Product) in reinforcing it: *"But even if we act to erase material poverty, there is another greater task, it is to confront the poverty of satisfaction – purpose and dignity – that afflicts us all. Too much and for too long, we seemed to have surrendered personal excellence and community values in the mere accumulation of material things. Our Gross National Product, now, is over $800 billion dollars a year, but that Gross National Product – if we judge the United States of America by that – that Gross National*

Product counts air pollution and cigarette advertising, and ambulances to clear our highways of carnage. It counts special locks for our doors and the jails for the people who break them. It counts the destruction of the redwood and the loss of our natural wonder in chaotic sprawl. It counts napalm and counts nuclear warheads and armored cars for the police to fight the riots in our cities. It counts Whitman's rifle and Speck's knife, and the television programs which glorify violence in order to sell toys to our children. Yet the gross national product does not allow for the health of our children, the quality of their education or the joy of their play. It does not include the beauty of our poetry or the strength of our marriages, the intelligence of our public debate or the integrity of our public officials. It measures neither our wit nor our courage, neither our wisdom nor our learning, neither our compassion nor our devotion to our country, it measures everything in short, except that which makes life worthwhile. And it can tell us everything about America except why we are proud that we are Americans."

In more recent years the arguments against GDP have been building. Aided by the ex-chief economist of the World Bank, Joseph Stiglitz, the EU's Sarkozy Commission was established in 2008 by then-French President Nicolas Sarkozy. Officially known as the Commission on the Measurement of Economic Performance and Social Progress, its main objective was to assess the limitations of GDP as a measure of economic performance and to explore alternative indicators that could better capture the wellbeing of individuals and societies. That is not to say that GDP doesn't have its uses in a Wellbeing Economy. It is one potentially very useful metric, if we understand its strengths and don't rely on the metric for more than that. As Tim Jackson in his book *The Care Economy* outlines, it is a sophisticated measure of how busy the market is with transactions, and potentially how busy society is – but that is where its use probably ends. Despite the problems of the measure and the urgent unsustainability that has resulted, we continue to operate with it as the basis of governance direction. Without a critical mass of leaders armed with an argument for a clear alternative it is easy to see why. Because we are bought into Logic 1, merely the expectation that GDP is falling creates real impacts – what Michael Tory writing in Bloomberg calls a "recursive loop".[12] In other words: "A gloomy growth outlook diminishes expectations for fiscal revenue, driving up borrowing costs and prompting speculation about ... future tax increases." While the leaders of the past had this fear, or ignorance, to excuse making the shift away from GDP, we have no excuse for inaction now, and the risks of not moving to Logic 3, and the rewards if we do, are too great. In the words of the former Prime Minister of New Zealand, Jacinda Ardern, another courageous contemporary leader, instead of focusing attention on financial wellbeing, *"We need to address the societal wellbeing of our nation."*

TAKEAWAY

GDP must no longer be the goal of economic and governance decision-making. Instead, it should be seen as one of many partial and imperfect indicators of progress – recognising that a decline in GDP could signal genuine advancement towards long-term wellbeing for all.

RETHINK 2: Wellbeing – from a side topic to the point

By recognising GDP as a partial and imperfect performance indicator, we free ourselves to place collective long-term wellbeing at the heart of national governance in the context of all nations being part of one world community. This redefines the purpose of government: to serve as a driver and protector of collective long-term wellbeing, ensuring that this guides decisions, shapes priorities, and becomes the measure by which progress is assessed and success is ultimately judged by them and citizens alike. In other words, we need purpose-driven governments. Clarity about this shift is an important first step in governing for a sustainable future. Pedro Saraiva, Director of PLANAPP, explained in the case of Portugal: *"The Portuguese government is clear that GDP is no longer good enough. There is a single thing where everyone should agree – to make sure that we contribute to a planet which is sustainable – where human beings can be happy and have the highest standards of quality of life. So I'd say if we don't agree even on this, then, there is no point in agreeing to anything else."*

Focusing directly on the real goal, rather than inefficient and ineffective intermediary assumptions, overcomes the strategic blockages that a focus on GDP has caused. Wellbeing has always been the assumed, or stated, mandate of governments. The International Public Sector Accounting Standards Board states: "The primary function of governments and other public sector entities is to provide services that enhance or maintain the wellbeing of citizens and other eligible residents."[13] The UK Local Authorities are a case in point at a national level. They are incorporated as formalised organisations and the duties of their directors are hinged to delivering wellbeing. The UK Local Government Act 2000 – purpose of Local Authorities (Corporations) states:

"Promotion of Wellbeing: Every local authority are to have power to do anything which they consider is likely to achieve any one or more of the following:

   a) the promotion or improvement of the economic wellbeing of their area

   b) the promotion or improvement of the social wellbeing of their area and

   c) the promotion or improvement of the environmental wellbeing of their area."

As such, they have wide-ranging power to remove policy obstacles that get in the way of this core duty.

A common concern about moving to a Logic 3 world is "how will we measure wellbeing?" Although this is a perpetually subjective question for the current generation to agree on, how we can measure wellbeing is perhaps the question humanity has spent more time on than anything else, even if we don't realise it. While there is currently no consensus on measuring wellbeing, the foundations of how we can measure what matters goes back to early spiritual leaders and philosophers. They have been advanced over the centuries in academia and practice and across all areas of the world. Consolidation is starting to happen, for example, as evidenced in the 2024 paper by Kedi Liu and colleagues "A comprehensive Beyond-GDP database to accelerate wellbeing, inclusion, and sustainability research" which gathered one million data points across 244 metrics, covering 218 countries looking at both direct and indirect measures of wellbeing.[14]

Furthermore, as we outline later, work to consolidate and advance an accounting system anchored to long-term wellbeing for all and purpose-driven governance is in motion. While there will never be a precise measure of something so rich and subjective as wellbeing – this extends to anything of meaningful value. As John Carver said in his book *Boards that Make a Difference*: "A crude measure of the right thing beats a precise measure of the wrong thing."[15]

GOVERNMENTS FOR WELLBEING

For decades, governments worldwide have been rediscovering their true mandate. They are beginning to recognise the shortcomings of governing for a Logic 1 GDP economy – not only in failing to deliver their core mandate of citizen wellbeing but often actively undermining it. This gradual, intuitive shift away from GDP-driven Logic 1 governance towards a Logic 3 Wellbeing Economy has gained momentum. Initiatives like the Purpose-Economy project in Canada and others across the world are testament to this. An early culmination of momentum was the formation of the Wellbeing Economy Governments (WEGo) initiative.

Sparked by an idea by one of the authors, Lorenzo, WEGo was instigated in 2018 by Katherine Trebeck when a groundbreaking group of countries came together to support each other on the journey, and to lead other countries to do the same. These countries were Scotland and New Zealand who were then joined by Finland and Wales. Additionally, Canada, Costa Rica and Brazil have been aligned with WEGo in a number of ways. The journey Katherine took to get WEGo off the ground is documented in the remarkable 2024 film *Purpose*, created by Martin Oetting who shadowed Katherine and Lorenzo's journey in person for years.

WEGo in turn created a leadership platform to encourage other countries to join suit when Sarkozy's mantle was picked up by Finland, who took over the EU presidency in 2019. They made the "Economy of Wellbeing" a priority for their time in office, something that was supported by the EU Council as a whole which concluded the very heart of the Logic 3 arguments made in this book:

- The Economy of Wellbeing is a policy orientation and governance approach which aims to put people and their wellbeing at the centre of policy and decision-making.

- Taking wellbeing into account in all policies is vitally important to the Union's economic growth, productivity, long-term fiscal sustainability and societal stability.

- People's wellbeing is a principal aim of the European Union.

- The Economy of Wellbeing brings into focus the raison d'être of the Union as enshrined in the Treaties and in the Charter of Fundamental Rights of the European Union.

- The creation of an environment that enables people to reach their full potential and to enjoy their fundamental rights is a central component of the Economy of Wellbeing. At the same time, sustainable and inclusive economic growth and resilience function as enablers for the wellbeing of people, societies and the planet.

WEGo is supported by the international non-governmental association Wellbeing Economy Alliance (WEAll) which operates through an international network of country-level hubs members from around the world. It undertakes collaboration on projects such as policy briefings and training, communications work and advocacy. Katherine was co-founder of WEAll which was formed with a view to bring together different groups loosely associated with the Wellbeing Economy movement. WEAll speaks of the need to position long-term wellbeing for all as the anchoring purpose of economies with WEAll's goal being that: "The purpose of the economy becomes exclusively to deliver human and ecological wellbeing." As Katherine explains: "It's not about trying to be happy in the world we have. Quite the opposite: it's about not being happy with the world we have. It's about changing this world through principles of equity, justice and sustainability."

GROWING AN ECONOMY THAT WORKS

When we shift our focus from economic growth as the increase in financial income – to economic growth as the increase in wellbeing, the concept of economic growth takes on a new and valuable meaning. Celebrating economic growth will mean celebrating improvements in wellbeing, ensuring that progress is equitable, sustainable and enduring over the long term. If GDP rises, we will recognise that this could be beneficial, but it might not be – additional information will always be needed to determine whether our decisions are leading us in the right direction. Our daily news and business-focused reports will be centred on how wellbeing has improved or not, what has made the difference and what companies are doing the best job. What will be clear is that GDP alone can never again serve as a guide for economic success.

The harmful consequences of prioritising GDP growth in a Logic 1 economy have led to movements advocating for "post-growth" or "degrowth", both of which seek to move beyond the destructive assumptions of our current economic model. Many individuals and organisations working under these banners provide crucial insights into how we can break free from Logic 1 thinking. The Wellbeing Economy, as part of an overall move to Logic 3, is different in that it expresses what we want to move *towards*: an economy used as a tool for wellbeing by purpose-driven governments and purpose-driven citizens, enabled by Purpose-Driven Organisations and Purpose-Driven Leaders.

There now exists a global structure of organisations supporting and coordinating the move to a Wellbeing Economy. This includes:

OECD: Has a workstream dedicated to understanding how to go beyond GDP and how to measure wellbeing as the alternative. It organises an annual global Wellbeing Economy Forum.

Earth4All: This global initiative has a Transformational Economics Commission to understand alternatives to GDP, of which the Wellbeing Economy is a key aspect.

DEAL: The Doughnut Economics Action Lab has a Wellbeing Economy Policy Design course

Iceland's Wellbeing Economy Forum: An annual Wellbeing Economy Forum is held in Iceland, of which President Halla Tómasdóttir has become the patron.

Japan's Nikkei Wellbeing Symposium: Now in its sixth year this symposium provides a forum for experts and business leaders from Japan and abroad for "lively exchanges of opinions on how to increase wellbeing, with reference to practical examples, research findings, and policy proposals".

TAKEAWAY

A Wellbeing Economy is the core tool of purpose-driven governments that put long-term wellbeing for all at the heart of their governance – aligning decisions and actions across society with a sustainable future.

RETHINK 3: From politicians to all leaders

One of the key reasons that the Logic 1 GDP economy has remained entrenched – despite its harmful consequences – is the widespread belief that economics is a field reserved for economists and that the economy is controlled by politicians. As the Logic 1 economy advanced, it shifted from being understood as a guiding philosophy to a rigid framework of equations managed by econometricians, further distancing everyday leaders and citizens from the conversation.

Yet, we are at a pivotal moment where all those who can lead – and who care about a sustainable future – must extend their leadership to the Macro-economic level. While this may seem daunting, it is both possible and essential.

Leadership for a Logic 3 Wellbeing Economy takes different forms depending on each person's context and sphere of influence. Actions could range from: signing petitions for change; creating regular citizen or organisational groups that debate how well the economy is delivering wellbeing; or persuading your company to join a lobbying group for a Wellbeing Economy. All actions that give energy and credence matter. Some leaders may go further by sitting in government, at least putting themselves in the running with a Logic 3 mandate to at least increase the "Overton window" of what people think is possible. We can take inspiration from actors worldwide who have been embodying the leadership needed.

Katherine Trebeck's story is a case in point. She was not a politician and does not describe herself as an economist, but her hard work to shift the conversation about what the economy is about and how to best measure economic success has had great success. She helped lay the groundwork for a gathering hosted by the Scottish Government at the University of Glasgow, the symbolic academic home of Adam Smith. "It was an extraordinary event," she recalls. "Scientists, opinion makers and politicians called on our Scottish government to change its approach to economic prosperity." It was the first step in a long journey of many setbacks and sudden advancements.

Eventually, her relentless dedication made it possible to formally launch WEGo, as already discussed, at the OECD in South Korea in 2018. She notes what it means to rest your ambitions on the political world: *"Working with politicians means taking many steps forward and then,"* she adds, *"suddenly, many more steps backward. "Leaders come and go, new governments are elected and priorities change. One needs to be patient."* Katherine was indeed patient, travelling the world preparing briefing notes, organising workshops and persuading presidents, ministers, mayors and local councillors to embrace the principles of the Wellbeing Economy.

In order to guarantee that the first reforms towards a Wellbeing Economy are not dropped due to the electoral cycle, Katherine recommends focusing not only on political leaders in parliament but also on public servants in government: *"Political leaders are often more concerned with being re-elected than with long-term impact,"* she notes. *"They can be wonderful in getting the message out there and giving impetus to reforms, but then you need the public servants to do the critical job of turning ideas into real action."* In every country she visited, she was always eager to connect with the chiefs of staff, the economic attachés, the advisors and the director generals that would not only help land the projects but also guarantee continuity in the long term.

In Scotland, in particular, Katherine's work would not have been possible without another leader – Gary Gillespie, who was inside the government system as the Chief Economist. *"It was Gary who ran with the project and turned it into a reality,"* she explains. *"He knew the procedures and had access to all key people in the administration. He also had the authority to pick up the phone and call his peers in other governments, which is what made it possible to extend the WEGo alliance to other countries."*

Enrico Giovannini shares this conviction and has worked tirelessly for macro level change. *"We have won the statistical battle. Now we need to win the political one,"* he said after dedicating his entire life to developing new tools for governments to move beyond GDP. When he was the Chief Statistician of the Organisation for Economic Cooperation and Development (OECD), he inaugurated a series of Beyond GDP conferences, with a first large international forum in Palermo, Italy, in 2004. It was the "institutional" genesis of an unstoppable movement that would grow over time and inspire the scientific community, statistical offices, data analysts, private companies and banks as well as international organisations the world over.

When Enrico was appointed president of the Italian Statistical office in 2010, he developed a new index of Equitable and Sustainable Wellbeing (known as BES), proposing *"it should become the 'compass' through which the government should assess the compliance of national policies with long-term wellbeing"*. The invention of BES predated the launch of the United Nations Sustainable Development Goals (SDGs) and was arguably the first case internationally of a wellbeing-based national headline indicator. After this work he became Minister of Labour in Italy and then Minister of Sustainable Mobility and Infrastructure. Enrico is clear: *"The planet will continue being here for billions of years. It's us that will go extinct unless we embed sustainable wellbeing in everything we do. A Wellbeing Economy is critical to reorganise how we produce, how we work, how we move and why."* Enrico also promoted the 2022 historical change of fundamental principles of the Italian Constitution, which now calls the Republic to "protect the environment, the biodiversity and the ecosystems, also in the interest of future generations" and states that economic activities cannot create damage "to health and to the environment".

Katherine Trebeck, like Lorenzo, is now a member of the Club of Rome, an international organisation traditionally devoted to building a post-growth economy. Back in the 1970s, the Club of Rome published the seminal report, Limits to Growth. This is one of the first pioneering reports on the systemic risks for humanity caused by an economy obsessed with growth of production and consumption and growing demands on natural resources due to expected population growth. One of the historic leaders of the club is another inspiring change-maker, Sandrine Dixson-Declève, co-author of *Earth for All: A Survival Guide for Humanity* and Executive Chair of the Earth4All initiative. *"We want to accelerate the systems-change we need for an equitable future on a finite planet,"* she says. *"We have assembled the best available science with new economic thinking and we have concluded that the next decade must see the fastest economic transformation in history if we want to steer humanity away from social and ecological catastrophe."*

According to Sandrine there are five critical turnarounds that must be achieved on issues that pertain to poverty eradication, empowerment, inequality, food and energy. *"We propose, for instance, to eliminate all debt owed by low-income countries coupled with a special allocation of US 1 trillion to support sustainable jobs and investment in these fledgling economies. We also advocate for the introduction of a wealth tax and some forms of basic income or a basic dividend framework that takes us away from our current over-financialised economy, together with an emphasis on the empowerment of workers and especially women. When it comes to food and energy, we focus on healthy diets, farm-to-fork reforms and a massive electrification powered by renewable energy through a decentralised infrastructure."* Sandrine concludes: *"To achieve that, however, we need a systemic shift in our mindsets and policy frameworks as we need to ensure that these 5 Turnarounds are implemented in sync."*

We can look to indigenous populations for many examples of leaders working tirelessly to influence the Macro level and create change to Logic 3. Wakan Wahohipi Win (also known as Wakan Zephier) is one such leader. An Oceti Sakowin and the daughter of Chief Arvol Looking Horse, Wakan's life is immersed in such leadership efforts that go way beyond her immediate place, with her leadership spanning indigenous peoples across the globe. Place is central to indigenous cultures and she described to us the ongoing battle to create parameters that would protect sacred sites like Mni Wiconi (Water is Life). These were central to the Standing Rock Dakota Access Pipeline protests where a sacred water source and land was threatened by new infrastructure. She described how these protests *reflect the Lakota and Dakota People's deep spiritual connection with the resources, systems and stakeholders that underpin collective intergenerational wellbeing, making it irreconcilable that we would liquidate them thoughtlessly into financial capital. Water, for example, is viewed as both sacred and essential to life, and its protection is a moral and collective responsibility.*

This cultural understanding sits deep in indigenous knowledge systems. The Māori concept of *kaitiakitanga* (guardianship), for example, situates resources as something to be cared for in relationship, as an interconnected source of wellbeing, rather than exploited for short-term personal gain. The essence is captured in an anonymous quote known to be a Native American proverb: "When the last tree has been cut down, the last fish caught, the last river poisoned, only then will we realise that one cannot eat money."

With a different, closer, relationship between the human and non-human world, the move to being purpose-driven becomes much easier or perhaps intuitive and "common sense", where one day we may no longer need conscious Logic 3 governance. But we have created a world where common sense has been severely distorted. However, we cannot afford to wait until people move naturally to rediscover this deep wisdom, especially given the deliberate Logic 1 governance to the contrary. We will have to actively create the conditions for this way of thinking and acting to become routine and eventually, once again just natural. This is why governance at all levels and particularly at the potent legal or governmental level is so essential.

Two leaders, also from Italy, Paolo Di Cesare and Eric Ezechieli, demonstrate how purpose provides the energy that spans action across the Micro, Meso and Macro levels. Paolo and Eric are active systems actors who could see the toxic effect of Logic 1 and how it was baked into governance systems, including company law. When they started their company, NATIVA, the available Italian law didn't match the intent they had. Rather than adjust to the context they decided to change it. The then-Prime Minister of Italy had created a stakeholder forum to collect and discuss ideas for the future of the country. Eric and Paolo, upon invitation of Senator Mauro Del Barba, proposed the idea of Benefit Corporation, which they had seen come to life in the US with the Public Benefit Corporation Act. This legal model is obliged to include social and environmental reasons to exist, alongside the default shareholder financial value creation. They worked for several months, starting in the autumn of 2014, helping draft the new law, and their efforts eventually saw Italy's Società Benefit become reality at the end of 2015, just 14 months after igniting the process. They explained how their motivation comes from wanting to fix the 'bug' in the system that has disconnected companies from the real world of humans and nature. The law, Eric outlined, ... *was a tool to accelerate action. Let's remember that this is officially recognised by legislation, by a country, by a state, right? So, it gives you the official recognition that you are flowing in the right direction. The law protects and aligns the mission and it assigns a wider mandate from the shareholders to board, and management.*

From there they triggered the introduction of legislation across jurisdictions in Latin America such as Ecuador, Colombia and Peru. They also work nationally with municipalities, such as the City of Rome, where there are 140,000 companies, to help as many companies as possible become Benefit Corporations and use this to coordinate and embed action in practice and by-laws such as climate change targets.

Canada has a strong base of action towards Logic 3 which has been spearheaded by dedicated leaders, some of whom we mention later in the book. One leader that demonstrates this spirit is Ryan Turnbull, a social entrepreneur who became a Canadian Member of Parliament and served as Parliamentary Secretary to the Minister of Finance and the Minister of Innovation, Science and Industry. He explained to us that he was not a born politician but started as a purpose-driven entrepreneur wanting to make the world better. He focused this energy in a Purpose-Driven Organisation "EcoEthonomics" – that sought to achieve a "more ethical economy" as a route to increasing wellbeing for everyone. Through this work, he learned first-hand just how many missed opportunities for increasing wellbeing there were all around. In many cases it was government policy with the intent to benefit which in fact got in the way. This led him to the heart of politics. As he summarised: *"All of my work always ran up against policy. People will say, if only we had the right conditions within our economy or within our area ... if only we had the right enabling conditions, if we only we had a government that really understood how citizens and communities needed to be leading the change, that understood how collective efforts really needed to be empowered and enabled by the systems – then that really could make the difference. So it seemed like every project ended up being about how do we change the policy so that we then have the conditions that we can then actually solve the problems that we've been working on. That gradually moved me into politics".*

A Purpose-Driven Leader is a leader for a Wellbeing Economy and Purpose-Driven governments. We all have the ability to effect and speed up the move away from Logic 1 GDP economies and support governments to make the shift to Logic 3.

TAKEAWAY

Shaping how the economy is understood, designed and guided by policy is not the sole responsibility of economists or politicians. As leaders, we all have a vital role in helping to build purpose-driven governments that shift the economy from short-term financial self-interest (Logic 1) to Logic 3 Wellbeing Economies – where long-term wellbeing for all is the central goal.

RETOOL

Once we understand the urgency of the issue and the call to action outlined above, we often find we can achieve far more change at the Macro level through our sphere of influence than we imagined (Chapter 4 will explore this in more depth). To do so effectively, a technical understanding of macro-level decision-making is essential. In this section, we introduce three key tools that support leadership for a Wellbeing Economy: first, a framework for understanding national governance for wellbeing; second, a view of how national accounts would change to reflect changes to long-term wellbeing for all; and third, a way of approaching fiscal policy.

RETOOL 1: National governance for wellbeing

GOVERNING THE ECONOMY FOR LONG-TERM WELLBEING FOR ALL
When we think of government decision-making, we often equate it with policy. However, clarity around the distinction between governance and policy remains elusive, even within the heart of government.

Hal Colebatch provides one of the clearest explanations of what policy in a government context is, in his 2009 third edition of his book *Policy*.[16] Within the section "policy as the systematic pursuit of goals" he summarises the mainstream definitions of policy: "Projected program of goals, values and practices" or "A course of action by government designed to achieve certain results".

To bring deeper clarity we can turn to the foundations of decision-making and how this decision-making is governed – which we touched on in Chapter 1 (see specifically Figure 1.3) and will go into more detail in Chapter 3. This tells us that the maximising goal of government, like for any organisation, represents the value it exists to generate. This goal, along with the boundary parameters that it says shouldn't be crossed in the process, forms the basis of governance direction.

In governments, like all organisations, this direction is the basis of the best approach to optimise achieving the goal within the parameters, given the dynamic context faced (i.e. it is the basis of strategy). In a well-governed organisations, all decisions should ultimately be able to be justified against the goal, within the parameters. This is no different for a government. Therefore, how governments govern – how they understand, embed and communicate their ultimate goal and parameters (governance direction) – is core to all the decisions then made across the government system, and those that interact with it, including all organisations that it governs.

The governmental purpose and parameters are translated into sub-objectives – which, if achieved, are expected to fulfil the purpose. This constitutes governance direction and is embedded in written governance policy and used to design strategy that cascades throughout the government system and beyond to those outsourced to or contracted.

For a Logic 1 government guided by BAU assumptions, the emphasis of the direction given in policy will be tied to GDP as the goal – and healthy stocks and flows of financial capital as the key parameter. This will guide and constrain the strategic choices made.

For a Logic 3 Wellbeing Economy government, direction is explicitly nested against the purpose of long-term wellbeing for all within the government's remit and parameters that ensure the protection, regeneration and enhancement of the resources, stakeholders, social and environmental systems that underpin long-term wellbeing for all.

In other words, in order to enact a Logic 3 Wellbeing Economy, governments need to act and govern as a Purpose-Driven Organisation. In fact, a government should be the archetypal Purpose-Driven Organisation and should be held to account against the behaviours specified in the forthcoming ISO 37011 (see Chapter 3).

As the ultimate purpose of economic development moves from GDP growth (which is the current purpose), to long-term wellbeing for all, all economic actors will need to understand this system of decision-making and their role in leading and upholding a new fully aligned Logic 3 governance system. Trying to achieve wellbeing optimisation in a governance and policy setting designed for GDP optimisation would be like swimming upstream against a flood of rules, regulations, sanctions and incentives that push every one of us, every single day, in the opposite direction. We need to align our governance frameworks and associated policies to long-term wellbeing for all if we really want to generate the systemic change we need. What is sure is that if we act to serve the current economic system in the hope it may one day serve us, is pure foolishness. The more we uphold the current system the more we lose.

PRINCIPLES FOR CHANGE

In the 2024 paper, "The Wellbeing Economy in Brief", Dr Katherine Trebeck and Warwick Smith state how they view the variability of strategy (approaches) in transitioning to a Wellbeing Economy: "The practical changes a Wellbeing Economy agenda entails range from local practices to substantial shifts in governance architecture. The approaches and pathways to get there will be different in different localities, of course, given different starting points, different challenges, different opportunities, different technologies, and different institutions and societal norms. They constitute the substance of the Wellbeing Economy agenda."[17]

The principles of direction, oversight and accountability are the same for all organisations, including political ones, and will be covered in detail in Chapter 2. The optimal strategies for each context will result from the direction given in the organisational direction (purpose and parameters) and nested in policy. When consider useful approaches for a Wellbeing Economy, WEAll outline three principles, in addition to Purpose: predistribution, prevention and people-powered.

Predistribution. "We don't leave it to people to fend for themselves or rely on limited redistributive mechanisms, but predistribute power, wealth, time, and income so that the heavy lifting is done by the economy itself." The concept of "predistribution" is of the essence here. In a Wellbeing Economy, it is critical that the governance mechanisms be redesigned to ensure that all economic actors produce wellbeing in their day-to-day activities, without the need to rely excessively on redistribution to "rectify" what is distorted by the market. For example, new forms of sustainable business (e.g. benefit corporations, cooperatives, social enterprises) pay decent salaries, avoid significant wage gaps, invest directly and indirectly in community development, make a positive contribution to personal and collective wellbeing, hence reducing the need to use the taxation system to redistribute income.

Prevention. "Rather than being content with just fixing the harm we do to nature and people, we adopt preventive measures that stop harm from happening in the first place." The importance of prevention is closely connected with predistribution: why would a country spend so much time and resources on fixing social and environmental problems when it could focus on not generating these problems in the first place? As we know, the belief in GDP growth at all costs has made us blind to the massive costs of BAU production and consumption. In a Wellbeing Economy, the so-called "negative externalities" are to be prevented at the source instead of being tackled after the fact. Incentives, investment and technologies should be deployed to ensure that the economy is producing positive wellbeing while minimising (and eventually eliminating) negative outputs. For example, circular economy innovations massively reduce waste, thereby avoiding the need to extract more natural resources and limiting environmental pollution.

People-powered. "Economic decisions are powered by the people, who become directly involved in decision-making and agenda setting." As we have explained, a well-governed Wellbeing Economy will result not only in a healthy environment, but also a socially empowering one. Our wellbeing is underpinned by human needs, one of which is established to be a sense of participation. As outlined in Chapter 1 BAU economy has relegated people to the passive role of consumers, which can be alienating and disempowering. By contrast, the Wellbeing Economy is advanced by understanding people as "prosumers" where the boundaries between production and consumption become blurry and collaboration between producers and users is the norm. Moreover, at the governance level, citizens, given the principle of subsidiarity, are empowered to be primarily able to decide economic policy – depending on their cultural and social preferences for driving, and not harming, collective long-term wellbeing.

The economist Manfred Max-Neef established that the *ways* in which wellbeing is created via universal need satisfaction will vary by cultural context and how meaning is constructed. At a governmental level, countries may therefore decide to pursue wellbeing in different ways and measure their performance to the overall goal of wellbeing according to other standards, without the need to adopt a one-size-fits-all approach as is the case with the Logic 1 approach. That said, learning and growing together to establish common global measures that relate to the universal aspects of growing, and not harming, wellbeing is likely to be of use. Also central to useful decision making is a shared set of measures, and thresholds, that reflect our best, current, understanding of the healthy regenerative functioning of planetary social and environmental systems – as well as variabilities in bioregions which are distinct in their socio-ecological requirements.

An example of a people-powered shift is where the so-called fourth-industrial revolution is making it possible to shift from mass production (which views users as passive consumers of large industrial processes) to customisation (which views users as co-designers of unique products), while governance innovations such as participatory budgeting allow citizens to collectively decide how to spend public budgets at the local and national level. Overt governance to counter the negative pressures on people-power, such as the concentration of wealth and the dominance of a few social media organisations will also be vital.

TAKEAWAY

We cannot achieve a Wellbeing Economy without designing and implementing a robust Logic 3 governance system to make it a reality. This begins with developing governance literacy across all spheres – enabling all of us to see how governance connects and shapes decision-making across citizens, governments, organisations and individuals.

RETOOL 2: Wellbeing accountability

To recap, the three core functions of governance are direction, oversight of that direction and accountability for it. Accountability sits at the heart of a functioning democracy. For accountability to work, it requires the ability and willingness to account to those stakeholders where an obligation exists. This accounting needs to explain and justify whether the intended value encompassed by its goals has been generated, while protecting the value intended through appropriate parameters. This goes along with appropriate resolutions or consequences if harms are done from underperformance. Further, there needs to be a nuanced dialogue about how change happened, including ensuring that any success hasn't happened by chance but is repeatable, and that appropriate actions have been taken to correct course in a timely way when needed. This includes assessing whether decisions are appropriately free from rules.

The economy is society's central tool, and so the primary tool of government, because the economy, in effect, decides how our shared resources are transformed and allocated in order to optimise our long-term collective wellbeing. True accountability requires government leaders to report back to citizens as to whether long-term wellbeing for all has been optimised through the governance direction and associated strategy (approach) they have pursued. They also need to demonstrate how they are overseeing this and ensuring continual learning and adaptation to the complex systems they are in a relationship with. This accountability is not only essential for democratic legitimacy but also for internal governance, ensuring that policies are actually useful.

Accounting sits at the heart of accountability. An effective system of accounts should enable evaluation regarding progress towards the value generation goal of the purpose while making clear if, and how, the value intended to be protected through the parameters has or has not been. Without this evaluation and reporting, government could be acting completely counter to the long-term wellbeing of the collective and it would be hard, or perhaps impossible for the collective to know. For example – are the countries greenhouse gas emissions this year on track to be aligned with a healthy global climate? Therefore, a core component of moving from Logic 1 to Logic 3 is to free the concept of "accounting" from measuring financial results and inputs – just as we need to unleash the concept of the "economic" or "economy" from a measure of finance. As Mark Carney, Prime Minister of Canada, neatly reinforced: "Finance is utility, a means to an end with the ends determined by society."[18]

A Wellbeing Economy requires a new system of national accounts that account properly for alignment of decisions to long-term wellbeing for all: National Wellbeing Accounts. These accounts in turn enable well-crafted KPIs and support iterative learning about what policies, based on what theories of change, produce better results. Wellbeing measures, indicators and dashboards are all potential aspects of a system of National Wellbeing Accounts, to evaluate the success of economic policies and strategies.

For an economy that has made a short step to Logic 2 (long-term financial self-interest) from Logic 1 (short-term financial self-interest) GDP will be supplemented with metrics like mental health, community cohesion and environmental sustainability. For instance, the EU employs a range of wellbeing indicators, such as employment rates, educational attainment and social inclusion to inform its policies but to not take centre stage. However, to be Logic 3 means going further. It requires that countries not limit themselves to "complementing" GDP growth: they must fully transcend it, which means abandoning GDP as a headline indicator. This requires accounting systems that roll up from communities, to organisations to a national and global level. This enables full visibility of how well governments, and organisations in their remit, are supporting and enabling the current and future wellbeing of communities. This should empower people and communities to determine the best approach – within the outer most governance frame that drives and secures the long-term wellbeing of the collective. In Logic 3, governments, and other organisations would naturally want to account for how well they were enabling and empowering people and communities. This is because they would recognise that *how* to achieve wellbeing (or meet universal needs) will ultimately always be subjective to citizens. Any details of an accounting system could only be generalised to the extent this was of use to long-term wellbeing for all.

Developing a harmonised basis of accounting for a Purpose-Driven Organisation is yet to be developed. However, the world has come a long way in developing the basis of accounting for wellbeing. In

December 2023, Social Value International published a report Impact Transparency in Public Sector Accounting, as a requested input into the independent, industry-led Impact Taskforce run by GSG and supported by the G7 under the UK's presidency.[19] The paper summarised developments in public sector accounting from across the world towards an accounting system for wellbeing across national, regional and organisational domains. This included the UNDP SDG Impact Standards reference to wellbeing as the basic unit of account.

Encouraged by what the research found, the authors stated: "Now is an opportunity to pull all of these threads together and adopt the necessary public sector accounting and reporting practices so that government expenditure meets demands for transparency, accountability and integrity of impact." They see this as an indication the world may be ready for a new wellbeing-oriented system of accounting that would be the basis for management accountants, company and public sector reporting and national accounts. The question of whether this is the case is progressing formally at the international level with work initiated alongside the development of the International Standard in Purpose-Driven Organisations (ISO 37011). The ad-hoc group that has been convened will assess the current international consensus on what this could look like, how it could be operationalised within Purpose-Driven Organisations and their accounting systems (including, of course, within government as an organisation) and whether the world is ready to create a consensus-based standard on this.

Some of the progress indicated above, can be seen in decades of advancements in wellbeing measurement. There now exist a wide range of alternative or complementary systems that seek to measure and account for wellbeing that balance both subjective and objective measures. These have been developed by academics, individuals, countries and groups of countries. With the adoption of the UN Sustainable Development Goals (SDGs) in 2015, many other countries and institutions followed suit, developing hundreds of new indicators, metrics and dashboards. The OECD states that over 70 per cent of all OECD countries now have some form of framework for assessing wellbeing.[20] While we cannot list them all here, a range of some major systems of measurement and accounting can be seen in Table 2.1:

TABLE 2.1 EXAMPLES OF EXISTING SYSTEMS OF WELLBEING MEASUREMENT AND ACCOUNTING

Name	Source	Methodology	Date
International			
Measure of Economic Welfare	Nordhaus and Tobin (1973)	Corrects GDP by adding household production, excluding military expenses and controlling for some environmental impacts.	1973
Index of Sustainable Economic Welfare (Genuine Progress Indicator)	Daly and Cobb 1989; Redefining Progress	Adds household activities and volunteering and subtracts 'bads' like crime, pollution, social breakdown.	1989
Human Development Index	United Nations Development Programme	Aggregates income, literacy and life expectancy (adjusted for inequality).	1990
Adjusted Net Savings	World Bank	Deducts depreciation of produced capital and depletion of natural capital depletion but adds human capital.	1991
Ecological Footprint	Global Footprint Network	Represents the productive area required to provide the renewable resources humanity is using and to absorb its waste.	1995

Name	Source	Methodology	Date
Legatum Prosperity Index	Legatum Institute	Operationalises prosperity along eight dimensions, including economy, entrepreneurship, governance, education, health, safety, personal freedom and social capital. Sources include World Development Indicators, Gallup World Poll, World Values Survey and International Communication Union.	2008
Better Life Index	OECD	Measures 11 dimensions (housing, income, jobs, community, education, environment, civic engagement, health, life satisfaction, safety and work–life balance) and allows users to customise weights.	2011
Happy Planet Index	New Economics Foundation	Multiplies subjective wellbeing (as measured in Gallup World Poll's "Ladder of Life") by life expectancy and divides it by ecological footprint as an efficiency measure of how long and happy lives are in comparison to environmental impacts.	2012

(Continued)

Name	Source	Methodology	Date
World Happiness Index	UN Sustainable Development Solutions Network	Uses the Ladder of Life evaluations from the Gallup World Poll. The English wording of the question is "Please imagine a ladder, with steps numbered from 0 at the bottom to 10 at the top. The top of the ladder represents the best possible life for you and the bottom of the ladder represents the worst possible life for you. On which step of the ladder would you say you personally feel you stand at this time?"	2012
Inclusive Wealth Index	UN Environment Programme and UNU-IHDP	Measures stocks rather than flows and specifically assesses the value of human and natural capital besides produced capital.	2012
Social Progress Index	Social Progress Imperative	Result-based index focusing on three dimensions: basic human needs, foundations of wellbeing, and opportunity. It uses data produced by a variety of institutions, including the World Health Organization, World Bank, International Energy Agency, Gallup and the Economist Intelligence Unit. It allows users to customise the set of variables included in the final calculations.	2014

Name	Source	Methodology	Date
National Level			
Gross National Happiness	Centre for Bhutan Studies	Conceives "national happiness" as founded on four pillars (good governance, sustainable socio-economic development, preservation and promotion of culture and environmental conservation). The survey is operationalised into nine domains: living standards, education, health, environment, community vitality, time-use, psychological wellbeing, good governance, cultural resilience and promotion.	2008
The Canadian Wellbeing Index (CWI)	Canada	Developed by the University of Waterloo, tracks multiple dimensions of wellbeing, such as health, education, and community vitality, as alternatives to GDP. This index is used as a tool for informing policy decisions and tracking the nation's progress in these areas	2011
Index of Equitable and Sustainable Wellbeing (BES)	Italy	Measures the wellbeing of citizens through dimensions such as health, education, environment, social relationships, and security. The index is also designed to highlight inequalities and current wellbeing as well as the basis for this in the future.	2010

(Continued)

Name	Source	Methodology	Date
Social and Emotional Wellbeing Framework (SEWB)	Aboriginal and Torres Strait Islanders	The framework of 2004 and 2017 were developed during a "Ways Forward" national consultation. The framework sets out nine guiding principles for SEWB: • health as holistic • the right to self-determination • the need for cultural understanding • the impact of history in trauma and loss • recognition of human rights • the impact of racism and stigma • recognition of the centrality of kinship • recognition of cultural diversity • recognition of Aboriginal strengths	2017
National Performance Framework (NPF)	Scotland	A tool to assess national progress setting out a vision for collective wellbeing based on a ground-up understanding of what wellbeing means for the population.	2018
Living Standards Framework (LSF)	New Zealand	Assesses policy decisions across 12 domains such as social connection, safety, environmental quality and work–life balance.	2021

Name	Source	Methodology	Date
National Well-being Dashboard and Nikkei Gross Domestic Wellbeing	Japan	Published since 2019, these initiatives are based on an annual survey of the population. A group of companies, supported by the Nikkei created an alternative to GDP – Gross Domestic Wellbeing and committed to report on it.	2019 2021
National Wellbeing Dashboard	Portugal	A tool as part of the country moving away from EU and other official statistics to measure wellbeing progress – towards a set of 20 to 30 high-level KPIs, which derived from existing official measures and the perceptions of citizens.	Forth-coming
Life in the UK, UK Measures of National Wellbeing	UK	An alternative metric to GDP that Carnegie UK has created, built on existing work to measure collective wellbeing across the UK. It identifies where progress is being made and the areas that require policy intervention. The UK has a set of national wellbeing indicators compiled under the UK Measures of National Well-being (UK MNW) framework. This framework encompasses	2023

(Continued)

Name	Source	Methodology	Date
		around 60 measures following a national debate and public consultation on what matters most to people. These data underpin the government's Wellbeing Green Book as a framework for analysts to assess wellbeing impacts to support decision-making in public spending and policy design. As part of this Green Book a metric called a WELLBY (Wellbeing-Adjusted Life Year) is used to quantify changes in a person's overall wellbeing represents a one-point change in life satisfaction on a 0-to-10 scale for one individual sustained over one year. One WELLBY is currently valued at approximately £13,000 (2019 prices).	2011 - 2021

Ultimately, a system of international accounting standards would seem to be necessary to advance quality progress, accountability and capital allocations, regardless of the progress on this, any country can develop a wellbeing measurement system to support a shift to a Wellbeing Economy as long as it focuses wellbeing as the goal and on social and ecological system health as the outlying parameter. Regardless of the system, there are three categories of measures that are useful to consider:

Mental and physical health are the two aspects that underpin wellbeing of living creatures and are achieved by the satisfaction of universal human needs. Many wellbeing indexes use life expectancy, mental health surveys, and access to healthcare as direct indicators of how "well" a society is functioning. New Zealand's Wellbeing Budget was used to prioritise mental health funding to address the rising rates of depression and suicide, recognising that GDP growth did not correlate with improved mental health.

Relational health is a core aspect of mental health, physical health and hence wellbeing. The quality of our interrelations is vital as humans, and many non-human species, cannot thrive in isolation. Hence, community and participatory wellbeing is indispensable. For humans, indicators like social trust, community engagement, and work–life balance are central to gauging how supported and connected people feel in their societies and hence lives. The OECD Better Life Index allows people to compare wellbeing across countries based on factors like housing, jobs, work–life balance, income, education, environment, health, and more. Countries like Denmark and Finland rank highly on these indices due to strong social safety nets and high levels of trust in government.

Environmental health is a commonly used term in these indices and emphasises that non-human wellbeing underpins human wellbeing. Environmental health measures are therefore typically focused on non-human wellbeing as a means to human wellbeing, rather than as an end in themselves. Metrics such as carbon footprint, air quality, biodiversity, and resource depletion rates are increasingly incorporated into wellbeing frameworks. For example, the Ecological Footprint measures how much land and water resources a population requires to produce what it consumes and to absorb its waste. Countries like Costa Rica, which prioritise conservation and renewable energy, consistently perform well on these measures. It is worth remembering that healthy human societies (i.e. with high wellbeing) are also essential to sustaining – rather than destroying – the health of the environment.

TAKEAWAY

Accountability requires an aligned accounting system. There has been huge progress across the world on the basis of measuring and reporting wellbeing, and acting on the results. Work is progressing to develop international consensus on an integrated system of accounts that can underpin accountability for long-term wellbeing for all.

RETOOL 3: Fiscal policy for wellbeing

If money is a flexible tool with the potential to direct energy, fiscal policy is a powerful tool to direct energy in ways that either destroy long-term wellbeing for all, or drive it. Once the role of financial capital is clear as a core *means* to a meaningful end – but never a goal in itself – we can begin to reimagine how financial capital, including through fiscal reform, could be optimally harnessed as a powerful driver of collective wellbeing.

In a Wellbeing Economy, fiscal reforms should align government budgets with a governmental purpose (maximising long-term wellbeing for all within the jurisdiction) and its parameters (at a minimum, protecting the basis of long-term wellbeing, in the context of one planet). A system of National Wellbeing Accounts would provide the anchoring for sophisticated fiscal policy that results in aligned budgets and budget accountability. Public spending can then be redirected to prioritise investments that achieve the purpose within its parameters and enable organisations, households and individuals to do the same.

This involves shifting funds away from activities that harm the environment and society in order to mitigate harm and redirect those funds to driving long-term wellbeing for all. In Logic 1 governments, national budgets and the laws surrounding them are dominated by financial objectives and parameters. In a Logic 3 governed Wellbeing Economy these would be redesigned as National Wellbeing Budgets and laws changed to support this.

As a result of these changes, policies in a Wellbeing Economy enable strategy that can shift from prioritising extractive, short-term income to long-term investments like human capital, infrastructure and environmental health that don't just protect but also enhance wellbeing. Those that give the highest wellbeing-return-on-finance-invested will win out. Governments already on the journey are known to increase spending on healthcare, education, housing and social services to improve wellbeing, with reduction in inequality a core means to that. They expand access to affordable housing and healthcare ensuring that a range of human needs are met for citizens such as subsistence, security and the means to participate in social life. Public funds are invested in securing reliable, clean infrastructure, for example, through distributed renewable energy, public transportation and energy-efficient buildings. These investments increase wellbeing directly by improving physical and mental health but also indirectly by creating jobs and reducing emissions. A move to purpose-driven governments running Wellbeing Economies tends to result in some key fiscal policy shifts, including:[21]

Reimagining fiscal policy. Taxes and subsidies for industries, companies and individuals are used in a sophisticated way to move away from harm rapidly, towards growth in long-term wellbeing. This ensures a "polluter pays" principle and generates funds that can be reinvested in the purpose via a market economy serviced by Purpose-Driven Organisations – including the government as a purpose-driven market actor. For example, in Bolivia, a tax on hydrocarbons is used to fund a healthy meals initiative in schools. In countries with significant financial inequality, which is a known legacy of BAU Logic 1 economies, this mechanism is particularly necessary. For all countries, proactive reimagining the entire system of fiscal policy is essential for transitioning to a Wellbeing Economy and ensuring a just transition for those locked into harm.

Progressive Taxes. Taxes are publicly reframed from a burden to a necessary corrective action to address Logic 1 legacy. Taxes can move the burden from those who create negative impacts towards organisations that can show they are governed to be purpose-driven. These organisations operationally align with government's and society's purpose and hence best interest – and so should be given every opportunity to flourish. This should show up in the National Wellbeing Accounts and provide evidence that the economy is growing wellbeing.

While taxes will always remain a necessary and important tool, the need for them can be reduced as an economy adopts the principles of predistribution, prevention and people-powered governance – where wellbeing issues are prevented and dealt with at source. In a Wellbeing Economy, fewer resources are therefore needed to fix issues downstream which creates a virtuous cycle of wellbeing growth. This means fewer resources are drained meaning more resources can be used to improve wellbeing foundations – which in turn prevents other wellbeing issues arising that would need funds to fix. For example, instead of taxing companies in order to fund large social support systems to support people suffering from mental and physical health issues (often caused by those very companies) the need for such taxes can be reduced by helping all organisations become well-governed, purpose-driven entities. When workforce wellbeing is treated as a core parameter, stress and unhealthy lifestyles are addressed through well-governed decision-making parameters. The more we perpetuate unsustainability, the higher the taxes and societal costs. Only by transitioning to a Logic 3 economy can we systematically reduce these burdens and prevent future escalations.

Redirecting subsidies. As outlined in the World of Withering Wellbeing in Chapter 1, current subsidies and financial incentives often support industries that undermine collective long-term wellbeing. Reforming these subsidies is essential – not merely removing them but redirecting them towards activities that enhance wellbeing. Redirecting these subsidies where they are needed most requires purpose-driven governments. Purpose-driven governments can govern with a strong frame to enhance and protect collective long-term wellbeing. This allows them, and all other organisations in the nation, to be free to engage in agile collaborative strategy building that isn't held back by unnecessary subsidies that may be "betting on the wrong horse", for instance, subsidising "clean energy solutions" that accelerate the transition to a low-carbon economy, reduce pollution and create green jobs, but without prescribing specific technologies or timelines. Wales, for example, has been piloting basic minimum income with a specific group: young people who are required to care for others at home – with promising results. This may not work for all regions. Farming subsidies should be redirected towards those that can optimise for the maximisation of long-term wellbeing for all, while protecting and restoring ecosystem and social system health in the process. This would be a high-level goal strongly directed, overseen and accounted through clear measurement regimes. The key is that this leaves farmers free to innovate the strategy depending on their unique context, whether that is a particular organic method, small-scale mixed farming, forest gardens or a different regenerative agriculture approach. Agricultural organisations would be free to adopt whichever organisational and governance strategy they deemed most appropriate to get the best results for as a Purpose-Driven Organisation (see Chapter 2), from highly participatory to highly structured. Citizens could rest easy knowing that whatever approach was taken it would not be harming the foundations of their wellbeing and would be doing the best job to make their lives better. Just imagine how this could pivot the decline in pollinators and nutrition in food – results that would be counted and reported by farmers to government and government to citizens.

Activating private capital. Mobilising the financial capital needed to transform infrastructure and systems – both to prevent harm and accelerate innovation for collective long-term wellbeing – will require the mobilising of finance from diverse sources. To enable this, the governance of financing organisations must shift from Logic 1 to Logic 3. During transition, governments have a crucial role to play in proactively embedding purpose-driven governance systems into the projects, and the organisations that finance others – and to bring them together to solve system problems in purpose-driven projects and governed as such. The 2025 UN policy brief authored by Marianna Mazzucato and based on the Sustainable Development Goals, highlights essential reforms required in this area. It underscores the importance of embedding clear conditionalities in public-private partnerships to ensure that public investment drives genuine transformation, rather than merely subsidising private sector activities.[22]

The implementation of "wellbeing budgets". This represents a key innovation in fiscal policy. These budgets allocate funding based on measures of wellbeing.

A number of countries have been experimenting with these innovations and beyond. We note a few of the key examples below:

Scotland. Scotland, another founding member of WEGo, launched its new National Performance Framework to track progress towards achieving wellbeing goals and, as a consequence, committed to reducing inequality, improving public health, increasing access to green spaces, improving social capital and transitioning to a low-carbon economy. The country has since focused on work–life balance and mental health, leading to targeted interventions aimed at reducing burnout, particularly among young people. The country's strong public health system and comprehensive mental health support programmes are also crucial to these wellbeing goals, and Scotland's work–life balance and high levels of community trust are regularly praised in global wellbeing reports.

Iceland. Since becoming a member of WEGo, Iceland's government has been committed to measuring societal progress in ways that go beyond GDP growth, focusing on key areas such as education, healthcare, environmental sustainability and gender equality. Iceland is frequently ranked as one of the most gender-equal countries in the world. The Icelandic government implements policies that promote work–life balance and support for families, including generous parental leave and affordable childcare. Among others, it passed legislation requiring companies to prove that they offer equal pay to employees regardless of gender. This policy has made Iceland a leader in gender equity, contributing to broader social wellbeing and economic stability

Italy. Changing governance so that policy decisions align with longterm wellbeing for all represents deep systemic change involving many stakeholders. Therefore, momentum can persist regardless of political cycles. Although not widely known, Italy is an example of a country on a journey of progress towards being a Wellbeing Economy. After pioneering the adoption of the Index of Equitable and Sustainable Wellbeing (BES), the country incorporated it into a review framework for the national budget, whereby every year all financial decisions of government must be vetted through wellbeing indicators. Moreover, driven by Lorenzo as then-Italian Minister for Education, University and Research, the country was the first to introduce mandatory sustainability education in all schools with a view to developing a wellbeing culture among the population. It was also the first to approve a national law in favour of "Benefit Corporations" – businesses that, by law, embed social and environmental objectives as part of their stated reason to exist. The country also instituted a national wellbeing commission in the office of the Prime Minister, tasked with overseeing coherence in all national programmes.

Canada. Supported by its Canadian Wellbeing Index (CWI), Canada has started incorporating wellbeing metrics into its budgeting process, with a focus on mental health, gender equality and reducing poverty. For example, the 2021 federal budget included a National Child Care Plan, aimed at making childcare more affordable, which directly improves family wellbeing.

Japan. The Japanese government has incorporated key performance indicators (KPIs) related to wellbeing into its policy development since 2021. Utilising the OECD Well-being Framework, the Cabinet Office created a national Well-being Dashboard, which has been published annually since 2019. These initiatives are based on an annual survey of the population, with the results guiding the establishment of KPIs and policy agendas.

New Zealand. The country underwent a fundamental retooling of development indicators. The government's Wellbeing Budget was first introduced in 2019. One major result was the increase in mental health funding by $1.9 billion over five years, underscoring a significant commitment to addressing issues such as suicide prevention, addiction and mental health services for children. The government focused on five key areas:

- Mental Health: Addressing the mental health crisis, which had become a significant social issue
- Child Wellbeing: Reducing child poverty and improving lives of young New Zealanders
- Māori and Pacific Peoples: Supporting indigenous communities with tailored programmes to reduce inequities
- Productive Nation: Transitioning to a low-emissions, high-wage economy
- Digital Transformation: Investing in technology to improve digital infrastructure.

In the words of the then-Prime Minister Jacinda Ardern: *"We are embedding wellbeing into the heart of what we do as a government. This is not woolly; it's critical."*

Wales. Wales is the only country in the world to have the Wellbeing Economy written into the heart of the constitution with the "Wellbeing of Future Generations Act (2015)" and this creates financial budgets that emanate and are justified against this. Resource health is also turned into budgets that act as decision-making parameters to drive the transition to operating within thresholds of system health country-wide – for example, carbon emissions (2016) and amount of non-recycled waste (since 2009). The amount of permitted emissions and waste is reduced over time and laid out in law, so that everyone is sure about the trajectory. This is combined with hard penalties for non-compliance. As a consequence, Wales is the third best country in the world for recycling and is due to improve their gains even further – demonstrating the tangible change that can be achieved with clear and effective governance.

Portugal. Portugal has had three years of allocating its financial budgets in ways that are able to show how they relate to all 17 SDGs. It is now moving towards a synthesised wellbeing-focused dashboard to also allow for making and justifying financial budgetary decisions. Different ministries are asked more and more to relate budget requests with wellbeing results. This also serves to move from budgets based on historical expenditure to performance-based budgeting based on sound wellbeing investment cases and impacts.

Finland. Following its membership of WEGo, Finland's government has formally adopted an "economy of wellbeing" approach, integrating wellbeing as a core objective in its policy making. This framework is built on the premise that social and environmental wellbeing are not just desirable goals but essential drivers of economic success. Finland has been one of the first countries to trial a Universal Basic Income (UBI) and has proposed the introduction of a four-day work week. The Finnish UBI trial showed that guaranteed income can improve life satisfaction and wellbeing. While employment effects were minimal, recipients reported higher wellbeing, reduced stress, and better financial stability, making this experiment a significant case study in how financial security can enhance mental health and resilience. A Steering Group on the Economy of Wellbeing started its work in February 2021 and prepared the Finnish National Action Plan for the Economy of Well-being, which was launched in March 2023. The National Action Plan includes five key directions for promoting the Economy of Wellbeing between 2023 and 2025, namely:

- The preparation of a governance model for the economy of wellbeing
- An examination of how wellbeing monitoring can be integrated more prominently in the decision-making power of the state, regions and municipalities
- Development of impact assessments and building capacity in this area
- Work to influence the EU, including through the European Semester
- Strengthening inclusion.

Finland has also developed a range of dedicated tools to keep sight of long-term societal goals in policy. For instance, the Committee for the Future in Finland's Parliament as well as the Government Report on the Future (a cross-governmental effort prepared by the Prime Minister's office once every electoral term and supported by the ministries' joint foresight working group) are both mechanisms that date back to 1993 and have developed a culture of long-term, cross-silo thinking in Finnish society and politics.

TAKEAWAY

Once GDP, and hence financial capital, is recognised as a means to a meaningful end, Purpose-Driven Governments can govern the economy so that this finance can be strategically deployed to drive long-term wellbeing for all and prevent harm to it. Several countries are already implementing innovative Wellbeing Economy fiscal policy.

REALISE

When governments shift from Logic 1 to Logic 3, they unlock a range of benefits that, in turn, accelerate progress. This section will draw from the personal insights of macro level purpose-driven leaders who are instrumental in taking their nations on this journey. These represent just a small proportion of the leaders around the world helping their countries realise the benefits of becoming Wellbeing Economies.

REALISE 1: Enduring direction

How do we achieve a sustainable world when governments change all the time and appear to act in their own self-interest? This is a fundamental issue that the shift to a Logic 3 Wellbeing Economy, governed by Purpose-Driven Governments is well placed to help overcome.

As will be addressed in Chapter 3, a move from Logic 1 to Logic 3 governance changes the nature of the goal from being abstract, self-interested and short-term to being meaningful, shared and stable. In a macro context, this means that a deep shared understanding between citizens and government can be developed about what it means to optimise for collective long-term wellbeing, whilst assuring the health of the underpinning resources, stakeholders and systems. This, in turn, enables citizens to embed and uphold a governance system that directs government action towards their long-term wellbeing – independent of political cycles or party ideologies which may have very different ideas about the best strategy to achieve this. This, in turn, supports a move away from relying on the next big "strategic idea" from the new president or set of ministers as the primary basis of accountability – and instead towards a more stable foundation of purpose and parameters that reflect what matters most for both current and future citizens.

As will be outlined in Chapter 3, the governing body is a collective decision-making entity. While its members may change over time, its core remit persists over time. Government is an organisation, including civil servants, that carries out the governance remit given to them by citizens. Political parties step into this pre-set governance system. Making appropriate adjustments to it is one aspect of their role that in principle should not happen without explicit wish of the governing body (citizens). However, for the short time they are allowed to be in office it is useful to see their role as enacting the particular approach (strategy) to advancing and protecting the long-term wellbeing of the country. This is the strategic "mandate" that citizens have delegated to them via their vote. The persistent and grounded nature of the shared purpose, supported by quality governance, would help ensure that government decision-making remains aligned with the long-term wellbeing of citizens, in the context of a shared planet, despite any political upheaval or external shocks. This, along with citizen-led governance, would prevent parties from veering off course. The strategies of a particular government may vary in quality, but with a clear collective understanding of the maximising goal and foundational parameters, significant misalignment with society's long-term best interest is avoided.

Hence Logic 3 purpose-driven governments, running Logic 3 Wellbeing Economies offers a vital course correction. While long-term wellbeing for all may be the intent of many constitutions worldwide, the absence of shared governance literacy by citizens and governments alike – particularly as a multi-level practice that spans the self to the international – has prevented progress to it and in fact driven the opposite. It's no surprise that without this literacy, Logic 1 gradually came to dominate government priorities and take us way off course from the goal. We can no longer afford to let it guide the future. We need to embed long-term wellbeing for all in the heart of decision-making, through Logic 3 governance.

Pedro Saraiva from PLANAPP, an arm of the Portuguese government, explained to us that they are working towards clarifying the long-term wellbeing of Portugal as the common goal all can share, regardless of political party. As part of this, they initiated a *"citizen-focused effort to come up with a consensus on what Portugal should aim to be by 2050".* He explained: *"Of course, it will be a very high-level ambition, but that's the kind of compass … guiding what society we want to be by 2050. Then, everything we do in the shorter term should be aligned and inspired by that ambition."* He further shared some specifics of this governance system: *"You need to make sure you have a proper monitoring system in place and that you make things happen in reality. But based on a long-term, conceptual framework. So, we'll have a plan for 2040, another one for 2030. And then every year, we want to make sure that more and more of this alignment is reinforced."*

Pedro described how this is aligned with an emerging wellbeing-oriented accountability system. Whilst demanding at the beginning because government officials and entities were used to financial budgets and financial measures of success, he outlined how replacing these with wellbeing results is changing and shaping the foundation of how the government and public administration thinks and acts. Based on the positive feedback from citizens and other entities about these changes he thinks they may have passed a point where it might roll back with a new political cycle: *"I think entities and people take it for granted. So, it's not any longer a discussion about keeping these changes or not even across election cycles – that's very important. I believe that in these domains we should not change the foundational goals every four years."*

As we have described in detail in Chapter 1, what seems like a rational decision from a Logic 1 viewpoint, just isn't from Logic 3 – and vice versa. While people may take a while to adapt to a new way of seeing the world and solving problems, putting a meaningful, collective goal and parameters at the centre of the room creates a chain reaction. This is especially effective when this governance direction is encoded in hard law – which are universal governance parameters that are particularly enduring.

Jane Davidson is an example of a Macro level Logic 3 leader, working at the heart of the Welsh Government for decades to move the long-term wellbeing of current and future generations of Wales to become the explicit goal of government (along with key parameters for how it should be achieved). Success came with the "Well-being of Future Generations Act" (2015). This is a journey she outlines in detail in her 2020 book *#futuregen: Lessons from a Small Country.*[23] The approach Wales has taken has inspired the UN Secretary-General's proposal to appoint a Special Envoy for Future Generations as laid out in the annex to the Pact for Future Generations agreed by the UN General Assembly in New York in September 2024. In her discussions with us, Jane kept coming back to how the goal and parameters encoded in the Act naturally motivated Logic 3 thinking and acting over time. This is despite early protestations that making long-term wellbeing for all the goal was "utopian" or wasn't going to change anything.

For governments moving to Logic 3 and wanting to embed a durable governance foundation that can persist beyond their term in office, or for purpose-driven civil servants, there are a number of ways to create momentum. All organisations moving to Logic 3 have legal and non-legal mechanisms to embed durable yet adaptive governance systems. This starts with the core functions of direction, oversight and accountability as well as governance levers to further translate this into influence over cultural hardware, e.g. structures, processes, and artefacts as well as cultural software, or e.g. ways of thinking, feeling and acting. The hardware and software are intertwined. For example, as a result of the change in law, Wales famously created the role of a Future Generations Commissioner who serves as a protector of the wellbeing of future generations and assists public institutions in adopting a long-term perspective. While symbolically important and influencing cultural software, the role has a legal mandate to monitor and assess the extent to which public bodies are meeting their wellbeing objectives – thereby also enabling cultural hardware.

The emphasis on wellbeing that is long-term – spanning both current and ongoing generations – is enduringly central to the macro governance of indigenous economies. As Wakan Wahohipi Win outlined to us: 'The concept of the *"Seventh Generation Principle' in Haudenosaunee (Iroquois) governance ensures decisions consider their impact on seven generations into the future. This reflects indigenous knowledge systems in general – it isn't possible for us to make a collective decision that would not consider the impact of those decisions on the wellbeing of those coming after us."*

TAKEAWAY

A Logic 3 Wellbeing Economy – underpinned by purpose-driven government – establishes a foundation for stable, resilient governance that serves the long-term interests of all citizens and diminishes the influence of short-term political cycles.

REALISE 2: Citizen engagement

Creating the level of change in the "governance of government", as outlined above, could not happen without citizen debate and engagement to establish where common ground exists in how to achieve long-term wellbeing for citizens – in the context of the world. We can think of national citizens as the national governing body (and everyone a citizen of planet Earth). Therefore, if we are to deliver Wellbeing Economies that serve long-term wellbeing for all we need citizens to become governance literate and able to use that literacy to become fully involved in the governance needed. Statistics covering mainly G20 countries were published recently by Earth4All and the Global Commons Alliance.[24] This suggests that there is a very strong basis for more governance – literate citizenship. Their 2024 report found, for example, that for G20 countries: 59 per cent are "extremely or very worried about the state of nature today and 62% about the state in which we will leave nature for future generations". Furthermore "72% agreed that it should be a criminal offence for leaders of large businesses or senior government officials to approve or permit actions they know are likely to cause damage to nature and climate that is widespread, long term or cannot be reversed".

As discussed in Chapter 1, one consequence of Logic 1 has been the outsourcing of much of civic and personal life to the "market," where solutions to wellbeing challenges – and definitions of what is valuable – are now largely determined. This shift was by design – a key appeal of Logic 1 was its promise to reduce the need for civic deliberation over complex and often controversial questions about wellbeing and value. These, it was argued, could be efficiently revealed through market mechanisms.

This change has had important and often seemingly appealing democratic effects on civic life that are hard to see: no single authority could dictate the path to wellbeing; instead, everyone had a "vote" through their purchasing choices. Theoretically, money was available for anyone to attain if they worked hard enough, a notion that reinforced money as the currency of success, pride and social worth, and dictated that the poor deserved their lot because they must be lazy and worthless.

These effects of Logic 1 most probably helped avert global and national conflicts in some cases by externalising responsibility to "the market". For example, blame for the rising price of staple goods following the 1997/98 Asian currency crises could be attributed to "market forces" rather than the choices of individual leaders or governments, or even the investors behind the trades who were "just doing their jobs".

This very same mechanism also means that a Logic 1 market economy creates distance: moral, philosophical and physical. This, compounded by its size, speed and globalised nature, has had obvious effects on our ability to see and act as citizens, that is, to be engaged in the act of governing and holding to account those we delegate to (government). The comforts resulting from transforming natural and social assets into goods and services has also dulled the motivation to look further beyond to recognise the toxic consequences. Over time, the perceived lack of motivation for citizenship has naturally resulted in a lack of skill in it along with a lack of opportunity to exercise it. Of course, as caveated in the front of this book, this generalises the unique experiences of countries who have conditions provoking more or less citizenship. France is known for its active civic engagement and South Africa and others are still new democracies with an observable level of heightened civic engagement. What matters is that this Logic 1 consequence affects all countries in one way or another.

Moving to a Logic 3 Wellbeing Economy therefore brings the need for citizenship back into the room, and as a result acts to enable it.

REQUIRING CITIZENSHIP

A Logic 3 Wellbeing Economy restores true value to the heart of government by embedding long-term wellbeing for all as the central purpose of decision-making. When citizen wellbeing shifts from being a distant, assumed result of financial growth to becoming the strategic focus itself, the role of citizen wisdom becomes not just valuable, but essential to success. This transformation ensures that governance is no longer detached from the realities of people's lives but actively directed by their voices, experiences, and collective aspirations – which become embedded in the governance of the nation.

Jane Davidson, the ex-Welsh Minister, described to us how Logic 3 is motivating opportunities for real citizen engagement: *"The 'Wellbeing of Future Generations Act' forces collaboration, because you have to involve citizens about whom decisions are being made, which is forcing the government into Logic 3 way of thinking and acting and I think that's incredibly exciting. And that's exactly what I wanted the Act to do. I wanted the Act to force good behaviour."* Jane described to us how she is both hopeful yet realistic about how far there is to go for citizens to be central to governance of government: *"Seeing citizenship as a reciprocal relationship is really new to democratic-elected governments of whatever form. It doesn't matter whether you're in a proportional representation system or first past the post; it's about the fact that you understand that old-fashioned parliamentary democracy is no longer enough for democracy. So active citizenship becomes the big democratic hope ..."* She went on to say: *"I don't think we're anywhere near far enough on in those discussions ... but what's really interesting to me is, because of wellbeing now being at the heart of the Welsh constitution, for the first time, the government actually wants to do deliberative engagement, it has questions it wants to ask and have answered by understanding citizens."*

For many countries the foundational point of citizen engagement revolves around how it will measure success. This requires having at least a starting answer to the core question: what does it mean to achieve long-term wellbeing for citizens? For Iceland, formally becoming a Wellbeing Economy government was a reflection of the country's desire for change. Dora Gudrun Gudmundsdottir, Director of Public Health, Directorate of Health in Iceland, Founder and Chair of Wellbeing Economy Forum, explained to us that when the Icelandic government became a Wellbeing Economy government, they founded a committee on wellbeing indicators with representatives from each political party in the parliament. This committee decided to have a survey among the citizens about what was most important for their wellbeing. Dora elaborated: *"Rather than the way some governments decide upon a specialist or expert or derive the best way to measure well-being, they engaged citizens, asking them 'what is most important for you' using a survey. Then the indicators were chosen based on what citizens said was most important for their wellbeing. Based on these results, 39 objective wellbeing indicators were chosen as well as one subjective wellbeing measure. The indicators were chosen based on what citizens said was most important for their wellbeing."* The top scoring indicators included good health and healthcare, secure housing, job satisfaction, work–life balance, a healthy environment and having influence in their community.

ENABLING CITIZENSHIP

As Logic 3 has a need for citizenship, mechanisms are therefore logically created to enable citizens to influence how to best achieve their collective long-term wellbeing.

Decentralised decision-making governance systems are central to many indigenous peoples, with the aim of actively developing collaboration and decisions close to the area of concern. For governments moving to Logic 3, similar ways of making decisions, in line with the principle of subsidiarity, has been an organic step. Pedro Saraiva, Director of PLANAPP, which belongs to the Portuguese Centre of Government, explained to us how their move to Logic 3 went hand in hand with devolving decisions to the most local level appropriate: *"You need to make sure that you don't stay at the very high level because things happen in a very localised way ... So bringing the engagement of organisations and citizens is part of what needs to be done. In our case in Portugal, this happens in territories of a smaller scale, such as regions, or in municipalities at the very local level."* He went on to explain how they were giving away control to enable a citizen-led approach: *"We have been in touch with some NGOs in Portugal, which are very strong and we did agree that it's even better for them to lead certain citizen-driven initiatives ... Then, once they have a proposal of the wording of specific proposals, they will introduce them to different entities and parties in the Parliament. Then, once and if such proposals are approved by the Parliament, the Government will assure that they are fully deployed, with the support of different public agencies, and the help of PLANAPP."*

Because in Logic 3 it is recognised that success cannot be achieved without understanding and shaping the constructed realities of citizens that shape wellbeing consequences, new engagement infrastructure becomes vital. This starts with recognition of the current lack of citizenship trust and infrastructure that is a natural consequence of Logic 1 governance. Jane Davidson reflected on the impasse of the status quo and the change that the country's move to Logic 3 is making: *"Governments historically consult and, and if we're brutally honest, they know what they want when they consult. So, they frame the question in the way that they want the answer. And even if people put in different answers, if they've got enough people giving them the answers they want, that gives them the confidence to do that. So, consultation can contribute to citizens not trusting government. In terms of government engaging with citizens over what it should do on behalf of citizens, then citizens have to feel that whatever process they're involved in – when they're being asked to put time and effort into considering something, that their views have been heard and acted upon."*

She went on to explain her view on where we have ended up after the erosion of trust: *"I've looked at polling over the years, and don't think trust in government will have ever been as low as it probably is generally in the Western world as it is now. And that is because of our current economic systems and the related disengagement from citizens."* She further outlined the difference that moving to a Wellbeing Economy government has had: *"We are starting to build citizens into the process in a range of ways but specifically through our five ways of working, which are written into law, thinking long term, being preventative, collaborating, integrating outcomes and particularly to involve people about whom decisions are being made. This change in how decisions are made has started pushing serious discussion and research about all sorts of deliberative democracy mechanisms."*

If people's wellbeing is put first then change can happen in a few years. Cyber hacker turned Taiwanese government Minister, Audrey Tang, helped raise trust and approval in government from 10 per cent to more than 70 per cent in 2014–2023, against the backdrop of rapid decline across most of the rest of the world. She did this through "humble government", focused on improving collective wellbeing and seeking active citizen participation. Jon Alexander, author of the 2023 book *Citizens: Why the Key to Fixing Everything Is All of Us*,[25] explained how for him Taiwan's approach in particular exemplifies what can be achieved when government approach citizens with a very different mindset: *"Taiwan, a nation of 23 million people, was pretty much the only nation in the world to start from the perspective that the best way to get through COVID would be to get everyone involved. They saw citizens as sources of ideas and energy and resources. They publicly announced three principles for the response, which roughly translate as fast, fun and fair. They set challenge prizes for the tech community to create apps for vital tasks like tracking availability of personal protective equipment. And they even set up a phone line where anyone could ring in with ideas on how the country's response could be better, with ideas coming through to improve the national response from all sources, even young children. The result was arguably the most successful COVID response anywhere in the world: the second lowest death rate after only New Zealand, and they never went into full lockdown"*. The approach taken by the Taiwanese government reflects a Logic 3 'guide-and-co-create' approach to value creation, which supports Purpose-Driven Organisations, as outlined in Chapter 3.

What this points to is, as demonstrated in a variety of case studies in Rebecca Solnit's 2010 book *A Paradise Built in Hell: The Extraordinary Communities That Arise in Disaster*, that when given half a chance to be purposeful, humans will come alive to this deep drive.[26] And further, that this drive, when unleashed from Logic 1 governance systems and enabled within Logic 3, provides the basis of all the change we seek. The Canadian politician Ryan Turnball attests to this: *"I have continually witnessed in my work, that communities, when they come together, when people think innovatively, when they're unchained and can get outside of the power dynamics that seem to prevail and hold them down or hold them in their place; when they can relinquish the system holding them back, then they're able to think really creatively and start to conceive of a new system."*

TAKEAWAY

A Logic 3 Wellbeing Economy depends on citizen engagement to govern government and design and deliver the best approaches (strategies) for collective long-term wellbeing. In a virtuous cycle, purpose-driven governments create the necessary governance infrastructure to enable citizens to play a full role in government decision-making.

REALISE 3: Purpose-Driven Organisations

The realisation of a Wellbeing Economy relies on a Purpose-Driven Government. At the same time it relies on the understanding that an economy is only as good as the organisations that enact it. If a government wants to drive a Wellbeing Economy then it cannot do this without being a Purpose-Driven Organisation itself – and without enabling and governing Purpose-Driven Organisations of all kinds, operating across all sectors. Transformation of government and all other organisations to being purpose-driven not only drives wellbeing progress, but stops the harms created by governments that support profit-maximising companies that do harm – often with their blessing, support or active negligence. This was starkly demonstrated in the case of South Korea, when the "mass exportation of children" by private agencies that were driven by profit was enabled by government.[27]

For some countries, support for Purpose-Driven Organisations is being felt as a consequence of the overall journey to being Wellbeing Economy governments. Dora Gudrun Gudmundsdottir explained: *"The fact that Iceland became a Wellbeing Economy government is in line with values of the nation, which embraces peace, equity, welfare and wellbeing. Being a Wellbeing Economy Government has most likely had an indirect impact on organisations, including businesses, in Iceland but more work is needed to support them directly towards aligning with a Wellbeing Economy – which will then lead to more wellbeing for both people and the planet."*

Strong active change is now required – and governments have the power to introduce laws which can change the operating environment very quickly.

Where purpose-driven government leaders meet Purpose-Driven Organisational actors, significant success can result. Eric and Paolo, who we discussed previously, created the Purpose-Driven Organisation NATIVA and through that worked hand-in-hand with government officials to create a change in law to bring Italy's version of the Public Benefit Act. They realised: *"The typical legal governance structure is an impediment, a hurdle, an obstacle to that positive energy to be expressed, you know, because, of course, governance of the last century, was built for different reasons. And so, if you liberate the energy, the entrepreneurs come together, they start to feel that they need also to have a specific path, governance, structures and models to unleash that energy."* After successfully supporting the government to change the law, they became the first Benefit Corporation in Europe. They then became the first BCorp in Italy. BCorp is a standard designed and certified by BLab which makes use of the Public Benefit Act where available. This legal model obliges inclusion of social and environmental reasons to exist, alongside the default obligations to the company and shareholders. Following their lead, NATIVA estimates that there are now almost 20,000 BCorps across the world, with 5000 in Italy – so many that if all Italian Benefit Corporations were a single company, they would be the largest in the country, counting over 200.000 employees and a revenue of €60+ billion.

The case of Italy is emblematic of law to support organisations to move from Logic 1 towards Logic 3 – or at least not force them into Logic 1 as is normal across the world at the moment. A summary of the emerging legal situation in how governments globally are starting to support purpose-driven legal forms can be found in the paper (Phase 1, Part 2) published as part of the multi-year University of Cambridge Institute for Sustainability Leadership and DLA Piper research collaboration that Victoria was part of.

Actors in some countries are pushing governments to go further. The Better Business Act in the UK backed by 2800 companies seeks to ensure Logic 1 is not possible. Instead they seek to ensure that governance allowing Logic 2 is the minimum condition – and are enabling progress towards Logic 3. However, if we want to align with a sustainable future, it is important we work together to urgently push for changes to full Logic 3 and a phase out of BAU organisations altogether, as outlined in the University of Cambridge Institute for Sustainability Leadership working paper Unleashing Governance that Victoria authored. Hybrid corporate forms, also known as "Zebra" companies, where profit maximisation and purpose maximisation sit alongside each other, in effect, create two very different "gods" which need to be prioritised. This is a less-than-ideal basis for governance of any kind – and in a world where Logic 1 dominates, when they clash, profit is likely to be the victor. During the current transition that requires those holding power (e.g. shareholders or governments in the case of some state-owned enterprises) to rescind that power for the good of everyone, hybridity may be necessary. But time is short. We need to help move organisations to full Logic 3 governance where tensions can be relieved and the full power of organisations can be unleashed in service of a Wellbeing Economy and, through that – long-term wellbeing for all.

As the next chapter will outline in detail, we are on the cusp of an international consensus on what an organisational governance system fully aligned with long-term wellbeing for all should look like. This framework will provide Macro-level leaders with the clarity and tools needed to move towards Purpose-Driven Organisations (including goverments) as the norm and to be part of co-creating new forms of this norm moving forwards. Without policies and action that enable Logic 3 organisations and put a halt to Logic 1 organisations, it won't be possible for the Wellbeing Economy intent to be translated into reality and therefore not possible for us to attain long-term wellbeing for all (sustainability).

TAKEAWAY

A Wellbeing Economy is realised through Purpose-Driven Organisations and Logic 3 purpose-driven governments will ensure a swift transition to becoming well governed Purpose-Driven Organisations and making this kind of organisation the norm.

CHAPTER 3

MESO

Leading for Purpose-Driven Organisations

● ● ●

If we want a sustainable world, supported by a Wellbeing Economy aligned with this, then organisations need to be governed for long-term wellbeing for all. This means organisations need to do more than just not harm our resources and people. Reversing harm has been a dominant narrative of sustainability discussions. However, to solve our issues and unleash the human enterprise required, we need organisations that exist to *drive* our wellbeing, while also not harming our resources in the process. This is what Purpose-Driven Organisations do. They exist, not to serve themselves and their stakeholders, but to ultimately serve all stakeholders (long-term wellbeing for all), via a specific, ambitious, and measurable contribution to this ultimate goal – and to ensure that the basis of this wellbeing is protected, regenerated and enhanced in the process. They do this through routine decisions that are created and held in place by a Logic 3 governance system.

Purpose-Driven Organisations, including purpose-driven governments that govern the economy, are therefore both the rationale for, and the life blood of, a Wellbeing Economy. It could be argued that Purpose-Driven Organisations have been around as long as human organisations have – people coming together to do something specific that betters the wellbeing of the collective over the long-term. However, since BAU Logic 1 took the world down an accelerated path of unsustainability, a more conscious design of the organisational governance that can assure collective benefits has become necessary. Despite the inevitable distortion from Logic 1 and 2 organisations, the increasing imperative for urgent change has helped progress purpose from an intuitive, fragmented global response, to an increasingly supported worldwide umbrella solution that unites organisations of all types. After all, why wouldn't we want every organisation that is given access to shared resources to fully align with our collective long-term wellbeing?

Governed well, Purpose-Driven Organisations ensure positive value is generated and protected while maintaining the freedom to learn from mistakes and experiment boldly and transparently through a shared vision of a governance system that has the best chance of making the optimal decisions for long-term wellbeing for all – one that puts this problem at the centre of the room. Otherwise, we will continue to design and use important tools like AI in ways that do not actually contribute to long-term wellbeing for all – or make it worse. "What is the purpose of humanity?" was presented by Bill Gates as the most critical question we need to answer in the closing section first episode of the Netflix documentary *What's Next?* He was reflecting on AI and what it could do for, or to, us. As an earlier innovator of powerful technology, Einstein also reflected at his UCT speech in 1931: "Why does this magnificent applied science which saves work and makes life easier bring us so little happiness? The simple answer runs: because we have not yet learned to make sensible use of it."

We are now on the cusp of a global consensus about precisely how a Purpose-Driven Organisation is governed with the right problem at the centre and guardrails at the edge. The forthcoming international standard in Purpose-Driven Organisations (ISO 37011) is intended to both complement, and extend to its logical conclusion, important legacy initiatives like Public Benefit Corporations and the associated BCorps standard, which have helped move the world towards being purpose-driven. ISO 37011 will specify the current global view on how to govern for a sustainable future. In revealing what Logic 3, Purpose-Driven governance looks like, it will shine a light on how this diverges or overlaps with Logic 1 or 2 governance. Having this shared clarity, and hence accountability, is crucial if we are to avoid the 'Groundhog Day' effects we have been stuck in until now. Sustainability concepts such as CSR and the triple bottom line were all designed to address the problems of Logic 1, but in not doing this directly or deeply enough, inevitably became co-opted by this very system. Hopeful proponents end up distancing themselves from these then watered-down concepts and new ones are created in their wake (or given new names such as "broad versus narrow CSR"). John Elkington famously "withdrew" his Triple Bottom Line concept due to misinterpretation and dilution that led to superficial applications rather than meaningful change.

It is our assessment that the concept of Purpose-Driven Organisations is one that finally challenges the very heart of the BAU system and its core self-interested profit motive. In tackling the very heart of the problem, purpose represents a necessary paradigm shift in the heart of organisations and their governance. To navigate this transformation, we must feel both empowered by the potential of these changes and realistic about the significant shifts required in organisational structures and leadership capabilities.

This chapter explores what it means to make decisions as a Logic 3 Purpose-Driven Organisation. It explains that to become Purpose-Driven Leaders shaping Purpose-Driven Organisations, we must RETHINK the organisation's point of being – shifting from financial CAPTURE to wellbeing CREATION; move beyond a focus on STRATEGY and recognise quality GOVERNANCE as the overarching decision frame; and we must transition from market RESPONSE to actively MAKING markets. We need to RETOOL using three essential frameworks: International ISO standard in Governance of Organisations (ISO 37000); the national (PAS 808) and forthcoming international (ISO 37011) standards in Purpose-Driven Organisations; and finally the Evolved Value Framework (EVF), which defines six purpose-driven marketing principles. We then outline how, when implemented effectively, the organisational-level benefits of Purpose-Driven Organisations are numerous, including COHERENCE, CREATIVITY and COMMITMENT.

RETHINK 1: From financial capture to wellbeing creation

- "How can we reduce the cost of X so that customer group Y can access it more easily?"

- "How can we create more positive impact X in market Y through a different product or service?"

- "Organisation X is becoming really effective at delivering impact X, and we can't compete. If they can create the impact better than we can, should we exit that market and do something that needs us more or consider joining forces?"

These are not normal questions for the average Logic 1 organisation, but they are normal questions for a well-governed Logic 3 Purpose-Driven Organisation.

This is because Logic 3 leaders have fundamentally reframed their understanding of what organisations are for – from vehicles for financial value extraction to systems for innovating wellbeing value generation. With this logic, markets are no longer battlegrounds for out-competing others, but as places of opportunity and collaboration for generating and amplifying wellbeing in a financially viable way. The problems of governance, management, communications etc. don't go away, but they look different and the strategies to deal with them are different – and more plentiful.

It is easy to think that Logic 1 organisations are also set up to create real value that makes people's lives better, but in reality, as set out in Chapter 1, this is, at best, a by-product of financial capture for the organisation's benefit, or because of purpose-driven individuals who are temporarily given bandwidth in a badly governed system.

Logic 1 upholds the mantra of 'customer is king' – but only, of course, *in order* to maximise financial income. People's preferences will be 'discovered' and 'supplied' only to the extent that products and services, pricing, promotions and distributions channels don't forfeit this profit potential. And if generating harm creates a profit, then there are very few decision-making constraints for an organisation to 'leave this profit on the table' and do something else.

In Logic 1, the very core of the language reflects the primacy of money. When we say 'economic' we mean money, when we talk of business case we often mean 'case for maximising money'. When we say 'value' in a Logic 1 system, we usually mean money or a pathway to it. This has infiltrated all types of organisations, where normal questions (implicit or explicit) in universities, government and business organisations alike, includes:

- 'What's the maximum we can persuade customers to pay for this service?'
- 'Can we reduce the quality / size of the product without customers noticing?'
- 'How can we increase our share of this market in the next quarter?'
- 'How can we lobby to stop changes that will harm our income?'

These questions reveal how deeply financial value dominates decision-making in Logic 1. The thinking of a Logic 3 organisation is starkly different.

ANCHORING TRUE VALUE

Decision-makers in Purpose-Driven Organisations see a market-place of potential wellbeing creation, not a market of potential financial value capture.

Dr. Tayba Hatimy, a former dentist from Mombasa, Kenya, whose near-death experience inspired her to set up a purpose-driven organisation to tackle the city waste management issue, encapsulates this: *"When I came in with the idea of venturing into waste management because of my near-death experience because of illegal dumping of waste, everybody was telling me you are crazy. You cannot leave the hospital to go into waste management? First of all, what woman ventures into waste management. You studied dentistry. How can you leave a career to want to go and save people just because you almost died because of illegal waste dumped on a roundabout?"*

It didn't take Tayba long to identify that Logic 1 was at the heart of the issue and that it required a Logic 3 enterprise to really make the right change. *"I realised that the root problem was that waste management was all about making money. It was all just about profit, whether you are having outbreaks of cholera or chikungunya – a disease that was not here in Mombasa before, but it came about because of waste staying in open areas for a really long time in communities. When I approached the business world, people were like, 'Yeah, let's do this, but only if we can make a large amount of money'. And that's when I realised we have a problem. Why can't you venture into waste management because you want to make a positive difference in the community? Instead, the answer of why do you want to venture into waste management was – because we're going to make money. So, I decided, we're going to be a purpose-driven company."*

Her company Baus Taku is systematically shaking up the world of waste management in her country and beyond. It's making big headway in changing how waste is processed and who benefits with enough financial income to drive the purpose, pay the bills and meet stakeholder expectations, but not forfeiting innovation for strategic decisions that would instead maximise profits. A chosen purpose can, and should, evolve and while Baus Taku's company's purpose was originally to solve the waste problem, speaking with Tayba it was clear that this is moving to a core parameter that guides strategy. Instead, the purpose of the company has become about empowering local women with the skills and independence from earning and being waste processing entrepreneurs in their own right. Resolving the waste industry has become a means to a different meaningful end.

Similarly, the Gates Foundation and their Gavi Alliance have shaken up the entire vaccine market, including how incumbent companies innovate, price and distribute. By pooling and leveraging their financial capital, they were able to purchase vaccines in large volumes at reduced prices, which they then passed on to end users. Crucially, their distribution strategy was driven by medical need, not profit. This approach fundamentally disrupted the Logic 1, profit-first model, where vaccines were typically sold at high prices to recoup costs quickly, often delaying access for those most in need by a decade or more, if they became available at all.

A similar shift was championed by Michelle Obama, who launched a Purpose-Driven initiative to challenge the food industry to enter a "race to the top" – prioritising children's nutrition over profit margins. These examples illustrate how Logic 3 organisations redefine markets by putting long-term wellbeing at the centre.

MAKING THE LAW USEFUL

Conventional corporate law, like the UK's Companies Act, instruct their directors to serve two stakeholders: the organisation itself and through that, its members (shareholders) – while not giving a clear priority to either. While financial benefit is not explicitly mandated to be the goal of these entities, it is almost universally assumed that it is. Benefit Corporations, (discussed earlier), and other "hybrid" constitutional forms, extend and start to challenge the Logic 1 foundation by requiring them to specify an "other serving" benefit. This supplements the default Logic 1 emphasis on financial self-interest, requiring the organisation to work out how to trade off these two fundamentally different goals so both can be considered to have been "maximised". In most cases, however, the law implies that organisations are owned by their members, for the benefit of their members. We say "implies" because, as discussed in Victoria's University of Cambridge Institute for Sustainability Leadership paper "Unleashing Governance", legal experts show that it is only in the US Delaware case law that the obligation to put the financial interests of shareholders first.[1] Juan Diego Mujica Filippi, a purpose legal expert and employee of NATIVA explained to us: *"The 'shareholder primacy' assumption is in fact one normative view of a possible interpretation of the law by judges. It is this global norm, fuelled by the fear of legal judgement that drives boards of directors to pursue profit maximisation for shareholders in decisions.' He went on to outline: 'We treat this interpretation as if it's normal – which isn't surprising, given that much of the pre-1970s reality has been systematically erased by corporate practice and legal decisions. However, this way of governing organisations is actually quite recent."*

For a cooperative or partnership, members are the organisations or individuals that, in effect, run the organisation; for others, employees are the members. Like with publicly listed companies, these "owners" are considered to be part of the organisation, not something outside.[2] In all cases, this positions the reason the organisation exists – its innovative goal – as benefitting itself. In other words, other than a few specific legal forms where a third party can be the focus, we assume that organisations exist to benefit themselves, normally financially – we generally assume they are not, or should not, be concerned about maximising value for others.

REAL ACCOUNTABILITY

If we want fast, effective change then we need to give up "pragmatically" trying to tweak a system set up to financially serve itself and its stakeholders align with the long-term good of the collective. Instead, we need to set up the governance of organisations to be accountable to directly innovating for and protecting long-term wellbeing for all.

The British Standard in Purpose-Driven Organisations (PAS 808), the precursor to ISO 37011, makes this foundational point, – which is expressed in its first principle as: "Long-term wellbeing for all people and planet (sustainability) is the anchor for the purpose of a Purpose-Driven Organisation and hence the ultimate frame for all Purpose-Driven Organisation decision-making. This means that all people (including future generations) and our planet, are the ultimate beneficiaries and current society is considered to have ultimate control rights over a Purpose-Driven Organisation on behalf of all people and planet, even if these rights are devolved, e.g. to a board of directors of an organisation."

The organisation then, in having the right to access and transform shared resources that are part of one global ecosystem that all generations of life rely on for wellbeing, is ultimately owned by, and in service of, all life forever – a collective that is represented by the current generation who become the rights-holders.[3] Recognising this core foundation is especially important if an organisation is allowed to benefit from the right to distance itself from harms made (e.g. limited liability for directors and no liability for financial investors). This, by extension, requires governing bodies to be entirely accountable to the stated purpose and stated parameters – which includes ensuring its contribution to the health of the stakeholders that it relies on and affects and be independent enough from ALL other stakeholders to do this optimally.

For true accountability and value creation to happen, being purpose-driven must become far more than stating a general ambition. It depends on a shared, precise and measurable understanding of the wellbeing value that an organisation exists to optimise. Without this clarity, the oversight of success, including continuous improvement as well as the accountability for it, is impossible. This level of governance quality and precision is the leap in leadership we need to make together. Without that, even the most well-intentioned purpose-driven efforts risk moving forward in constantly shifting sand.

Too often, we rely on flexible and aspirational terms like "sustainability", "flourish", "good", "responsible", "regenerative" or "prosperity" – without clarifying the common terminal value they imply: long-term wellbeing for all. When this value remains obscured, and detached from organisational governance, it is not possible to properly evaluate alternative approaches (strategies); accountability weakens, and engagement risks becoming superficial or confused. This "blurriness" is helpful to smooth over tensions or invite people to the discussion because it allows us to feel we agree on far more than we actually might. However, given the urgency and magnitude of transformation required we are dependent on united action that we can hold to account.

Practically, the shared language about value creation inherent in the standards on Purpose-Driven Organisations, gives us a collectively negotiable anchor to consider, debate, tradeoff and decide the merits of various strategic options as they present themselves – and to design appropriate ways of justifying and being accountable for them to those affected by them.

This precision, in turn, allows us to properly assess current legal, financial and all other systems that hold Logic 1 governance in place and then challenge them with practical suggestions for change. In this way, barriers can be removed and these systems can actively enable the governance behaviours required.

This is likely to provoke the question: perhaps we only need one purpose-driven umbrella legal form for all organisations? To ensure a sustainable future is embedded across all organisations that access shared resources, it would be logical to establish a single, standardised commitment within the constituting documents of any organisation. This could be grounded in the conceptualisation of organisational purpose that will be established in ISO37011. This could be similar to that currently in PAS 808 – "to exist to achieve an optimal strategic contribution to the long-term wellbeing of all people and the planet and to make a fair and adequate contribution to the healthy functioning of the social and environmental systems that underpin long-term wellbeing for all people and the planet". From there other specific legal forms may be necessary, but this foundation, and governance system, unites them all.

The anchor for accountability is the purpose itself. No one organisation can ensure long-term wellbeing for all. Hence, an organisation can only work for its best contribution to it – although you would be forgiven for thinking otherwise when reading the many organisational purposes that in essence repeat the meta-purpose, e.g. "to create brilliant sustainable lives for everyone, forever". This is not strategically specific enough to be the basis of a governance system.

A Purpose-Driven Organisation justifies to society as a whole a specific reason for existence and the impact that is expected to ensue: Why is this the thing that most needs doing? Why is the organisation the one to do it? Why is this a good use of collective resources? It also needs to give a justification that it can achieve this purpose through an operating model that will not harm long-term wellbeing for all in the process – even if not immediately but through a governed transition plan. Delegated national committees, citizen's jury's or even carefully designed AI could be utilised to decide if, on the basis above, an organisation should exist. It makes this organisational purpose the focus of the governing body – achieving the purpose, within the parameters, is what the governing body exists to direct, oversee and what they are publicly accountable to achieve.

This is not entirely new. Any organisation's incorporation is effectively approved by a nation. This approach, described earlier, also merely effectively modernises, globalises and standardises how the first organisations were given the right to exist. As Colin Mayer outlined in his book *Prosperity*, historically, sovereign rulers decided if a company could exist and access resources and rights, based on a justification that it was of benefit to the nation.[4] This also conforms with the concept of the theory of the common good of the firm, as summarised by Alberada and Sison in 2020, which states that organisations, including businesses, exist to act in common for the common good, they have a shared goal and support meaningful work.[5]

BEYOND "ALL STAKEHOLDERS"

It is common for those working for a sustainable future to talk of the need to 'create value for all stakeholders'. While this is the ultimate "meta goal" (if we consider all stakeholders to be everyone that is affected by, or affects, the organisation), if we want real change, we need far greater precision – both in terms of what we mean by value and particularly in how we specify stakeholders in relation to the governance of decision-making. An organisation *could* choose to define its maximising goal as "serving all stakeholders", positioning this as its organisational purpose. However, this approach to being purpose-driven, though admirable, presents several fundamental challenges:

1. It could be seen as, in effect, repeating the meta-purpose of long-term wellbeing for all which no one organisation can achieve. If not then questions include: If it is some other kind of value to wellbeing, what is it? Achieved over what timescale? What happens to those that aren't stakeholders?

2. It is not easy to communicate and hence drive energy and creativity.

3. It is very hard to govern and drive useful results. Michael Jensen, a Harvard-based business professor has claimed "it is logically impossible to maximise in more than one dimension. Purposeful behavior requires a single valued objective function".[6] This means that the ability of an organisation to align with long-term wellbeing for all through enterprising efforts is hamstrung if all stakeholders

are its pinnacle goal. It should be noted this pinnacle goal can be as broad an umbrella as needed, containing sub-objectives, but there comes a point of abstraction where it isn't useful or governable.

4. It gives energy to the arguments that allowed Logic 1 to become so popular in the first place. Friedman was countering entrenched "managerialism" arguing that use of investor resources should not be decided opaquely between managers and governments based on "pet social projects". In being unclear about what and whose "values" were driving what decisions, a rationale for putting values entirely out of mainstream organisations was created. Purpose-Driven Organisations enable values to shape governance direction (purpose and parameters) precisely because they are clear, transparently embedded in the organisational purpose and parameters, anchored to our collective meta-purpose and therefore able to be governed.

Therefore, while all stakeholders (everyone), forever, are indeed the *ultimate* beneficiaries of Logic 3, an organisation must clearly define how its chosen purpose translates into:

- specific stakeholder(s) it is actively maximising specific value for,
- what kind of decision-making relationship it holds with other stakeholder groups, and
- what value it will or will not seek to protect for them in the process.

This goes beyond a list of categories of stakeholders like government, community, or customers. It overcomes the limitations of vague commitments to "engage stakeholders" that lack a rationale linking that engagement to actual decision-making and governance. Instead, a Purpose-Driven Organisation starts by identifying stakeholders based on their relationship with them: their obligation to them, or dependency on them. The British Standard details five specific stakeholder categories and outlines the logical basis for a Purpose-Driven Organisation's relationship with each. These categories will be detailed in the RETOOL section.

In summary, Purpose-Driven Organisations overtly change who and how they exist to serve. They move from serving themselves and investors with money they capture from markets, to serving an optimal strategic contribution to long-term wellbeing for all, through wellbeing value created in markets, and beyond – and of course making enough profits in the process to achieve this goal. This creates a new basis on which to govern and be held to account that is aligned with a sustainable future. In turn, this changes how an organisation regards and engages in markets. Purpose-Driven Organisations are strategically laser focused on creating and protecting value – real value anchored against the end goal of long-term wellbeing for all. With this biggest possible frame – translated into context – they are able to create maximum freedom to learn and adapt the "how" to the ever changing realities around them. Finally, the shared idea of the "marketplace" moves from being narrowly defined markets of potential financial value capture to expansive marketplaces of potential wellbeing creation. Leaders of Purpose-Driven Organisations don't stop trying to capture financial capital – they need enough money to run the show, and do it well – but they see money as a necessary "hygiene factor" for a decision, not the maximising goal.

TAKEAWAY

Well governed Purpose-Driven Organisations exist not to capture financial value for themselves but to do its best job to serve and protect collective long-term wellbeing. This is a fundamental shift in how an organisation views its role in society.

RETHINK 2: From strategy to governance

We have said a lot about governance, but here we delve one level deeper. The second big rethink in organisations, is to move from seeing strategy as the pinnacle decisions made in an organisation – to recognising that it is governance where the power over decisions really lies and where the initial and primary focus of change should be. Without directing energy primarily into changing the governance system, the existing system and resulting culture will continue to be an uphill struggle that even the most dynamic CEO and workforce can't fight against. As Catherine Wood, Chief Product, Marketing and Wealth Officer at the purpose-driven Canadian mutual, Coast Capital Savings, stated clearly: *"If you do not have governance structures that support change, you will be drawn back into Logic 1."*

Furthermore, it is essential to understand governance as something that extends far beyond the governing body, though it plays a unique and central role (to be outlined later). Governance is relevant to all employees and even external stakeholders and citizens who are part of the organisation's governance system. If you are involved in directing (e.g. setting goals and parameters), overseeing or ensuring accountability, then you are part of the governance system. This system nests from the governing body, which holds ultimate accountability for everything the organisation does, to all levels of organisational decision-making – and the stakeholders, including citizens, that govern organisations as a whole. As introduced in Chapter 1, all leaders wear two hats: a governance hat (directing, overseeing and ensuring accountability) and a management hat (planning, doing, checking and acting). This dual role even applies to the governing body itself, as it must both govern the organisation and manage its own operations as a governing body.

The current reality, however, is that most leaders are fixated on strategy – crafting and executing the "plan" for "doing" (i.e. enter X market in Y way, with Z resource and F suppliers) – rather than anchoring their work in a clear and robust governance frame that should guide strategy in the first place.

If you have ever worked in a typical organisation, you will recognise the elevated status given to strategy. The more senior you are, the more you are involved in "strategic" conversations and decisions. If you have a new idea then, if the organisation is even half well run, you will be required to justify this against the current strategy. When a new CEO or senior leader takes the helm, the defining question quickly becomes: *What's their strategy?* – because it often reshapes everything. Until they leave. Then, the cycle begins again. It's as if nothing exists beyond strategy – when, in fact, it should be strategy that follows governance, not the other way around.

As outlined in Chapter 1, strategy is simply the answer to the question: How do I optimally maximise the goal within the set parameters, given the dynamic reality I face? Therefore, these two elements – purpose and parameters – hold the real power in decision-making. And it is the governance system that determines and embeds them … or fails to. This is why strategy is often mistaken as the pinnacle of leadership:

when governance is weak or unclear, it is strategy that fills the vacuum. But without a clear governance direction, strategy is baseless.

In Logic 1 the ultimate goal and parameters are so deeply assumed to be about financial capital that they guide strategy across an organisation, but aren't explicit enough to be questioned or changed. Logic 3 leaders need to learn to re-question the basis of strategic tools that are *always* relative to the organisational goal and parameters. For example:

Risk – can only be understood in relation to achieving a goal within set parameters.

Strategy – is about achieving a goal within the set parameters.

Quality – is a measure of consistently and to a high degree, achieving a goal within set parameters.

Material – what material is what matters. For the organisation, what matters will be in relation to achieving its goal within its parameters, and for other stakeholders is will always be in relation to achieving *their* goal within their parameters.

When defined within a collective and in the understanding that our fates are intricately intertwined, then these concepts will need to be anchored to long-term wellbeing for all. With this, most vital, goal at stake, Purpose-Driven Organisations cannot afford murkiness in how they consider these and other important terms. Neither do they need to be opaque. Well governed Purpose-Driven Organisations have no reason to hide their maximising goal and parameters. In fact, the opposite. They will be emotionally attractive, as their reason to exist is based on tangible results that really matter to our collective future. Because of this, and the fact that the purpose persists over time, culture, meaning and expertise can all be built-up around the purpose in a way that Logic 1 would find hard, if not impossible. For example, the clarity and persistence of the goal and parameters means that stakeholders are enabled and empowered to invest in changes to their capabilities and process to better strategically support the organisation.

DEGREES OF FREEDOM

This brings us to the central reason why anchoring to a wide governance frame and not a narrow strategic response to it, is a core "rethink":

the agility it gives an organisational system to work as an adaptive learning system and solve the problems of long-term wellbeing for all without being hemmed in by outdated rules and structures.

The issues facing our collective long-term wellbeing are immense and getting tougher every day. By the time you finish reading this sentence, the optimal strategic response will be different. We could never really afford the problems created by rigid strategy that treats organisations like machines and not living systems, but now, more than ever, keeping a broad but appropriately aligned direction and letting the solutions adapt, is critical.

By going heavy on getting governance right, you can go much lighter on strategy and rules dictating specific behaviour to achieve it. Rather than try to force the route, by creating a clear, wide, shared and strong (but adaptive) frame for decision-making, the path to achieve it can be set free to be far more adaptive and innovative. Focusing on the broadest possible governance frame to guide collective dynamic strategy also tends to motivate and support flatter hierarchies that remain well governed yet adaptive. Here more decision-making groups anchor to the same organisational level goal and parameters, and are enabled to decide the best approach in situ – rather than there being many layers of nested translations between the organisational level and decision-makers on the ground.

There is no hard evidence to suggest that a particular number of layers or particular level of specificity of "rules" is universally "right" for Purpose-Driven Organisations. At the same time, given the worldviews and logic of Purpose-Driven Organisations, there is a notable shift towards asking:

- What are the minimum layers of translation of the organisational purpose and parameters required? *(The lower the number of layers of translation, the more decision-makers stay connected to what the organisation exists for and to their contribution to long-term wellbeing for all.)*

- How can I enable the highest levels of organic participatory structure that can strategically adapt to the external realities against the governance direction?

- How can I stay true to the principle of subsidiarity – where decisions are made closest to the consequences of them?

In his seminal book *Reinventing Organisations*, Frederick Laloux described Purpose-Driven Organisations as evolutionarily advanced "Teal" organisations tended to have flat hierarchies with few levels of strategic translation.[7] Purpose works better with a "governance over bureaucracy" mindset.

ENABLING MEANING

It's not just that strategy in Purpose-Driven Organisations can be more agile – it's that greater degrees of freedom allow them to tap into the deepest source of human motivation: the desire to live a meaningful life. We experience our lives as meaningful when we see evidence that we've improved someone else's life. This is the essence of purpose.

The work of well-known thinkers and researchers such as Mihaly Csikszentmihalyi, Daniel Pink, Edward Deci and Richard Ryan all point to how purpose underpins motivation and the rewards we get from feeling that we, personally, are doing a skilled job at it (mastery and autonomy).

Purpose-Driven Organisations therefore don't just benefit from creating governance systems that tend to naturally be more organic and participatory. They are also better equipped to benefit from these adaptive structures because the human spirit is unleashed and the human spirit is most welcome in Logic 3. It is not, however, welcome in Logic 1 organisations. Additionally, without a clear sense of goal and parameters, or where they are clear but uninspiring and not meaningful, Logic 1 organisations are naturally more likely to rely on hierarchy, rules and plans to drive action.

At the same time, while Logic 3 leaders need to ensure that inappropriate parameters don't create unnecessary rules, they should also recognise that constraints are the "mother of innovation" and not be afraid to create them where needed.

THE ART OF GOVERNANCE DESIGN

The ideal may be to have minimum layers of strategic translation – but where to draw the line of specificity and strength in governing those layers? Where does the benefit of autonomy end and issues of incoherence begin? The more specific and stronger the governance frame, the more compliance, consistency and accountability there is likely to be. However, simultaneously, there is less room to adjust if long-term wellbeing for all requires a different approach in that instance. The broader and looser the frame, the more degrees of freedom that employees and other stakeholders will have to make decisions to achieve the ambition,

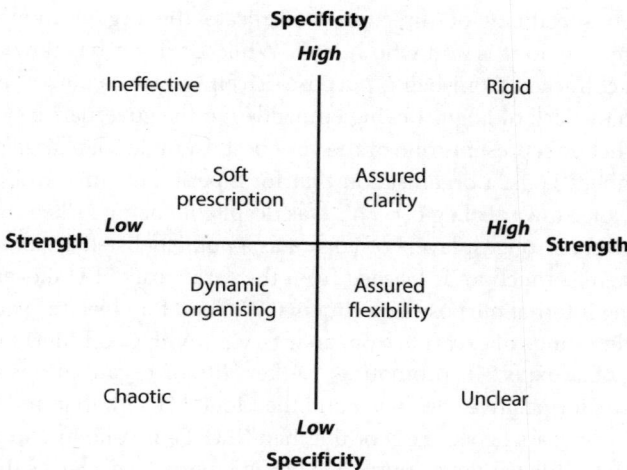

Figure 3.1 Specificity versus strength choices in governance

but the less clear and accountable it may be. This, and the resulting types of governance systems, can be seen in Figure 3.1.

Specificity. It may be tempting to think that using the largest possible governance frame is the best approach – why pin down any more detail at all beyond the optimal contribution to long-term wellbeing for all and the key parameters to ensure its health? Given the long list of critical social and environmental systems we need to regenerate and keep healthy, this resulting list of decision-making parameters will already be long, so why not stop there? There are in fact many reasons why the governance frame may need to be more specific than that.

First, the global economy and the organisations that run it are largely governed to be Logic 1. That means that a well governed Logic 3 Purpose-Driven Organisation is, in effect, creating a strong frame for decision-making that is misaligned with the world around it. This will create tensions and will require enough specificity in the governance system to guide behaviour through tough times when adaptation to the status quo would be easier, e.g. when an important client wants you to work on a project supporting an oil and gas project that is misaligned with your purpose or values (parameters).

Second, a strong culture and supported brand relies on stakeholders understanding the organisation's identity – and this relies on having enough specificity of direction to indicate the organisation's brand identity – who it is and who it isn't. While Unilever has now observably backtracked from being purpose-driven (which is almost certainly due to the lack of Logic 3 being embedded in the governance system), it nonetheless represents one of the very best examples of a large complex incumbent Logic 1 organisation that for a period of time, worked hard to advance towards Logic 3. This was despite its being locked into some of the very strongest layers of Logic 1 as a publicly listed organisation.

There is much to be learned from the early years of Unilever's wide-ranging internal purpose experiments. We therefore feel it is valuable to include a range of excerpts from an interview with Geoff McDonald who is a global expert in promoting the benefits of organisations creating contexts for positive Wellbeing and the Mental Health that underpins it. For many years he was part of the then-CEO, Paul Polman's, inner team that took Unilever on its journey to become purpose-driven as the Global Vice President HR for Marketing, Communications and Sustainability. He explains how important it was for Unilever to get the right level of understanding of purpose and what it meant: *"So you get this wonderful purpose, but then what does that actually mean? You have to translate that statement into strategic imperatives. I think it's only then that you get real coherence around the shared goal. So, being clear about how the brands were going to contribute to the goals / strategic imperatives was key."* Nakamura and Csikszentmihalyi (2002) state that to create the highly favourable conditions for "flow" (see the Realise 2 section of Chapter 4) requires clear proximal goals along with clear and fairly immediate feedback on what has been done at key stages of actioning.[8]

Strength. The strength of the governance frame depends on how well communicated and understood it is, how fast and hard digressions from it are treated and how often it changes. For a Logic 3 Purpose-Driven Organisation the governance frame needs to be strong enough to be both trusted and effective at consistently guiding behaviour that runs counter to a Logic 1 world, but not so strong that it cannot itself learn from and so adapt to its external, or indeed internal, context. It needs to act like a living system and not a machine, ensuring that there is a sense of co-ownership for the governance frame, that it is monitored by everyone for appropriateness to long-term wellbeing for all. It is also crucial that there are in-built mechanisms that allow stakeholders to raise concerns where strategic responses to the purpose and parameters result in actions that may run counter to long-term wellbeing for all.

Elinor Ostrom's work on self-organising systems, as outlined in Chapter 1, reinforced the vital insight: governance strength and specificity are not fixed – they are choices. Determining the most effective balance between flexibility and precision in a governance system is always a contextual art. Senior leadership in a Purpose-Driven Organisation should focus less on creating the right strategy and far more on designing a governance system that maintains the right balance of specificity and strength, depending on the context and the organisation's risk appetite. This, in turn, enables strategy-making to be made close to the consequences and be the dynamic, responsive process it needs to be. Strategy can be rethought, and rethought over and over again and those designing and enacting the strategy can be sure that the shared goal and guardrails around them will keep them on track to what they really care about. This applies to all organisations, including governments and global institutions.

Having this clear, strong (but adaptive) governance frame also reinforces psychological safety, not just by reducing the fear of harming the world around them but also enabling fewer rules that they may inadvertently contravene.

In focusing on governance, the role of the leader then becomes less about setting the path and the rules and more about holding the frame and keeping the system on track. The core question becomes: "Am I creating the conditions for those I lead to make sound, adaptive strategic decisions within the outermost boundaries of our organisational purpose, and ultimately in service of long-term wellbeing for all?"

TAKEAWAY

A well-governed Purpose-Driven Organisation enables stakeholders to anchor their strategy dynamically to a strong, clear governance frame. This positively transforms the clarity and agility of the organisation.

RETHINK 3: From market response to market making

"We're all about delivering safe sanitation through market development and market creation. So, it's not about just trying to sell affordable toilets. The market ecosystem does not exist, so we actually work with the community serving the base of the pyramid to build the value chain necessary to create this new market ecosystem for communities that are moving from open defecation to their first household toilet." This is a clear example Logic 3 thinking shared by Jin Montesano, Chief People officer at Lixil, about a sub-business called Sato. Sato is a Japanese housing technology company whose purpose is to "make better homes a reality for everyone, everywhere". Sato's purpose, in service to Lixil's, is to help achieve Sustainable Development Goal 6 (Clean Water and Sanitation) through delivering safe toilets to 1.3 billion people. Jin Montesano, a seasoned Purpose-Driven Leader, was instrumental in the founding of SATO at LIXIL and still oversees this growing business.

Market making, like for Sato and other Purpose-Driven Organisations, is just a natural approach. When markets are seen as places of potential wellbeing creation, armed with an intent to maximise wellbeing in them, and without all the baggage of BAU assumptions, then markets and marketing can take on new roles. They are seen as tools to co-create future modes of consumption in line with long-term wellbeing for all. Furthermore, the idea of what is a "market" expands beyond the formal market where money is exchanged for goods and services. Instead, markets are seen as any place where people are in relationship and engaged in formalised exchange – including where no money changes hands. This matters. The World Bank estimates that up to 70 per cent of employment is situated in the informal economy.[9] This explodes the size of the permitted remit of marketing to engage in creating long-term wellbeing for all compared to Logic 1 and 2 organisations. To become a Logic 3 leader for a Purpose-Driven Organisation is to make a conscious shift in how markets, marketing and human behaviour that shapes it, are regarded.

MARKETING AT THE HEART OF UNSUSTAINABILITY

If a company claims to be "sustainable", a good first question to ask is "show me your marketing" – and of course "show me how you govern your marketing".

As anyone who studied business will know by heart, if an organisation is to be successful, marketing must sit at its core. Marketing is what makes the intentions of the governance system turn into something real that changes the world. As Peter Drucker famously said: "The business enterprise has two – and only two – basic functions: marketing and innovation. Marketing and innovation produce results; all the rest are costs. Marketing is the distinguishing, unique function of the business."

In truth, marketing and innovation should be intricately connected. Marketing happens through decisions about what products and services are created, how they are made available, how they are priced and how promotions and communications bring awareness, understanding and action. Governance sets the direction and assures it, but it is marketing that centrally brings ideas, resources and stakeholders together to bring that direction to life. Or at least it should. Unfortunately, Logic 1 with its drive for short-term financial returns has largely relegated marketing to be an end of pipe sales tool too often synonymous with advertising. This not only limits its potential but also disconnects it from the deeper value marketing can create and protect if put to work in a Purpose-Driven Organisation.

As early as the 1970s, Philip Kotler, the godfather of modern marketing, proposed that marketing should be Societal Marketing – which meant that marketing should be focused on the long-term wellbeing of customers. Continuing this thread,[10] Victoria (and colleague's) "Characterising Marketing Paradigms" paper outlines how marketing is shaped by economic thinking and how marketing must urgently align with purpose and hence long-term wellbeing for all.[11] With BAU assumptions, markets are either places you sell to, in order to maximise financial income directly (make-and-sell marketing) or places you gather insights from and respond to in order to maximise financial income (sense-and-respond marketing). Both are arms-length from wellbeing value generation and protection and totally inadequate for driving a sustainable future. Sense-and-respond is the aspiration for most Logic 1 companies and represents the genesis of the more enlightened Logic 2 way of thinking – where it is recognised to be in your longer-term financial interest to serve customer demands so they buy more from you. From either perspective, competitors reveal ideas and winning strategies to be benchmarked against, manoeuvred against and replicated. Preferences are revealed by rational "consumers", and the role of organisations, through marketing, is to use customer insights to understand and respond to demand, but not manipulate it – which would be a distortion of the market.

In reality, attempts to manipulate how we meet our wellbeing in order to maximise profits are everywhere, but this intangible influence (that we can call brainprint) is not acknowledged or the costs counted.

To be fully purpose-driven requires rethinking marketing to be the core strategic capability that works sensitively and hand in hand with stakeholder to co-create markets, behaviours and outputs that can deliver on purpose-driven intent in a way that is viable (including financially profitable) over the long term. This means moving deliberately away from either a make-and-sell or sense-and-respond mode of marketing and deliberately moving to a purpose-aligned "guide-and-co-create" approach.

GUIDING POWERFULLY

Freed from the BAU assumption that people are self-interested, rational and capable of knowing and maximising their wellbeing, Logic 3 leaders are able to embrace a more accurate and evidence-based view of human nature. Research shows that humans are purpose-driven, complex, and inherently collaborative – whose level of wellbeing is underpinned by satisfying universal human needs. While these needs are universal, routes to achieve needs, and hence wellbeing, are infinitely varied. This is because these routes are dynamically "constructed" and "reconstructed" through "symbolic interactions" in a social context – where people actively shape and create the world around them through symbols in artifacts such as objects, gestures and language. This changes what we value – and what reach for when we feel lacking in something important. A compelling example comes from a study by Bauer and colleagues which showed that if you take a large sample of people and use the identity cue "consumer" rather than "citizen", then the results are significantly different. Even if just that one word changes. people will respond in ways that are significantly more self-enhancing, competitive and selfish.

Manfred Max-Neef provides a useful basis for understanding how this "constructed" view of human behaviour shines a light on the power that organisations have to shape our wellbeing through their marketing decisions.[12] Max-Neef was an economist who spent time living and researching a huge variety of communities across the world, in order to understand what unites us as humans, regardless of context. From this he established a powerful suite of universal human needs. These are needs that all humans require to be satisfied for wellbeing, but the way that these are satisfied – the particular modes of consumption and specific products and services – depends on the systems of symbolic meaning in a particular context. This is why the way people relax, for example sitting in a massage chair, meeting with friends, or running, will not be the same for each cultural context and can be very different to how we may have relaxed 100 years ago.

Max-Neef created a categorisation for how effective, ineffective or oppositional a market offering could be considered in meeting needs, and hence creating wellbeing. These range from *synergistic satisfiers* that meet more than one need without harming any others, to *pseudo-satisfiers* and *destroyers* which appear to meet a need but don't meet that need or destroy the very need they purport to meet. The important learning is that we have the innate desire to satisfy our universal needs and enhance our wellbeing but *how* we go about that is based on the narratives and connections (symbolic associations) we are exposed to.

Hence, through massive budgets, marketing's influence extends beyond the physical impact of its design, promotion and distribution influence to a profound influence on people's identities, society's power structures and cultural realities, and these, in turn, affect our physical world. Statista reports that global marketing and advertising spend exceeds \$1.6 trillion, the size of South Korean GDP and the 12th largest economy in the world. All messages have impacts. Therefore, what messages should be constructed, who will be exposed to them and how they do, or do not create wellbeing are powerful and vital questions that those that govern an organisation should be obliged to ask, and answer.

Through our faith in BAU assumptions, marketing has been allowed, and even encouraged, to disrupt our ability to achieve wellbeing for financial gain, without assuming responsibility for this. We can consider our understanding of wellbeing to be a social system at "the bottom of the triangle" (see Figure 1.1 in Chapter 1) that has been asset-stripped for profit. Direct harms on wellbeing such as reducing self-esteem, and indirect harms via the promotion of unsustainable consumption and patterns of valuing that underpin this, has almost no knock-on consequences for the organisations that create these effects and benefit in the short term from them.

The increasing raft of greenwashing legislation such as the EU Green Claims Directive and China's Guidelines for Environmental Claims in Product Advertising go some very small way to addressing these harms by trying to reduce the worst kinds of tangible misinformation. But the most powerful effects are subtle and intangible. Hence, it is hard to see how we will ever legislate our way out of a Logic 1 system that seeks ever more creative and subtle ways to fulfil the socially sanctioned motive of financial self-interest. Without a move to transparent, accountable, Logic 3 governance systems we will drown enterprise in red tape trying. This is another reason why moving to purpose-driven Logic 3 organisations will reduce bureaucratic costs – when we create the conditions for ethical behaviour, we need to spend less energy (and laws) addressing the consequences of the self-interest that we have institutionalised.

When we rethink the science of human behaviour, the damaging consequences of distorting meaning in society for profit become unmistakably clear. This directly confronts the moralised Logic 1 belief that simply making money through markets inherently results in good. Despite this, some powerful and vocal Logic 1 marketing industry leaders still hold true to business-as-usual assumptions that harm is not being created. They insist that marketing has no important effect on society or on persuading people to demand particular products and services; rather, it merely informs society of the choices available. Hence the only contributing role of marketing to sustainable future is to better inform people of the alternative ways of consuming. At the same time, a number of organisations are actively calling out the ungrounded nature of these assumptions and seeking real accountability in the marketing industry.

For example, the global organisation Purpose Disruptors have set out the case for Advertised Emissions, the carbon emissions that result from the uplift in sales generated by advertising, and argued that advertising agencies should take ownership of this pollution. In a similar vein, the UN's Race to Zero and Oxford Net Zero launched the

Serviced Emissions Principles to stem harm from the advice offered by an extended range of professional service providers, such as management consultants and lawyers. Organisations such as Clean Creatives are further pushing for change by shining a light on the raft of agencies who choose to work with problematic fossil fuel clients.

One of the first mainstream initiatives to recognise marketing's societal impact was the Unstereotype Alliance, launched in 2017 by Unilever, in collaboration with UN Women (who now convene it). This alliance focuses on eliminating harmful stereotypes in advertising – an important early step in acknowledging and addressing marketing's power to shape culture. A Logic 3 Purpose-Driven Organisation would go much further. It would understand potential harms across a wide range of areas. It would transparently use its influence over society's brainprint to advance its purpose, and embed this accountability within its governance system. Systematic auditing – not just of emissions, but of cultural and behavioural impact – would become a core part of oversight. This is the level of integrity and consciousness the future demands.

If all marketing decisions and related actions have an effect, then we need organisations to be intentional about the consequence on long-term wellbeing for all that its marketing decisions create or avoid – and oversee and account for this through governance.

CO-CREATING THE PATH, PROFITABLY

Seeking to create a positive future state (to actively "guide") is one thing, but ensuring an effective and appropriate approach is equally important. As demand for products and services that "do good" has risen, Logic 1 and 2 organisations have swept in to meet this, leading to claims of "green growth" and "doing well by doing good". This has resulted in beneficial market innovations in materials, processes and messaging – to a point. Once opportunities for quick financial gains and reputational rewards have been exhausted, these organisations are left with a choice. For those firmly in Logic 1 they often need to admit their 'green growth' ambitions have come to an untimely end. For organisations developing their enlightened self-interest (Logic 2) it will feel risky to retreat. Here such firms face a problem. Markets have been shaped by decades of Logic 1 marketing activity and governance systems. This creates a "wicked problem" – you want to build your income from more sustainable markets but the demand isn't strong or certain enough to make investment worthwhile instead of staying in safe market territory. This often leads to an "educate customers" approach – because "you can't go beyond what the customer demands".

This "educate customers" approach for Logic 2 firms also faces massive barriers making success unlikely:

1. Actively trying to change preferences is fundamentally anti-BAU because the preferences of customers are not supposed to be influenced (see Chapter 1). Because this tends to be sub-consciously understood, marketers merely have a nagging feeling that they shouldn't be trying to change people – something Rory Sutherland as chair of the Advertising Association famously exposed when he chastised the marketers for hiding their skills in preference manipulation – "I would rather be evil than a bad marketer" he proclaimed. The valid dissonance marketers feel holds back creative progress.

2. Changing markets is hard; it takes persistence and requires new collaborative efforts, therefore involving a whole range of risks that just don't apply to continuing to capture financial value from existing markets. This is the essence of Clayton Christensen's *Innovator's Dilemma* where incumbents find it hard to take risks that jeopardise privileged positions in markets they have hard-earned.[13] The extra risk will likely be judged as unnecessary by Logic 1 leaders, making it challenging to achieve and retain support from senior leaders and the governing body.

3. They may not have the levels of customer trust required – it takes a highly trusted organisation to be able to take customers on a journey to a place they haven't been before. If your primary motive has been financial self-interest then deep trust is not easy to create and sustain. Finally, and perhaps most significantly, the specific business-as-usual assumptions about humans being self-interested and rational make it impossible to create the step change in markets required, through truly excellent customer and citizen insights.

Therefore, the "educate customers" approach falls into trap in trying to tweak or break loose from Logic 1 short-termism – but without tackling the assumptions at the heart of BAU, it isn't feasible to move forwards as boldly as needed. The result: the ambition appears unachievable and the organisation drifts back to Logic 1.

Because Logic 3 organisations and their leaders are consciously free from BAU assumptions, as well as being motivated to take risks to solve problems that really matter, they approach markets differently. They can openly act on the existing evidence that identities, society, cultures, and hence markets, are constructed. They are then creatively freed to walk hand in hand with stakeholders to reconstruct them. In seeing existing markets as being socially and physcially constructed for profit maximisation, they recognise marketing as the act of dealing with this problem head on and making new markets – not responding or tweaking existing unsustainable ones.

This means that Logic 3 organisations will avoid another trap which is to, in effect, "make-and-sell for sustainability". An organisation can be purpose-driven in its intent but fail to adjust their marketing approach, including their view of human behaviour. As a result, they focus on internal expertise to devise the "best solution" and hand marketing the role of persuading people to buy it. This misses the core reality that people, and the company, need to go on a dialogic journey together to reconstruct meaning – away from the current market and landscape of wellbeing that is built around profit, towards as yet unknown markets, products and services that maximise wellbeing. Only through this relational journeying can optimal solutions for the current reality be created which synergistically progressing towards the ultimate goal.

MAKING MARKETS

Being a viable Purpose-Driven Organisation now, while making the viable sustainability-aligned markets of the future, will almost certainly involve one or more of the following:

1. **Operating in a harmful market while changing that market.** Just as Netflix had to cannibalise its physical distribution of films to create a strong digital film market, Ørsted, the Danish multinational energy company, cannibalised its position in coal to transition to be one of the largest wind turbine and renewable energy companies in the world in order to work towards its purpose to "create a world that runs entirely on green energy". The heart of the job is not to be perfect before engaging stakeholders, but to co-create and enact strategy together. Marks & Spencer, the UK-based retailer turned global brand, offered a powerful example of Logic 3 leadership

when it launched "Plan A" in 2007. Reflecting on the initiative in 2015, the company echoed the openness it had shown from the outset: "Launching Plan A was bold. We didn't have all the answers. We didn't know exactly where it would take us. But despite this uncertainty, we were clear that we had to change. We had to find a better way of using resources, managing waste, and demonstrating our social legitimacy. All we could be sure of was that business as usual was not an option." Rather than waiting to present polished plans or proven successes, Marks & Spencer began with an honest conversation with its stakeholders. This approach highlights how marketing communications – often seen as merely reputational – becomes a core capability for Logic 3 leaders. It's not just about staying legally compliant; it's about activating the organisation's purpose, within defined parameters, by engaging and aligning the energy of all stakeholders around a shared direction.

2. **Operating in a "sustainable" market and eliminating hidden harms.** It is hard to think of a supply network that doesn't currently do harm in some way, so this harm is almost inevitable for any organisation. For example, Tony's Chocolonely is a purpose-driven chocolate company with the mission to "end exploitation in cocoa together." Yet, like any organisation, it inevitably creates some harm – such as the health impacts associated with sugar consumption or its reliance on retailers who may themselves contribute to harm through unsustainable energy use and other practices. Their ambition is going to involve what might be termed "transition trade-offs" in how an organisation moves towards achieving an optimal strategic contribution to long-term wellbeing for all, and getting its operating model to do this within thresholds of system, stakeholder and resource health. Once they have "arrived" at a governance system aligned with long-term wellbeing for all (see details of ISO 37011 below) then there will be "maintenance trade-offs". However, the challenges of transition and the need for transparency and stakeholder support/ help with accountability, are notable and need to be tackled head on.

3. **Unusual collaborations.** This is a strong feature of purpose-driven marketing. An example is the partnership between Allbirds and Adidas to create low carbon shoes. As Marianna Mazzucato convincingly outlines in her book *The Entrepreneurial State*, this

will invariably benefit from, or even require, active government involvement.

No matter how authentic the purpose-driven intent of the organisation and its leaders is, realising this intent will always be very hard – but it is the work to be done. Marketing is at the very heart of this task and we need to make it fit-for-purpose.

TAKEAWAY

Well governed Purpose-Driven Organisations move from responding to market demand to making the markets needed to achieve long-term wellbeing for all. Through guide-and-co-create marketing, they develop a clear vision of the impacts to be created and actively co-create the path with stakeholders.

RETOOL

In this section we outline tools that you as a leader can lean on when moving your organisation from Logic 1 or Logic 2 to being a Purpose-Driven Logic 3 organisation. We focus on three tools in three key areas: foundational governance literacy, specifically governing Purpose-Driven Organisations and establishing purpose-aligned guide-and-co-create marketing.

RETOOL 1: Governance of Organisations: ISO 37000

We are all involved in bringing about Logic 3 governance regardless of where we sit in the system. As Indian social change leader Rohini Nilekani summarises on her website: "We cannot be mere consumers of good governance, we must be participants; we have to co-create it."[14] For this to happen, we need mass foundational governance literacy.

ONE TOOL TO UNLOCK ALL LEVELS

Luckily governance shares the same core features that can be applied across all three levels:

> **MACRO:** National governments governing a country, its economy and its organisations – and being governed by citizens
>
> **MESO:** organisations being governed by governing bodies and all stakeholders
>
> **MICRO:** Individuals governing themselves

This means that while the following information about governance may feel detailed at first, once armed with foundational governance literacy we can govern in any domain – including applying the foundations to ourselves.

How, then, can leaders start a journey to governance excellence? The most important core tool for this is without doubt the International Organization for Standardization (ISO)[15] in "Governance of organisations". While an author of this book (Victoria) co-led its development, her enthusiasm for it is shared widely.[16]

In his role as Chair of the International Corporate Governance Network (ICGN), George Dallas summarised: "Beginning with corporate purpose as its guiding principle, the ISO 37000 guidance provides a rigorous and systematic framework on the governance of organisations. It is thoughtful and carefully crafted. It serves as a valuable frame of reference for companies, boards, investors, policymakers, regulators and other governance professionals." Renowned Governance Professor at the University of Oxford, Colin Mayer, perhaps sums up best its global significance: "ISO 37000 is of profound significance in establishing the global standards of governance that are required to meet the challenges of business, society and the environment in the 21st century. It meets the needs of boards, management teams, governance bodies and other stakeholders in providing practical, forward-looking guidance on governance matters. ISO is to be congratulated on reaching consensus between nations on the fundamental principles of good governance."[17]

The reason this standard represents a watershed in governance literacy is because it is the first standard that pins down a common language and set of principles for organisational governance that is designed to be applicable across any country, any sector and any type of organisation. It is also based on the widest possible consensus – using ISO's carefully designed and international multi-stakeholder process. ISO 37000 was approved via a voting round of 164 countries.

Before ISO 37000 there was just a scattering of definitions and codes leaving some organisations with no guidance but covering some organisations more than once, e.g. stock exchange codes, regulatory bodies, sector/country level guidance. The nuances in the language used was wide, and none described the complete governance system. This meant that our understanding of governance – our most critical tool – had been fragmented, incomplete and most importantly, anchored almost entirely to BAU Logic 1.[18] BAU Logic 1 is the context that governance as a domain and professionalised discipline has grown up in. At the core of this "growing up" was stock exchange codes and laws that were created against a backdrop of financial crashes and scandals, for example, the globally influential 1992 London Stock Exchange-commissioned Cadbury Report and the 2002, Sarbanes–Oxley Act in the US. These governance advances were created primarily to protect financial income for investors.

Alongside these efforts, a whole legal-based topic was formed called "corporate governance". Although charities, public benefit companies and community interest companies are also "incorporated", corporate governance has been overwhelmingly focused and associated with Logic 1 BAU profit-maximising corporations. This has captured much research and other attention, amplifying the idea that organisational governance is about protecting financial capital for investors and giving the impression that governance of NGOs, government and all other organisations is somehow something entirely different. Therefore, the tools just didn't exist to have joined up mature conversations about the foundations of good governance.

Without a foundational and shared understanding of governance, driving real progress in the "G" of Environmental Social and Governance (ESG) reporting factors also remained out of reach. As Paul Druckman, a global leader in sustainable organisations summarised: "There is momentum in disclosure and reporting around ESG, however the emphasis is hardly ever on the 'G' – governance. I have long held the view that governance is central to any conceptual framework for disclosure which then leads to an accountability mechanism. The ISO standard can provide such an underpinning for governance."

Underlining Druckman's observation, work to develop a standard in "Indicators of Effective Governance" (ISO 37006) is now ongoing and will provide the basis for far more useful indicators of good governance that can be used in ESG metrics.

In the above context, it is easier to see how ISO 37000 provides a leap forward in our ability to create a shared vision of how, practically, we can govern organisational decision-making so that it is, as far as reasonably possible, aligned with a sustainable future.

In this section, we will offer a foundational overview of ISO 37000, with the full standard available from the ISO website. ISO 37000 also embeds some aspects of how to support an adaptive, learning organisation. Leslie Thiele outlines three key parameters for how an organisation should go about decision-making: "(1) diverse, distributed, and transparent participation; (2) safe-to-fail experimentation; and (3) exploratory foresight."[19] All these are built into the standard in different ways. Additionally, as already emphasised, Logic 3 governance allows experimentation to flourish through a shared clear frame within which there is much flexibility. We outline safe-to-fail experimentation in more detail through the role of a Purpose-Driven Leader in creating psychological safety in Chapter 4.

ISO 37000 has three key parts which we will now summarise:

1. Core definitions
2. Foundations of integrated governance
3. The 11 principles of governance

CORE DEFINITIONS AND WHY THEY MATTER

In ISO standards, terms and definitions always come up front. Having solid shared ground about what we are basing ideas of good practice on really matters – as any academic will tell you. Table 3.1 provides a selection of core terms and their definitions in ISO 37000, along with an interpretation of why they matter. There are further clarifying notes that come with these definitions, which you can find in ISO 37000 or are freely available via the ISO Online Browsing Platform if you select "terms and definitions":

TABLE 3.1 KEY GOVERNANCE TERMS IN ISO 37000

TERM	DEFINITION	WHY IT MATTERS IN PRACTICE
Govern-ance of organi-sations	*Human-based system by which an organisation is directed, overseen and held accounta-ble for achieving its defined purpose*	When thinking about the remit of governance, it is useful to return to the basics. There are three key functions: direction, oversight (of that direction), and accountability for it (for performance against that direction).
Govern-ing body	*Person or group of people who have ultimate accounta-bility for the whole organisation*	A governing body is accountable for the whole organisation and is respon-sible for designing and maintaining the integrated, organisational-wide governance system. In an organisation of one, that person will be both the governing body and the executive. The governing body is where align-ment and misalignment with long-term wellbeing for all stems from – or should … In reality many governing bodies do not fully embody their role and often, in effect, take their direc-tion (and oversight information) from the CEO/executive without due reflec-tion that it is ultimately their choice and responsibility.

(*Continued*)

TERM	DEFINITION	WHY IT MATTERS IN PRACTICE
Governing group	*Person or group of people who govern an organisation*	Governing groups is a term that includes the governing body as a special kind of governing group (see above), but extends to all other delegated collective decision-making bodies in the organisation that do not have ultimate accountability. This includes executive boards, main boards of subsidiary companies but also groups that direct, oversee and account for actions at an operational level. This supports and gives structure to a formal "thread" of governance that reaches across the organisation. The design of this network of delegation to governing groups also determines how distributed an organisation is. In the case of the cooperative organisation Buurtzog, governance direction starts with the individual patient and works outwards, respecting the principle of "subsidiarity" where decisions are made closest to the impact. What system structure is most useful will ultimately be the decision of an overall governing body which remains accountable for all decisions made in the other governing groups and the organisation as a whole.

TERM	DEFINITION	WHY IT MATTERS IN PRACTICE
Accountability	*Obligation to another for the fulfilment of a responsibility*	The world talks a lot about accountability but an internationally agreed definition didn't exist before ISO 37000 – in Brazil they don't traditionally have a word for accountability. The ISO 37000 process built the consensus to clarify that accountability involves responsibility to fulfil an obligation. The notes to the definition specify that this, in turn, creates an obligation to inform and explain how this responsibility was fulfilled. This means the stakeholder you account to is, in effect, given the right to judge your success.
Delegation	*Assignment of authority and responsibility from one that holds them to another*	All delegation starts with the governing body and it is a well designed system of delegation that enables accountability and the freedom to act and lead well. When responsibility is delegated to someone, it needs to come with the necessary authority to fulfil that responsibility. This delegation can be highly structured and hierarchical. It can also be highly distributed as in the case of a Decentralised Autonomous Organisation (DAOs) which is governed through rules encoded as "smart contracts" on a blockchain.

(Continued)

TERM	DEFINITION	WHY IT MATTERS IN PRACTICE
Governance policy	*Intentions and direction of an organisation as formally expressed by its governing body*	Governance is as much about writing down, communicating and bringing to life the governance direction as it is about creating it. Governance policies are the main tool for clarifying the maximising goal, parameters, sub-objectives and any other guidance for strategy and actions. If these are not clear, useful and coherent then the governance system cannot be effective.
Member stakeholder	*Stakeholder who has a legal obligation or defined right to make decisions in relation to the governing body and to whom the governing body is to account*	Members of an organisation are considered an internal part of it. Registered shareholders are members, even when they have almost no legal influence over the organisation. The global norm is to consider shareholders as "owners", but this definition reminds us that shareholder relationships with the organisation are about specific legal rights or obligations to influence the decision-making of the governing body in specific areas. This is what makes them powerful – or not – because often these rights are very constrained or almost non-existent (as are the responsibilities and hence accountabilities on those "owners").

TERM	DEFINITION	WHY IT MATTERS IN PRACTICE
Reference stakeholder	*Stakeholder to whom the governing body has decided to account to when making decisions pertaining to the organisational purpose*	Beyond member stakeholders who have legal rights of influence, the governing body is free to decide to create an obligation to account to other stakeholders for the nature and fulfilment of the organisational direction. These stakeholders then become influential as they are able to guide governing body decisions, judge success and provoke governance change. These stakeholders can also be referred to as "moral stakeholders".
Ethical behaviour	*Behaviour that is in accordance with accepted principles of right or good conduct in the context of a particular situation and is consistent with international norms of behaviour*	This definition enables the vital and commonly used concept of ethical behaviour to be clear and practical, anchoring it to the normative context of international conventions of "good".
International norms of behaviour	*Expectations of socially responsible organisational behaviour derived from customary international law, generally accepted principles of international law, or intergovernmental agreements that are universally or nearly universally recognised*	This definition helps us get beyond the idea that there is no shared ethical mandate to act just because the world is complex. This reminds us that the first principles of long-term wellbeing for all are encoded in already established and agreed international principles, law and agreements, e.g. the International Human Rights law and UN Guiding Principles.

(*Continued*)

TERM	DEFINITION	WHY IT MATTERS IN PRACTICE
Compliance obligations	*Requirements that an organisation mandatorily has to comply with as well as those that an organisation voluntarily chooses to comply with*	Compliance and "compliance culture" are often seen as negative because of their association with mindless tick-boxing for a third party. This issue is exacerbated with Logic 1 short-term self-interest where the interest of the company and society are perpetually at odds and compliance is done because it "has to be" – not because decision-makers are invested in the reasons why. This definition shows that compliance is both to the law but also to parameters that the organisation chooses to commit to. For Logic 3 organisations this will be, at a minimum, the voluntary obligation to do no harm to foundational social and environmental systems – something stakeholders of a purpose-driven would care deeply about.
Risk	*Effect of uncertainty on objectives*	This definition is taken directly from the popular ISO in Risk Management (ISO 31000) which establishes risk as both the positive and negative effects of uncertainty on what you are trying to achieve. Both positive and negative aspects are important for setting risk appetite and risk tolerance because too much or too little risk taking can reduce optimal performance. The governing body exercises risk governance of itself, and the organisation as a whole, as well as carrying out risk management of its own actions.

TERM	DEFINITION	WHY IT MATTERS IN PRACTICE
Risk appetite	*Amount and type of risk that an organisation is willing to pursue or retain*	Taking risk at a certain level is a choice. This choice is subjective and completely anchored to what you are trying to achieve and what you want to avoid when pursuing an organisational direction – i.e. the organisational goal and parameters. This appetite needs to be translated into risk criteria and limits which then shape decision-making through clear behavioural parameters that can be overseen and accounted for through a useful accounting system.

FOUNDATIONS OF INTEGRATED GOVERNANCE

In this section of ISO 37000, some key points include:

Distinguishing between governance and management "hats". All members of an organisation need to be clear when they are governing, that is, whether they are acting as part of a governing group or just directing, overseeing or accounting for action, versus when they are "doing". In other words, an executive director ceases to be an executive when they are acting in their capacity as part of the governing body. Clear role definition is critical for good governance.

Governing competence. Those governing, particularly the governing body, must have the right skills, experience and knowledge to govern well, including understanding the changing organisational strategic context. They need to establish an ongoing system to assess the quality of governance, publish these findings and draw on independent professionals as needed

The system of delegation is vital to get right and anchored to governance direction, oversight and accountability. Delegation is core to the thread of governance. It connects: Direction – what is being delegated; Oversight – the information required to be gathered and reported by delegates, which enables co-creative success, failure and correction or improvement; Accountability – the ability to take responsibility and explain whether and how (or how not) the responsibility was fulfilled to stakeholders.

THE 11 PRINCIPLES OF GOVERNANCE

ISO 37000 outlines 11 principles of governance. Figure 3.2 shows how these are separated into primary, foundational and enabling principles, with the consequences of an effective integrated system including responsible stewardship, effective performance and ethical behaviour. Table 3.2 offers a top-level summary of each of these principles, which operate as one integrated system, anchored to the purpose. The table offers an interpretation of the principles with the precise text found in the original standard:

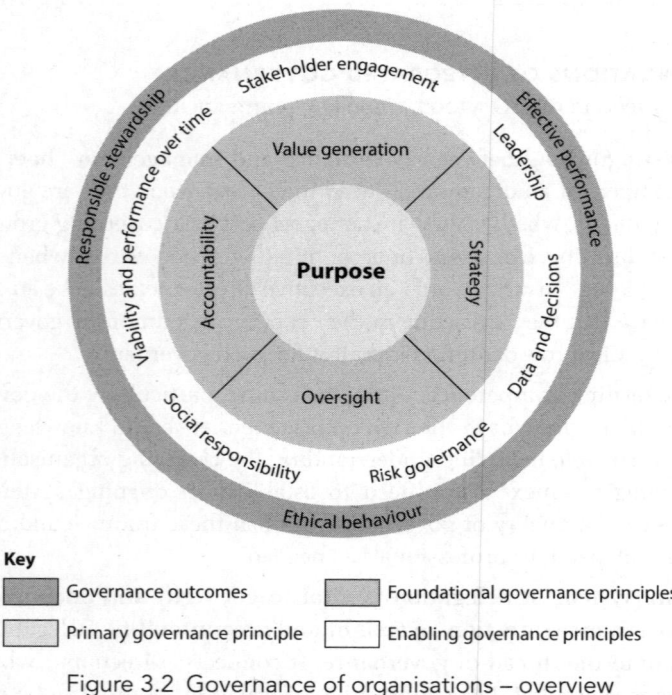

Figure 3.2 Governance of organisations – overview
Source: ISO37000:2021

TABLE 3.2 THE 11 GOVERNANCE PRINCIPLES OF ISO 37000

NO.	PRINCIPLE	SUMMARY POINTS
1	Purpose	The governing body should define and govern to a clear and stakeholder relevant purpose that is its meaningful reason to exist. This is informed by clear and authentic values which need to be defined and governed. The purpose and values specify the pinnacle organisational value generation objective and all other principles should be interpreted and enacted against this.
2	Value generation	The governing body should clarify the value generation model. In other words: **Define**: Define what value should be created to optimally deliver the purpose. **Create**: Set parameters for the firm to deliver the value. **Deliver**: Ensure appropriate delivery of the value. **Sustain**: Ensure value is retained and distributed in order to maximise the value generation objectives and achieve the purpose.
3	Strategy	The governing body should direct and engage with strategy by setting strategic outcomes that it believes can best achieve the purpose. It also needs to establish governance policies to guide the strategy development and engage with strategy. It does this by being involved in strategic planning and through dynamically steering the strategy with governance levers.

(Continued)

NO.	PRINCIPLE	SUMMARY POINTS

4	Oversight	The governing body should ensure that the organisational purpose is achieved in the way intended by overseeing performance and obtaining assurance:
		
		• Require timely and accurate reports from delegated parties on material matters.
		• Ensure a well-functioning internal control system including:
		  ○ a risk management system
		  ○ a compliance management system
		  ○ a system of financial controls
		• Ensure corrective action is taken as and when needed.
		• Assure itself that the reports and evidence it receives are accurate, and that the internal control system is effective.

5	Accountability	The governing body is responsible for, and accountable to, the organisation as a whole and holds to account those it has delegated to. It needs to demonstrate accountability through effective reports and disclosures about *how* the purpose was achieved.
6	Stakeholder engagement	The governing body should identify and prioritise all relevant stakeholder groups, engaging stakeholders to help achieve purpose through organisational strategy. It should ensure: • a "stakeholder responsive" organisational culture • collaborative relationships • open and transparent stakeholder communication • coherent reporting to stakeholders

NO.	PRINCIPLE	SUMMARY POINTS
7	Leadership	The governing body should demonstrate ethical and effective leadership. This applies in relation to, itself, across the organisation and also in relation to external stakeholders and wider context.
8	Data and decisions	The governing body should ensure that the decisions it and everyone in the organisation takes are effective, and that data is recognised as a strategic resource throughout the organisation and used responsibly.
9	Risk governance	The governing body governs risk to generate value and effectively oversee the organisation. It does this by establishing an organisational risk framework to set the tone for management of risk, practicing effective risk management itself and overseeing risk management across the organisation as a whole.
10	Social responsibility	Organisational decisions should be transparent and aligned with societal expectations. In this way, decisions are supported, the organisational purpose will be valid, value is generated in a way that meets longer-term stakeholder needs and strategy is effective and implemented.
11	Viability and performance over time	The governing body should govern for viability and performance over a future time horizon, in a way that assures the success of the organisation and protects and restores the basis of wellbeing for future generations. As part of this it should ensure that its disclosed value generation model includes an integrated view of its dependencies as well as resulting risks to the organisation and to external systems.

(Continued)

On the launch of the ISO 37000, Saker Nusseibeh, CEO of Federated Hermes warmly welcomed it, stating: "It fills a gap that should have been addressed long ago. Further, with a strong multi-stakeholder focus, it brings corporate governance into the modern economy." All Logic 3 leaders can lean on ISO 37000 knowing it has global credibility, is universally applicable and has been freed from the constraints of BAU Logic 1.

There now exists a wide variety of training globally on ISO 37000 and it is increasingly integrated into bespoke and mass market courses, for example the University of Cambridge Institute for Sustainability Leadership's eight-week online course in Governance for a Sustainable Future.

TAKEAWAY

We all need to become governance literate if we are to lead for a sustainable future. ISO 37000 is a multi-stakeholder global consensus on the foundations of good governance, relevant to any organisation, country or sector. It is free from the constraints of Logic 1 thinking.

RETOOL 2: Governance of Purpose-Driven Organisations: PAS 808 and ISO 37011

"It's all well and good talking about purpose, but we need to be able to describe what it looks like and know when it is being done!" This is the view of a leading impact investor Luca Zerbini who started a purpose-driven venture capital firm Una Terra where Victoria is on the Sustainability Impact Advisory Committee. Trying to demonstrate what a purpose-driven venture capital organisation would look like is not an easy or quick task – but it is impossible without a clear view on what it means to govern a Purpose-Driven Organisation. This clarity is vital because:

- It is core to allocating capital to advance long-term wellbeing for all.
- It helps organisations to progress and to professionalise the Logic 3 governance capabilities needed.

- If we can't establish what good governance to align with long-term wellbeing for all looks like, then we are all in effect "washing". Washing is about misrepresenting how well you are doing in relation to a goal. If we are unable to clarify the destination, we cannot properly represent how far from that destination we are.

- If we try to avoid "washing" without clarifying universal purpose-driven governance behaviours to gauge true progress against, then we end up "hushing" – a phenomenon where organisations hesitate to discuss or advance sustainability efforts for fear of being accused of overstating progress or facing legal challenges. This is a natural risk-aware consequence of a lack of clarity.

- Our collective understanding of sustainability has often been limited to specific strategies such as technologies, products, services or approaches. These strategies might be assessed as "sustainable" today but may fall short tomorrow or in the coming years.

A strong shared view of specific governance behaviours for a Purpose-Driven Organisation should demonstrate should therefore be front of mind for anyone wanting to lead for a sustainable future.

Establishing a global shared view of governance via ISO 37000, gave the world the first possibility to ask, and answer, the ultimate question: "What are the universal aspects of an organisational governance system that will result in decisions that are fully aligned with long-term wellbeing for all?"

Work to establish the current consensus on this question began with a national process between 2020 and 2022, created by a group of representative experts, convened by Britain's standards body, British Standards Institute or BSi, and supported by Victoria as the Technical Author. The result was the standard "PAS 808: Purpose-Driven Organisations: Worldviews, Principles and Behaviors for Delivering Sustainability – Guide". It is available free online and we invite you to download it now and read it alongside the insights below.[20] This standard has enabled many organisations to start or progress their practice to be purpose-driven, including via a peer group of implementers. Andrew Brown, ex-Group Chief Sustainability Officer at the Anglian Water Group, a privately owned international water services company involved in developing the standard and the peer group, summarises: *"Members of the implementers group have said how transformational PAS 808 is in laying out what it really looks like to be a Purpose-Driven Organisation, especially understanding what behaviours an organisation and its governing body should be displaying. The standard is particularly useful as it can be used by any type of organisation, at any stage in their journey to becoming purpose-driven; from using it as a framework to develop your organisational purpose and approach, through undertaking a full maturity assessment on how well your purpose is embedded and functioning."*

While it was important to have a "first draft" from a national standards body, the move to Logic 3 is an international problem and requires an international shared view of the way forwards. A proposal to ISO by the British Standards Institute, with the PAS 808 attached as the working draft, received overwhelming approval after a three-month member ballot. Work to develop the standard kicked off in 2024 with Victoria as the project leader and the standard is set to be published in 2026.

After reading the summary below, it will be clear that these standards aren't about codifying norms around what board committees should exist (e.g. a sustainability specific committee), who should sit on a board (e.g. nature), who should have the right over governance decisions and a share in the benefits (e.g. employees) and how distributed or centralised decision-making should be. These are all potentially vital governance system *strategies*. In other words, they are all potential routes to achieve the goal of governance. Many options and examples of governance strategies are available: for example, Employee Ownership or Steward Ownership and the use of Purpose Trusts, as utilised by Patagonia, where a trust holds voting rights and non-voting shares are owned by an organisation that reinvests profits or gives them to a designated charity. Open AI gave us an example of how to set parameters for financial returns when they attracted investment through a capped return model. This strategy meant that those who invested could only earn dividends up to a declared point and did not have decision-making influence – something made very clear at the time of investment. Many thought-leaders, organisations and actors have carried out groundbreaking work weighing up choices about the design of governance systems. This includes organisations such as DEAL, Dark Matter Labs, Common Trust, Chapter Zero and others.

However, as established earlier, we can only properly debate and decide the best strategy for a particular organisation or context if we have a shared view of the goal and parameters of the governance direction. In other words, we first need to establish what the outer governance direction is. Only once armed with this clear view of the point of the governance system can we employ a governance strategy that is the most effective for the context faced – and continually adapt it as needed.

ISO 37011 is in development and is set to be be published at the end of 2026. As well as from countries including: Argentina, Austria, Brazil, Canada, China, Costa Rica, Cyprus, Denmark, Egypt, France, Germany, Iran, Ireland, Italy, Jamaica, Japan, Peru, Portugal, South Africa, Sweden, Trinidad and Tobago and the UK, liaisons to this work include the International Finance Organisation (IFC), the Capitals Coalition, Social Value international, the EU Commission, the ACCA (Association for Chartered Certified Accountants) and the United Nations Development Programme (UNDP). Below is a synthesis of four key areas of Logic 3 governance and organisational practice, drawing from PAS 808 and the emerging consensus on ISO 37011.

1) DIAGNOSE YOUR CURRENT GOVERNANCE SYSTEM
The first step is to understand what organisation you are, or want to be. The Logic that dominates depends on the system's prevalent worldviews – i.e. the set of base assumptions about what is valuable in the world to protect and enhance, the current state of value and how the world works. This forms the initial stance for action in the world. We have already outlined the worldviews of BAU Logic 1 and the governance system, behaviours consequences that rationally result. If we want to be a Logic 3 Purpose-Driven Organisation and supportive governance system then it is critical to understand how far the worldviews of the organisation, and particularly key decision-makers, are aligned with Logic 3. If weak, then doing pre-work to build or strengthen these worldviews is probably the best strategy. PAS 808 has a section that lists worldviews that are most likely to be held, more often, by Purpose-Driven Organisations. These worldview descriptors can be used in various ways, such as, conversation starters for board members, a company-wide survey or a stakeholder analysis. For instance, Victoria collaborates with Pat Dwyer and The Purpose Business with a presence in Hong Kong, Singapore and the Philippines. In a "tour" in late 2024 of these locations, they ran Masterclasses with local leaders which included asking people to reflect on a sample of the worldviews and

score how far they agreed with them on a simple Likert scale, and then step into their organisations and key stakeholders' shoes to answer the same questions. This quickly gets to the heart of where issues and opportunities for alignment are. A set of common purpose-driven worldviews are listed from page 11 onwards in PAS 808.

The University of Cambridge Institute for Sustainability Leadership, in collaboration with Victoria, created a Business Transformation Framework based on the three logics. This includes the specific behaviours across an organisation that you would expect to see for each logic – providing a practical way to diagnose and plan for change.[21]

2) DECIDE THE PURPOSE

There is a wealth of resources about how you can establish your organisational purpose. The standards distil the vital aspects. This includes that the governing body has ultimate accountability to establish and achieve the purpose (within the established parameters) in alignment with long-term wellbeing for all. Even if they delegate to others, they can only delegate the obligation to fulfil a responsibility. They cannot delegate away the accountability for what results. Other stakeholder interests, including that of any shareholder, are secondary and in service to this goal. In an ideal world, the purpose would be formally recognised in an organisation's constituting documents from the outset. However, this is not sufficient to achieve a Purpose-Driven Organisation – there is much more work to be done. This work creates the ground conditions for buy-in for a purpose-driven constitution – so it is in effect a "chicken or egg" situation, where either can come first.

3) DESIGN THE PARAMETERS

The value the organisation intends to protect while achieving the purpose needs to be translated into behavioural boundaries that shouldn't be crossed when achieving the purpose.

For a Purpose-Driven Organisation, its parameters need to, at a minimum, include those that ensure a fair and adequate contribution to the health of social and environmental systems. For any organisation parameters that support the healthy stocks and flows of all capitals will be vital for continuity and performance. For a Purpose-Driven Organisation, this will almost certainly require creating an explicit cap on the expected returns for financial investors and embedding this, and any decided minimum, into decision-making parameters to transparently guide strategic choices. In addition to these "resource parameters" are "strategic parameters" about how the organisation acts while achieving the purpose within the resource parameters – for example, that the law must be obeyed, the best scientific data available is used, the organisation is set up to continually learn and adapt, win-wins are sought where possible to go beyond minimum levels of health without diverting resources from the purpose, a maximum differential between what people in the organisation earn and treating people a certain way based on organisational values.

Values are important parameters – as well as informing the purpose, as covered earlier. Values are derived from worldviews and are beliefs about the valuable states that should be established and protected. They remain a nice idea until they are turned into specific behaviours (conduct) that are guided by decision-making parameters. They then become part of governance direction that can be overseen and accounted for. For example, if an organisational value is to respect human dignity, then a decision-making parameter could be zero modern day enslavement in all tiers of the value network, with interim targets based on what is, or could be, feasible. In this way, values ensure that stakeholders (even those that the purpose is directed towards) are treated as human beings in their own right, with treatment that doesn't fall below a certain threshold.

There are a huge number of credible organisations worldwide that, in effect, help organisations establish both resource and strategic parameters aligned with collective long-term wellbeing. This includes those helping organisations achieve the globally agreed Sustainable Development Goals, which are largely expressions of minimum thresholds we need to get within for a minimum level of wellbeing.

4) CREATE THE PURPOSE STATEMENT
The purpose statement
More than a purpose summary (described below), the purpose statement should be a clear written and public document that establishes and justifies the value generation and protection intent of a Purpose-Driven Organisation in relation to the long-term wellbeing of all people and the planet. At a minimum this should clarify why the value generation intent of its purpose is an optimal strategic contribution

to the long-term wellbeing of all people and the planet. The purpose statement exposes the organisational (and governing body) view on the most urgent crises faced now, and in the future, the associated "theory of change" about how to resolve them, and the organisation's ability, compared to others' ability, to tackle them. In other words, whether an organisation exists to achieve self-esteem in populations of craftspeople in a particular area of Addis Ababa or to stop the degradation of peatland globally, it would need to convincingly establish why this is an optimal reason for it to exist in relation to collective long-term wellbeing. Alongside this would be a statement of a commitment, regardless of the purpose, to contributing fairly and adequately to the health of the environmental and social systems it affects. This should be supplemented by any other value it intends to protect in the process of achieving the purpose and the foundational parameters it commits to keeping within to make this protection a reality (and any interim parameters, if doing no harm immediately isn't possible).

Importantly, the purpose statement should include clarification of the value the organisation intends to generate and protect for specific stakeholders. PAS 808 categorises the universe of stakeholders into five types based on the organisations' obligations and commitments to them.

Those whom value is generated for:

1. **Ultimate beneficiary stakeholders:** all people and the planet over the longer-term, including future generations as the primary decision-making anchor

2. **Primary/ focal beneficiary stakeholders:** those whose wellbeing the purpose primarily serves. In the case where the purpose is focused on addressing an ultimate social or environmental system problem (e.g. climate change or inequality), the ultimate beneficiary stakeholders would be all people and the planet.

Those whom value is protected for:

3. **Influential stakeholders:** those the governing body is legally bound to (e.g. member stakeholders as defined in ISO 37000) and those it chooses to account to (e.g. reference stakeholders as defined in ISO 37000)

4. **Enabling stakeholders:** those who the organisation relies on to achieve the purpose in the way intended

5. **Affected stakeholders:** those who are affected by the decisions the organisation makes, even if their effect on the organisation is non-existent, imperceivable or very limited

The purpose summary

This is a pithy, easily communicable summary of the essence of the organisation's maximising goal which should be its commitment to protecting the basis of long-term wellbeing for all in the process. If the organisation has established a well-functioning purpose-driven governance system then this short collection of words should unlock a whole system, of meaning that bridges to the purpose statement. Many organisations only create this short summary as an inspiring positioning statement without it being anchored to a robust purpose statement that allows it to be directed, overseen and accounted for across the organisation. Hence, although sometimes this purpose summary can be central to orientating decisions, it can also be merely a PR tool. Other issues are that often these summaries are not actually about a purpose (e.g. "we create the best products in market X") or they inadvertently are so ambitious and broad that they replicate the ultimate purpose of long-term wellbeing for all (e.g. "sustainable lives for everyone into the future") and offer no strategic orientation for decision-makers. Ørsted's summary is: "To drive green energy transformation and help shape a world that runs entirely on green energy." Beyond Meat's is: "By shifting from animal to plant-based meat, we can positively affect growing global issues such as constraints on natural resources and animal welfare." These are both good examples of summaries that are strategically rich enough to help direct decision-makers and other stakeholders.

5) MAKE IT A LIVING, LEARNING SYSTEM

Having a clear and meaningful reason to exist that is aligned with a sustainable future is the foundation of establishing shared purpose-driven intent in an organisation. However, intent is not the full story. That intent needs to be realised. Realising that intent requires a wide range of governance skills and practices. Four of these that are contained in PAS 808 will be outlined below:

Embedding in all systems and processes and strategy. Governance direction should be the basis for strategy and aligned decision-making by all organisational decision-makers. This involves embedding this direction (purpose and parameters) in the whole governance system through clear, usable and well communicated written governance policies. For a purpose-driven start-up, the leaders have the luxury of designing the governance system and associated policies from scratch. Doing this well is vital in order to harness and maintain the central and positive role of the purpose as the organisation grows in size and complexity. For existing organisations, diagnosing the current governance system and culture that has resulted is the first step – no matter how opaque or fragmented it is – and then assessing and implementing the change needed.

Aligning the stakeholder constellation. An organisation is an adaptive living system made up of humans who are themselves adapted living systems. As such, it can only achieve its objective, within its parameters, to the extent that the stakeholders that it depends and interacts with are aligned and functioning well, into the longer term. We have talked previously about the need to help ensure the health of enabling stakeholders (see Create the Purpose Statement in this chapter for a definition) and about treating them well via organisational values. However, a further question is how aligned they are to achieving the organisational purpose. Therefore, absolutely key to realising purpose-driven intent, is to establish and govern a stakeholder constellation strategy. The goal of this strategy is to keep expanding the "head room" for action through greater alignment, for example, investors being willing to expect lower returns because they place value on the meaningful value the organisation generates and protects. There are different ways in which the stakeholder constellation can be actively aligned through strategy:

- Most organisational decisions shape stakeholders, but of specific note are those made in marketing, communications and PR, human resource and procurement or other contracting. The governing body should create an overarching stakeholder constellation strategy which supports all decision-makers to improve stakeholder alignment. As part of this, engaging with "influential stakeholders" (see Create the Purpose Statement in this chapter for the definition) is particularly important. The Canadian Purpose Economy Project (CPEP), for example, has created a declaration to move Canada to a Purpose Economy (i.e. Wellbeing Economy) with signatories including over 100 Canadian CEOs. As part of this, CPEP have created a set of "Purpose Due-diligence Questions for Investors". This supports asset managers in their duty to understand what types of organisations they are investing in, whether these are aligned with their clients' best interest and whether those investee organisations are indeed governing their stated purpose.

- Where stakeholders are not amenable or able to change, and especially where they are particularly powerful, another strategy is to swap out stakeholders with those that are more aligned. This could be changing the people employed or changing suppliers. It can also mean changing customers through market making (see in Rethink 3 in this chapter) or trying to attract new organisational members (e.g. shareholders). Paul Polman, the ex-CEO of Unilever took this approach when he made a public announcement in effect stating that investors should only continue to invest in Unilever if they believed in the company's purpose of making sustainable living commonplace – and its long-term multi-stakeholder focus to achieve this. He made clear that the purpose-driven innovations and the change in business model would prioritise long-term value creation away from chasing quarterly performance goals. He further stated that if some were still interested in single-mindedly pursuing shareholder value at any cost, they should take their money elsewhere. He subsequently abolished quarterly reporting guidance and moved investor compensation to the longer term. These actions were reported to have helped reduce the share of hedge-fund investors in Unilever from 15 per cent to 5 per cent between 2011 and 2013. It also reportedly helped increase shareholder return by nearly 300 per cent during his ten-year tenure.[22] An aligned approach is to bring alternative, more aligned, stakeholders into the organisation's orbit. Other options include, the use of different classes of shares, removing voting rights or restricting the extraction of financial capital to investors: setting a cap on returns and making it a clear decision-making parameter (vital to being purpose-driven).

Oversight. As well as following the principles of effective purpose-driven oversight that will be detailed in ISO 37011, auditing an organisation directly against the standards can be an easy way to move forwards. Both PAS 808 and ISO 37011 are not certification standards – they are written as guidance. However, that does not preclude their being used in a similar way. For example, Anglian Water has undergone two audits against

PAS 808 – an initial self-assessment and then a full audit by a respected independent third party using an in-house maturity assessment methodology. As Andy Brown explained: *"One of the key outcomes of this audit was the implementation of an 'internal purpose dashboard' which allowed the governing body, and other internal stakeholders to quickly and regularly assess how well they were doing in delivering their purpose. PAS 808 has become a vital part of how we ensure we are operating in line with our purpose."* It is useful to note that measuring the cultural embeddedness of purpose is a supporting tool for oversight.

Accountability. Logic 1 accounting departments are traditionally set up to account for financial capital accumulation (the goal) and stocks and flows of financial capital (the core parameter) mostly via numeric data. This reflects a Logic 1 governance system. Accountability for a Logic 3 governance system, on the other hand, is about whether, and how, the purpose has been achieved within the parameters – and how strong that performance is. This includes accounting for healthy stocks and flows of financial capital and will also include accounting for: all its non-financial capital stocks and flows; health of stakeholders; a fair and adequate contribution to the health of social and environmental systems; as well as adherence to any other voluntary parameters.

The basis of this accounting is the value generation and protection intentions embedded in the purpose statement which are then cascaded throughout the organisation. Governance supports decision-makers being able to decide well between options and the trade-offs they encompass – and to account properly for these decisions. This in turn enables accountability for how and why/why not wellbeing (and pathways to it) is generated, protected or destroyed. These organisational purpose-driven accounting systems should be no different for government accounting for itself as an organisation or for it accounting for the nation it governs. This is also the way that organisations can be held to account by Purpose-Driven governments, operating Wellbeing Economies. An effective purpose-aligned accounting system (which we might call "Wellbeing Accounting"), starting with organisations and rolling up to the national level, should be the basis of national accounting.

There have been decades of work experimenting with measuring and reporting wellbeing at the economy level (as detailed in Chapter 2). This sits in parallel to Meso organisational-level reporting advancements – for example, by r3.0 and the United Nations

Research Institute for Social Development (UNRISD) Sustainability Development Performance Indicators. These indicators and associated reporting regime are designed to connect organisational accounting to the realities of the social and environmental systems that are affected as a result. This enables the reporting of actual, not relative, performance towards long-term wellbeing for all. Other organisations that have spearheaded aspects of improved accountability are Social Value International, CDP, Global Reporting Initiative, the Capitals Coalition, BLab, TNFD, Value Balancing Alliance, A4S, World Benchmarking Alliance, Impact Management Platform, the Science-Based Targets Initiative as well as academic centres like the Value Research Center at Doshisha University in Japan and internal decision-making tools like Sustainability Balanced Scorecards and the MultiCapital scorecard. These are in addition to the legal frameworks for reporting impacts and mitigation in financial reporting and national legislation (largely under the ESG banner) – amongst many other examples.

However, this is one planet and one set of organisations that currently exist. Thus, one clear accounting system is needed. This doesn't preclude the space for an infinite number of self-created context rich indicators of progress, but the base foundations of wellbeing and the systems that support it are universal. Therefore we can, and need, comparability where possible and useful. Without a system of accounting aligned with achieving long-term wellbeing for all there can be no real accountability for it.

Jeremy Nicholls' forthcoming 2026 book *The Accounting Paradox: How Financial Accounting Is Damaging the World (But Can Help Repair It)*[23] will provide an outline of how accounting needs to change. This work is vital because a governance system can't operate without an aligned system of accounts. At the same time, even if we establish a unified "Wellbeing Accounting" system, it will remain an irrational administrative burden on organisations, subject to massive lobbying and never fully addressing the scale and urgency of change needed unless the worldviews and logic of the governance system becomes Logic 3.

In the interim, stop-gap innovations are being created for Logic 1 and 2 firms. As an example of a Logic 3 accountability innovation, Social Value International, in collaboration with Jeremy, are using the legal obligation for directors only to sign off accounts if they are "True and Fair" to motivate the use of "notes to the accounts" below the main formulas. These notes detail the accumulated unpaid costs created via by carbon emissions and other social and environmental harms. It is easy to see how this simple use of existing rules could make it difficult for auditors to approve accounts that don't make this simple step.

In summary, ISO 37011 will describe the current consensus view on what a system fully governed for long-term wellbeing for all needs to looks like. Every organisation will be on a different journey to get there and these guidance standards can be used flexibly to support Purpose-Driven Leaders to understand and drive this necessary transformation in a credible and robust way.

TAKEAWAY

High quality purpose-driven governance is our best chance of creating, driving, and not destroying, long-term wellbeing for all (sustainability). PAS 808 and the forthcoming ISO37011 give us the consensus-built clarity to move forwards with confidence.

RETOOL 3: The Evolved Value Framework (EVF) – unlocking purpose-driven marketing

Marketing holds the key to solving one of the most complex creative challenges that Purpose-Driven Organisations face: How do we urgently create financially viable markets that optimise organisational purpose within clearly defined, purpose-aligned governance parameters?

As outlined in Rethink 3: From market response to market making in this chapter, traditional marketing modes tied to Logic 1 and 2 – make-and-sell and sense-and-respond – are not fit for a sustainable future. These approaches focus on pushing products or reacting to demand rather than co-constructing markets in alignment with long-term wellbeing for all.

In contrast, the guide-and-co-create approach to marketing is essential for Purpose-Driven Organisations. It enables the kind of value-creation creativity required to build feasible, purpose-aligned markets by actively involving stakeholders, shaping demand, and innovating responsibly within governance boundaries.

But what are the core practices at the heart of this guide-and-co-create marketing that can deliver on the promise of purpose-driven governance?

The Evolved Value Framework was created by Victoria and the late, pioneer in sustainable marketing, Carole Bond, in order to answer just this question. Its early basis can be found in a paper by multiple authors, including Victoria, entitled "Reforming marketing for sustainability" which was written as part of a Friends of the Earth UK's "Big Ideas" research programme in 2015, which was further developed in the paper "Characterizing paradigm of marketing".[24]

The Evolved Value Framework has six key principles across three key sections which are depicted in Figure 3.3 and unpacked in Table 3.3. These six principles need to be considered together, as a whole system, in order to effectively shift marketing practice.

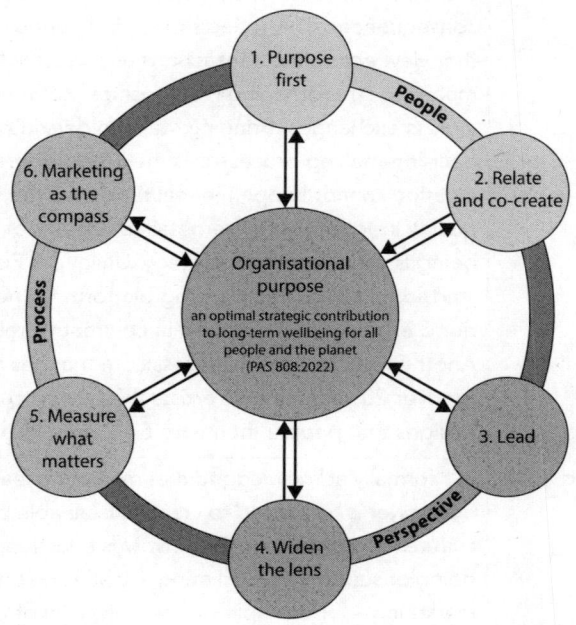

Figure 3.3 Evolved Value Framework (EVF): Bringing Guide-and-Co-Create marketing to life

TABLE 3.3 SIX KEY PRINCIPLES OF THE EVOLVED VALUE FRAMEWORK

NO.	PRINCIPLE	WHAT THIS MEANS IN PRACTICE
1	Purpose first	The purpose, parameters and associated value generation objectives are clear to all and used to test, improve and justify decisions. The ultimate purpose of long-term wellbeing for all is the fallback test for decisions and misalignments with this are elevated. Profits are consciously used as a parameter and explicitly not the goal.
2	Relate-and-co-create	Building long-term, collaborative relationships with customers and other stakeholders is understood as central to being able to achieve the purpose within parameters. These stakeholders are recognised as holding the key to impact – the behaviours and markets that can achieve long-term wellbeing for all can only be achieved in co-creation with those affected by them or close to the consequences. This reflects many indigenous societies that view economic transactions as sacred acts that are a means to strengthening relationships, not merely meaningless exchanges. Bringing stakeholders into real time decision-making processes is the ideal. Where co-creation cannot happen in real time then the highest quality insights about the detailed aspects of their wellbeing is used to inform strategy. Unilever's Foundry, which started off as a crowdsourcing platform for new ideas, is a good example of innovation in co-creative relationships. Another example is Threadless.com that has been running for over 20 years to give artists the power to propose designs that people then vote on to turn into products.
3	Lead	It is formally acknowledged that marketing leads – and then this power is harnessed to create sustainable behaviours, cultures and processes. This involves educating everyone doing or supporting marketing activities on the power of marketing – for example via the University of Cambridge Institute for Sustainability Leadership Sustainable Marketing course that Victoria co-designed and heads up.

NO.	PRINCIPLE	WHAT THIS MEANS IN PRACTICE
4	Widen the lens	Decisions are based on long-term systemic success. The Logic 1 pressure for a narrow line of sight and short-term expediency is brought to light and designed out of the system. This involves thoroughly understanding the governance system that surrounds and shapes marketing decisions and then advocating for change to broader ways of shaping and judging success. For example, addressing systems that override longer-term marketing strategy to "hit quarterly financial targets", or the expectation of a return on investment within such a short time frame that long-term investment projects and relationships isn't possible.
5	Measure what matters	Commonly used marketing metrics are founded in Logic 1 and support the governance system that optimises for financial short-term self-interest. Delivering value creation within a Logic 3 Purpose-Driven Organisation will require new ways to account for how marketing decisions have worked to achieve the purpose, within the parameters. These should feed into the overall governance system and ultimately roll up into the macro level system National Wellbeing Accounts discussed in Chapter 2. Creating new metrics will involve experimenting and collaborating with the wider system to establish, where possible, standard metrics that can be used for benchmarking. This can aid national and global accountability as opposed to those measures that relate only to the organisation. Measures come in a variety of forms and should always support learning organisations that adapt to their ever changing contexts. They should actively avoid "Goodhart's law" where the measure (or strategy) becomes the goal – or otherwise hinders decision-making for long-term wellbeing for all.

(Continued)

NO.	PRINCIPLE	WHAT THIS MEANS IN PRACTICE
6	Marketing as the compass	Marketing is the intersect between the organisation and its stakeholders and the basis of any value creation. If marketing is aligned with principles 1–5 then the organisation will not realise its full purpose potential unless marketing is at the very root of strategic decisions on value creation. This includes at the governing body level and governing group levels regarding market choice, along with functional decisions that affect product, price, distribution and promotions, e.g. research and development, human resource and procurement. As the conduit with stakeholders, marketing should also be central to decisions about the overall organisational direction – the value it generates through its purpose and protects through its parameters. Seeing marketing as an end-of-pipe sales tool is a function of Logic 1. Logic 3 flips this.

These six principles can be understood and made practical through a set of questions that can be asked by leaders at different strata of the organisation as outlined in Figure 3.4.

For any individual marketer – or leader who didn't realise they were a marketer but may now be suspecting they are (spoiler: most leaders are making marketing decisions, even if this is not their professional background), Guide-and-Co-Create marketing may feel out of reach: How can you begin to ask and act on these questions if you are just one part of the system that dictates the answers? The response to this mirrors what we outlined with purpose in general in Chapter 1 and will explore in detail in the next chapter. Every person, team, department, organisation, country, etc., are all trapped by layers of Logic 1 governance systems and underlying worldviews that seem impossible to change. This is also true in functional areas like marketing. The only possible way for this to change is to develop a keen view of the landscape and develop purpose-driven energy. This will enable better strategic analysis of the best route forward and provide the persistence to overcome and remove barriers along the way.

	People			Perspective	Process	
	1. Purpose first	2. Relate and co-create	3. Lead	4. Widen the lens	5. Measure what matters	6. Marketing as the compass
CMO	a. Is your reason to exist (purpose) optimal strategic contribution to long-term wellbeing for all? Is this clear, meaningful and authentic?	a. Is the delivery of your purpose based on building genuine, long-term collaborative relationships?	a. Do you acknowledge your footprint and brainprint power to create long-term wellbeing – and work to make this impact always positive?	a. Do you have a justified theory of change to drive long-term wellbeing, profitably? Do you identify and remove constraints (hardware and software) to win-wins and sacrifice firm gain as needed?	a. Are your core measures designed around your purpose or do they prioritise financial gain for the firm?	a. Are the voices and long-term wellbeing of those you serve at the core of your strategic decision-making and those you lead?
Middle management	b. Do all your systems, targets, processes and ways of working incentivise value generation that supports long-term wellbeing?	b. Do you actively facilitate ongoing collaborative relationships between your staff, stakeholders and customers?	b. Do you motivate staff to consider and optimise their positive footprint and brainprint impacts?	b. Do you consider the knock-on impacts of your value creation decisions? Do you enable and empower others to make such decisions?	b. Have you audited and altered your KPIs to track your contribution to long-term wellbeing for all?	b. Do the voices and long-term wellbeing of those you serve underpin your decision-making and those you lead?
Marketing/ brand associates etc.	c. Is long-term, wellbeing, via serving real needs, at the heart of all your marketing decisions?	c. Do your programmes and projects advocate, build and sustain long-term collaborative relationships?	c. Do you make footprint and brainprint decisions in the interest of long-term wellbeing and encourage others?	c. Do you consider the long-term consequences of your decisions and push back where long-term wellbeing is threatened?	c. Are you collaborating to develop and argue for meaningful measures that align with long-term wellbeing for all?	c. Are you ensuring the voice of those you serve and their long-term wellbeing is front of mind in your decisions?

Figure 3.4 Using questions to advance the Evolved Value Framework in practice

Here are some practical steps to move forwards with the Evolved Value Framework:

1. Diagnose how you and your organisation understand marketing (Make-and-Sell, Sense-and-Respond or Guide-and-Co-Create). This includes establishing what "value" means to your organisation and how this aligns to Logics 1, 2 and 3.

2. Establish a clear ambition of where you want to be, aligned with which Logic you, and your team, department or organisation want to be in – i.e. if you want to be in Logic 3 then you will need guide-and-co-create marketing practice.

3. Assess the gap between this and what you are measuring as value, and what you are asking and rewarding your "marketers" to produce / do through the governance system.

4. Create a strategy and plan to bridge the gap between the two.

5. Help everyone see the vital importance of aligned, excellent marketing to achieving your purpose-driven ambitions. Ensure everyone in the organisation recognises that they are either a marketer or support marketers – and that either way, becoming a capable marketer is a journey all employees need to embrace

6. Use the Evolved Value Framework to develop a reporting system that assesses the extent to which marketing decisions align with the six principles. Identify which aspects of the governance system may be limiting progress, and who within that system holds the authority to drive change. Use these insights to inform strategy, guide planning, and shape action.

Finally, you can consider joining a collaborative group to support you on your journey. For example, creatives for Climate Collective is dedicated to supporting marketers in their journey to Logic 3. They are part of a growing ecosystem of marketing-focused organisations helping the industry move beyond Logic 1.

TAKEAWAY

Guide-and-Co-create marketing is the heartbeat of a Purpose-Driven Organisation and achieves the promise of a purpose-driven governance system. The Evolved Value Framework sets out the 6 Principles to guide progress towards marketing that can deliver on long-term wellbeing for all.

REALISE

The world is not short of consultant reports and annual progress updates on the benefits of becoming purpose-driven. These are based on the huge rise in attention and experimentation that has happened over the past two decades. Benefits commonly cited include increased employee engagement and retention, stronger stakeholder trust and relationships, enhanced innovation and long-term resilience. Stories supporting this are widespread.

While this intuitively makes sense and can be seen as good news, we need to view, and use, these subjective experiences and summaries sceptically. It is not that purpose doesn't, or couldn't, produce all these results, but any transformative change is complex, nuanced and never linear or always positive. Furthermore, robust studies that properly test the relationships between purpose and its effects are thin on the ground. This may not be a bad thing because the third factor we need to consider is that, as outlined previously, we are only just moving properly into the consolidation and clarity phase of what it is to be a Purpose-Driven Organisation. ISO 37011 will give the world the first shared basis that we can use as a starting point to improve on. What is certain is that it is unlikely that any organisation can claim to be fully purpose-driven, given the Logic 1 systems that surround us all. Instead of presenting examples of Logic 3 organisations, we will focus on drawing from the foundations outlined in this book to provide a robust understanding of three key consequences that purpose when done well is logically likely to result in. These are coherence, enterprise and commitment.

REALISE 1: Coherence

"We could see how starved employees were for a clear, meaningful purpose. And till this day our purpose statement is the statement that all employees can rally around when they make decisions in the company.

People are more motivated when they are united in their purpose at work. Today, our purpose helps us to recruit and retain the best talent." These are the words of Jin Montesano, Chief People Officer at Lixil, talking about the coherence that comes from the company having a clear purpose to "Make Better Homes a Reality for Everyone, Everywhere". A Logic 3 organisation, because of a clear purpose and parameters, has the conditions to create a salient identity, a strong culture and aligned stakeholders. The following are aspects of that coherence.

CLEAR SHARED AMBITION

It has long been known that a clear, organisation-wide, and well-communicated ambition is key to organisational success. For example, Collins and Porras gained much traction with their summary of a "Big Hairy Audacious" Goal,[25] and the *Financial Times* promotes their "North Star Strategy". While ambitious goals – whether focused on product quality, customer satisfaction or technological breakthroughs – can drive performance, their impact is significantly amplified when the goal is a genuine purpose. That is because purpose is a distinct kind of goal – the pinnacle shared ambition that gets to the heart of why the organisation exists – and why anyone would want it to.

A SPECIAL TYPE OF DESTINATION

Purpose is a meaningful goal anchored to ambitious tangible impacts on the long-term wellbeing of human or non-human species. Even if this organisational purpose is anchored to small steps along the way – for example, to "support the healthy recovery of bullying victims in the construction sector in Nova Scotia" or "protect small garden birds in Singapore" – this purpose will have been chosen and justified to stakeholders in relation to the effects on long-term wellbeing for all – and so will be emotionally, humanly, meaningful. The fact that the goal is tangible, meaningful and connected to impacts, in turn, builds coherence.

The nature of purpose means that it can endure over a long period in a way that strategy-based goals can't. In a well governed organisation, the governing body will be the ultimate custodians of the purpose – a perpetual body that endures even if members change.

In her additional role as Non-Executive Director for the British Columbia Lottery Corporation, as a large established Crown Corporation in Canada, Coro Strandberg described how the board took responsibility for the purpose as the organisation's pinnacle goal: *"We started from the board down, we started to make some changes. The board amended its terms of reference to state that the board had oversight of the purpose and delegated detailed oversight to the Governance Committee. We supported management's direction to include questions in the employee engagement survey so the board and management could track our success in creating a purpose-driven culture. We went into a CEO search, and, in the process, updated the job description to make oversight of the purpose fundamental to the role. We sought a candidate who had this perspective. We use a third-party Social Purpose Assessment Tool to track the degree to which purpose is integrated into the company, and that drove a 3-year strategy target. The board adopted that target and put it into the CEO's performance objectives to foster accountability for increasing the degree of integration year over year."* This ownership by the governing body, combined with the emotionally engaged relationships that stakeholders can build for a meaningful purpose deepens the foundations of purpose. This means that the governance system, and consequently the organisational culture and expertise, can be developed with care over time – something that is true both internally and within the broader external value network. This is in contrast to a BAU organisation where the highest visible organisational goal is ultimately anchored to following money around markets based on the latest insights or the new CEO's agenda – even where it appears to be other-serving.

Another reason that the nature of purpose builds coherence is the fact that the goal is fundamentally aligned with society's best long-term interest. This systematically helps reduce tensions that arise from societal discontent with Logic 1 or 2 organisations. The ability to be proudly open about the purpose with stakeholders means that the organisation will receive less pressure from society to change course. Even when challenged by Logic 1 stakeholders focused on short-term gains, a well-governed Purpose-Driven Organisation can lean on its purpose to justify its decisions, stand firm in its long-term commitments and stay on course with integrity. Geoff McDonald (ex-Unilever) describes this: *"Having that sense of purpose and the clear translation of it, allowed us to better justify decisions like an acquisition that aligned to that sense of purpose, or selling parts of the business off, you know, which might've led to lots of redundancies and difficult decisions around people's lives. But that decision could be justified to those people who might've been losing their job, that this didn't fit within the frame of Unilever's purpose."*

AGILITY THROUGH STABILITY

Having a clear, shared, meaningful, stable and socially aligned reason to exist, made real through a purpose-driven governance system, results in a level of certainty for decision-makers that reduces anxiety. This, in turn, creates some base conditions for a psychologically safe context where teams can experiment, fail, involve stakeholders, and pivot strategy as needed. It also enables a cornerstone for teams to quickly debate and decide where trade-offs arise. Chapter 4 will delve more into the ways that leaders can further create psychologically safe contexts.

The mistake many start-ups make is to believe that the early coherence that comes from their infectious commitment to and clarity of purpose is enough to carry the organisation forwards. However, it can't be stressed enough that the benefits of coherence are likely to be diluted or wither if reliant on charismatic leaders and not deliberately embedded in the governance system. The Scottish craft brewing company Brewdog fell foul of this. They hired employees and galvanised other stakeholders who were committed to what they felt was a clear, enduring and meaningful purpose – to support the craft beer industry in the face of profit maximising large producers. When employees instead felt that pursuit of this shared purpose was being replaced by decisions based on "growth, at all costs" and as a result creating a "culture of fear", they posted a public letter outlining their concerns.

TAKEAWAY

Well governed Purpose-Driven Organisations create high levels of coherence through a clear, shared ambition, and the enduring and meaningful nature of the ambition. This coherence enables deep culture, expertise and resilience.

REALISE 2: Enterprise

The second benefit realised is enterprise – i.e. actions that are *enterprising*, which are achieved through an *enterprise*. An enterprise is "a project or undertaking that is especially difficult, complicated, or risky" or "a purposeful or industrious undertaking (especially one that requires effort or boldness)". These Merriam Webster definitions seem to sum up the starting point of a Purpose-Driven Organisation. The appropriate and purposeful risk-taking of true enterprise is the real promise of a sustainable market economy: the ability to harness the best of human creativity, bravery and persistence and direct to achieve collective well-being rather than destroying it.

A well governed Purpose-Driven Organisation realises the full potential of the human enterprising spirit. There are three central aspects of this: right risk, bounded blue oceans and market agility.

RIGHT RISK

"The current briefs are nearly always built in a short-term vision and locked towards a budget that makes it also more difficult to do something a bit more long-term, more complex to develop. They come with a lot of these financial constraints regarding, say: 'We want it to be sold at that price unit with this kind of margin'. This kind of brief is a way to still play the 'sustainability' game but inside the traditional box." This is Joachim Froment, a leading designer based out of Brussels and Copenhagen who runs the company Futurewave, describing his typical client brief. He spends much of his time meeting these briefs with a short list of product designs.

Joachim sees first-hand how the decision-making of Logic 1, which he estimated forms the decision-making box for 70–90 per cent of them, shapes how briefs are written, conversations about which to choose and eventually what solution is backed. *"It's not only big corporates – smaller enterprises are in this box too. Start-ups will often think, okay, well if I want to have a profitable business, I use a business model that is like this, that is a traditional business model."* In his view, as well as focusing on which option will make the most money, rather than have the most impact, it is about how much risk is willing to be taken in achieving high levels of income that has massive influence.

He summarised to us how brilliant solutions to sustainability issues are left on the table because the financial payback is a bit longer than normal, or the market is less certain. This is true even when the design option passes all the tests of viability (including financial) desirability and feasibility. Sometimes discussions get really far down the line with the most senior people in the company, but invariably these better solutions will be shelved for "sometime later", while solutions in known markets with more certain financial returns are preferred. He described one situation where *"There was really a purpose in the brief itself – stating they wanted to push the innovation to be more sustainable. We suggested about ten different solutions from some very feasible, some very viable, but some that were really innovatively sustainable and also had really good viability – one that is as close as possible to their current brief – but like is usually the case, they went with the less risky option."*

Well governed Purpose-Driven Organisations can overcome this myopia that plagues decision after decision for Logic 1 organisations. The reason for this is that being purpose-driven creates a new way of approaching and experiencing risk.

Approaching risk differently. Risk is an effect of uncertainty on about what you want to achieve, therefore always subjective. Risk assessment helps decision-making between viable alternative options. When the organisation's goal is to solve some of the most important problems threatening the pinnacle goal of long-term wellbeing for all, then the risk of not acting creates a counterbalancing risk that is highly potent. This provides the basis for accepting more uncertainty about objectives such as financial income and reputation – or trying harder to mitigate them in order to maximise the goal (while, of course, assuring the non-negotiable parameters protect the basis of long-term wellbeing for all). In other words, in a Logic 3 organisation there will be boldness towards achieving the goal. At the same time correct parameters ensure a necessary level of precaution towards protecting the health of the underlying social and environmental systems (see PAS 808 for details).

This is the opposite of the risk approach that characterises a Logic 1 organisation. Aversion to financial loss, combined with a governance frame that embeds blindness to the risks beyond, creates the conditions for what Clayton Christensen coined 'The Innovator's Dilemma'.[26] Faced with the urgent need to transform business models due to rampant unsustainability, Logic 1 incumbents do not have the decision-making structures to enable them to routinely take risk related to current financial income streams, in order to ensure them for the long-term. While a handful of Logic 1 organisations like Netflix have been able to do this (in relation to profit maximising trends) they are held up as unique examples – precisely because it is not normal. This is perhaps the biggest barrier for organisations that want to move from Logic 1 (short-term self-interest) to Logic 2 (long-term self-interest). While in theory, acting for the longer term and leaving easy, quick financial returns on the table sounds like the right thing to do, creating a governance culture that results in decisions that run counter to decades of Logic 1 lock-in is hard. Furthermore, even if an organisation is fully Logic 2, decisions are filtered through those that maximise financial income and self-enhancement or survival remains the core goal.

On the other hand, for Logic 3 organisations, because profit is a tool and not the goal, and risk is defined against bigger, riskier issues facing long-term wellbeing, it becomes rational to act more boldly. The drive for "survival at all costs" that constrains Logic 1 and 2 is not a drag either. Although a Purpose-Driven Organisation will be motivated to be extremely well run, the only reason it is exists is to achieve its purpose. The logical starting position for a truly Purpose-Driven Organisation is therefore: "Why would I want to continue to survive if I have achieved the purpose? Either we should find a new purpose that needs achieving or we should pack up and go home. Someone else could better use the resources we are utilising."

There are many examples of organisations that, fuelled by purpose-driven intent, completely transformed their business and shunned the excess profits they could make from staying put. Interface Flor made dramatic business model changes and invested heavily in it, fuelled by purpose. DSM, the Dutch multinational and Ørsted, the Danish energy company, are examples of singular fossil fuel actors that completely changed markets – DSM diversifying into a wide range of industries including health, nutrition and materials and Ørsted becoming one of the largest wind turbine and renewable energy companies in the world.

Experiencing risk differently. Risk will also be experienced differently by Logic 3 organisations. The reduced "cognitive lock-in" that comes with walking away from BAU assumptions gives decision-makers greater degrees of freedom to think systemically and implement new ideas and navigate obstacles – supported by the governance system. This is enhanced by the fact that purpose is a big, clear, stable goal as outlined previously, resulting in expertise and cultural infrastructure supporting it. Finally, purpose enables the development of deeper, more meaningful relationships with stakeholders creating a tangible reduction in risk; risk is more likely to be spread amongst the value network and there is more resilience to foresee and mitigate problems. This is underpinned by more open, vulnerable relationships where potential issues can be dynamically pre-empted by stakeholders.

BOUNDED BLUE OCEANS

Alongside a shift in risk perception, a well-governed Purpose-Driven Organisation can make far more creative decisions than Logic 1 or 2 organisations. Why? Firstly, they are free from the BAU assumptions that create a box around decisions such as how contracts work, what kinds of partnerships are normal and the types of payback times expected. Combined with the clarity of a stable purpose, Purpose-Driven Organisations can navigate the formal market, and informal, routes to impact with blue ocean creativity.

At the same time, having hard clear governance parameters that reflect actual constraints in the real world, serve to bound and amplify this blue ocean creativity in technically sound ways.

Constraints are the mother of innovation as they say. These constraints include making enough money to be able to pay the bills, invest in the purpose and meet the expectations of stakeholders. For example, even establishing financial capital as a parameter can have profound effects on creativity. Jin Montesano, the groundbreaking Purpose-Driven Leader explained how introducing healthy stocks and flows of financial capital as a hard constraint transformed the innovation of a philanthropic endeavour in her company: *"When our new CEO, Kinya Seto, arrived at LIXIL, we sat down to review the SATO initiative. He challenged us as a team by saying, 'I give you 5 years to try and break even. Please design a business model that enables SATO to be self-sufficient.' The goal of SATO was to improve the lives of 100 million people by 2025 through basic sanitation. But with the P&L challenge in front of us, it gave us the opportunity to build a team and put investments behind a budget that allowed the team to build a scalable business. This supercharged our creativity because we had to create a business model, markets and market offerings that could do all this."*

This wasn't the first time in her career that Jin had to wield transformational marketing creativity to achieve a purpose within hard constraints. Jin described a time she presented to the CEO of a large pharmaceutical company on its journey to being purpose-driven, on the realities of moving from a high margin / low creativity situation to being purpose-driven – often lower margin / high creativity: 'You know that all we have to do is completely change our product mix. You know you're gonna have to change the product mix to get the margins that we need to break even.'

While financial profits, as a parameter, are central to being purpose-driven, but, as Dr Tayba Hatimy of the purpose-driven waste management company Baus Taka describes, profits as a goal is a deadweight for the level and type of innovation the world needs: *"When you're thinking about empowering communities, you get to be more creative, and you explore more ideas, too, as compared to you just wanting to go to a community and make money. Like, is this going to make me money? I need to do one, two, get paid, and I'm out. But for us, it's like, we go down to the communities, we interact one on one, with the women, with the youth, with the children – we empathise and want to walk in their shoes. We go back to the drawing board and see how can we come up with a solution that is a local solution – a localised solution, but an innovative solution."*

Similarly, when Dole Sunshine Co. outsourced the Chief Marketing Office to The Shed 28, co-founders Rupen Desai and Ranjit Jathanna took on the roles of being global CMO and CCO. Their roles were to lead how the company embedded a more purpose-driven approach at the heart of its business model. In doing so, creativity at the company was transformed. Over three years, they systematically integrated this purpose-driven approach into the economic model and entered new market categories with valuable resources that had previously been discarded. As they described to us: *"We believe purposeful is what purposeful does and we did not let existing ways of doing things limit our thinking. Instead, we focused on creating as many 'win–win-wins' as possible including ensuring we met necessary margins."* This included the collaboration with Ananas Anam to turn waste pineapple leaves into Piñatex, a vegan leather alternative, as well as repurposing fruit side streams into high-value natural products like enzymes, extracts seed oils and fibres. The company entered new categories by upcycling fruit by-products into fermented drinks, vitamin gummies and healthy snacks.

MARKET SENSITIVITY

The final driver of enterprise is that well governed Purpose-Driven Organisations can engage in innovation which sensitively flexes to create markets that count – not just service the demands of easy to charge customers or those customers that can pay the most. It is widely recognised and well-documented that BAU Logic 1 enterprise routinely services just a small proportion of the population, leaving aside a vast range of viable markets where people are in real need of wellbeing solutions.

The 2002 article by Stuart Hart and Clayton Christensen outlined the underserved markets at the "base of the pyramid" (BOP) and from there, the notion of serving BOP markets to tap into unseen profit maximising opportunities became popular.[27] Logic 1 firms should have poured in. Despite this, unsurprisingly given what we have outlined about the Logic 1 approach to risk, these markets continue to be ignored in favour of more certain and familiar market returns. For Purpose-Driven Organisations, BOP markets are a natural place to focus efforts. Jin Montesano of Lixil describes how the purpose of *"Make Better Homes a Reality for Everyone, Everywhere"* automatically led them there: *"If we're really aiming for everyone everywhere, then we can't just be selling premium products or targeting only a specific segment of consumers. We need to find a way to meet the needs of everyone. And we need to be doing this in a way that protects the planet and supports people in society."*

Further bringing this to life, Cambridge University scholar, Professor Jaideep Prabhu, along with his colleague Navi Radjou, shone a light on the Indian concept of Jugaad Innovation to the mainstream with their book *Frugal Innovation.*[28] The book is full of examples of organisations started and run by enterprising leaders that are looking to solve the important problems of wellbeing for the largest number of local populations. In summary Jugaad is about "doing more with less". This often requires getting close to the source of the problem, leveraging local resources, knowledge and talent and adapting traditional methods.

Beyond BOP markets, the literature is full of new products and markets that leaders note only happened because of the enterprising spirit they gained on their journey to becoming purpose-driven. Geoff McDonald's tenure at Unilever spanned the time before Paul Polman became CEO. He explained to us the difference purpose made to spurring innovation that created a massive wellbeing-return-on-financial-investment, through market sensitivity: *"When we put purpose and the goals to achieve it at the centre of decision-making, our brands brought innovations to the market that Unilever would never, ever have thought about ... for example one of the goals was to reduce water consumption and based on that we innovated a brand called One Rinse. All over the world people who were using our washing powders in rural communities were rinsing garments six or seven times – I saw it in China. We responded with One Rinse. So, one of the things that purpose did was it created a far more innovative organisation. Having that goal around reducing our water footprint led to innovations that just wouldn't have happened otherwise".*

TAKEAWAY

Well-governed Purpose-Driven Organisations will realise high levels of enterprising action through taking the right risk, thinking in "bounded blue oceans" and being able to navigate markets in an agile way. This results in the bold and wellbeing relevant innovation needed, without harming the people and systems we depend on in the process.

REALISE 3: Commitment

The final likely result of being a well governed Purpose-Driven Organisation that we want to highlight is the higher levels of ongoing, resilient and committed support from the humans who are in the organisation's stakeholder constellation. It is only something that an organisation can properly benefit from when they cross the divide from being a Logic 1 or 2 self-interested organisation, to a Logic 3 organisation authentically doing their best work for the common good. There are three key aspects that underpin this level of enhanced commitment: care, connectivity and collaboration.

CARE

It is well established that when people care about achieving a goal, they will go further and faster to achieve it. Purpose taps into the central motivation of humans – to avoid a sense that our lives are meaningless and instead to wake up every day feeling that the world is better because we exist. This primes us to act in a purposeful way towards long-term wellbeing for all simultaneously using and expanding our sphere of influence to move organisations, the economy and themselves to Logic 3. The search for meaning and the role leaders play in enabling Purposeful Work and Lives is explored in more detail in Chapter 4.

When the core reason for the organisation to exist is anchored to long-term wellbeing for all, and brought to life by brilliant governance and leadership, then a high level of energy and commitment by personnel and all stakeholders is possible. This is a level that is just logically less likely in self-interested, financially focused Logic 1 or 2 organisations. Geoff McDonald, gave us a prime example of the results of Unilever going on a purpose-driven journey: *"The other consequence was this attractiveness as an organisation: to want to work for an organisation that was trying to give something back to the world. I remember us recruiting a very, very senior market insight guy, the senior vice president for market insights. And he worked for Coca-Cola in Atlanta as their Senior Vice President. We made an offer to him. I remember making that offer to him and he looked at me and he said, Geoff, why? I mean, he said, why would I come as a local to London, work for a brand that hardly anybody knows about called Unilever? I'm now working for the probably most recognised brand in the world called Coca Cola. I said, you know what I'd like you to do is just pause and I want you to take this booklet on Unilever's sustainable living plan and I want you to read about what it is that we want to try and do in the world. Two days later, he came back and said, Geoff, where can I sign? I want to be part of an organisation that wants to do some of that. So, our ability to attract talent into the organisation by having that greater sense of purpose was off the scale."* He went on to explain to us what that meant in terms of engagement scores across the organisation: *"We sat in the lower end of the upper quartile. You know, at the end of five years of beginning to embed this type of stuff those engagement scores moved to the top end of the upper quartile 85% plus."*

CONNECTIVITY

As outlined previously, it is one thing to state a purpose and another to live it. This requires the right governance system to support leaders to really bring the system to life – and this happens through building emotional and relational connective tissue throughout the internal and wider value network. A Purpose-Driven Organisation recognises the value of emotional engagement and feelings of ownership and inclusivity with the organisation. Leaders make themselves informed of the systems that comprise this value network. As a result, there is a logical foundation for integrating stakeholders as co-decision makers (depending on the nature of those stakeholders as outlined in Chapter 2, Retool 2). Connectivity extends beyond current stakeholders and to affected stakeholders who are often voiceless. For example, designating a decision-maker to represent future generations, non-human life ("nature") and / or non-human systems (a particular ecosystem such as a river).

Coro Strandberg, Non-executive Director at the British Columbia Lottery Corporation, described for us how their journey to purpose, led them to governance questions being asked to create better connectivity between the company and stakeholders. She explains: *"The board realised it didn't have sufficient perspective on the status of the stakeholder relationships at the company. That's what began the stakeholder governance framework that the Board adopted which names our primary and secondary stakeholders upon whom we depend for our success. Management is creating stakeholder engagement strategies for each of our primary stakeholders over maybe five or seven years completing one or two a year. And in those stakeholder engagement strategies, management sets out how it wants to collaborate with that stakeholder to achieve our purpose, create stakeholder value and foster meaningful and reciprocal relationships. As part of that we are developing KPIs with our stakeholder groups that is a perception type survey about our purpose. We ask questions around how they feel about collaborating with us on our purpose, these kinds of things, it basically makes real the fact that we need to collaborate with our stakeholders on our purpose as we can't fulfil our purpose on our own."*

Well-governed Purpose-Driven Organisations also build a level of intellectual as well as emotional connectivity over time. Catherine Wood of Coast Capital Savings describes how the rich attractiveness of the purpose moves parts of the organisation to connect with it, and each other: *"We started with the desired outcomes for our purpose. These outcomes were human-centric, meaning they played a role in someone's overall wellbeing. Money is part of this, but it's not holistic enough. To achieve our aspirations, we needed to rely on the creativity of people who resonated with our purpose. As a result, our strategy and culture shifted to be less siloed and hierarchical. This attracted people who resonated with our purpose and brought new ideas to the table."* She went on to explain that this resulted in an informal obligation to those stakeholders – to deliver on the promise to those that had made that connection and those that had taken the leap to invest.

CO-CREATION

As outlined in this chapter in Retool 3: The Evolved Value Framework, co-creation, instead of arms-length innovation, is essential because markets are symbolically constructed. A further reason for leaning into co-creation, a form of collaboration, is because Purpose-Driven Organisations are tackling tough stretch goals to make an optimal contribution to complex and urgent issues threatening long-term well-being for all. This means they cannot achieve that goal alone.

Catherine Wood describes the necessity of broad-reach collaboration to achieve their purpose: *"We recognised that government and community-based institutions weren't capable of doing it on their own. By creating an ecosystem, we can better find and serve vulnerable, equity-seeking, and marginalised groups."* Because of this, Coast Capital actively collaborates with and helps fund many of these community-based organisations, which enables them to access those they seek to benefit through their purpose.

Geoff McDonald, ex-Global Vice President of Unilever, confirmed that the purpose led to strategies that transformed collaborations at Unilever, way beyond what a normal Logic 1 organisation would either conceive of or be able to realise: *"So if I take India and the brand Lifebuoy, what it required was to collaborate with the Indian government, the education department to get hand washing into the national curriculum. Why? Because Lifebuoy was a brand that was positioned as saving lives by teaching young children to wash their hands after they had been to the toilet and thus prevent diarrhoea. And, we were authentic and the product was authentic in its formulation. The other organisation that we had to collaborate with was Unicef because Unilever didn't have the distribution capabilities that Unicef had to get this brand into the most rural parts of India and other developing markets."*

The nature of the purpose goal also logically supports co-creation and collaboration in general, for reasons that include:

1. The organisation is acting for the good of others, not themselves – breaking down issues of distrust and lack of motivation that can plague Logic 1 collaborations where self-interest is known goal.

2. Organisations identifying, declaring and communicating their purpose publicly enables full view by potential collaborative partners, of where synergies are likely to exist.

3. Anchoring to a shared ultimate goal of long-term wellbeing for all, means that while the organisation's distinct purpose will be individual, there is always a shared goal that any purpose-driven actor can return to when strategic conversations get fraught or personal. Even if the collaboration isn't with a purpose-driven actor, long-term wellbeing for all is also the closest we may get to a shared purpose for humanity as a whole, so with humans in the room, the chances of getting sustained buy-in is greater.

TAKEAWAY

Well governed Purpose-Driven Organisations will build commitment through care, connectivity and commitment. This provides the foundation for deep wisdom, resilience and sustained energy from stakeholders.

In conclusion, achieving a Wellbeing Economy will be impossible without a deliberate global shift towards Purpose-Driven Organisations – including Purpose-Driven governments. These organisations must be consciously governed to translate the ambition of long-term wellbeing for all into practical, systemic change. This chapter has explored how leaders can begin that shift by challenging foundational assumptions, engaging with key tools and seeing the potential of the positive flywheels they can set in motion. To build Purpose-Driven Organisations and realise a Wellbeing Economy, leaders must tap into and unleash the purpose-driven energy that already exists within themselves and those they lead.

Chapter 4 will bring this to life through Ben's experience coaching CEOs and senior teams – offering real-world stories, insights and inspiration to energise this vital journey.

CHAPTER 4

MICRO

Leading for Purposeful Work and Lives

● ● ●

So far in *Beyond Profit*, we have explored the creation of long-term wellbeing for all, which represents humanity's enduring shared purpose, the definition of sustainability and the ultimate goal of governments and the economy.

Chapter 3 connected the Macro and Meso levels by explaining why ideas about the economy, success and measurement remain theoretical until they are actively brought to life within organisations. To transform ideas into action, the most powerful system leaders need to understand, and leverage, the governance system which shapes routine decision-making and organisational culture. Both the Macro and Meso levels are human-made systems brought to life by us as individuals. Who we are, the energy we bring, and how we see the world ultimately direct this energy, defining whether we create a world of declining wellbeing or one of collective long-term wellbeing for all, where better lives nourish and replenish the systems that sustain them.

At the heart of this dynamic lies our deepest human motivations. Previously, we explored how Logic 1 conditions our motivations towards financial self-interest, implying that accumulating wealth and purchasing more goods and services leads to a better life. This narrative, reinforced by marketing messages and governmental systems, leaves us without the tools to truly understand what wellbeing means for ourselves and those around us or how to achieve it effectively within the organisations where we work.

A shift to Logic 3 at the Micro level involves refocusing our motivations – and those of the people we influence – onto the ultimate goal: collective long-term wellbeing. This shift taps into the most powerful, infinite resource available: our desire for a meaningful life, fulfilled by positively impacting the wellbeing of others. While spiritual leaders have emphasised this for millennia, Viktor Frankl famously outlined this motivation in his 1985 book *Man's Search for Meaning*, Einstein referenced this sentiment in a 1948 interview: "I believe in one thing – that only a life lived for others is a life worth living." Similarly, Winston Churchill said: "We make a living by what we get, but we make a life by what we give."

Our innate purpose-driven nature, often suppressed under Logic 1 decision-making, holds this potential. If we are human, we are capable of being purpose-driven. It doesn't matter if we work in an organisation that isn't. Wherever you are in a system you can be purpose-driven and surrounded by people and systems in Logic 1 or 2. Given we live in a Logic 1 world, this is the reality we face. While it is harder to realise Purpose-Driven Leadership when your immediate surroundings are not, the task that comes with purpose is to work to shift the system around, as much and as far as you can.

While the purpose potential exists within all of us, it is a capability that requires conscious development. Modern science reinforces what ancient wisdom has long understood: our wellbeing is intricately tied to the wellbeing of all people and the planet. Behavioural science reminds us that our deepest sense of worth depends on the wellbeing of others, not merely for physical needs but for emotional and psychological fulfilment.

To fully harness this energy, it is not enough to adopt Logic 3 leadership principles – we must also actively break free from Logic 1 tendencies, which have long been presented as the hallmarks of successful leadership. The global movements shifting from GDP-driven economies to Wellbeing Economies and from profit-driven to Purpose-Driven Organisations mirror a broader shift in individual lives from financially-driven work to meaningful work. Though these shifts often operate independently, they are accelerating in parallel, as evidenced in people rejecting self-interested companies, academics advocating for a redefinition of "human resources", a surge in purpose-driven coaching and professional bodies evolving their leadership training frameworks. As with Macro and Meso systems, the opportunity lies in uniting this collective energy to become fully conscious of what we are moving from – and what we are moving towards.

A vast body of knowledge from diverse global traditions and increasingly enriched by longstanding indigenous wisdom offers profound insights into what constitutes a meaningful life and how to achieve it. Attempting to summarise this wealth of knowledge would be impossible. Instead, our task here is more focused but equally important: to help you develop your capacity as a Logic 3 Purpose-Driven Leader through rethinking, retooling and realising leadership insights drawn from real-life experience. While the examples primarily reflect the hard-earned wisdom of Ben as a global CEO business coach, the foundational principles shared are equally relevant to community, government and NGO leaders.

RETHINK

Leaders are paid to think. It is one of the most critical facets of leadership. Yet in our hyperactive lives, most leaders are too busy to truly think. This is not smart. Better thinking leads to better outcomes, and in a world teetering on late-stage unsustainability, there has never been a greater need to apply our best thinking possible.

As discussed in Chapter 1, leading *Beyond Profit* is the leadership agenda of the 21st century. Our work and lives are shaped by theories – beliefs about how the world works. Everything that has happened in the past and everything we perceive about the future stems from a theory we hold.

These theories directly shape the outcomes we create. They define what problems we consider ours to solve and which we accept as inevitable, who we believe we are influencing and how we think we can create that influence. Therefore, now more than ever, we must strive for clarity about the theories we rely on and critically assess whether they are truly serving us – and the world – well.

Rethink invites you to explore three of the most fundamental shifts required to become a Purpose-Driven Leader:

1. Money to Meaning
2. Doing to Being
3. Fear to Love

These shifts may challenge the paradigms you currently use to make decisions. However, by approaching this personal inquiry with intense curiosity, you can create a coherent mental map that is essential for building clarity and confidence as you engage with change at the Meso (organisational) and Macro (economic) levels.

There are no neutral points of view, and therefore, no value-neutral acts – whether we are conscious of them or not. By rethinking your leadership, you become more aware of the beliefs you hold about what is valuable. This awareness allows you to intentionally align your actions with what matters most.

Arriving at a clear understanding of what truly matters will unlock your potential to contribute meaningfully to the fundamental objective that unites us all: long-term wellbeing for all.

RETHINK 1: Money to Meaning

Above all, leaders can be considered meaning makers. A Purpose-Driven Leader fulfils this role in three primary areas:

1. MEANING FOR SELF

It is vital for leaders to be clear about what things mean to them personally. Developing an informed point of view requires integrating multiple data points that reflect the complex realities around us. However, many leaders fail to take the time to consider diverse perspectives or deepen their understanding of critical systemic issues, such as the breakdown in social and environmental health, which shape the context in which they operate. These gaps in understanding can limit their ability to make informed decisions, communicate effectively and guide others.

By making sense of this complexity emotionally and strategically, leaders can gain a broader perspective, enabling them to navigate challenges with clarity and confidence while developing resilience in themselves and their teams.

2. MEANING FOR OTHERS

As a leader, you bear the responsibility of creating environments where others can reflect deeply, make sense of their experiences and connect to a greater purpose. This goes beyond transactional conversations; it involves creating spaces for meaningful dialogue that inspires and aligns.

Justin Reese, CEO of Ghirardelli, highlights this role: "In today's world, employees have different expectations from their leaders. They want leaders to provide clear direction, set the strategy, and inspire. They expect leaders to make meaningful connections with them at every level of the organisation. Leaders must be able to respond to questions on geopolitical and socio-economic issues, translating the noise from the press into actionable insights. Your ability as a leader to hold a meaningful perspective on a wide range of topics and connect deeply with people is incredibly powerful."

By providing meaning for others, leaders empower their teams to see how their roles contribute to a greater purpose. This not only enhances individual motivation but also strengthens collective understanding and alignment.

3. MEANING FOR THE ORGANISATION

A Purpose-Driven Leader serves as a custodian of the organisation's purpose and its evolution towards becoming fully purpose-driven. This responsibility spans both governance and management:

- **Governance:** Directing, overseeing and being accountable for the organisation's purpose. This includes ensuring that the organisation operates within clear parameters that prioritise and safeguard long-term wellbeing for all stakeholders.
- **Management:** Planning and executing strategies that align with the organisation's purpose and governance framework.

By clarifying and consistently living out the organisation's purpose in a transparent and authentic way, Purpose-Driven Leaders inform, engage and inspire employees, stakeholders and collaborators. This alignment infuses the organisation with a shared sense of meaning and direction, creating a unified and motivated culture.

In the following sections, we will explore these three dimensions of meaning in greater depth. Each area offers unique opportunities for leaders to unlock purpose and create lasting impact.

Meaning for self

Sindy was tasked with leading the delivery of a multi-billion-dollar infrastructure programme in a highly regulated industry. The company's reputation – and its share price – were heavily tied to the successful and timely completion of the programme. The Board was hyper-focused on performance, having suffered a costly project failure in the past that had resulted in financial losses, job terminations and reputational damage. Sindy operated in a high-pressure environment where the CEO demanded daily data reviews, intensely scrutinising performance metrics.

While trying to manage Board expectations, lead her team and collaborate across the organisation, Sindy faced a dilemma. Her detailed oversight was perceived as micromanagement by her team, undermining their sense of autonomy and trust. Yet, from her perspective, staying deeply involved was essential for keeping the Board satisfied and avoiding further scrutiny.

Sindy's situation reflected a classic Logic 1 environment where short-term financial self-interest dominates decision-making. Logic 1 pressures often crowd out the capacity to address broader systemic factors, such as long-term sustainability, employee wellbeing and organisational culture. Many leaders, like Sindy, feel trapped in this cycle of relentless task focus, leaving little room for reflection on deeper systemic challenges.

However, leaders worldwide are beginning to shift from this limited paradigm towards Logic 3, where the emphasis is on purpose and long-term wellbeing. This transition involves rethinking personal success, moving beyond short-term gains to focus on deeper meaning and sustainable impact.

A 2023 report from the Great Place To Work institute, "The power of purpose in the workplace", highlighted this shift.[1] It found that employees increasingly seek meaningful work and often reflect on questions such as:

- "How does what I do here matter?"
- "What is my purpose?"
- "Why am I doing the work I'm doing?"

Michael C. Bush, CEO of Great Place to Work, encapsulated this evolution, stating: "For me, purpose transcends P&Ls, balance sheets, and

EBITDA calculations. Purpose is the reason we miss family dinners and important events – it's why we question our priorities and life choices. Yet many leaders still default to financial incentives instead of providing the deeper sense of purpose employees crave."

Sindy's CEO, aware of the mounting challenges, approached us for support. He expressed concerns about her ability to sustain the project's demands and pace without sacrificing her wellbeing or leadership effectiveness. When we met Sindy, she was transparent about the tensions she faced in balancing the Board's expectations, satisfying the CEO, and maintaining the morale of her team. When asked what success truly looked like for her leadership, Sindy described aspirations far beyond the project's deliverables. She wanted to build a culture where people could thrive, progress in their careers, nourish their wellbeing, build trust and find fulfilment at work. Yet, under constant task pressure, she realised she had not clearly communicated these values with her CEO.

This realisation marked a turning point. We encouraged Sindy to shift from a performance-driven mindset to a purpose-driven one, redefining success not just as meeting deadlines but creating an environment where people could contribute meaningfully.

To initiate this shift, we asked Sindy to step back from the relentless task-focus and reflect. She created a leadership framework anchored in purpose and crafted a compelling narrative for her CEO and team. The three pillars of her new leadership approach included:

- **Aligning performance with purpose:** Deliver results not for their own sake but as a way to contribute to societal progress.

- **Fostering relationships and community:** Build a culture of trust and collaboration where people could bring their best selves to work.

- **Providing growth opportunities:** Create an environment where continuous learning and personal development were prioritised alongside operational targets.

This clarity reinvigorated Sindy, providing her with renewed energy and direction. When she presented her thinking to the CEO, he responded positively, recognising the potential for a more engaged and motivated workforce. Together, they introduced new cultural practices, such as storytelling workshops and purpose-aligned performance reviews, to inspire the team.

Sindy's transformation illustrates the critical leadership shift from Money to Meaning. By reconnecting her work with a broader sense of purpose, she was able to unlock greater resilience and motivation not only for herself but for her entire team.

The importance of this shift is reinforced by insights from thought leaders like Clayton Christensen who in his *Harvard Business Review* article "How will you measure your life?" posed three profound questions:

- "How can I be happy in my career?"
- "How can I ensure my relationships remain a source of happiness?"
- "How can I live my life with integrity?"[2]

Psychologist Frederick Herzberg, cited by Christensen, further emphasised: "The most powerful motivator isn't money. It's the opportunity to learn, grow, contribute, and be recognised."

This insight aligns with findings from McKinsey & Company, which identified a "meaning quotient" as a critical factor for workplace success.[3] Their research concluded that employees crave more than financial rewards. They also seek to feel that their work truly matters and makes a difference to others.

Like Sindy, to be a Purpose-Driven Leader requires rethinking your relationship with money and clarifying what is most meaningful to you. Without this clarity, it's easy to remain trapped in a Logic 1 system, chasing short-term outcomes that fail to deliver lasting fulfilment or wellbeing.

By consciously anchoring leadership in purpose, leaders can create environments where both performance and personal growth thrive – unlocking the full potential of people and organisations alike.

Meaning for others

A core responsibility of a Purpose-Driven Leader is to consciously create conditions where others can experience work as meaningful – beyond financial gain. The shift from Money to Meaning reflects a deeper understanding of human motivation. People are driven not only by external rewards but also by the desire to contribute to something greater than themselves. It is this intrinsic motivation that fuels purpose, resilience and long-term success, moving leadership from self-interest to serving others. As leaders, we have the capacity to enable this deeper sense of meaning within our teams and organisations.

Bestselling author Daniel Pink explores this dynamic in his landmark book *Drive*, where he highlights the importance of creating environments centred on purpose, autonomy and mastery – core elements of intrinsic motivation.[4] Pink emphasises that while external rewards like bonuses may generate short-term results, they often undermine long-term performance and engagement. He explains: "The people who are intrinsically motivated to do amazing work don't make career decisions based solely on salary and perks. They choose a job because they'll do work with great people. Or they'll get to use their strengths. Or it's a place where they can accomplish something meaningful. A place where they can learn and grow as a person."

When leaders create environments where autonomy, mastery and purpose are aligned, they unlock powerful, sustainable sources of motivation. Employees feel connected to their work in ways that transcend financial incentives – enabling higher performance, creativity and personal fulfilment.

Few have captured the transformative power of meaning more profoundly than Viktor Frankl. Born in Vienna in 1905, Frankl was a neurologist, psychiatrist and Holocaust survivor whose family perished in Nazi concentration camps. His personal experiences of suffering and survival led him to develop *logotherapy* – a psychological approach based on the belief that our primary drive as humans is the search for meaning.

In his seminal work, *Man's Search for Meaning*, Frankl shares his reflections from Auschwitz, revealing that those who found meaning – even in the direst circumstances – were more likely to endure.[5] He wrote:

"It was the men who comforted others and who gave away their last piece of bread who survived the longest – and who offered proof that everything can be taken away from us except the ability to choose our attitude in any given set of circumstances. The sort of person the prisoner became was the result of an inner decision and not of camp influences alone."

Frankl's insights reveal a powerful truth: our capacity for meaning-making is not contingent on our environment but on our internal choices. He further observed:

"For success, like happiness, cannot be pursued; it must ensue, and it only does so as the unintended side-effect of one's personal dedication to a cause greater than oneself."

To enable meaning for others we resonated with the sentiment of Justin Basini, CEO and Co-founder of The ClearScore Group, a British financial technology business. In our inspiring interview he recounted: "Building a business, especially as a founder, you need to tap into both the rational and irrational, more emotional, aspects of people. The odds are stacked against you as a start-up and any rational view alone, any sane person, might conclude that it's futile so why bother founding or joining a start-up. So, you have to demonstrate that your mission is important enough for people to take the risk. That's where purpose comes in and, in my opinion, for most people, you have to go beyond money. This was one of the founding beliefs of ClearScore – the numbers are of course important, but for most people our mission, helping our users master their finances, is much more motivating. The majority of people connect with stories that evoke emotion – tapping into the human side of the impact that your business is having is powerful. Bringing people back to a consistent storyline, the mission, as well as the financial fundamentals, means you combine both the rational and emotional to maximise motivation."

This perspective underscores the role of leaders as meaning-makers. Purpose-Driven Leadership is not just about guiding teams towards organisational objectives; it is about helping individuals connect their daily contributions to a greater cause. It is in this connection where the deepest motivation and fulfilment reside.

Meaning for your organisation

To help others live meaningful work and lives while developing as Purpose-Driven Leaders, leadership must extend beyond the personal or team level. It requires actively engaging with the Meso level of the organisation where governance systems are designed, cultural norms are embedded and daily decisions are shaped. Purpose-Driven Leaders have a responsibility to create and implement governance structures that embed meaning, aligning the organisation's day-to-day realities with the ultimate goal of long-term wellbeing for all.

Renowned academics Sumantra Ghoshal and Christopher Bartlett highlighted the consequences of Logic 1 thinking, which obscures the true purpose of organisations, in their seminal article "Beyond strategy to purpose":[6]

"In most corporations today, people no longer know – or even care – what or why their companies are. In such an environment, leaders have an urgent role to play. Obviously, they must retain control over the processes that frame the company's strategic priorities. But strategies can engender strong, enduring emotional attachments only when they are embedded in a broader organisational purpose. This means creating an organisation with which members can identify, in which they share a sense of pride, and to which they are willing to commit. In short, senior managers must convert the contractual employees of an economic entity into committed members of a purposeful organisation."

This reflection underscores how essential it is for leaders to elevate the organisation's sense of purpose beyond financial metrics. Without a broader purpose, even the most capable employees can become disconnected from the true value their work brings to society.

Even within financially driven environments, some of the world's most influential leaders have publicly recognised the need to embed meaning and purpose into the core of organisational leadership. Larry Fink, CEO of BlackRock, the world's largest asset manager, has consistently emphasised the importance of Purpose-Driven Leadership in his annual letters to CEOs.

In his widely discussed 2018 letter "A Sense of Purpose"[6], Fink stressed the need for companies to serve a social purpose, shifting away from short-term profit maximisation:[7]

"Society is demanding that companies, both public and private, serve a social purpose ... Without a sense of purpose, no company, either public or private, can achieve its full potential. It will ultimately lose the license to operate from key stakeholders. It will succumb to short-term pressures to distribute earnings, and, in the process, sacrifice investments in employee development, innovation, and capital expenditures necessary for long-term growth."

He argued that long-term sustainability and financial performance are deeply linked to purpose-driven strategies that consider employee development, innovation and stakeholder relationships. Fink reinforced this message in his 2022 letter, "The Power of Capitalism":[8]

"Over the past three decades, I've had the opportunity to talk with countless CEOs and to learn what distinguishes truly great companies. Time and again, what they all share is that they have a clear sense of purpose, consistent values, and, crucially, they recognise the importance of engaging with and delivering for their key stakeholders."

These reflections highlight a pivotal leadership truth: Organisations that anchor themselves in purpose can inspire deeper employee commitment, create long-term resilience and build stronger relationships with stakeholders.

Justin Basini, CEO and Co-Founder of the ClearScore Group brought this to life in our conversation. He shared: "When I started ClearScore I committed the business to making a positive impact on the financial wellbeing of our users. This was a personal passion of mine and motivates me and others in the team. As a result, I think we have a workplace which is unique. We've spent the last 9 years disrupting an industry and having a positive impact on millions of users around the world. At the heart of this success is our unique culture, where we work hard, embrace change and treat each other with respect. We want everyone to reach their potential and deliver results that make a difference to our users. We have developed a focus on being user first, our partners (financial institutions) second, and revenue third. This helps us understand that the financials of the business are a result of delivering for our users and our partners. This has become very meaningful for our team to be part of delivering our mission. It drives our productivity, focus, attraction and retention of talent and ultimately is the core of our success."

Shifting from a Logic 1 mindset (short-term self-interest) to a Logic 3 approach (long-term wellbeing for all) requires structural change. Leaders must go beyond rhetoric and actively design governance systems with direction, oversight and accountability that ensure the purpose is clearly articulated and integrated into decision-making, not just as a vision statement but as a basis for all policies, incentives and success measures. This ensures decisions are aligned with long-term wellbeing for all (see Chapter 3 for details).

In Chapter 3, we explored the practical governance and management details of a Purpose-Driven Organisation, one that contributes actively to a Wellbeing Economy. While every structural element of this system matters, its success hinges on a central leadership responsibility: creating an emotional connection between people's work and the meaningful impacts the organisation generates.

This emotional connection transcends individual tasks and roles. It links personal contributions to the broader organisational purpose – the ultimate goal of collective long-term wellbeing for all. Leaders play a critical role in ensuring this alignment by weaving information-rich stories that resonate with employees, stakeholders and the wider community. These stories help clarify how daily efforts contribute to the organisation's higher purpose and societal impact, bridging the gap between individual work and long-term collective outcomes.

A Purpose-Driven Organisation thrives when its people feel genuinely connected to its purpose. Emotional resonance fuels engagement, commitment and a sense of belonging, qualities essential for sustained impact. Leaders must actively cultivate this emotional clarity by consistently reinforcing the connection between work and purpose through storytelling, transparent communication and visible actions.

This emotional link is not a peripheral aspect of leadership but the foundation of meaningful work. It generates the energy and motivation required for a Purpose-Driven Organisation to succeed and fulfil its role in creating a Wellbeing Economy.

TAKEAWAY

Being clear about what matters beyond money anchors your decisions in what matters most.

RETHINK 2: Doing to Being

Craig was a high-performing C-suite executive in a publicly listed company. From humble beginnings in northern Scotland, his grandfather worked in coal mines, his father was a professional footballer who retrained as a plumber after a career-ending accident and his mother was the steady anchor raising five children. Seeking financial stability, Craig pursued a career in accountancy, working his way to the top. Now married with three loving children, he juggled multiple leadership responsibilities – serving on the Board, leading his function, managing stakeholders and contributing to the Executive Committee – while also struggling to maintain his personal wellbeing.

When we met Craig, he was on the brink of burnout. Approaching 50, he admitted his primary strategy for wellbeing was "retirement" – enduring another ten years of "hardship", believing that only then could he enjoy life.

To shift his mindset, we encouraged Craig to revisit what it truly means to be human. Initially sceptical, he acknowledged that his current path was unsustainable. We asked him about his morning habits – what was on his mind upon waking? His answers were task-driven: checking overnight numbers, managing crises, attending meetings, monitoring traffic and calculating how many times he could hit snooze before facing the day. His thinking was task-focused, reflecting a pattern we've observed in many leaders – prioritising doing over being.

This overemphasis on doing begins early. Children from financially stable families often face overpacked schedules – ballet, gymnastics, tutoring – pushing achievement as a path to external validation and financial success. Even parents without financial means frequently make significant sacrifices to fit this mould, often at the cost of intrinsic joy and connection. The long-term consequences of this obsession can be severe, from personal breakdowns to tragic outcomes such as the death of a loved one due to overwhelming pressure.

This relentless focus on doing carries into the workplace, where busyness is often worn as a badge of honour. Long hours, "all-nighters" and the stigma of leaving on time as being a "part-timer" create a toxic culture. Extreme cases, such as Japan's widespread issue of *karoshi* (death from overwork), underscore the dangers of this mentality. In one widely reported case by the BBC, Dentsu advertising agency was charged after employee Matsuri Takahashi took her life, having worked such excessive hours that she averaged only ten hours of sleep a week.[9]

In March 2021, a group of first-year analysts at Goldman Sachs created a detailed report highlighting the extreme working conditions they faced.[10] The report, which gained widespread media attention,

painted a stark picture of a macho work culture in the banking industry. Key Findings from the survey were:

- **Working hours**: Analysts reported working an average of 98 hours
  per week. Many claimed they were sleeping only 5 hours a night.

- **Mental health**: 77 per cent said their working conditions had negatively affected their physical health, and 75 per cent reported mental health deterioration.

- **Mistreatment**: Analysts cited instances of workplace abuse, such as
  being "screamed at" and publicly humiliated over mistakes.

- **Culture**: The unwritten expectation to work excessive hours and
  "tough it out" reflected the longstanding macho ethos of proving
  one's worth through endurance and sacrifice.

The majority of success measures have traditionally focused on financial outputs, which drive task-based, "doing" behaviours. This narrow
focus can create a toxic work culture, as illustrated when we were
invited into a hyper-growth, Logic 1 digital start-up. The UK Managing
Director, concerned about the culture, described a high-pressure environment where the average tenure for talented employees was only
18 months, with multiple cases of mental health struggles. Employees
referred to the culture as "dog-eat-dog". When we inquired about the
influence of global leadership, we learned the CEO was notorious for
narcissistic behaviour – craving authority, control, and prioritising
short-term self-interest over the wellbeing of others. When the CEO
heard about our proposal to explore Purpose-Driven Leadership, we
were dismissed without engagement. The company's continued
issues with regulatory bodies eventually led to the CEO's termination.
Unfortunately, this story is all too common, with the resulting financial
and emotional damage often borne not just by employees but by their
families and society at large.

Craig, however, was more fortunate. He realised he didn't need to
wait ten years for retirement to reclaim his sense of self. We introduced
Craig to a powerful mindset shift: from Doing to Being. We often tell
ourselves that once we have what we want, we will do the things we
desire and become the person we aspire to be. As explored in Chapter 1,
this conditioning stems from a fixation on money as the gateway to
wellbeing, leading to a common belief: "When I have enough money,

I will have great things, do great things and be fulfilled." In the meantime, who we *are* gets postponed. The invitation is to reverse this pattern by prioritising Being first.

Craig developed a personal plan to be human again. As someone from a finance background, he created a personal dashboard that measured success across all areas of his life, including work and relationships. His top ten areas included:

1. Being the best father
2. Being the best partner
3. Being the best son
4. Being the best friend
5. Being the best community member
6. Being the best CFO
7. Being the best Board member
8. Being the best strategic advisor
9. Being the best leader
10. Being the best mentor

He then attached specific measures to each area. For example:

- As a father: Having meaningful conversations with his children rather than sending quick texts.
- As a partner: Prioritising one sacred date night per month instead of canceling due to exhaustion.
- As a CFO: Partnering with the CEO at a strategic level rather than focusing solely on managing numbers.

By moving from Doing to Being, Craig shifted both his leadership and his personal life to being purpose-driven.

We are called *human beings*, not *human doings*, for a reason. When we become consumed by constant doing, we risk disconnecting from our humanity and the intrinsic motivations that inspire meaningful action. Centuries of spiritual and philosophical teachings, along with modern research on wellbeing, emphasise this principle. More recently, the professionalisation of the wellness and workplace wellbeing sectors has brought these insights into personal and organisational development spaces, highlighting the enabling role of personal purpose.

The rapid growth of these industries reflects a natural shift from Logic 1 (short-term financial self-interest) to Logic 3 (long-term wellbeing for all). However, some Logic 1 organisations exploit these fields for profit-driven reasons. For wellbeing initiatives to genuinely support the transition to a Wellbeing Economy, they must be integrated into the broader goal of long-term wellbeing for all, rather than existing as separate or superficial add-ons. Chapter 2 established that economic wellbeing emerges when people achieve sustained wellbeing in their daily lives. As further detailed in Chapter 3, to lead a Logic 3 Purpose-Driven Organisation requires, at a minimum, establishing strong governance frameworks for decision-making that safeguard the wellbeing of employees, stakeholders and the social and environmental systems on which they depend.

How do you want to be? This is the central question we encourage you to explore as a Purpose-Driven Leader. Making the shift from Doing to Being is Nick Dent, Director of Customer Operations at London Underground, part of Transport for London (TfL), the public body overseeing most of London's transport network. Nick leads approximately 10,000 colleagues in one of the most demanding operational environments, ensuring safety, reliability and resilience while delivering the UK's most intensive passenger service – moving over a billion customers annually.

Historically, the belief was that running such a complex operation required a command-and-control leadership style. However, Nick challenged this mindset, reflecting deeply on how he wanted *to be* as a leader. His answer? *Leading with humanity.*

Nick's humanity became especially evident during the COVID-19 crisis when London Underground remained operational as an essential service despite immense uncertainty, personal hardships, and health risks for staff. During this challenging period, his leadership was tested further by the merger of two key teams. Recognising the critical need for trust in such difficult circumstances, Nick made it a priority to establish a strong foundation for how the leadership team wanted to *be* together, grounded in openness, empathy and shared purpose.

With our support, he took a significant risk, designing an online session where every team member shared a personal story illustrating one of their core values. This experience humanised the team, revealing personal insights that reshaped perspectives, particularly among long-serving colleagues. Years later, team members still reference this as a pivotal moment in building trust and strengthening the team's culture, driven by Nick's commitment to *being* human.

This example illustrates that leadership transformation begins with consciously deciding *how to be*, especially in challenging environments where resilience and shared humanity matter most.

We have long encouraged leaders to begin each day with a deliberate "to be" decision – clarifying the qualities they wish to embody rather than focusing solely on tasks to complete. This principle was reinforced in a McKinsey & Company article titled "Making a daily 'to be' list: How a hospital system CEO is navigating the coronavirus crisis".[11]

In the article, Michael Fisher, CEO of Cincinnati Children's Hospital, shared his leadership approach during a challenging period. While he had always maintained a disciplined task list, he realised the importance of being equally intentional about how he wanted to show up as a leader each day:

"I've always had a decent amount of discipline around writing down 'to-dos' – what I want to accomplish for the day. But I never purposefully gave thought to whether there's a way to be really intentional about how I want to show up every day. So I've added a 'to be' list to my routine. For example, today I want to be generous and genuine. I have key meetings, and I want to ensure people feel valued and appreciated."

The good news is that no matter how deeply ingrained you have become in Doing, you can make the shift to Being. As explored in Chapter 3, extensive research into human behaviour demonstrates that our lives are continuously shaped by how we interact with the world of meaning around us. Neuroscience shows that this ongoing change, known as *neuroplasticity*, rewires our brains based on our experiences. Through this process – essentially the brain's ability to "build muscle" – we become what we think and repeatedly do. This means we can deliberately develop our mindset and choose how we want to *be*, transforming our way of leading and living at a physiological level.

Purpose-Driven Leadership is grounded in this intentional Being.

Roland Fasel, COO of Maybourne Hotel Group, reflected on the importance of anchoring leadership in purpose: "As a leader, you need to be committed to being purpose-driven. Bring it into the organisation.

Be passionate about it. Get advocates to spread the word. It is not complicated once you put in the work. Bring the business back to purpose at every opportunity. People want to follow those who inspire and provide the right filters for effective decision-making and implementation."

The shift from Doing to Being invites you to challenge long-held assumptions. If you believe that more Doing leads to greater success, better outcomes, or long-term wellbeing for yourself, your family, or the world – think again. Doing is essential for progress, but it's the quality of Being that shapes the right kind of action.

You don't *do* Purpose-Driven. You *be* Purpose-Driven – expressing it through the way you lead, inspire and empower others to reconnect with their own sense of purpose.

TAKEAWAY

Set a deliberate intent to be – letting your humanity become the foundation of who you are, how you lead and the impact you create.

RETHINK 3: Me to We

At the heart of Purpose-Driven Leadership lies a commitment to working in partnership to serve others. True, lasting impact doesn't come from individual heroics but from collaboration and collective effort.

Sarah, as President of the Americas for a global hospitality company, embodied this philosophy through her relational approach to leadership. Despite overseeing thousands of hotels and leading a large workforce, she prioritised personal connection. At leadership development events, she prepared meticulously – learning the names and accomplishments of each delegate to create genuine, lasting memories through thoughtful, individualised recognition. Rather than relying on scripted messages, Sarah engaged through storytelling, asking personal questions and responding with meaningful anecdotes. Her clarity was profound: "I don't do anything. I simply spend time meeting people and sharing with them the great work you do!" Sarah understood that leadership is fundamentally relationship-based. Her focus on shifting from "Me" to "We" reflected a deeper belief: *business is relationship.*

Roland Fasel, COO of Maybourne Hotel Group, echoed this senti-ment, emphasising the importance of human connection in leadership: "As humanistic capitalism evolves, we need to recognise that business is all about people. Organisational purpose and values must embrace this understanding. We must do everything possible to support the individuals in a business, from inclusion and mental health to sustain-ability and community."

He further highlighted the need for empathy in modern leadership: "We lead four generations of employees, and the complexity of multi-generational teams requires curiosity and the ability to help people connect. Leaders need to engage people at a higher level of purpose to ensure their involvement. It's essential to show empathy by under-standing people's backgrounds, recognising their contexts, and inte-grating this understanding into leadership."

Purpose-Driven Leadership calls for creating people-focused organ-isations where individuals can connect, thrive and contribute to meaningful, sustainable outcomes. The most effective leaders build environments where people feel valued, heard and inspired to make a difference together.

We are fortunate to work with Matt Palmer, Executive Director of the Lower Thames Crossing, a major infrastructure project set to connect Kent and Essex through a tunnel beneath the River Thames. As the UK's most ambitious road project in over 35 years, it aims to nearly double road capacity east of London, strengthening community connections and expanding opportunities for where people live, work and learn.

Our journey with Matt began more than a decade ago at Heathrow Airport, where he led multiple large-scale infrastructure projects. At the time, he described himself as operating in a "washing machine" – constantly caught in a cycle of endless tasks and reactive leadership. When introduced to the concept of Purpose-Driven Leadership, Matt was initially sceptical but chose to engage in a reflective process. Through this journey, he realised that much of his leadership had been centred on delivering physical infrastructure rather than deeply investing in the growth and wellbeing of people. As he stepped into the immense responsibility of leading Lower Thames Crossing – facing challenges from influencing government officials to unifying diverse delivery partners and cultures – Matt saw that success required a mind-set shift from "Me" to "We".

To explore this shift, we facilitated a series of leadership dialogues with Matt's executive team, focusing on how to create a more inclusive and engaged workforce. The team identified that *trust* had to be the foundation of their cultural transformation, but this required clarity on what trust meant and how it could be developed across the organisation.

A key moment in this journey came when we invited the executive team and delivery partners to accelerate trust through shared vulnerability. Each leader prepared a personal story about when trust was either built or broken and shared it over a long dinner. Matt set the tone by recounting a personal experience while ice climbing, where trust in a partner was severely tested during an accident. Despite the risk, Matt emphasised his belief in starting all relationships from a position of trust.

The stories shared were raw and personal, especially in an industry where safety is paramount and the stakes are high. Some leaders expressed a belief that trust must be earned, while others believed it should be given freely. The outcome of these conversations was profound. The team gained clarity and alignment around creating a culture of inclusion aligning the leadership team and driving cultural transformation throughout the organisation.

Research strongly supports the emphasis on trust as the foundation for moving from "Me" to "We". One of the most powerful illustrations comes from the pioneering work of Paul Zak. In his *Harvard Business Review* article, "The Neuroscience of Trust", Zak writes: "In my research, I've found that building a culture of trust is what makes a meaningful difference. Employees in high-trust organisations are more productive, have more energy at work, collaborate better with their colleagues, and stay with their employers longer than people working at low-trust companies. They also suffer less chronic stress and are happier with their lives, and these factors fuel stronger performance."[12]

Zak's research highlights the role of oxytocin, a brain chemical that facilitates collaboration and teamwork, as central to building trust in organisations. By measuring oxytocin levels in response to workplace experiences, Zak identified eight key leadership behaviours that stimulate trust:

1. Recognise excellence.
2. Induce "challenge stress".

3. Give people discretion in how they do their work.

4. Enable job crafting.

5. Share information broadly.

6. Intentionally build relationships.

7. Facilitate whole-person growth.

8. Show vulnerability.

Zak concludes that leaders cultivate trust by setting a clear direction, providing people with the tools and autonomy to achieve it and then stepping back. Ultimately, developing trust means treating people like responsible adults, an approach that aligns with the governance principles outlined in Chapter 3. This science underscores the importance of trust not just as an interpersonal value but as a structural foundation for driving performance, engagement and collective wellbeing.

Unleashing the power of oxytocin and creating a high-trust environment doesn't happen by chance – it requires deliberate effort. Brian Woodhead, Heathrow Terminal 2's Operations Director, exemplified this in his leadership during the opening of The Queen's Terminal at Heathrow Airport, Europe's largest and most connected hub. Tasked with delivering the project on time and on budget for its opening on 4 June 2014, Brian recognised that success depended not just on operational excellence but on cultivating a Purpose-Driven Leadership approach. Reflecting his belief in the importance of a unifying "North Star", he scheduled an offsite meeting to shift his team from a 'Me' to 'We' mindset. Despite initial resistance – some influential team members considered it a waste of time – the session opened space for critical dialogue. Tensions eased as Brian shared his vision of providing Purpose-Driven Leadership, working collaboratively, and aligning with Heathrow's vision: 'To give passengers the best airport service in the world.'

The team explored the implications of moving from self-interest to collective success, weighing both the benefits and perceived risks:

Pros:

- Shared focus on what matters most
- A unified culture around core values and behaviours
- Clear decision-making and accountability framework

Cons:

- Time investment with no guarantee of long-term relationships
- Reduced pace due to collaborative processes
- Potential difficulties in aligning all contributors

To deepen understanding, we guided the team through an exercise where they identified adjectives that captured the reasons for shifting from "Me" to "We". Themes such as *growth, inspiration, delivery, people* and *opportunity* emerged, leading to the co-creation of this unifying statement: "To inspire people to go beyond what they think is possible and to maximise the power of everyone."

This shared intent went beyond operational goals, serving as a foundation for how the team worked together. Over the following 18 months, we met quarterly to ensure alignment and progress, anchoring the shift around six key focus areas:

1. **Talent:** Aligning recruitment and development with the 'We' mindset
2. **Culture:** Embedding company values of safety, respect and collaboration
3. **Performance Management:** Balancing delivery metrics with behavioural expectations
4. **Supply Chain:** Integrating trust-based behavioural contracts with suppliers
5. **Operations:** Streamlining processes to support collective success
6. **Communication:** Tailoring messaging to reflect the power of collective achievement

The terminal's grand opening, officiated by the late Queen on 27 June 2014, was a defining moment for the team. The culture of collaboration remained strong as new members seamlessly integrated into the high-trust environment. This impact endured, with Terminal 2 being awarded "Best Terminal in the World" by Skytrax in 2018, a lasting testament to the power of Purpose-Driven Leadership and the 'We' mindset.

Expanding our sphere of influence beyond perceived limits requires heightened awareness and intentional commitments. In *Me to We: Finding Meaning in a Material World,* authors Craig Kielburger and Marc Kielburger capture this mindset, stating: *"Me to We* is an approach to life that leads us to recognise what is truly valuable, make new decisions about the way we want to live, and redefine the goals we set for ourselves and the legacy we want to leave."

Their insights mirror the shift from Money to Meaning and the profound impact leaders can have when they help others find Purposeful Work and Lives – an essential step in becoming a Purpose-Driven Leader and moving from Me to We.[13]

Andy Cosslett, CBE, Chair of ITV, a British media company, and formerly Kingfisher, a British multinational retailing company, exemplified this "We" approach. As CEO of IHG (InterContinental Hotels Group), a global hospitality company, he prioritised creating a shared sense of identity across the organisation. Understanding the challenge of uniting leaders in a multinational setting, he brought his top 100 leaders together for dedicated forums to build relationships, create deeper understanding and align on shared aspirations.

Andy encouraged a "Yes and" mindset in decision-making, emphasising curiosity and collaboration over defensiveness and fixed perspectives. His focus on constructive partnerships extended to IHG's owner relationships, where he shifted traditionally adversarial dynamics by investing time in understanding stakeholder priorities and building mutual trust. Moreover, Andy's commitment extended to frontline colleagues. He prioritised visiting key regions, emphasising the collective importance of everyone's contributions. His actions resonated across the organisation, with stories circulating about his "We" leadership, inspiring others to follow his example and embrace Purpose-Driven Leadership.

It is essential to examine how Logic 1 conditioning, with its business-as-usual economic assumptions and overemphasis on self-interest, creates significant barriers to adopting a "We" mindset. This worldview often limits leadership potential and prevents the creation of Purpose-Driven Organisations. To move forward, leaders must critically reflect on their base assumptions – the worldviews driving their decisions and behaviours – and explore how these manifest in both their hopes and fears.

Some common Logic 1 assumptions that hold leaders back from moving to a "We" mindset include:

- Being overlooked for promotion if they focus on helping others
- Not receiving recognition for their own achievements if they prioritise lifting others up
- Sacrificing local resources like finances and talent for the greater good of the business
- Losing influence and impact if they listen more and talk less.

These concerns are deeply rooted in traditional leadership models. Shifting from a mindset centred on self-interest to one that prioritises collective success requires conscious effort and structural support. However, when leaders commit to Purpose-Driven Leadership, these barriers can be addressed intentionally, creating space for more collaborative, inclusive and effective leadership. To explore the shift from "Me" to "We", consider reflecting on the impact you want to have as a leader:

What would you want people to say, feel and do as a result of your shift from "Me" to "We"?

Say:

- It's refreshing to be led by someone who genuinely cares about others' success.
- Our leader actively creates the conditions for us to grow and progress.
- It's inspiring to see consistent actions aligned with a focus on others.

Feel:

- I feel energised knowing my leader prioritises our success.
- I feel supported and empowered by a leader who puts people first.
- I feel motivated to contribute more and support others' growth.

Do:

- Develop stakeholder plans focused on understanding others' realities and success metrics.
- Schedule collaboration meetings to strengthen cross-functional teamwork.
- Communicate with a united voice, emphasising shared goals and alignment.

Moving from "Me" to "We" is one of the most transformative shifts a leader can make. It's the foundation of a Purpose-Driven Organisation – one where collective wellbeing, trust and long-term impact drive sustainable success.

TAKEAWAY

A Purpose-Driven Leader is wired to serve the best interest of others and adopts a "We" mindset to make it happen.

RETOOL

Purpose-Driven Leadership requires a fundamental shift in how we perceive leadership – moving from Logic 1, which emphasises short-term financial self-interest and individual achievement, to Logic 3, where leadership is anchored in collective long-term wellbeing and positive societal impact. To make this shift, leaders need to embrace a core set of tools that transform both mindset and behaviour: Lead with Love, Lead with Vision and Lead with Perspective.

Lead with Love focuses on cultivating genuine care, empathy and trust within relationships. It challenges the transactional, output-driven tendencies of Logic 1 by emphasising emotional connection, mutual respect and a deep commitment to the wellbeing of people. Love in leadership means prioritising personal growth, valuing human dignity and creating environments where everyone can contribute their best.

Lead with Vision reframes leadership as the ability to inspire others through a shared, meaningful purpose. Instead of focusing solely on financial outcomes, vision-centred leadership aligns daily actions with a clear and compelling long-term goal, one rooted in collective wellbeing. It offers clarity and motivation, helping teams see how their work contributes to a larger purpose beyond profit.

Lead with Perspective moves leadership from narrow, isolated decision-making to an understanding of interconnectedness.

A Logic 1 mindset often reduces complex challenges to financial metrics or short-term outputs, whereas leading with perspective adopts systems thinking enabling leaders to see the broader web of relationships, impacts and dependencies. This tool ensures decisions support holistic success, balancing economic, social and environmental wellbeing.

Together, these tools enable Purpose-Driven Leaders to make the profound shift from self-interest to collective impact. They equip leaders to inspire positive change, align organisational strategies with long-term wellbeing and navigate complexity with wisdom and care. This shift is essential not just for organisational success but for the creation of Logic 3 organisations and economies that serve the wellbeing of all.

RETOOL 1: Lead with Love

We were invited to deliver a leadership and cultural development programme for an operational division in the retail sector. To design the programme effectively, we conducted our customary diagnostic interviews with a range of stakeholders. Before the interviews, we met with Lara, the new Senior Director, who advised us to put away our laptops and engage in open conversations instead. She explained that it was a low-trust environment, where external consultants were often viewed with suspicion, and formal note-taking might increase cynicism about our presence. Sure enough, we were met with a mix of responses from outright hostility to mild caution. What emerged in our conversations was more than simply not trusting external people. It was a classic Logic 1 environment which had built up over the years through dysfunctional leadership creating a toxic culture of fear. We heard stories of past leaders' behaviours including:

- Lurching from one priority to another, resulting in confusion and fear of failing.
- Humiliating people in performance meetings in front of peers without seeking to understand root causal factors if there was perceived underperformance.

- Shouting at people on morning calls when giving directions for the day.
- Talking behind people's backs about issues or concerns.
- Creating in and out groups through favouritism, causing pockets of isolation and toxic competitive behaviour.
- Micro-managing people by getting into inappropriate levels of detail and control.
- Failing to give constructive feedback in real time resulting in lists of unspoken issues.
- Avoiding accountability for results and blaming others or external factors for underperformance.
- Using leadership development activity intended to improve organisational effectiveness as a way to inform people of job losses.

An interesting picture emerged regarding Lara's leadership since she took charge. People appeared suspicious because they couldn't figure her out. She made time for others, asked meaningful questions, sought to understand issues and genuinely wanted to help, qualities that were unfamiliar and even unsettling in a culture used to the opposite. When we shared our findings with Lara and her HR Business Partner, there were no surprises. However, two key priorities became clear:

- Lara needed to explain her leadership approach to manage expectations, as it was so different from what the team had experienced before.
- She needed to help shift the organisational culture from one of fear to one of safety.
- This shift was critical to enabling the team to begin their journey towards becoming purpose-driven, where serving the greater good is the core driver. The starting point was creating the conditions for psychological safety – an essential foundation for quieting fears and building trust.

In our conversations with Amy Edmondson, Novartis Professor of Leadership and Management at Harvard Business School and author of the 2018 book *The Fearless Organisation: Creating Psychological Safety in the Workplace*,[14] she shared the following: *"To do their best work people need to feel secure and safe in their workplace. I define psychological safety as a shared belief held by members of a team that it is a safe environment for interpersonal risk taking. Individuals feel they can speak up, express their concerns, and be heard. This is not to say that people are 'nice'. A psychologically safe workplace is one where people are not full of fear and not trying to cover their tracks to avoid being embarrassed or punished. What I am advocating is candor. Being open. And sometimes that might mean being direct to a fault, knowing that you have a right and a responsibility to ask hard questions about the work such as: Is this the right decision? Are we collecting the right data? Do we know the impact this might have on others?"* Psychological safety is a core foundation of good governance, enabling both effective oversight and accountability, as well as developing an environment where people feel free to take appropriate risks to achieve goals within defined parameters.

Amy went on to say: *"If you don't have psychological safety, it's hard to feel a sense of love for your work. If we are caught up in survival it means that we can't be as focused on and available for our work. When in self-protection our first inclination is to not get hurt, or to get expelled. We tiptoe. We hide our tracks. We try to read the tea leaves. Having psychological safety assumes that your voice is welcome. You go for it, ask your questions, offer your ideas and are available for people. In truth you can't go wrong by assuming that your voice needs to be heard because if you get feedback that it's unhelpful for you to speak up then you have two options. Either you are not in the right environment and need to leave, or you need to take the feedback on board to keep learning and become more effective. It's not a given that every word that comes out of your mouth is gold. Part of the reason we need to take interpersonal risks and speak up is so that we can learn and grow.' Amy acknowledges: 'Psychological safety feels better than fear, but it's not comfortable. Working in a psychologically safe workplace is a stretch environment."*

Creating psychological safety has become a key focal area for the work we do with leaders, teams and organisations. We are not alone. In 2012, Google embarked on an initiative, code-named Project Aristotle, which set out to answer the following question using data and rigorous analysis: what makes a Google team effective? Over two years they conducted in excess of 200 interviews with Googlers (their employees) and looked at more than 250 attributes of over 180 active Google teams. They thought that if they found the perfect mix of traits and skills necessary for a brilliant team, they would solve the problem. What they actually found was: "Who is on a team matters less than how the team members interact, structure their work and view their contributions."[15] They learned that there were five key dynamics which set successful teams apart from other teams at Google and the number one factor was psychological safety. At Google psychological safety refers to: "An individual's perception of the consequences of taking an interpersonal risk or a belief that a team is safe for risk taking in the face of being seen as ignorant, incompetent, negative, or disruptive. In a team with high psychological safety, teammates feel safe to take risks around their team members. They feel confident that no one on the team will embarrass or punish anyone else for admitting a mistake, asking a question, or offering a new idea."

Back to our leader of the operational division in the retail sector. Lara brought the team together to share the insight from our diagnostic interviews. She set the stage by thanking them for their honesty and saying that in order for the business to have a better future it was imperative to move from a fearful culture to an environment of high trust and transparency. Lara explained her leadership approach. She described how in previous roles she was used to working in highly competitive environments where people jostled for hierarchy and were happy to throw others under the bus to get ahead. She had developed sharp elbows to protect her from the threat of others, but it drained her energy and went against her open and collaborative personality. Lara came into this division determined to be driven by love not fear. She shared how in her last role she had come across the concept of psychological safety and started communicating about it through her social network and introduced it to campaigns at work. She found that it caught a wave. With the increased lens on topics like diversity, inclusion and mental health, psychological safety had caught a nerve. Lara gave examples of what psychological safety could look like for the team, including:

- Speaking up in a meeting to propose a risky or untested idea
- Admitting publicly that the project you championed failed, and offering lessons learned in the process

- Disagreeing with her or offering a different way forward than had been previously considered
- Willingly giving up time or resources to help out someone on the team, taking away from the resources you have to achieve your own goals
- Sticking up for a teammate in the face of unfair criticism
- Volunteering to do something you don't know how to do
- Showing emotions when you're under pressure or stressed out.

Lara paused and asked the team for their reflections and if this was a direction they wanted to pursue together. One by one team members affirmed their support; however, given the history and the turnover of leaders, suspicions remained. Lara acknowledged the mood in the room and promised that they would use a 1:1 say / do ratio to move anything forward, saying that any commitment would need to have a clear, evidenced plan of action attached.

One of the team's biggest challenges was breaking down silos with other functions, which hindered collaboration across the business. We met with the support functions to get feedback about how the operation was perceived. "Closed, cynical and scary" were three key messages played back. The operation was described as an island which was difficult to work with. As a result of the feedback Lara and the team made some clear decisions with supporting actions:

- We are open for business – schedule collaboration meetings with the support functions focused on how to work better together.
- We seek to understand – invite the support functions to share their experience about working together and to get feedback about how the operations team could be more collaborative.
- We will deliver together – agree specific actions to move the agenda forward including refreshing the governance for mutual accountability.

By addressing both internal team culture and cross-functional collaboration, Lara modelled a Purpose-Driven Leadership approach that was transparent, inclusive and action-oriented, laying the foundation for lasting organisational change.

Moving yourself and your teams out of a place of fear is critical because fear is the single greatest barrier to being purpose-driven. Psychological safety, therefore, becomes one of the most essential tools a leader can use to unleash purpose. As described in Chapter 1, transitioning from a BAU Logic 1 or 2 approach to Logic 3 is fundamentally a shift from governance systems designed for self-interest to systems designed for other-serving interest. To be purpose-driven – whether as an economy, organisation or individual – is to be governed in service of the greatest possible good: long-term wellbeing for all.

At its core, Purpose-Driven Leadership is about acting with love – being in service of the wellbeing of others. Elisabeth Kübler-Ross, the Swiss-American psychiatrist, captured this essence beautifully in *On Death & Dying* when she wrote: "There are only two emotions: love and fear. They're opposites. If we're in fear, we are not in a place of love. When we're in a place of love, we cannot be in a place of fear."[16] Purpose, then, is a system that enables love to flourish – and it cannot thrive in an environment governed by fear, a logical byproduct of economies and organisations driven by self-interest.

On a technical level, creating psychological safety in the workplace reduces the energy people spend on self-protection, freeing them to step into a mindset of love, openness and creativity. This shift is vital for enabling the bold, collaborative innovation required to halt harm to our collective wellbeing and drive equitable, thriving futures.

At the organisational level, a strong purpose-driven governance system – described in Chapter 3 – creates the structures and incentives that ensure dynamic activity remains within safe thresholds while building processes and cultural norms that promote psychological safety. This Logic 3, purpose-driven intent inherently supports the creation of a fearless environment. As Amy Edmondson explains: "There will be conflict and upset because people will disagree, but it's recognised as necessary to do good work. People will experience discomfort, but they can withstand it because of what's at stake. There will be higher degrees of commitment to the purpose and goals for the work because they surpass personal comfort."

By freeing ourselves to lead from love, we unlock the untapped energy of our desire to serve others and bring this powerful force directly into our day-to-day work. Paul Zak emphasises this connection in his work on the neuroscience of trust and purpose, explaining:

"I love to be of service to others. I believe that work is always about being of service. If we know our purpose and keep it on the tip of our tongues every day, it will make a significant difference in our energy and in feeling like a valuable member of the community."[17]

Leading with Love as a Purpose-Driven Leader means grounding your leadership in care, service and compassion for those around you. John Mackey, co-founder of Whole Foods Market, embodied this mindset throughout his 44 years of leadership. In his article "Lead with Love" (2023), Mackey wrote: "Love helps us understand what all the different stakeholders need and desire, making it easier to help fulfill them. When stakeholders feel loved by a company, they love it back. Love is one of the most human things we can do. It builds trust and a sense of community that elevates business to more than just a place for transactions."[18]

Mackey emphasised that love in leadership isn't just theoretical – it requires consistent action through qualities such as service, generosity, gratitude, care, compassion and forgiveness. These qualities create a deeper connection between leaders, teams, and the broader organisational purpose, making work a source of meaning rather than a transactional experience.

Laura Miller, former Executive Vice President and Chief Information Officer at Macy's, reflected on the personal side of leading with love: "Whether it's making a difference for a company, team, or individual, there are days you feel caught on the hamster wheel, spinning so hard it's hard to recognise your impact. When this happens, I have to remind myself that making a difference for even one person – helping their work feel easier or supporting their success – fulfils my purpose for that day."

Joel Burrows, CEO of Lindt UK & Ireland, further emphasises the importance of aligning love with leadership: "You get one life. If you're going to spend a large portion of it at work, make it meaningful by being your authentic self. I didn't want a gap between the home me and the work me." He encourages leaders to explore their intrinsic motivations, asking: "What makes you happy? What drives you? What do you love about your work? Once you gain clarity, seek feedback from others on when they see you energised and at your best."

To lead with love is to prioritise humanity and embody Purpose-Driven Leadership. Fear inhibits love, but by replacing fear with trust, empathy and genuine connection, leaders create organisations where people feel safe, valued and inspired to contribute their best in service of others. This shift at the micro level is essential for enabling organisations – and, through them, entire economies – to work collaboratively towards long-term wellbeing for all, ensuring progress without causing harm along the way.

TAKEAWAY

A Purpose-Driven Leader has the capability to quieten fear within themselves, their teams and the organisation as a whole. In doing so, they unleash the innate human drive to serve the good of others – the essence of purpose.

RETOOL 2: Lead with Vision

We are creatures of imagination. What we envision – both the positive outcomes we aspire to create and the negative consequences we seek to avoid – shapes our daily decision-making. However, in Logic 1 organisations, this imagination is constrained by governance systems focused primarily on financial self-interest, with financial health as the core success measure. Broader impacts on the systems that sustain long-term wellbeing are often overlooked or dismissed as irrelevant in decision-making.

This narrow focus limits leadership potential, preventing leaders from imagining and pursuing holistic success or addressing systemic challenges meaningfully. For Purpose-Driven Leaders operating with Logic 3, a clear and compelling vision – of both the positive impact they seek to create and the harm they aim to prevent – is essential for making agile, effective decisions. Vision provides the clarity and energy required to sustain leadership through barriers and complexity.

Developing the ability to craft both personal and shared visions is a foundational skill for Purpose-Driven Leadership. It bridges the gap between personal humanity and collective possibility, inspiring action, aligning teams and creating a shared sense of responsibility for long-term wellbeing for all.

Ben had the privilege of coaching Nyala, who managed the real estate portfolio of a luxury hospitality brand valued at several billion dollars. Her role offered a profound leadership opportunity: to transform an exceptional collection of properties towards a more sustainable future. Achieving this, however, required Nyala to envision a future not yet realised – demanding a significant leap in imagination, not just for her company but for the entire market.

Yet, during early conversations, it became clear that Nyala was consumed by operational demands, constantly juggling emails, meetings and calls. This relentless focus on day-to-day tasks had eclipsed her capacity to engage in forward-looking leadership. When asked how she might rebalance her focus, Nyala struggled to identify a clear path forward.

Together, they revisited the company's emerging purpose which included caring for others through exceptional guest experiences, developing the next generation of hoteliers, and positively impacting local communities. As Nyala reflected on this deeper intent, it reignited her sense of meaning, yet she realised she hadn't connected this purpose to a personal, motivating vision of the future she wanted to create. Without this personal connection, her leadership focus remained anchored in operational demands rather than the transformative potential of her role.

This experience highlights a critical insight: while a clearly defined organisational purpose can inspire, it only becomes a driver of transformative leadership when translated into a personal, motivating vision that guides daily decision-making.

It's rare for leaders to intentionally let operational demands overshadow their leadership impact. Yet most report spending around 80 per cent of their time on task-related work – emails, meetings and immediate operational needs – while just 20 per cent are invested in vision-driven activities like strategy, deep problem-solving, stakeholder engagement and team development.

This imbalance often signals gaps in governance and culture, revealing that the foundational structures, habits and accountabilities to support Purpose-Driven Leadership are not yet in place. Creating these conditions is essential for shifting from reactive task management to leading with clarity, imagination and long-term impact.

When asked about the importance of vision, Jeff Weiner, Executive Chairman of LinkedIn, shared: "Simply put, it's the ability to inspire others to achieve shared objectives, and I think the most important word there by far is 'inspire'. I think that's the difference between leading and managing. Managers will tell people what to do, whereas leaders will inspire them to do it, and there are a few things that go into the ability to inspire. It starts with vision, and the clarity of vision that the leader has, and the ability to think about where they ultimately want to take the business, take the company, take the team, take a particular product."

In today's urgent context, where the need to reconnect with our shared humanity has never been greater – both to address widespread harm and unlock the vast potential for wellbeing – vision becomes more than a leadership tool. It becomes a guiding force that helps leaders and organisations rise above immediate pressures to recognise their role in shaping a better future. When anchored in a purpose-driven approach, vision provides clarity not only for strategic direction but also for a deeper human responsibility: to contribute positively to the systems we are part of.

Otto Scharmer, Senior Lecturer at MIT Sloan School of Management and co-founder of the Presencing Institute, explores the profound importance of vision in his seminal work, *Theory U*.[19] He describes visioning as a future-oriented process that involves connecting with deeper levels of awareness and intuition, tapping into both personal and collective potential while becoming attuned to emerging possibilities.

This transformative approach enables individuals and organisations to move beyond reactive, habitual patterns towards more conscious, purpose-driven action. Scharmer's model mirrors the shift from Logic 1 to Logic 3 governance – at the economic, organisational and personal leadership levels – by emphasising forward-looking, human-centred leadership rooted in long-term wellbeing.

Developing a compelling vision requires imagining the details of a future not yet realised, connecting others with that future both cognitively and emotionally, building scenario plans for different pathways to achieve it and using storytelling to inspire and sustain momentum. These visionary capabilities are essential for leaders committed to systemic change that uplifts wellbeing for all.

In our interview with Richard Boyatzis, an academic in the field of the mechanics of vision, Boyatzis shared insights from his latest book,

The Science of Change:[20] *"A rational strategic plan does not motivate change. It is emotional 'swarming' that drives change, which is a phenomenon where emotions spread rapidly and collectively within a group, creating a shared emotional state. It occurs when individuals emotionally resonate with one another, often triggered by shared experiences, storytelling, or vision-driven leadership. It is clear that it is only when you focus on the bigger picture that you activate the positive emotions and brain functioning which makes you open to new ideas. In other words, if you want to initiate change, you need to develop a compelling vision."* Given the urgent need to lead deep change in our world of withering wellbeing, our ability to develop expertise in the creation and application of vision is vital.

In our conversation with Richard Solomons, Chairman of Rentokil Initial plc, the global experts in pest control, he reinforced, from a practical point of view, the theory Richard described: *"You have to decide what you do and where to spend your time. There is a job description, but it is sterile. Every day there is a different situation to handle. What needs to inform your decision making and where you spend your time is your vision for the business. Be clear about what success looks like from a cultural, operational, and competitive perspective."*

Aligning your personal vision with your organisation's vision can be a profound source of inspiration and resilience on your leadership journey. The true power that sustains Purpose-Driven Leadership arises from the deeply human experience of knowing your efforts are making a positive difference in the lives of others.

Purpose-Driven Organisations flourish when they create the conditions to harness and amplify this energy. However, this potential is only fully realised when leaders craft imaginative pathways – narratives and frameworks that engage both the hearts and minds of their teams, connecting daily work to a meaningful future. This often requires navigating complex, uncertain pathways towards long-term positive impact.

This is why vision-building is more than just a leadership skill. It is a critical tool for Purpose-Driven Leadership. A clear, inspiring vision helps leaders align, motivate and sustain collective energy, even in the face of challenges, keeping purpose at the heart of decision-making and long-term success.

In Ben's experience, five fundamental steps are essential for vision creation as a Purpose-Driven Leader in an organisation with a clearly articulated purpose:

- **Create time and space:** Prioritise moments for open, curious exploration of the possibilities that could emerge from the organisation's purpose, free from daily operational pressures.

- **Understand current reality:** Engage in deep listening and seek diverse stakeholder perspectives to develop a sense of interconnectedness, ensuring the vision is grounded in real needs and realities.

- **Let go of preconceptions:** Release assumptions about 'how things are done' to open space for fresh thinking, allowing clarity and new possibilities for the future to surface.

- **Shape the vision through experimentation:** Use rapid prototyping and small-scale initiatives to test and refine the emerging vision, encouraging continuous learning, feedback and adaptation.

- **Embody the vision:** Scale the vision across the organisation through partnerships and collaboration, embedding it in strategic decision-making, culture and leadership practices, always making the link between the vision and the organisation's purpose clear and actionable.

On one occasion, Ben worked with a Purpose-Driven Leader who actively used vision to bring the organisation's purpose to life. Sanjay, the CEO for the UK & Ireland region of a global FMCG company, held a firm belief that leadership extended beyond titles and pay grades – everyone was a leader. Inspired by this philosophy, we co-created a leadership development initiative called "Game-Changing Leadership", engaging 1,000 leaders from the shop floor to the Executive Committee over a three-year journey. The five steps of vision creation outlined earlier formed the foundation of this programme.

In the initial phase, we facilitated workshops bringing together leaders from all areas of the business. Sanjay understood that to fully realise the company's purpose – providing high-quality, great-tasting and nutritious food that brings joy to mealtimes while supporting community wellbeing – leaders needed to co-create a clear, collective vision of future possibilities.

- **Step 1: Create time and space.** The workshops created intentional space for leaders to explore bold possibilities. One insight that emerged was the opportunity to expand the company's health-focused product range and deepen its positive impact on communities.

- **Step 2: Understand current reality.** To ground this vision, we held listening workshops across the organisation. A particularly profound session occurred with frontline factory workers, whose deep knowledge and passion revealed daily challenges and barriers to progress. Hearing their stories strengthened the urgency for change and highlighted the untapped expertise already present within the business.

- **Step 3: Let go of preconceptions.** Leaders were brought together in cross-functional groups to reflect on the insights gathered. Sanjay challenged them to let go of outdated assumptions, questioning historical approaches and decision-making habits to allow space for a more innovative future to emerge.

- **Step 4: Shape the vision through experimentation.** Sanjay took bold action to test the evolving vision. He identified a group of committed leaders, provided them with creative workspace separate from their P&L responsibilities and granted them the freedom to innovate. Within a year, they developed and tested new products that more fully aligned with the company's purpose. These successful prototypes demonstrated that the vision was achievable, boosting both credibility and momentum across the organisation.

- **Step 5: Embody the vision and use storytelling.** Storytelling played a pivotal role in scaling the vision throughout the organisation. Sanjay regularly shared emotionally resonant narratives to connect the company's purpose with the day-to-day contributions of its people. He modeled visible leadership by personally engaging with teams – spending time in factories, walking the office floors, hosting town halls and using both internal channels and public platforms like social media to reinforce the vision consistently.

The impact of this visioning process was measured through employee engagement surveys, specifically asking: "I understand and feel personally connected to the organisation's vision and how my role contributes to achieving it." Engagement levels rose consistently throughout the programme, underscoring the power of a well-crafted, purpose-driven vision to unite and inspire an entire organisation. This growth further highlighted the importance of proactive leadership, consistent communication, and emotional connection in transforming purpose into tangible outcomes.

In the words of Steve Jobs: "The most powerful person in the world is the storyteller. The storyteller sets the vision, values, and agenda of an entire generation that is to come." Zoë Arden has spent decades working with organisations and their leaders to develop storytelling skills in support of purpose-driven journeys. In her new book *Story-Centred Leadership* she outlines the intrinsic connection between stories, vision and purpose. She summarised for us: "Stories motivate, engage and inspire others to contribute towards making the vision a reality. Stories bring the leader's vision to life, making it tangible and meaningful. And with purpose at the heart of our stories, we can tap into the power of a new collective story to unlock positive change."

A Logic 3 leader leverages vision not just as a strategic tool but as a way to build emotional connection and inspire action towards a shared purpose. By making the desired future tangible and relatable, vision deepens commitment to long-term collective wellbeing. It transforms abstract goals into felt experiences, motivating individuals across all levels of an organisation to stay engaged and contribute meaningfully, no matter their role. This emotionally-anchored clarity sustains energy, focus and alignment, even in the face of complexity and challenge.

TAKEAWAY

Creating a personal and collective vision by imagining a future that doesn't yet exist; connecting others with this future cognitively and emotionally; building scenario plans to bring it to life and using storytelling to reinforce and sustain momentum are core tools for a Purpose-Driven Leader.

RETOOL 3: Lead with Perspective

Transitioning from self-interest to serving others is a fundamental element of being a Purpose-Driven Leader. This shift mirrors the evolution from Logic 1 leadership, where siloed thinking and profit-driven priorities dominate, to Logic 3 leadership, where interconnectedness, shared outcomes and long-term wellbeing guide decision-making. Siloed thinking spurs fragmented efforts, limiting collaboration and focusing on isolated success, whereas systems thinking recognises the complex, nested relationships between individuals, teams, organisations, communities, and the planet. By embracing systems thinking, leaders can break down barriers, promote cooperation and drive long-term, regenerative success across all levels of impact.

We referenced the pioneering work of Donella Meadows on environmental and social analysis in Chapter 1. In her classic book *Thinking in Systems*, she describes how working on systems thinking reinforces the transition from Logic 1 to Logic 3 leadership by emphasising the importance of interconnectedness, feedback loop and holistic decision-making.[21] Her principles highlight how narrow, self-focused actions can disrupt the entire system, whereas a focus on collective wellbeing and systemic health can drive long-term success. This systems-based approach encourages leaders to break down silos, foster collaboration, and consider the impact of decisions across all levels of influence, aligning with the values of a Wellbeing Economy.

A powerful example of leading with perspective and embracing systems thinking emerged during one of our team and leadership development programmes in the transportation sector. The company had an organisational purpose focused on creating better journeys for a better world. However, this intent was not reflected in practice, as functions often operated in silos. The COVID-19 pandemic, which resulted in significant financial losses, made it critical to break down these silos and unify functions to optimise resources and drive efficiencies.

Following recent organisational change, Warun, a leader without direct operational experience, was appointed to head a key operational division known for its siloed and intimidating approach. The division had a history of absorbing disproportionate resources and using aggressive tactics, including the threat of strikes, to maintain its influence. Warun was selected for his reputation as a high-trust, low-ego and collaborative leader, qualities seen as essential for transforming the division from a self-serving entity into an integrated and cooperative part of the business, ultimately advancing the company's customer-focused approach.

At the start of his tenure, Warun collaborated with Ben to navigate the existing climate. Ben conducted a series of diagnostic conversations with Warun's leadership team to assess the current state and explore what it would take to embrace systems thinking as a leadership approach. The findings revealed deep-rooted challenges stemming from a culture of fear, a lack of cooperation with other business units and a tendency to prioritise individual interests over collective success.

We used Donella Meadows' "Iceberg Model" to help the team shift their perspective, see beyond the immediate events of what is going on, help discover root causal factors behind events and to understand the system. The model consists of four levels:

1. **Events:** This level focuses on observable facts and occurrences. It's the surface level where most people tend to focus, often leading to reactive decisions without deeper understanding.

2. **Patterns of behaviour:** By examining events over time, recurring trends and behaviours emerge. This level helps identify broader patterns that influence outcomes.

3. **Systems structure:** At this level, the focus shifts to understanding the underlying structures, relationships and feedback loops that create the patterns observed.

4. **Mental models:** The deepest level, exploring the core values, beliefs and assumptions that shape how systems behave and influence decisions.

We brought Warun's leadership team together and began by asking, "What is happening right now?" Their summary of the events included:

- **Decision making:** Difficulty reaching joint decisions for the good of the organisation.

- **Duplication:** Wasted resources due to poor information sharing and lack of collaboration.

- **Delivery:** Targets being met late or over budget due to inefficiencies.

To explore Patterns of Behaviour, we asked, "What trends have you observed over time?" Key trends identified included:

- **Lack of trust:** Ongoing conflict had eroded trust, reducing collaboration between operations and the rest of the organisation.

- **Lack of communication:** Insufficient information sharing and limited efforts to keep others informed.
- **Lack of collaboration:** A breakdown in teamwork and genuine cooperation across the organisation.

At the Systems Structure level, the team examined the deeper influences behind these patterns. Insights included:

- **Leadership:** A history of COOs failing to address the operational silos, often reinforcing them.
- **Recognition:** Incentive systems that rewarded individual performance over collective success, promoting siloed behaviour.
- **Meetings:** A focus on transactional meetings rather than strategic discussions that could align functions.

Finally, at the Mental Models level, the team identified root assumptions and beliefs influencing the structure:

- **Opposition mentality:** Language reflecting 'us vs. them' thinking.
- **Assuming ill intent:** Unfounded suspicions of others deliberately undermining operations.
- **Perceived superiority:** A belief that operations were superior to other functions, viewing them as subservient rather than collaborative partners.

Following the "Iceberg Model" provided the team with a structured framework, leading to meaningful conversations and a deeper understanding of the underlying dynamics. It became crucial to explore how to disrupt the system and create a positive path forward. The team took ownership of the patterns that had developed over time and acknowledged the need for significant improvements. With the team's support, Warun sought permission to share their findings with the CEO and Executive Committee. This act of honesty and transparency was a notable shift – Operations had not previously demonstrated such proactive engagement. The Executive Committee welcomed this openness but requested that the intent be reinforced with tangible commitments.

Warun collaborated with each Executive Committee member to conduct focused deep dives into their collective plans with Operations. He prioritised these sessions as a matter of urgency, involving his team members as necessary to maintain momentum. Using the organisational purpose and strategy as the guiding framework, they developed joint plans across key areas, including people, commercial, financial, procurement and asset development. To ensure sustained progress, Warun assigned individual team members to lead each workstream, integrating regular updates and issue resolution into team meetings. Relevant Executive Committee members and their teams were invited into these meetings, supporting clarity and alignment.

This approach became reciprocal, with Operations being actively included in meetings across the business – clearly demonstrating their commitment to collaboration, being 'open for business' and to delivering the organisational purpose.

Another pioneer in Systems Thinking to create perspective is Peter Senge. In *The Fifth Discipline*, he introduced systems thinking as a powerful way to see organisations not as disconnected parts but as deeply interconnected systems where decisions ripple across the whole.[22] His work reminds us that focusing only on surface-level issues rarely leads to lasting change – real transformation comes from addressing the deeper patterns, structures, and beliefs that drive behaviour.

Senge outlined five core disciplines that support purpose-driven leadership:

- **Systems thinking:** Seeing the whole picture and how elements influence one another.

- **Personal mastery:** Committing to self-awareness and personal growth as a foundation for leadership.

- **Mental models:** Identifying and challenging the underlying beliefs shaping our decisions.

- **Shared vision:** Creating a collective sense of purpose that inspires action.

- **Team learning:** Building collaborative learning environments where insight and innovation can thrive.

His approach aligns closely with the "Iceberg Model" explored earlier, emphasising the importance of understanding the hidden structures and mental models shaping outcomes. For Purpose-Driven Leaders, Senge's principles offer a roadmap for making more thoughtful, long-term decisions. They encourage leaders to step back, ask better questions, and ensure their leadership supports the health of their organisations and the wellbeing of people and the planet – today and for the long term.

TAKEAWAY

Purpose is often the most crucial determinant of a system's behaviour and it is the role of a leader to bring perspective to the impact of purpose on the system.

REALISE

Choosing to become a Purpose-Driven Leader, actively creating Purpose-Driven Organisations, and contributing to a Wellbeing Economy is not the easy path – but it is the necessary one. It demands courage, resilience and a willingness to challenge the entrenched Logic 1 system. Yet, the rewards are profound. Leading with purpose fuels our energy, sustains our commitment, and drives us towards a future where long-term wellbeing for all is not just an aspiration, but a reality.

As we have described, moving from Logic 1 (or Logic 2) to Logic 3 shifts the focus from self-interest to serving the greater good – this is the essence of being purpose-driven. Brandon Peele, author of *Purpose Work Nation* shared: "People require two things to do their best work: 1. A life-giving organisational purpose that creates long-term wellbeing for all, and 2. the opportunity to fulfil their unique purpose at work. With peer learning methods, we now have the tools to do this swiftly, sustainably, and at scale. As we know, companies that do this greatly outperform those that do not. More bluntly, without the heart, soul, and purpose of every person in an organisation bringing forth their best ideas, humanity has no chance of surviving the polycrisis."

Exploring Purpose-Driven Leadership at the micro level highlights the deep personal and collective benefits of rethinking and retooling leadership. Investing in this approach unlocks three essential elements: Energy, Flow, and Impact. These not only drive success in fulfilling your purpose but also sustain your wellbeing, developing the resilience and optimism needed to navigate challenges and stay committed to meaningful transformation.

Equally significant is the ability to empower others. By enabling those around you to unlock their own energy, flow, and positive impact, you create a culture where collective wellbeing thrives and thereby purpose can scale. This ripple effect strengthens teams, organisations and communities, making Purpose-Driven Leadership one of the most meaningful and enduring acts a leader can take.

REALISE 1: Energy

Johan sat with his arms folded and legs crossed for most of Ben's three-day Leading with Purpose programme in Dubai. As CFO for the Middle East, Africa, and India at a global organisation, Johan played a critical leadership role in navigating the business through challenging times. Yet he showed up to the programme visibly disengaged and sceptical.

Towards the end of the programme, Ben took Johan aside to chat on the terrace overlooking the city skyline. After a long pause, Johan opened up. He shared that years of operating in a Logic 1 world – where short-term profit maximisation dominated – had left him exhausted and questioning his worth. The relentless quarterly drive to "crunch the numbers" and demonstrate growth had sapped his energy and sense of purpose.

Exploring the shift to Purpose-Driven Leadership during the programme sparked something in Johan. The idea of a Logic 3 organisation – where governance, culture and decision-making align with the collective goal of long-term wellbeing for all – resonated deeply with him. For the first time, he envisioned a future where finance could play a transformative role, driving value not just for shareholders but for colleagues, communities and the environment.

This shift in perspective showed Johan how his role as CFO could be more than just managing numbers – it could be a driving force for meaningful change. By redefining finance to prioritise purpose-aligned strategies, he saw an opportunity to ensure the organisation's financial health was intrinsically linked to creating lasting, collective wellbeing.

Recent research underscores a significant correlation between a lack of purpose and increased burnout among professionals. A study published in *Frontiers in Public Health* found that healthcare workers experiencing burnout reported notably lower scores in Purpose in Life compared to their non-burned-out counterparts.[23] Specifically, 62.7 per cent of those without burnout exhibited high purpose in Life, whereas only 37.3 per cent of those with burnout did so.

Further supporting this, an article by Taylor Tower from Concordia University in April 2024, highlights that uncertainty and a lack of meaning in work are significant contributors to burnout.[24] The research suggests that continuously working towards unclear goals without a clear sense of long-term purpose is more likely to lead to burnout than diligently working towards well-defined objectives that serve long-term purpose that matters. At the same time, without self-governance aligned with long-term wellbeing, purpose can also become a pathway to burnout. As Geoff McDonald, ex-Global Vice President of Unilever, reflected in our conversation: *"I wish we had made employee wellbeing one of those big parameters and one of those goals, because sometimes you rely so much on purpose as the driver of your wellbeing that you become overly attached to it – neglecting other aspects like physical, emotional, and mental health. True purpose-driven leadership requires setting boundaries that sustain personal wellbeing, ensuring that the drive to serve others does not come at the cost of one's own health and resilience."*

Angela, a seasoned CEO with extensive experience across commercial, technology, and operational roles, exemplified how being purpose-driven can amplify both individual and collective energy. At the heart of her leadership philosophy was a commitment to helping people understand how to align their roles with the organisational purpose, ensuring they had clarity about the difference they make every day. Angela prioritised setting objectives that integrated individual deliverables with the organisation's long-term commitment to serving others. These objectives combined tangible outcomes with key behaviours essential to realising the broader ambition – such as nurturing collaboration across stakeholders, developing others and contributing positively to the community.

People loved working for Angela. She was a talent magnet, consistently attracting individuals committed to meaningful work and lives. Her team members frequently referred to her as the "best boss", with many following her to new organisations throughout her career. Angela's leadership combined a mindset for being purpose-driven with a structured approach to sustaining energy.

Her daily routine began at 5 a.m., incorporating mindfulness and physical exercise, followed by intentional choices around nutrition, sleep and hydration to manage the demands of her busy schedule, including frequent travel. Angela worked closely with her Executive Assistant to optimise her calendar, incorporating 25- and 50-minute meetings to maintain focus and prevent burnout. She also introduced regular check-ins with her Executive Committee, creating space for open dialogues on purposeful topics such as meaning, love and service – bringing the strategic intent of Purpose-Driven Organisations to life. Her efforts extended across the organisation. Angela celebrated examples of value-adding energy during Town Halls, incorporated energy-related questions into engagement surveys and launched learning and development programmes focusing on being purpose-led. The results were tangible: higher employee engagement, a culture of collaboration and strong organisational performance.

Another important benefit of being purpose-driven is having a healthy emotional state which nourishes energy. Leaders grounded in purpose are more able to maintain emotional balance even in challenging situations. Emotional Intelligence (EI) – including self-awareness, social awareness, self-management, and social skills – supports this balance and develops resilience. Daniel Goleman, author of the groundbreaking book *Emotional Intelligence*[25] explains how purpose and emotional intelligence blend in an article about his latest book *Optimal*: "It's no wonder emotional intelligence and purpose have both become so critical to the conversation around work, leadership, and organisational culture. Empirical evidence from workplace research suggests that greater levels of EI make you more productive and engaged, and improve your performance in any job, at every stage. They help you go further in your career, be better at sales, be more effective, and feel more satisfied with your job and committed to your work. They even contribute to your being in better health. Goleman summarises: "These benefits ... correlate with a strong sense of meaning – things like increased engagement and higher levels of overall wellbeing."[26]

An example of putting Emotional Intelligence into action via being purpose-driven is Jeff Weiner, former CEO of LinkedIn, known for his compassionate approach which made a considerable difference to nourishing energy and enhancing organisational development. In a speech given at Wharton's graduation ceremony, Jeff Weiner shared: "The long-term value of a company is based on the speed and quality of its decision-making. It's hard to make better decisions faster when people on the team lack trust in one another and are constantly questioning each other's motivations. In an environment like that, you'll spend most of your time navigating corporate politics, rather than focusing on the task at hand. I've been there, and it's no fun. The flip side is developing a culture with a compassionate ethos. That's what our leadership team has tried to do at LinkedIn; create a culture where people take the time to understand the other person's perspective, and not assume nefarious intentions; build trust; and align around a shared mission. After nearly 10 years, I still celebrate the fact that we can make important decisions in minutes or hours that some companies debate for months. Create the right culture, and you create a competitive advantage."

A range of research suggests that Purpose-Driven Leaders not only manage their own emotions effectively but also inspire their teams to approach challenges with clarity, resilience and a shared commitment to the greater good. Emma Seppälä and Kim Cameron, writing in the *Harvard Business Review*, demonstrated the benefits of energy in an article entitled "The best leaders have a contagious positive energy":[27] "Researchers and leaders have looked for the secret to successful leadership for centuries. Dozens of new books each year promise to deliver the answer. We decided to examine this question empirically, and when we did, we found that the greatest predictor of success for leaders is not their charisma, influence or power. It is not personality, attractiveness or innovative genius. The one thing that supersedes all these factors is positive relational energy: the energy exchanged between people that helps uplift, enthuse and renew them." They went on to say: "Energisers' greatest secret is that, by uplifting others through authentic, values-based leadership, they end up lifting up both themselves and their organisations. Positive energisers demonstrate and cultivate virtuous actions, including forgiveness, compassion, humility, kindness, trust, integrity, honesty, generosity, gratitude, and recognition in the organisation. As a result, everyone flourishes."

The energy unleashed by Purpose-Driven Leadership connects people to a shared goal, creating workplaces that are vibrant, resilient, and impactful. By channelling purpose into action, leaders inspire their teams to align their efforts with meaningful, long-term contributions. This focus on purpose doesn't just sustain energy – it magnifies it, unlocking the full potential of individuals, teams and organisations to thrive and create lasting positive change.

TAKEAWAY

Energy is a direct outcome of being purpose-driven which in turn energises others.

REALISE 2: Flow

Flow – where focus, creativity and performance reach their peak – is a natural result of Purpose-Driven Leadership. Psychologist Mihaly Csikszentmihalyi, renowned for his work on flow, described it as "a state of concentration so focused that it amounts to complete absorption in an activity, resulting in the achievement of an ideal state of happiness:"[28] It's the experience of becoming so immersed in meaningful work that time seems to disappear, and you operate at your best.

Purpose-Driven Leadership creates the conditions for flow by aligning personal values and organisational goals with meaningful outcomes. When leaders work in a purposeful environment, they unlock sustained focus, emotional energy, and profound engagement. In his seminal book, *Flow: The Psychology of Optimal Experience*, Csikszentmihalyi wrote about how leaders in flow operate with an alignment to the wider context in which they are part and a sense of what they could create, which wouldn't have been possible without them. He states: "You know that what you need to do is possible, even though difficult, and a sense of time disappears. You feel part of something larger."

Steven Kotler highlighted the impact of flow in his 2019 *Harvard Business Review* article, "Create a Work Environment That Fosters Flow":[29] "In a 10-year study conducted by McKinsey, top executives reported being five times more productive in flow. If we could increase the time we spend in flow by 15–20%, overall workplace productivity would almost double."

Kotler explained that flow is neurochemically driven, involving a cascade of neurotransmitters like norepinephrine, dopamine, endorphins, anandamide and serotonin. These chemicals heighten focus, reduce pain, spark creativity and enhance collaboration, creating peak performance conditions essential for complex environments. While flow can emerge from deep immersion in challenging tasks like sports or creative work, Csikszentmihalyi and other researchers emphasise that transcending self-interest is key to activating it. Purpose, by its nature, is about serving something greater than oneself – diminishing the ego to contribute to a larger, more meaningful goal.

Kotler's research also shows how flow is triggered by purpose: "Purpose gives meaning and significance to your actions and goals. When your work aligns with your values, it's easier to get into a flow state. Purpose acts as a guiding compass, enabling you to stay resilient despite obstacles." Paul Snyder, Executive Vice President at Tillamook County Creamery Association, discovered flow through purpose-driven work: *"When you love what you do, there is a resonance and an experience of being in the flow. In some of my first sustainability projects, I felt like I was being who I was meant to be. It became self-fulfilling. What I discovered was focusing on bringing together sustainability, social justice and making business a force for good in the world translated into being the best version of me. When I came out of business school it was at the time of companies like Enron were imploding. It angered me to my core. At business school we were a bunch of good people coming out with MBAs and wanting to do good. It shaped my belief in conscious capitalism and that business can be the greatest advancement for human evolution in the world. Conversely, 'Crony Capitalism' is the most damaging and destructive for societies. Ever since those formative times I have wanted to prove that business is a force for good and that people need to recognise it. I love the fight."*

Jamie Bunce, Entrepreneur in Later Living, exemplified flow through Purpose-Driven Leadership. *"My purpose is to make a tangible difference to people as they age. My simple outlook helped to create an organisation with the promise of a life less ordinary for today's generation of retirees. We put the health and happiness of our residents at the heart of everything we did. My empathy impacted my choices, for instance if I saw a colleague struggling, I would seek to understand what else was affecting their outputs and then focus on supporting them through their own challenges. My drive to make a positive difference to people's lives played itself out with colleagues, customers and investors so that I focused on what mattered most. Being purpose-driven kept me in a state of flow enabling me to achieve outcomes beyond what I thought was possible."*

Flow doesn't happen by chance; it requires intentionality. The shifts in practice outlined in the earlier instructional part of this chapter create the conditions for flow – focusing on clarity, removing distractions, and aligning efforts with a world we want. Flow is also not just an individual experience; it is a state that Purpose-Driven Leaders can cultivate within themselves and inspire in others through purpose. Purpose-Driven Leadership, as we have outlined, creates the conditions where people feel inspired, challenged and fully immersed in their work and these are core conditions that underpin flow. When teams experience flow collectively, they can feed others, feed from others and reduce their potential to derail flow. As Csikszentmihalyi outlined in his 1990 book: "Surgeons say that during a difficult operation they have the sensation that the entire operating team is a single organism, moved by the same purpose; they describe it as a 'ballet' in which the individual [emphasis added] is subordinated to the group performance, and all involved share in a feeling of harmony and power."[30] This appears to neatly describe conditions whereby organisms acting together can create emergent benefits that are greater than the sum of the parts.

Flow happens naturally when people are deeply connected to what matters most, finding meaning in their work rather than being driven by external pressure. Purpose-Driven Leaders unlock this powerful state for themselves and their organisations, driving performance and creating long-term meaningful impact.

TAKEAWAY

Flow results from Purpose-Driven Leadership by aligning values, focus, intrinsic motivation and doing meaningful work.

REALISE 3: Impact

Perhaps the most profound outcome of being a Purpose-Driven Leader is the deep sense of fulfilment that comes from knowing your life and work serve the ultimate collective goal of long-term wellbeing for all. As we've explored, purpose isn't just a driver of engagement – it's a source of profound meaning.

When leaders see their impact reflected in the lives of others and when they receive confirmation that their work has made a difference, it reinforces a sense of worth that is essential to their own wellbeing. Susan, a senior technology executive, discovered the difference she wanted to make through being purpose-driven. Though successful on paper, she felt unfulfilled. After reflecting on the impact that she wanted to have, she realised her true motivation was to help others succeed. This realisation led her to mentor a colleague, Nina, a single mother navigating a challenging work culture. Susan championed a shift in her company's culture, challenging presenteeism and advocating for more dynamic, flexible working environments.

Observing the difference that it made on Nina's ability to fulfil her responsibilities as a mother, and contribute in a meaningful way at word had a profound self-reinforcing effect on Susan who shared: *"I can now see that what was missing in my work and life was the opportunity to have a demonstrable impact on improving others' long-term wellbeing. I am now intentional everyday about being purpose-driven in order to strengthen the foundations of this being my reality regardless of circumstance."* Leading with purpose isn't just about shaping better organisations and economies. It is about creating a life of significance, where success is measured by the lives we touch and the lasting value we create.

For Ben, the journey towards purpose began during his time growing up at The Yehudi Menuhin School. While attending the world's most famous music school was seen as a privilege, for Ben, it felt like a gilded cage. Playing the violin all day did not fulfil his deeper desires or help him make sense of the world. His discontent persisted until a turning point came when he met Sally Trench, a guest speaker whose extraordinary story shifted his perspective.

Trench shared how her privileged upbringing masked deep unhappiness. Despite her father's success in the housing industry, she felt emotionally neglected. At the age of seven, she rebelled, and by fifteen, after multiple school expulsions, she felt disconnected and lost. Yet, this pain ignited a personal mission. One night, she encountered homeless individuals at Waterloo Station in central London. Compelled by a sense of compassion, she returned night after night, providing coffee and blankets while listening to their stories. This commitment grew into a lifelong mission of service.

Her experiences led to the bestselling book *Bury Me in My Boots*, which sold over a million copies and funded her youth intervention initiative, Project Spark. Spark supported young people at risk of addiction and crime, restoring self-respect and hope. Inspired by Sally's example, Ben visited her project and saw firsthand how a life dedicated to making a difference could inspire profound change. His own sense of purpose began to emerge.

This notion of impact resonates with many leaders. Leadership expert Richard Boyatzis emphasises that the path to meaningful impact begins with small steps: *"No matter where you are, you can set a vision and make progress. Surround yourself with mentors and a support network to stay true to your purpose."* Emily Chang, CEO of VML West, offers another perspective: *"Legacy is not reserved for extraordinary individuals. We are all meant to leave a legacy, to leave things better than we found them. We are each gifted with a unique set of experiences, talents, and personality. And when we identify the intersection of what we uniquely offer and the injustices we feel compelled to address, we uncover our own social legacy, the impact each of us was made to have on the world."*

Purpose-Driven Leaders understand that the drive to have a positive impact is a fundamental human need. The critical questions are: What impact do you want to have? What difference do you want to make? Edith Eger, a Holocaust survivor turned psychologist, exemplifies this. After surviving Auschwitz and unimaginable trauma, she chose to heal and help others. Her book, *The Choice*, shares her journey of using personal healing as a tool for global impact, proving that even the most challenging experiences can fuel positive change.[31]

Achieving meaningful impact requires courage and self-awareness. Tony Robbins, renowned life and business strategist, once observed, "Most people overestimate what they can accomplish in a year and underestimate what they can achieve in a decade."[32]

Purpose-driven leaders make a difference not through grand gestures but through taking consistent actions that lead to tangible impact on the long-term wellbeing for all that can be evidenced on Macro, Meso and Micro levels as shared in *Beyond Profit*.

TAKEAWAY

The most tangible result of being purpose-driven is the positive impact you create towards long-term wellbeing for all. By staying focused on this, you amplify the energy needed to sustain your purpose-driven journey.

Conclusion

Moving Forwards Together

"Each of us is put here in this time and in this place to personally decide the future of humankind. Do you think you were put here for something less?"

Chief Arvol Looking Horse

We don't choose when we are born or where we are put on this planet. We stand at a defining juncture for life on Earth: either we continue making decisions within the governance box of short-term financial self-interest, accelerating the decline of wellbeing, or we pivot our governing to directly deliver what we really care about: long-term wellbeing for all. If you are reading this book, you are likely to fall into a privileged category of humans with influence and resources amplifying the choice you make. *Beyond Profit* is created to support your journey and leapfrog you as a leader to your greatest potential. It shows how we need to operationally align the world with long-term wellbeing for all – our ultimate shared value creation goal and to deliberately kill off certain assumptions and governance systems.

Leadership is about inspiring others to move towards a forward future that doesn't yet exist. This requires shared clarity about what we are building together – which cannot be defined by products or services, as these will need to constantly adapt. The common, shared vision for practical change has to be a specification for how to govern routine decisions in a way that drives and protects what we collectively care about most: long-term wellbeing for all. From that foundation, the right solutions will naturally follow.

Almost as important as having shared clarity about what we are building, and for what end, is having a shared understanding of the governance box that has driven our unsustainability crisis and prevents us from addressing the grave problems when they hit this box. It is imperative that we collectively call out the problem (Logic 1), why Logic 2 is not enough, and what is truly necessary to align with reality – if we are to harness the market economy when we need it most. We have lost decades trying to work within a deeply flawed system. If we are to move forward as a global movement rather than fragmented pockets of concern, we need to give this decision-making prison a name and hold a clear, shared view of the new system we are creating.

Change in a seemingly inert system can seem very far out of reach. But systems are constantly changing.

The only way to consciously shift a locked system is through tapping into an energy source that makes the effort worthwhile and courageous action the norm – this is purpose-driven energy. This energy is everywhere if we choose to see it, building over the decades in every domain one can think of. We don't necessarily need more of this energy – but we desperately need to unite, amplify and direct it.

This book is designed as a handbook for doing just that: building collective clarity around what we want to build, and for showing how we can journey together as leaders across all parts of the system, uniting energy at every level to move from Logic 1 to Logic 3. *Beyond Profit* distils the core components of this shared journey – insights that are, in many ways, hidden in plain sight.

It begins with a surprisingly simple idea: that our collective goal must be the creation of wellbeing: not just for some, but for everyone; not just for now, but for the future. And if long-term wellbeing for all is the outcome we seek, then we must intentionally direct, oversee and account for decisions in ways that serve and safeguard this goal.

It is governance that has locked us into destruction and it is governance – coupled with purpose – that can release us. Governance is not a fragmented system that differs fundamentally between government, business or the self; it is the same foundational system, nested and replicated. Each layer shapes and is shaped by the others, and all are underpinned by the same core principles. If we become literate in these governance principles we can use them to transform all domains. And true transformation requires all of us to engage with governance at every level, simultaneously with the same clear intent to move Beyond Profit to intentional creation and protection of lasting, equitable wellbeing:

At the **MACRO** level – to create a Wellbeing Economy and move deliberately away from GDP economies

At the **MESO** level – to transition from profit-maximising organisations to Purpose-Driven Organisations that can realise the Wellbeing Economy

At the **MICRO** level – to build our capability as Purpose-Driven Leaders and enable Purposeful Work and Lives

What we need in terms of system actors is:

MACRO: Governments and citizens. To build a Wellbeing Economy, we need informed and engaged citizens who understand their governance role and, with clarity and unity, demand purpose-driven government. We need governments that are governance literate, in other words, able to use their legal powers to reflect and encode citizen support for Logic 3 in law. A key step is creating the governance framework for a Wellbeing Economy – ensuring alignment with long-term wellbeing for all, beyond the limits of any single political term. This shift must replace outdated systems that are difficult to reform and vulnerable to the self-interest Logic 1 enables. Crucially, it also means using both legal and non-legal levers to create the enabling conditions for Purpose-Driven Organisations to thrive. It is no longer enough to inch toward harm in the hope that change will follow. We need organisations to be fully enterprising, driven by design, to create wellbeing.

MESO: Organisations (beyond governments) We need all organisations to be governed as Logic 3 Purpose-Driven Organisations. Shortly, we will have a global consensus-built framework for what a purpose-driven governance system looks like (ISO 37011). We can all be involved in this and lean on it to hold ALL organisations to account and drive useful change. The fact that there is one co-created view of good governance for all organisations (ISO 37000) is incredibly powerful. We can all become proficient in this and progress with the really hard work of designing and constantly adapting strategy.

MICRO: Ourselves. We need individuals who govern themselves with purpose to become Purpose-Driven Leaders, enabling meaningful work and purposeful lives. When rooted in this clarity, they can feel confident that they are activating the nucleus of a flywheel that generates lasting, positive impact.

The substance of this book consists in the following:

To be successful in influencing these three levels and actors, *Beyond Profit* has brought to life the global shift already underway in each that we can learn from and put energy behind. We offered a chapter on each of the three levels, each outlining areas to rethink, retool for change and what you can realise as a result.

MACRO: At the economy level (Chapter 2) we brought to life the global movement towards Purpose-Driven Governments and Wellbeing Economies.

Rethink entailed moving from:

RETHINK 1: **GDP: From Goal to Parameter** outlines the numerous dangerous aspects of pinning our problem-solving to GDP.

RETHINK 2: **Wellbeing: From a Side Topic to the Point** shows why putting Wellbeing at the centre of the room for governments and the economy is transformational.

RETHINK 3: **From Politicians to All Leaders** reminds us that we are the ultimate governing body of the economy and we can all play a transformative role in it.

Retool focused on:

RETOOL 1: **National Governance for Wellbeing** clarifies the core tools of governance – showing that, at its foundation, it is no different from the governance of any other organisation.

RETOOL 2: **Wellbeing Accountability** focuses on the accounting system for a Wellbeing Economy that unites national accounts with organisational accounts.

RETOOL 3: **Fiscal Policy for Wellbeing** brings insights from countries around the world about how Wellbeing Economies use the tool of fiscal policy.

If everything from Chapter 2 is put into practice, the benefits Realised by Wellbeing Economies will unlock:

REALISE 1: **Enduring Direction** summarises the unifying force that anchoring to a meaningful goal can bring to a nation.

REALISE 2: **Citizen Engagement** emphasises how a move to a Logic 3 Wellbeing Economy would bring a rationale to citizen engagement and create the infrastructure needed to bring it to life.

REALISE 3: **Purpose-Driven Organisations** highlights the potential and imperative for purpose-driven governments that want to create Wellbeing Economies to swiftly enable Purpose-Driven Organisations that can realise this ambition.

MESO. In Chapter 3 we brought to life the global movement towards Purpose-Driven Organisations.

Rethink entailed moving from:

RETHINK 1: **Financial Capture to Wellbeing Creation** requires a shift from seeing organisations and markets within the lens of "financial capture" to "wellbeing creation" in service not to themselves but to all people and the planet, now and into the future.

RETHINK 2: **Strategy to Governance** focuses our attention as leaders on creating quality governance systems that enable adaptive, relevant and wellbeing-aligned strategy.

RETHINK 3: **Market Response to Market Making** is a call to create the bold, innovative and disruptive organisations that we need.

Retool focused on:

RETOOL 1: The foundation of governance that **ISO 37000 "Governance of Organisations"** provides.

RETOOL 2: The first national consensus build standard in how to govern **Purpose-Driven Organisations (PAS 808)** and the coming international consensus **ISO 37011.**

RETOOL 3: **The Evolved Value Framework** – a tool to realise purpose-driven marketing and drive value creation of Purpose-Driven Organisations.

If everything from Chapter 3 is put into practice, the benefits Realised by Purpose-Driven Organisations will be:

REALISE 1: **Coherence** – the foundation to move forward with confidence and skill towards a future we want.

REALISE 2: **Enterprise** – the ability to hyper-innovate the solutions we need at speed.

REALISE 3: **Commitment** – the emotional alignment within and beyond the organisational system to sustain the journey.

MICRO: In Chapter 4 we explored how to develop as a Purpose-Driven Leader who works actively at all three levels by utilising our human purpose-driven energy.

This chapter challenges us to Rethink three fundamental shifts required to be a Purpose-Driven Leader, moving from:

Money to Meaning equips leaders to help others pursue meaningful work and lives by creating and delivering governance systems that bring long-term wellbeing for all into the day-to-day reality of employees and stakeholders.

Doing to Being reminds us to bring humanity back to leadership. We are called "human beings," not "human doings", for a reason.

Me to We challenges leaders to move from self-interest to other-focus by removing the interference with our natural wiring to help others.

The Retool section at the Micro level enables leaders to inspire others to move in a shared direction, work cohesively and synchronise organisational performance through disciplined governance.

The tools leaders can use are:

Lead with Love is anchored in the tool of psychological safety. Operating in an environment of fear might produce short-term performance boosts, but building and leading an organisation dedicated to long-term wellbeing for all requires serving the good of others, which is love in action.

Lead with Vision is grounded in neuroscience research that explains the role of the positive emotional attractor critical to vision creation. Vision moves us beyond the grind of day-to-day activity and sustains us when challenged by Logic 1 thinkers focused on short-term results. A compelling vision shapes our desired futures and pushes us beyond perceived limits.

Lead with Perspective focuses on moving beyond isolated individuals, teams or functions to align mutual outcomes, share information, make joint decisions and deliver in partnership.

The potential benefits of Realising Purpose-Driven Leadership at the Micro level are:

Energy is a direct outcome of being purpose-driven and gives you the sustenance to unlock the potential of individuals, teams and organisations to thrive and make meaningful change.

Flow arises from being purpose-driven, giving meaning and significance to your actions and goals. Once in flow you become so immersed in doing work that matters that time and the self seem to disappear as you operate at your best.

Impact emerges from purpose and touches one of the deepest intrinsic motivations of knowing that your life and work serve the ultimate collective goal of long-term wellbeing for all.

So where will the drive to initiate and sustain such a leadership journey come from? From Purpose-Driven Leaders like you.

That is why our intent with this book is to fuel and develop your energy to choose to be Logic 3 Purpose-Driven Leaders – and your skills to govern yourself, your organisations and the economy so that long-term wellbeing for all becomes a reality. In our view, this is the fundamental task we all need to engage in to create the world we want. As you reflect on this, we invite you to consider:

'If not this, what?

'If not now, when?'

'If not you, who?

Armed with a shared destination and language to describe what we are trying to achieve, we can have the confidence to move forwards as Purpose-Driven Leaders, knowing we are on the right track that reflects a common aim.

Every reader is on a unique journey, but by developing a community of like-minded leaders with a shared understanding of the foundational requirements for being purpose-driven, we can create unstoppable momentum. This foundation includes:

- Harnessing our natural drive to serve others and unlock collective potential.

- Building the capacity to govern well, ensuring a strong shared frame that creates adaptability, learning and growth in the right direction – while encouraging others to do the same.

- Developing the imagination, knowledge and ability to help others understand why essential changes must be made for a sustainable world – and envisioning the destination that will resolve the challenges of our time.

- Clarifying the direction individuals and organisations must take, while deliberately moving away from the limiting constraints of Logic 1 and Logic 2.

- Co-creating and implementing Logic 3 governance to guide decision-making, holding us accountable, and ensuring we stay committed to the ultimate goal: long-term wellbeing for all.

The world stands at crisis point, and the need for Purpose-Driven Leaders, skilled in purpose-driven governance, has never been greater. You are now equipped with the context, knowledge and tools to propel the work already underway around the world and to make a global shift to Logic 3 Governance a reality – in our lives as leaders, our organisations and role as citizens.

We have the power to change the system that we are invested in. If not a change to Logic 3 Purpose-Driven Governance, then what? If not now, when?

Acknowledgements

Victoria: As well as all interviewees, I would like to give my heartfelt thanks to the following people for their support with various aspects of the long journey that led to this book: Alexandra Nikitina, Aljan de Boer, Alexis Eyre, Amelie Lambert, Andreea Sapunaru, Andrew Griffiths, Arun Kelshiker, Axel Kravazky, Ben Carpenter, Ben Kellard, Beth Knight, Bénédicte Peillon-Russo, Bill Baue, Bob Garrett, Brandon Peele, Carolynn Chalmers, Charles Ebert, Chidi Obihara, Chris Nichols, Colin Mayer, Coro Strandberg, Courtney Howard, Ed Freeman, Ed Gemmell, Erinch Sahan, Geoff Kendall, Ghada Haddad, Gillian Secrett, Graham Singh, Hamish Khamisa, Iain Stewart, Jaideep Prabhu, James Vaccaro, John Elkington, John O'Brien, John Rosling, Jonathan Wise, Kirsten Wright, Lou Drake, Louise La Gat, Lucy von Strumer, Mark Drewell, Mark Gough, Mark Kahn, Manjit Yadav, Mario Abela, Matt Bell, Matt Scott, Michele De Capitani, Mike Mongo, Michael Palmer, Mike Rowands, Neil Gaught, Nicole van der elst Desai, Pat Dwyer, Paul Polman, Paul Randle, Peter Lipman, Phillip Sugai, Philippe Joubert, Rick Alexander, Rob Hopkins, Roger Miles, Sarah Gillard, Shaun Chamberlin, Stephen Stirling, Stephen Huddart, Stephanie Bertels, TH Culhane, Vitto Cerruli, Will Gardner, all the wonderful people in the PAS 808 and ISO 37011 expert groups and so many more I have no room to mention. With very special thanks to Charlie Thompson for her unwavering hands-on support and David Wheeler for all you did especially at the beginning of my journey. To my wonderful mother for your detailed editing support – you are incredible (and Dad for just being amazing). To my loving son and broader family, and finally to my incomparable husband who has spent three decades being nothing but supportive of me and my life's purpose. I am so grateful for you all.

Ben: I am fortunate to partner with inspiring leaders who through our work together constantly challenge me to learn and develop my thinking about being purpose-driven. I am very grateful for the generous insight of all the contributors recognised at the beginning of the book. However, I do want to shout out to Amy C. Edmondson, Novartis Professor of Leadership and Management, Harvard Business School, who graciously wrote the foreword. Finally, thank you to my incredible children, India, Ziggy and Zebedee who bring the deepest meaning to my life every day.

Lorenzo: I would like to thank the many colleagues and friends who have accompanied me on this "long walk" to the establishment of a Wellbeing Economy. Whether in my capacity as an academic, as an entrepreneur or as a politician, I have been fortunate enough to meet amazing "doers", who are translating my ideas into actual realities. It is thanks to their daily commitment that the principles of the Wellbeing Economy are spreading to the four corners of the world. Despite the challenges and the complexities involved with "building a better world", my children have always been on my side. Thanks for your trust and patience.

Thank you from all of us to the brilliant team at John Murray Business for their expertise and commitment: Jonathan Shipley (commissioning editor); Alisha Raj (project editor); Matt Young (marketing manager).

Notes

Overview

1 Sachs, J. D., Lafortune, G., Fuller, G., & Lablonovski, G. (2025). Sustainable Development Report 2025: Executive summary. SDG Transformation Center. https://dashboards.sdgindex.org/chapters/executive-summary
2 PAS 808:2022. (2022). Purpose-Driven Organisations for delivering sustainability. British Standards Institution. https://www.bsigroup.com/en-GB/insights-and-media/insights/brochures/pas-808-purpose-driven-organisations-for-delivering-sustainability/
3 EU Monitor. (2009). GDP and beyond: Measuring progress in a changing world, available at: https://www.eea.europa.eu/policy-documents/com-2009-433-final-gdp.

Chapter 1

1 Goodland, R. & Ledec, G. (1987). "Neoclassical economics and principles of sustainable development". *Ecological Modelling*, 38(1–2), 19–46.
2 Marshall, A. (1890). *Principles of Economics*. London: Palgrave Macmillan.
3 WCED (1987). World Commission on Environment and Development; (WCED) (1987). Our Common Future.
4 Costanza, R., McGlade, J., Lovins, H. & Kubiszewski, I. (2014). "An overarching goal for the UN sustainable development goals". *Solutions*, 5(4), 13–16.
5 International Public Sector Accounting Standards Board, available at https://ifacweb.blob.core.windows.net/publicfiles/2023-12/IPSASB-Public-Sector-Conceptual-Framework_2023%20-%20Updated%2012-19-23_Secure.pdf
6 Reflecting a range of disciplinary traditions, the British Standard in Purpose-Driven Organisations defines Wellbeing as: "positive state of being where current and future needs are met, such that there is the capacity and opportunity to flourish".
7 Cardinal Naheyawin, J. (n.d.). *A Guide to Indigenous Concepts of Wellness & Wellbeing*. Naheyawin, available at https://www.edmonton.ca/sites/default/

files/public-files/assets/AGuidetoIndigenousConceptsofWellnessWellbeing. pdf

8 Smith, A. (1809). The theory of moral sentiments; or, An essay towards an analysis of the principles by which men naturally judge concerning the conduct and character, first of their neighbours, and afterward of themselves. To which is added, a dissertation on the origin of languages, available at https://www.loc.gov/item/18015943/

9 Brundtland Report, available at https://sustainabledevelopment.un.org/content/documents/5987our-common-future.pdf

10 Hagens, N. (2023). Economics. Nate Hagens. available at https://www.natehagens.com/economics

11 Ripple, W. J., Wolf, C., Gregg, J. W., Rockström, J., Mann, M. E., Oreskes, N., ... & Crowther, T. W. (2024). "The 2024 state of the climate report: Perilous times on planet Earth". *BioScience*, 74(12), 812–824.

12 Financial Times Special Report on Renewable Energy, available at https://www.ft.com/renewable-energy

13 World Health Organization (2024). Ambient (outdoor) air pollution. 25 October, available at https://www.who.int/news-room/fact-sheets/detail/ambient-(outdoor)-air-quality-and-health

14 Peters, R., Ee, N., Peters, J., Booth, A., Mudway, I. & Anstey, K. J. (2019). "Air pollution and dementia: a systematic review". *Journal of Alzheimer's Disease*, 70(s1), S145–S163.

15 National Ocean Service (2024). *What Is Ocean Acidification?* U.S. Department of Commerce, National Oceanic and Atmospheric Administration, 16 June, available at https://oceanservice.noaa.gov/facts/acidification.html

16 Burgherr, P. & Hirschberg, S. (2008). "Severe accident risks in fossil energy chains: a comparative analysis". *Energy*, 33(4), 538–553.

17 Fields, S. (2004). Global nitrogen: Cycling out of control. *Environmental Health Perspectives*, 112(10), A556–A563. https://doi.org/10.1289/ehp.112-a556

18 *European Nitrogen Assessment*, Cambridge University Press, 16, May 2011.

19 World Wildlife Fund (2024). *Living Planet Report 2024: A System in P{eril* [Press release], available at https://www.worldwildlife.org/publications/living-planet-report-2024

20 IPBES Transformative Change Assessment, available at https://www.ipbes.net/transformative-change/media-release

21 Food and Agriculture Organization of the United Nations. (2019). *Key messages: Global Symposium on Soil Erosion*. FAO available at https://www.fao.org/about/meetings/soil-erosion-symposium/key-messages/en/

22 World Bank (2021) *Water in circular economy and resilience*, available at: https://www.worldbank.org/en/topic/water/publication/wicer

23 World Wildlife Fund (n.d.). *Freshwater Facts and Challenges*, available at https://www.worldwildlife.org/places/freshwater

24 World Bank (2021) *Water in circular economy and resilience*, available at: https://www.worldbank.org/en/topic/water/publication/wicer

25 World Health Organization. (2023). *Antimicrobial Resistance*, 21 November, available at https://www.who.int/news-room/fact-sheets/detail/antimicrobial-resistance

26 World Bank Group (2017). *Drug-Resistant Infections: A Threat to Our Economic Future* (Final report). World Bank, available at https://documents1.worldbank.org/curated/en/323311493396993758/pdf/final-report.pdf

27 Trasande, L., et al. (2024). Prenatal phthalate exposure and adverse birth outcomes in the USA. *The Lancet Planetary Health*. Advance online publication. https://doi.org/10.1016/S2542-5196(23)00270-X

28 Mitchell, E. A., Mulhauser, B., Mulot, M., Mutabazi, A., Glauser, G. & Aebi, A. (2017). "A worldwide survey of neonicotinoids in honey". *Science*, 358(6359), 109–111.

29 Dennis, B. & Kemp, W.P. (2016) "How hives collapse: Allee effects, ecological resilience, and the honey bee". *PLoS ONE* 11(2): e0150055. doi:10.1371/journal.pone.0150055

30 Zheng, G., Schreder, E., Dempsey, J. C., Uding, N., Chu, V., Andres, G., ... & Salamova, A. (2021). "Per-and polyfluoroalkyl substances (PFAS) in breast milk: concerning trends for current-use PFAS". *Environmental Science & Technology*, 55(11), 7510–7520.

31 Ling, A.L. (2024). Estimated scale of costs to remove PFAS from the environment at current emission rates. Science of the Total Environment. https://doi.org/10.1016/j.scitotenv.2024.170647

32 Geyer, R., Jambeck, J. R. & Law, K. L. (2017). "Production, use, and fate of all plastics ever made". *Science Advances*, 3(7), e1700782.

33 World Health Organization (2022). *Mental Health*, available at https://www.who.int/news-room/fact-sheets/detail/mental-health-strengthening-our-response

34 Organisation for Economic Co-operation and Development (2023). *Health at a Glance 2023: Care for People with Mental Health Disorders*. OECD Publishing, available at https://www.oecd.org/en/publications/2023/11/health-at-a-glance-2023_e04f8239/full-report/mental-health_af4ca002.html

35 OECD (2021). "All the lonely people: Education and loneliness". Available at: https://www.oecd.org/content/dam/oecd/en/publications/reports/2021/06/all-the-lonely-people_69cfb1ff/23ac0e25-en.pdf

36 Ernst, M., Niederer, D., Werner, A. M., Czaja, S. J., Mikton, C., Ong, A. D. ... & Beutel, M. E. (2022) "Loneliness before and during the COVID-19 pandemic: A systematic review with meta-analysis". *American Psychologist*, 77(5), 660.

37 'Our epidemic of loneliness and isolation', The U.S. Surgeon General's Advisory on the Healing Effects of Social Connection and Community, 2023, available at: https://www.hhs.gov/sites/default/files/surgeon-general-social-connection-advisory.pdf

BEYOND PROFIT

38 Dugan, A. (2024). "Over 1 in 5 people worldwide feel lonely a lot", Gallup, 10 July, available at: https://news.gallup.com/poll/646718/people-worldwide-feel-lonely-lot.aspx

39 World Health Organization (2023). WHO launches commission to foster social connection=, 15 November, available at https://www.who.int/news/item/15-11-2023-who-launches-commission-to-foster-social-connection

40 Cuesta, J., López-Noval, B. & Niño-Zarazúa, M. (2024). Social exclusion concepts, measurement, and a global estimate. *PLOS ONE, 19*(2), e0298085. https://doi.org/10.1371/journal.pone.0298085

41 Gaspar, V., Poplawski-Ribeiro, M., & Yoo, J. (2023, September 13). *Global debt is returning to its rising trend.* International Monetary Fund available at https://www.imf.org/en/Blogs/Articles/2023/09/13/global-debt-is-returningto-its-rising-trend

42 United Nations Conference on Trade and Development (2024). *A World of Debt 2024*, available at https://unctad.org/publication/world-of-debt

43 World Bank (2024). *International Debt Report 2024*, 3 December, available at https://www.worldbank.org/en/news/press-release/2024/12/03/developing-countries-paid-record-1-4-trillion-on-foreign-debt-in-2023

44 Hickel, J., Barbour, F. & others (2024). Unequal exchange of labour in the world economy. *Nature Communications*, 15, 49687. https://doi.org/10.1038/s41467-024-49687-y

45 Juniper, T. (2025). *Just Earth: How a Fairer World Will Save the Planet.* Bloomsbury Publishing.

46 World Resources Institute (2023). How to sustainably feed 10 billion people by 2050, in 21 charts, available at https://www.wri.org/insights/how-sustainably-feed-10-billion-people-2050-21-charts

47 McMillan, J. (2003). *Reinventing the Bazaar: A Natural History of Markets.* WW Norton & Company.

48 Carrington, D. (2025, April 3). *Climate crisis on track to destroy capitalism, warns top insurer.* The Guardian. https://www.theguardian.com/environment/2025/apr/03/climate-crisis-on-track-to-destroy-capitalism-warns-allianz-insurer

49 Holland, J. H. (2018). "Can there be a unified theory of complex adaptive systems?" In *The Mind, The Brain and Complex Adaptive Systems* (pp. 45–50). Routledge.

50 Smith, A. (1809). The theory of moral sentiments; or, An essay towards an analysis of the principles by which men naturally judge concerning the conduct and character, first of their neighbours, and afterward of themselves. To which is added, a dissertation on the origin of languages, available at https://www.loc.gov/item/18015943/

51 Friedman, M. (n.d.). *Milton Friedman on Donahue Show: Greed, Markets, and Government* available at YouTube. https://www.youtube.com/watch?v=2BI7VpU3Ccw

52 Friedman, M. (1993). *Why Government Is the Problem* [Essay]. Hoover Institution, available at https://www.hoover.org/sites/default/files/uploads/documents/friedman-government-problem-1993.pdf

53 Also known as constraints, guardrails, red-lines or limitations.

54 We recognise that humans are natural but the term "natural capital" as opposed to human or social capital is the most widely used. See the work by Forum for the Future and the International Integrated Reporting Council for details on the breakdown of capital groups. Here we use a simplified version.

55 Herman Daly sadly passed away in 2023. Just prior to his death, he exoressed via emails with Victoria, his support of the adaptation of the triangle, particularly that it connected the macro to the meso and micro domains where change is operationalised – something he said he had thought about but not actioned.

56 Bio-regional systems of governance based on non-political boundaries based on organic socio-ecological boundaries are argued by many to be by far the most appropriate for governing for collective long-term wellbeing.

57 Thomas Paine, Rights of Man (1791). Penguin Classics.

58 Ostrom, E. (1990). *Governing the Commons: The Evolution of Institutions for Collective Action.* Cambridge University.

59 Johar, I. (2025). Linkedin post: Beyond Burning The RedTape available at: https://lnkd.in/p/esbxbkWN

60 Graeber, D., & Wengrow, D. (2021). *The dawn of everything: A new history of humanity.* Farrar, Straus and Giroux.

61 Bouchaud, J.-P. & Mézard, M. (2000). Wealth condensation in a simple model of economy. *Physica A: Statistical Mechanics and its Applications, 282*(3), 536–545. https://doi.org/10.1016/S0378-4371(00)00205-3[1]

62 Jensen, M. C. (1986). Agency costs of free cash flow, corporate finance and takeovers. *American Economic Review.*

63 University of St Andrews School of Medicine. (n.d.). *Government Revenue and Development Estimations (GRADE)* available at https://medicine.st-andrews.ac.uk/grade/

64 Nicoletti, L., Ma, M., & Bass, D. (2025, May 8). *How AI demand is draining local water supplies.* Bloomberg News available at https://www.bloomberg.com/graphics/2025-ai-impacts-data-centers-water-data/

65 Bowen, H. R. (2013). *Social Responsibilities of the Businessman.* University of Iowa Press.

66 Friedman, M. (1970(, September 13). The social responsibility of business is to increase its profits. *The New York Times Magazine*, 13 September.

67 Gallup. (2024). *State of the Global Workplace: From suffering to thriving.* Gallup. https://www.gallup.com/workplace/349484/state-of-the-global-workplace.aspx

68 Wilson, D. S., Ostrom, E. & Cox, M. E. (2013). Generalizing the core design principles for the efficacy of groups. *Journal of Economic Behavior & Organisation*, 90, S21–S32.

69 IBM Institute for Business Value. (2024). *Businesses Embedding Sustainability Outperforming on Profitability, Talent Attraction: IBM Survey* [Report]. IBM.

70 *Why business won't abandon sustainability — Long-term play.* Reuters. available at https://www.reuters.com/sustainability/sustainable-finance-reporting/why-business-wont-abandon-sustainability-long-term-play-2025-05-19

71 Deloitte (2024). "2024 Gen Z and Millennial Survey", available at: https://www.deloitte.com/content/dam/assets-shared/docs/campaigns/2024/deloitte-2024-genz-millennial-survey.pdf?dlva=1

72 ShareAction (2025). Voting Matters 2024: Are asset managers using their proxy votes for action on environmental and social issues? Available at https://shareaction.org/reports/voting-matters-2024

Chapter 2

1 Different terms are used that share all or many of the goal and parameters, such as "purpose economy", "mission economy", "regenerative economy" "care economy", "new economy" "Die Gemeinwohl-Ökonomie", "postgrowth economy" and "economy of wellbeing".

2 Many argue we should govern for biogregions rather than nations if we are to align with the realities of natural and human system functioning.

3 Fioramonti, L. (2013). *Gross Domestic Problem: The Politics Behind the World's Most Powerful Number.* Zed Books.

4 Piketty, T. (2014). *Capital in the Twenty-First Century* (A. Goldhammer, Trans.). Harvard University Press. (Original work published 2013)

5 Blas, J. (2024). "Cargill, America's largest private company, faces leaner times". Bloomberg UK, 4 September, available at: https://www.bloomberg.com/opinion/articles/2024-09-04/cargill-america-s-largest-private-company-faces-leaner-times

6 Food System Economics Commission (2023). *The Economics of the Food System Transformation: Global Policy Report*, available at https://foodsystemeconomics.org/wp-content/uploads/FSEC-Global_Policy_Report.pdf

7 Newman, R. & Noy, I. (2023). The global costs of extreme weather that are attributable to climate change. *Nature Communications*, 29 September, available at: https://www.nature.com/articles/s41467-023-41888-1

8 Better Homes, Cooler Planet: How Low-Carbon Technologies Can Reduce Bills and Increase House Value. (updated with July 2023 price cap data)

9 Offshore Energies UK (2024). Offshore Decommissioning Report 2024, available at https://oeuk.org.uk/wp-content/uploads/2024/11/OEUK-Decommissioning-Report-2024.pdf

10 Smith, A. (1937). *The Wealth of Nations* [1776] (Vol. 11937).

11 Kallis, G., Hickel, J., O'Neill, D. W., Jackson, T., Victor, P. A., Raworth, K., Schor, J. B., Steinberger, J. K. & Ürge-Vorsatz, D. (2025). Post-growth: The science of wellbeing within planetary boundaries. *The Lancet Planetary Health*, 9(1), e62–e78. https://doi.org/10.1016/S2542-5196(24)00310-3[4]

12 Tory, M. (2025). *A Novel Fiscal Fix for What Ails the UK Economy*, Bloomberg UK, 20 January, available at: https://www.bloomberg.com/opinion/articles/2025-01-20/a-novel-fiscal-fix-for-what-ails-the-uk-economy?embedded-checkout=true

13 International Public Sector Accounting Standards Board, available at https://ifacweb.blob.core.windows.net/publicfiles/2023-12/IPSASB-Public-Sector-Conceptual-Framework_2023%20-%20Updated%2012-19-23_Secure.pdf

14 Liu, K., Wang, R., Behrens, P., Schrijver, I., Jansen, A., A. Rum, I. & Hoekstra, R. (2024). "A comprehensive Beyond-GDP database to accelerate wellbeing, inclusion, and sustainability research". *Scientific Data*, 11(1), 1166.

15 Carver, J. (2006). *Boards that Make a Difference: A New Design for Leadership in Nonprofit and Public Organisations*. (Vol. 6). John Wiley & Sons.

16 Colebatch, H. (2009). *Policy*. McGraw-Hill Education (UK).

17 Trebeck, K. & Smith, W. (2024). The Wellbeing Economy in Brief: Understanding the growing agenda and its implications. Centre for Policy Development, available at https://cpd.org.au/wp-content/uploads/2024/03/Wellbeing-Economy-in-Brief.pdf

18 Carney, M. (2021). *Value(s): Building a Better World for All*. PublicAffairs.

19 Carpenter, B. & Nicholls, J. (2023). *Impact Transparency in Public Sector Accounting*. Social Value International, available at https://www.socialvalueint.org/publications

20 Organisation for Economic Co-operation and Development (OECD) (2024). *How's life? 2024: Measuring Well-Being and Progress*. OECD Publishing, available at https://www.oecd.org/en/publications/how-s-life-2024_bdcf2f9f.htm

21 Kallis, G., Hickel, J., O'Neill, D. W., Jackson, T., Victor, P. A., Raworth, K., Schor, J. B., Steinberger, J. K., & Ürge-Vorsatz, D. (2025). Post-growth: The science of wellbeing within planetary boundaries. *The Lancet Planetary Health*, 9(1), e62–e78. https://doi.org/10.1016/S2542-5196(24)00310-3[4]

22 Mazzucato, M. (2025). *Reimagining Financing for the SDGs: From Filling Gaps to Shaping Finance* (UN DESA Policy Brief No. 170, Special issue). United Nations Department of Economic and Social Affairs; UN High-level Advisory Board on Economic and Social Affairs; University College London Institute for Innovation and Public Purpose, available at https://desapublications.un.org/policy-briefs/un-desa-policy-brief-no-170-special-issue-reimagining-financing-sdgs-filling-gaps

23 Davidson, J. (2020). *#futuregen: Lessons from a Small Country*. Chelsea Green Publishing.

24 "G20 + Global Report: attitudes to planetary stewardship and segmentation", Global Commons Survey, September 2024, available at: https://earth4all.life/wp-content/uploads/2024/10/Global-Commons-Survey-2024-Global-2.pdf
25 Alexander, J. (2023). *Citizens: Why the Key to Fixing Everything Is All of Us.* Canbury Press.
26 Solnit, R. (2010). *A Paradise Built in Hell: The Extraordinary Communities that Arise in Disaster.* Penguin.
27 BBC. (2025, 26th March). *South Korea admits to "mass exporting" children for adoption* BBC News available at https://www.bbc.com/news/articles/cwyjryv1kpgo

Chapter 3

1 Hurth, V. (2023). "Unleashing governance for sustainable business". Cambridge, UK: University of Cambridge Institute for Sustainability Leadership.
2 A critical global debate is ongoing about what constitutes "owners" of an organisation particularly whether those with no responsibilities, and highly temporary shareholders who are speculators only trying to make money quickly, can be considered owners. For an overview of this debate, see Victoria's paper "Unleashing governance".
3 Rights-holders are individuals or social groups that have particular entitlements in relation to specific duty-bearers. In general terms, all human beings are rights-holders under the Universal Declaration of Human Rights.
4 Mayer, C. (2018). *Prosperity: Better Business Makes the Greater Good.* Oxford University Press.
5 Albareda, L. & Sison, A. J. G. (2020). "Commons organizing: Embedding common good and institutions for collective action. Insights from ethics and economics". *Journal of Business Ethics,* 166(4), 727–743.
6 Jensen, M. (2001). "Value maximisation, stakeholder theory, and the corporate objective function". *European Financial Management,* 7(3), 297–317
7 Laloux, F. (2014). *Reinventing Organisations* (Vol. 58). Brussels: Nelson Parker.
8 Nakamura, J. & Csikszentmihalyi, M. (2002). The concept of flow. In C. R. Snyder & S. J. Lopez (Eds.), *Handbook of Positive Psychology* (pp. 89–105). Oxford University Press.
9 "Widespread informality likely to slow recovery from COVID-19 in developing economies". World Bank Group, 11 May 2021, available at: https://www.worldbank.org/en/news/press-release/2021/05/11/widespread-informality-likely-to-slow-recovery-from-covid-19-in-developing-economies
10 Kotler, P. (1972). What consumerism means for marketers. *Harvard Business Review,* 50(3), 48-57.

11 Hurth, V. & Whittlesea, E. (2017). "Characterising marketing paradigms for sustainable marketing management". *Social Business*, 7(3–4), 359–390.

12 Max-Neef, M. A. (1991). Human scale development: conception, application and further reflections.

13 Christensen, C. M. (2016). *The Innovator's Dilemma: When New Technologies Cause Great Firms to Fail.* Harvard Business Review Press.

14 Nilekani, R. (n.d.) 'Samaaj, Sarkaar, Bazaar – a citizen-first approach', available at: https://rohininilekaniphilanthropies.org/approach/

15 ISO is a body made up of currently 174 national member bodies that share standard processes for drawing out and encoding the consensus view on a topic. Normally this is in the realm of organisations and international trade. Nations create standards and also propose topics to be standardised at the ISO international level. While ISO is generally known for management systems standards in products (e.g. plugs) in recent years it has become more known for requirement and guidance standards in organisational wide topics like quality (9001), environmental management (14001) and social responsibility (26000) and now the broadest topic – organisational governance.

16 A range of endorsements for ISO 37000, including some used in this chapter, can be found here: https://committee.iso.org/sites/tc309/home/projects/published/iso-37000-governance-of-organiza/iso-37000-endorsements.html

17 Mayer, C. (2018). *Prosperity: Better Business Makes the Greater Good.* Oxford University Press.

18 An important exception is the South African "King Codes" led by the governance expert Mervyn King, which was concertedly anchored to Logic 2. These codes are embedded in the South African stock exchange and have influenced the world in many ways.

19 Thiele, L. P. (2020). Integrating political and technological uncertainty into robust climate policy. *Climatic Change, 163*(1), 521–538. https://doi.org/10.1007/s10584-020-02853-9

20 BSi PA808:2021, available at: https://www.bsigroup.com/en-GB/insights-and-media/insights/brochures/pas-808-purpose-driven-organisations-for-delivering-sustainability/

21 https://www.cisl.cam.ac.uk/news-and-resources/publications/cisls-business-transformation-framework-preliminary-diagnostic

22 Confino, J. (2012). Unilever's Paul Polman: challenging the corporate status quo, *The Guardian*, 24 April, available at https://www.theguardian.com/sustainable-business/paul-polman-unilever-sustainable-living-plan

23 Nicholls, J (2026 forthcoming) *The Accounting Paradox: How Financial Accounting Is Damaging the World (But Can Help Repair It).* Practical Inspiration Publishing.

24 Hurth, V., Peck, J., Jackman, D. & Wensing, E. (2015). *Reforming Marketing for Sustainability: A Framework for Evolved Marketing.* Friends of the Earth,

available at https://friendsoftheeearth.uk/sites/default/files/downloads/reforming-marketing-sustainability-full-report-76676.pdf

25 Collins, J. C. & Porras, J. I. (1991). "Organisational vision and visionary organisations". *California Management Review*, 34(1), 30–52. https://doi.org/10.2307/41166682

26 Christensen, C., M. (2016). *The Innovator's Dilemma: When New Technologies Cause Great Firms to Fail*. Harvard Business Review Press.

27 Hart, S. L. & Christensen, C. M. (2002). "The great leap: Driving innovation from the base of the pyramid". *MIT Sloan Management Review*, 15 October, available at: https://sloanreview.mit.edu/article/the-great-leap-driving-innovation-from-the-base-of-the-pyramid/

28 Radjou, N. & Prabhu, J. (2015). *Frugal Innovation: How to Do More with Less*. The Economist.

Chapter 4

1 Great Place To Work (2023). "The power of purpose in the workplace". available at: https://www.greatplacetowork.com/resources/reports/the-power-of-purpose-in-the-workplace

2 Christensen, C. (2010). "How will you measure your life", *Havard Business Review*, July–August 2010, available at https://hbr.org/2010/07/how-will-you-measure-your-life

3 Cranston, S. & Keller, S. (2013). "Increasing the meaning quotient at work", McKinsey Quarterly, 1 January, available at: https://www.mckinsey.com/capabilities/people-and-organisational-performance/our-insights/increasing-the-meaning-quotient-of-work

4 Pink, D. (2011). *Drive: The Surprising Truth about What Motivates Us*, Canongate Books.

5 Frankl, V. (2008/1946). *Man's Search for Meaning*, Rider.

6 Bartlett, C. & Ghoshal, S. (1994). "Beyond strategy to purpose". *Harvard Business Review*, November–December, available at https://hbr.org/1994/11/beyond-strategy-to-purpose

7 Fink, L. (2018). "A sense of purpose", Larry Fink's 2018 letter to CEOS, available at: https://www.blackrock.com/jp/individual/ja/about-us/ceo-letter/archives/2018#

8 Fink, L. (2022). "The power of capitalism", Larry Fink's 2022 letter to CEOS, available at: https://www.blackrock.com/corporate/investor-relations/larry-fink-ceo-letter

9 BBC (2017). "Japan's Dentsu advertising agency charged over employee suicide", 8 July, available at: https://www.bbc.com/news/world-asia-40541609

10 Goldman Sachs & Co LLC (2021). "Working Conditions Survey", available at: cdn.worktechacademy.com/uploads/2021/03/Goldman-Sachs-employee-survey.pdf

11 McKinsey Quarterly (2020). "Making a daily 'to be' list: How a hospital system CEO is navigating the coronavirus crisis". McKinsey & Company, 23 July, available at: https://www.mckinsey.com/capabilities/strategy-and-corporate-finance/our-insights/making-a-daily-to-be-list-how-a-hospital-system-ceo-is-navigating-the-coronavirus-crisis

12 Zak, P. (2017). "The neuroscience of trust". *Harvard Business Review*. Jan–Feb 2017, available at: https://hbr.org/2017/01/the-neuroscience-of-trust

13 Kielburger, C. & Kielburger M. (2021). *Me to We. Finding Meaning in a Material World.* Simon and Schuster, available at https://www.simonandschuster.com/books/Me-to-We/Craig-Kielburger/9781982154578

14 Edmondson, A. (2018) *The Fearless Organisation: Creating Psycholgical Safety in the Workplace for Learning, Innovation and Growth.* Wiley, available at: https://fearlessorganisationscan.com/the-fearless-organisation

15 re:work. Tool: Foster psychological safety. Google. 2015, available at: https://rework.withgoogle.com/guides/understanding-team-effectiveness/steps/foster-psychological-safety/

16 Kübler-Ross, E. (2008). *On Death & Dying – What the Dying Have to Teach Doctors, Nurses, Clergy & Their Own Families.* Scribner Book Company.

17 Zak, P. (2017). "The neuroscience of trust". *Harvard Business Review*. Jan–Feb, available at: https://hbr.org/2017/01/the-neuroscience-of-trust

18 Mackey, J. (2023). *Lead with Love*, available at: https://johnpmackey.com/lead-with-love/

19 Scharmer, O. (2009). *Theory U: Learning from the Future as It Emerges*, Berrett-Koehler Publishers.

20 Boyatzis, R. (2024). *The Science of Change.* OUP USA.

21 Meadows, D. (2008). *Thinking in Systems.* Chelsea Green Publishing, available at: https://a.co/d/5izKBT1

22 Senge, M. P., (2006) *The Fifth Discipline*, Random House Business.

23 Yuguero, O. (2022). "Burnout, psychopathology and purpose in life in healthcare workers during COVID-19 pandemic". *Public Health*, 15 August, available at: https://www.frontiersin.org/journals/public-health/articles/10.3389/fpubh.2022.926328

24 Tower, T. (2024). "Uncertainty and lack of meaning at work fuel burnout", 2 April, available at: https://www.concordia.ca/cunews/jmsb/perspectives/articles/uncertainty-and-lack-of-meaning-at-work-fuel-burnout.html

25 Goleman, D. (1996) *Emotional Intelligence – Why it Can Matter More Than IQ*, Bloomsbury Publishing.

26 Korn Ferry, 2023 How Purpose and Emotional Intelligence Blend: https://www.kornferry.com/insights/this-week-in-leadership/how-purpose-and-emotiona-intelligence-blend

27 Cameron, K. & Seppälä, E. (2022) "The best leaders have a contagious positive energy". *Harvard Business Review*, 18 April, available at: https://hbr.org/2022/04/the-best-leaders-have-a-contagious-positive-energy

28 Csikszentmihalyi, M. (2008) *Flow: The Psychology of Optimal Experience.* Harper Perennial Modern Classics.
29 Kotler, S. (2014). "Create a work environment that fosters flow". *Harvard Business Review*, 6 May, available at: https://hbr.org/2014/05/create-a-work-environment-that-fosters-flow
30 Csikszentmihalyi, M. (1990). *Flow: The Psychology of Optimal Experience.* Harper & Row.
31 Eger, E. (2018) *The Choice*, Rider.
32 Robbins, T. (1991). *Awaken the giant within: How to Take Immediate Control of your Mental, Emotional, Physical and Financial Destiny!* Free Press.

Author Biographies

Victoria Hurth is an Independent Pracademic who works at the cutting edge of theory and practice to help the world clarify its consensus on foundational issues. She co-led the five-year development of the global ISO standard in Governance of Organisations (ISO 37000), was Technical Author for the first national standard in Purpose-Driven Organisations and is currently Project Leader of the development of an equivalent ISO (ISO 37011). Victoria is a regular global keynote speaker, executive leadership advisor and content creator. She is a Fellow of the University of Cambridge Institute for Sustainability Leadership, Director of the Soil Association Certification Ltd, Sustainability Academic Lead for the Common Ground Research Networks. She advises Planet Mark and Una Terra Early Growth Fund. She advised SACE (Italy's export credit agency) and the UN on the SDG methodology for the business reporting target 12.6.1. She has over 25 years' global experience in business transformation and as a full-time Associate Professor of Marketing and Sustainable Business. To find out more about Victoria's speaking and executive leadership work, or for media requests, please email connect@victoriahurth.com.

Linkedin: https://www.linkedin.com/in/dr-victoria-hurth/
Website: www.victoriahurth.com

Ben Renshaw is one of today's foremost leadership thinkers. A sought-after speaker, executive coach, and author, Ben's innovative work with leading organisations, senior executives, and entrepreneurs has earned him international acclaim. He writes about how to lead and succeed in today's volatile world and is the author of 12 acclaimed books, including *How to Be a CEO, LoveWork, Being, Purpose,* LEAD, and SuperCoaching. For speaking engagements, executive coaching, team and leadership development programmes, or media inquiries, please contact: info@ benrenshaw.com

Website: benrenshaw.com
LinkedIn: https://www.linkedin.com/in/ben-renshaw

Lorenzo Fioramonti is a distinguished political economist, member of the Club of Rome, former Italian Minister of Education, University, and Research and former Member of Parliament. Currently serving as the Academic Director of NATIVA Campus, a new training academy for regenerative leaders, Fioramonti has a rich academic and political background that spans continents and disciplines. He has published several influential books, including the bestselling *Wellbeing Economy: Success in a World Without Growth* (MacMillan 2017) and *The World After GDP: Economics, Politics and International Relations in the Post-Growth Era* (Polity 2017). His opinion pieces have been published by leading publications such as *The New York Times, The Guardian* and the *Financial Times.* To find out more about Lorenzo Fioramonti's speaking and coaching development programmes or for media requests, please visit lorenzofioramonti.org.

LinkedIn:https://www.linkedin.com/in/lorenzo-fioramonti-b5366b259/

We would love you to be part of the *Beyond Profit: Purpose-Driven Leadership for a Wellbeing Economy* community. To join the conversation and connect with fellow purpose-driven leaders, visit: https://www.linkedin.com/groups/13085230/

Index

RAISING READERS
Books Build Bright Futures

Dear Reader,

We'd love your attention for one more page to tell you about the crisis in children's reading, and what we can all do.

Studies have shown that reading for fun is the **single biggest predictor of a child's future life chances** – more than family circumstance, parents' educational background or income. It improves academic results, mental health, wealth, communication skills, ambition and happiness.[1]

The number of children reading for fun is in rapid decline. Young people have a lot of competition for their time. In 2024, 1 in 10 children and young people in the UK aged 5 to 18 did not own a single book at home.[2]

Hachette works extensively with schools, libraries and literacy charities, but here are some ways we can all raise more readers:

- Reading to children for just 10 minutes a day makes a difference
- Don't give up if children aren't regular readers – there will be books for them!
- Visit bookshops and libraries to get recommendations
- Encourage them to listen to audiobooks
- Support school libraries
- Give books as gifts

There's a lot more information about how to encourage children to read on our website: **www.RaisingReaders.co.uk**

Thank you for reading.

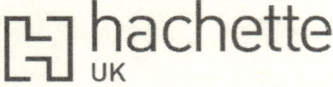

---

[1] OECD, '21st-Century Readers: Developing Literacy Skills in a Digital World', 2021, https://www.oecd.org/en/publications/21st-century-readers_a83d84cb-en.html

[2] National Literacy Trust, 'Book Ownership in 2024', November 2024, https://literacytrust.org.uk/research-services/research-reports/book-ownership-in-2024